Sin and Filth in Medieval Culture
The Devil in the Latrine

Martha Bayless

NEW YORK LONDON

First published 2012
by Routledge
711 Third Avenue, New York, NY 10017

Simultaneously published in the UK
by Routledge
2 Park Square, Milton Park, Abingdon, Oxon OX14 4RN

*Routledge is an imprint of the Taylor & Francis Group,
an informa business*

© 2012 Martha Bayless

The right of Martha Bayless to be identified as author of this work has been asserted by her in accordance with sections 77 and 78 of the Copyright, Designs and Patents Act 1988.

Typeset in Sabon by IBT Global.
Printed and bound in the United States of America on acid-free paper by IBT Global.

All rights reserved. No part of this book may be reprinted or reproduced or utilised in any form or by any electronic, mechanical, or other means, now known or hereafter invented, including photocopying and recording, or in any information storage or retrieval system, without permission in writing from the publishers.

Trademark Notice: Product or corporate names may be trademarks or registered trademarks, and are used only for identification and explanation without intent to infringe.

Library of Congress Cataloging-in-Publication Data
A catalog record has been requested for this book.

ISBN13: 978-0-415-89780-8 (hbk)
ISBN13: 978-0-203-13807-6 (ebk)

Contents

List of Illustrations	vii
Abbreviations	ix
A Note About the Translations	xi
Acknowledgements	xv
Preface	xvii

1	The Devil in the Latrine	1
2	Pollution and Filth in the Middle Ages: Material Realities	29
3	The Symbolic Order of the Body	65
4	The Realm of Corruption	98
5	In Conclusion	164

Notes	183
Bibliography	219
Subject Index	239
Index of Biblical Passages	243

Illustrations

1	The Devil in the latrine. *A New Discourse of a Stale Subject, called the Metamorphosis of Ajax* (1596), p. 18.	4
2	A man in a privy with a moon emblem. Vienna, Österreichische Nationalbibliothek 2561, fol. 307r.	36
3	An ape worshipping a bottom with no head. New York, Pierpont Morgan Library William S. Glazier Collection 24, fol. 78.	76
4	The Devil with faces on his bottom. The Queen Mary Psalter: London, British Library Royal 2.B.Vii, fol. 1v.	77
5	The witches' *osculum infame*. Oxford, Bodleian Library Rawlinson D.410, fol. 1.	86
6	The Devil's bottom and the maiden with the mirror. Illustration from *Der Ritter vom Türn*.	89
7	The backside at the carrying of the cross. Chicago, Art Institute, Charles H. and Mary F. S. Worcester Collection.	91
8	The rule of the backside at the mocking of Christ. Innsbruck, Tiroler Landesmuseum Ferdinandeum.	92
9	The fool and his backside at the crowning with thorns. Wallraf-Richartz-Museum, Graphische Sammlung, Inv.-Nr. 1961/32, p. 102.	93
10	Sinful reversal. London, British Library Stowe 17 (the Stowe Missal), fol. 214r.	97
11	The hanging of Judas. Holkham Bible Picture Book: London, British Library Add. MS 47682 (Holkham 666), fol. 30r.	126
12	St. Francis, birds, and the recalcitrant dog. Oxford, Bodleian Library Douce 49 (the Saint-Omer Psalter), fol. 64v.	173
13	The toilet as a place of demonic peril. *Weekly World News*, August 4, 1998.	182

Abbreviations

CCCM	Corpus Christianorum, Continuatio Mediaeualis
CCSL	Corpus Christianorum, Series Latina
CSEL	Corpus Scriptorum Ecclesiasticorum Latinorum
EETS	Early English Text Society
o.s.	original series
MGH	Monumenta Germaniae Historica
NRCF	*Nouveau recueil complet des fabliaux*, ed. Willem Noomen and Nico van den Boogaard, 10 vols. (Assen: Van Gorcum, 1983–98)
PG	Patrologiae cursus completus, Series Graeca, ed. J.-P. Migne. 161 vols. Paris: 1857–66
PL	Patrologiae cursus completus, Series Latina, ed. J.-P. Migne. 221 vols. Paris: 1844–58
Tubach	Frederic C. Tubach, *Index Exemplorum: A Handbook of Medieval Religious Tales*, FF Communications 204 (Helsinki: Suomalainen Tiedeakatedia, 1969)

A Note About the Translations

I have endeavored to provide an English translation of all quotations in other languages. In some cases the published critical editions of texts offer a facing English translation, and in these instances it seemed presumptuous to disregard the editor's translation and substitute my own, and so I have used the original editor's translation. In other examples, principally the *Cronica* of Salimbene de Adam and the *Dialogus Miraculorum* of Caesarius of Heisterbach, the editions of the original are difficult of access and the translations much easier to obtain; therefore (while using and quoting the original) I have cited the modern published translations so as not to obscure the fact that they are available for those who might wish to follow the trail. These are all footnoted to this effect. I also have often used standard published translations for Biblical passages. Further, in the cases of languages of which I am not very familiar (e.g., Old Norse, medieval German and Cornish), I have relied on the published translations of others. In all other cases, in Latin, Old English, Middle English, French and other languages, translations are, for better or for worse, my own.

Luxuriam ventris, lector, cognosce vorantis,
  Putrida qui sentis stercora nare tuo.
Ingluviem fugito ventris quapropter in ore:
  Tempore sit certo sobria vita tibi.
> —Alcuin (ed. E. Dümmler, MGH, Poetae Latini Aevi Carolini I (Berlin, 1881), p. 321)

Understand, reader, the excess of the devouring belly,
You who smell the putrid dung with your nose.
Flee therefore the gluttony of the belly and mouth:
May your life be sober at the certain day.

Reflection on dirt involves reflection on the relation of order to disorder, being to non-being, form to formlessness, life to death.
> —Mary Douglas

Ooh, there's a lovely lot of filth over here.
> —*Monty Python and the Holy Grail*

Acknowledgements

I would like to thank the University of Oregon for a Creative and Scholarly Development Award in support of this project, as well as Kate Rudy, whose expertise with images and permissions is surpassing, and Aletta Biersack, whose anthropological insights and encouragement have been invaluable. I am also particularly grateful to Robert D. Hughes for his help with Catalan and in pinning down the details of Francesc Eiximenis. In addition, I have received suggestions, references and help from dozens of people, among them Barbara Altmann, Debby Banham, Doris Beers, Tom Capuano, Edwin Duncan, Jennifer Fellows, Alison Hymes, Malcolm Jones, Lillian Kaiser, Enid Karr, Lee Kirk, Vicente Lledó-Guillem, James Mall, Jim Marchand, Susan Morrison, Pat Murphy, Jacque Pollard, Colin Richmond, John Sebastian, Bill Sullivan, Kathryn Talarico, Augustine Thompson, Belle Tuten, David Wacks, Jonas Wellendorf and, supplying helpful last-minute sustenance and dictionaries, Jill Mann and Michael Lapidge. I also benefited immensely from the comments of the anonymous reviewers for Routledge. I am grateful to everyone who contributed. All mistakes that may remain are, unfortunately, my own.

Preface

However much modern scholars may try to bridge the gulf between the medieval period and the twenty-first century, there is one perspective that unfailingly brings into view the famous Otherness of the Middle Ages: the medieval attitude toward filth and dung. I have found that it also tends to bring conversation to a halt. Like the fastidious Absolon in Chaucer's Miller's Tale, the modern age has proven itself "squeamish of farting"—and like Absolon, when we investigate matters more closely, we may find ourselves faced with a closer view of the lower anatomy than we like.

But the emblems of material corruption—the corrupt body and the filth it brings forth, particularly the filth found in latrines—are everywhere in medieval culture: in sermons, in saints' lives, in histories and chronicles, in Biblical commentaries, in fables and moral tales, in accounts of heresy and witch trials, in pious poetry, in religious plays, in depictions of hell, in manuscript illustrations, in paintings in cathedrals and houses and in both learned and popular stories. For the medieval world, excrement and dung were powerful moral and theological material, to a degree scarcely imaginable in today's world, where serious discussion of excrement is almost inconceivable in most realms. Like the modern world, the medieval world could regard dung as lowly, degrading, trivial and comic; but medieval thought could also understand dung as lowly, degrading, important and deadly serious. To comprehend that mindset, we must be prepared to put away the prejudices of modern social constraint and look realistically at medieval practice. Today excrement is a substance so taboo (despite being so universal and unavoidable) that it is still considered virtually unspeakable in modern scholarship. This is testimony to its power to disgust and embarrass, two reactions that dispassionate modern scholarship seeks to avoid. But these reactions were precisely the response serious medieval writers hoped to provoke.

In the current day, as in the Middle Ages, filth and dung are familiar symbols for sin, corruption and moral impurity. This is an obvious and predictable equivalence. What I aim to show in this book is that in the Middle Ages these relationships were not merely metaphorical. (The book does, however, agree with the groundbreaking thesis of Lakoff and Johnson, which contends that our worldview is constituted through metaphor, so that even metaphor is not "just" metaphorical.) As the following chapters will demonstrate, excrement was not merely used as a figure of speech but was central to a popular medieval metaphysics. It was not a symbol of sin or a consequence of sin: it *embodied* sin. It was an alternate manifestation of sin, as ice is an alternate manifestation of water. Excrement was sin made material. In the modern period, filth and excrement are deplorable but otherwise meaningless material realities, most useful as metaphors. In the Middle Ages, filth and excrement were the foundation of the understanding of human history. They were as important as sin because they *were* sin. This is a radical and crucial difference from modern attitudes.

This conception of excrement is expressed in both historical and fictional sources, by theologians and storytellers, by sophisticates, but most of all by popular writers who were not trying to argue a particular point of philosophy, but were reflecting the world as it was generally understood. This explains the otherwise perplexing pervasiveness of excremental motifs in medieval literature and art. Literary scholars have noted the popularity of latrine humor in medieval comedy, attributing it to a freewheeling crudity in medieval attitudes. But few scholars have remarked on the even more pervasive presence of excremental motifs in serious medieval religious material. This is not because even religious writers were crude, but because the material was theologically meaningful in a way that modern images of filth cannot be. Not only does this explain the otherwise inexplicable (and ignored) widespread use of filth in religious literature, but it throws new light on the use of filth in comedy, which operated against this backdrop of theological significance.

Part of what this book seeks to demonstrate is the central role of filth and excrement in medieval religious thought, and to this aim I have provided full examples from numerous sources, hoping to give some idea of how extensive and how commonplace such stories really were. Just glancing at or summarizing the evidence would obscure the very open, detailed, theological nature of the examples, and so I have quoted at length. What is more, these examples should demonstrate the level at which such thought was conducted: most are in Latin, the language of "official," elite culture, which modern scholarship has tended to suppose was too refined to deal with such low matters. But Latin was the language of the Church, and the Church understood the importance of filth more than any author of entertainment. There is more dung in theology than there is in Chaucer. Even in Chaucer, the subject is tied to religion. At the same time, the analysis of filth was not the province of abstruse theological writers; the sources reflect a culture-wide understanding most relevant to those concerned with the divine, with which filth was intimately connected.

For this reason, I have chosen to concentrate largely on the utilitarian, devotional and exemplary literature of the medieval period, rather than on "literary" authors such as Chaucer or Dante. Although the texts in this study can evince considerable sophistication, they are more ordinary than singular, witnesses to a commonplace understanding of the moral and material structure of the universe. I have included the original texts, despite their length and number, in part to show what a great number appear in Latin, the language of learned, "official" culture. The fact that they concern dung does not make these texts lowly, facetious, subversive or improper. On the contrary, they are entirely mainstream: commonplace, sober, exhortatory and moral. Dung could certainly be a staple of comedy in humorous genres, as today. That does not need a book to explain it. What this book explains is the non-comedic, moral, sober uses of the subject.

The scope of this book is broad: from the first glimmerings of the theological formulation of the subject in the early Christian period to the dawn of the Renaissance. Indeed, as examples will make clear, this understanding of filth outlasted the Middle Ages. In some ways it found its most aggressive form in the early modern period, and the whole of this book might form a prolegomenon to the work of Martin Luther, which is suffused with scatology. But the Reformation precipitated theological complexities which are beyond the scope of this already distended study, and so I have left later periods to future researchers. As a rough guide, the earliest substantial works examined here date from the fifth century, and the latest from the late fifteenth and very early sixteenth century. Culture, morals, resources and technology do not remain static over an eleven-hundred-year period, and I emphasize that I aim to avoid a totalizing view of the medieval period. Individual thinkers sometimes formulated individual answers to common medieval questions: the thirteenth-century philosopher and proto-scientist Roger Bacon, for example, developed mechanistic explanations for many phenomena in ways that differ from more popular interpretations. But what I aim to discuss are the elements that remained constant across the period: the ways in which medieval culture largely agreed, rather than the specifics of those who sometimes differed. Medieval Christian culture from the fifth century to the fifteenth had a steadfast understanding of the moral connotations of filth within a theological framework. Certainly this might take different forms in different periods. In the tenth and succeeding centuries, worries about the relationship between divinity and corrupt materiality found voice in the stercoran heresy and controversies about the Eucharist. In the eleventh and twelfth centuries, the same concerns are reflected in the beliefs of the Cathars and other heretical sects. The twelfth century saw the same understanding reflected in the rite of the stercory seat at the papal consecration, a practice that continued until the sixteenth century. With the rise of drama in the later medieval period, this understanding of filth begins to appear in plays about Judas, demons and sinners. In late fifteenth- and early sixteenth-century Continental painting, it took the form of images of Christ and the saints being insulted by the lower bodies of fools and sinners. Across the period it appears in theology, sermon literature and tales of the deaths of sinners. The methods and focuses of theology as a whole shifted from period to period, but many of the basic underlying assumptions were the same throughout; the understanding of filth was one of these. Thus this book intends to draw the broad picture that found expression in many forms, some of them taking different forms across the period, some enduring.

Similarly this understanding of filth was general throughout western Christendom, the area of focus in this book. To some extent I favor witnesses from Britain and France, particularly in the historical sections, although materials from Italy, Germany, the Low Countries and Scandinavia also come into play. This bias is largely because English materials were easiest to access and alone provided far more evidence than could be included in any single study. I hope that providing this more comprehensive background to English literature may encourage scholars of English to take account of this material when they look at vernacular texts on these themes. While I discuss differences between regions and periods in the second chapter, once again my focus is on the larger commonalities between disparate witnesses.

Chapter 1, "The Devil in the Latrine," introduces the subject: the role of dung and filth as moral agents in medieval thought and literature. These are set against a backdrop of modern scholarship on filth, disgust and the body, forming a theoretical context for the study of medieval social practices.

Chapter 2, "Pollution and Filth in the Middle Ages: Material Realities," examines filth and dung as the material, public reality it was, the underlying actuality upon which systems of thought were overlaid. It proceeds by analyzing the sanitation of four categories of medieval people: citydwellers, countrydwellers, the cloistered and the wealthy and identifies their concerns, ranging from shame, privacy and bodily vulnerability to the hoarding of waste as a vital resource and source of wealth. The latter part of the chapter examines the thought underlying filth-related taboos and euphemisms. The whole forms the first comprehensive overview of medieval sanitary systems to appear in scholarship. This explication of material conditions demonstrates that the medieval understanding of filth is a symbolic construct, shaped by Christianity, rather than an invariant reaction to a single objective reality.

Chapter 3, "The Symbolic Order of the Body," extends the current understanding of the cosmology of the Middle Ages, situating filth in relation to other material reflections of moral issues in the realm of the body and the wider cosmos. It begins by establishing the body as a moral realm: In the medieval understanding, the body could be read and interpreted no less than scripture or other components of the universe. Moreover, in medieval culture the material and moral were identical, not just metaphors: filth *was* sin, "up" was literally "superior." The chapter then uses this framework to analyze the literature of inversion, in which sinners invert the right order of the body, ceding lofty reason to the base animal desires of the lower half. As a whole, the chapter seeks to demonstrate the ways in which this medieval schema is vital to a full understanding of a variety of works, including hagiography, exempla, devotional treatises, heresy charges, altarpieces and religious images.

Chapter 4, "The Realm of Corruption," lays out the consequences of these systems: an understanding of human filth as both a symbol and a literal embodiment of sin. After laying out the ways in which divinity was associated with the immaterial and sin with the fleshly and corrupt, it identifies the many ways in which medieval people worried about conjunctions of the divine and the bodily, whether this concerned the attributes of God or the specifics of Christ's incarnation. As a wealth of examples demonstrate, sinners could be likened to excrement itself, often being *de facto* transformed into excrement as they suffer death in the latrine as punishment for their sins. I then discuss the theological understanding of dung as reflected in the Bible and its exegesis, including the ways exegetes introduce dung into a discussion of Biblical passages that do not specify it, such as the interpretation of the conditions on the ark. The chapter goes on to discuss the practical ramifications of this understanding of sin and excrement, such as the very concrete understanding that sin and treachery literally arose in the bowels, and the ways in which this was expressed in practices like the disemboweling of traitors and the "inverted execution." The moral system of the body was also reflected in images of the body and its processes as a figure of the Church, as examples show; and excrement became a marker of sin. This chapter analyzes these and many other instances of the symbolic force of filth and excrement, showing how an understanding of these beliefs makes sense of much that has been deemed crude or unwarranted in medieval culture.

The final chapter, "In Conclusion," sums up and applies the schema of previous chapters. Here I discuss the question of whether filth really embodies its own contradiction, whether that contradiction may be carnivalesque, fruitful or protective. With the meaning of filth clear from so many examples explored in previous chapters, it should be possible to shed light on some more enigmatic examples. Therefore, I look at four cases that have puzzled or bemused previous scholars: a key passage from the early gnostic theologian Valentinus, a thirteenth-century manuscript image of St. Francis, the devilish torments of St. Christina of Stommeln and the knockabout fabliau *Le sacristain*. Finally, the chapter traces the religious understanding of filth past the end of the Middle Ages, into the early modern period and the Enlightenment, and to its end.

To recognize the role of filth in the symbolic order is to expand our understanding of medieval thought, thought that assigned to even the lowliest of substances a key role in the universe and in relation to God. To put aside modern discomfiture and apprehend this in medieval terms is to understand the very real concerns represented by the Devil in the latrine.

1   The Devil in the Latrine

> A godly father sitting on a draught,
> To do as neede, and nature hath us taught;
> Mumbled (as was his manner) certen pray'rs,
> And unto him the Devil straight repayr's:
> And boldly to revile him he begins,
> Alledging that such pray'rs are deadly sins;
> And that it shewd, he was devoyd of grace,
> To speake to God, from so unmeete a place.
> The reverent man, though at the first dismaid;
> Yet strong in faith, to Satan thus he said.
> Thou damned spirit, wicked, false & lying,
> Dispairing thine own good, & ours envying:
> Ech take his due, and me thou canst not hurt,
> To God my pray'r I meant, to thee the durt.
> Pure prayr ascends to him that high doth sit.
> Down fals the filth, for fiends of hel more fit.
>
> —Sir John Harington, *The Metamorphosis of Ajax*[1]

Among the concerns of medieval theology, one debate was particularly down-to-earth: whether the latrine was a proper place for the praise of God. The thirteenth-century Italian chronicler Salimbene de Adam tells a story in which the devil weighs in on this question:

> Quidam religiosus, dum in loco privato *ad requisita nature* sederet et Deum laudaret, fuit reprehensus a demone quod locus ille non erat ydoneus, sed inhonestus ad Deum laudandum. Cui respondit frater et dixit: "Ita sum divinis laudibus assuetus, quod a laude Dei cessare non possum. Nam, Scriptura teste, didici quod Deus est ubique, ergo ubique est laudandus a suis.... Igitur qui omnem locum dicit nullum excludit. Quapropter et ventrem meum purgabo et Deum meum laudabo."[2]

> A certain man in religious orders was praising God while sitting on the privy "for the necessities of nature" [Deuteronomy 23.12]. And a demon came and rebuked him, saying that such a place was

2   *Sin and Filth in Medieval Culture*

not suitable and honorable for giving praise to God. But the Brother answered, "I am so accustomed to singing divine praises that I cannot cease praising God. For I learned in the Scripture that God is everywhere; therefore, everywhere is suitable for praising him. . . . Therefore, I shall praise God while emptying my bowels."³

The brother castigates the demon for some time, and finally expounds on the similarities between the demon and latrines:

> "similia similibus gaudent. Nam omne animal ad sibi simile convertetur. Tu porcus es, immundus es, immundus diceris, immunda diligis et immunda requiris. Factus enim eras ut habitares in celo, et nunc vadis per sterquilinia visitando latrinas." Cum igitur frater talia perorasset, demon erubuit et recessit ab eo confusus.⁴

> "like rejoices in like. For every animal seeks its own kind. You are a pig: you are impure, you speak impurities; you love impurities; you seek impurities. For you were created to live in heaven, and now you seek out toilets and go visiting latrines." After the Brother had said these things, the demon blushed and departed in confusion.⁵

In replying, the brother articulated an important theme of medieval thought: that moral impurity and material impurity are closely allied. Thus cleanliness was indeed next to godliness, and filth and material corruption, no less than sin, were the realm of the devil. So it should come as no surprise that the latrine was regarded as the haunt of demons and that this religious man was not alone in meeting the devil when he went to satisfy the necessities of nature. Similar tales were abundant in the Middle Ages. The story is found, for instance, attached to Gregory the Great.⁶ As in Salimbene's account, the devil reproaches the religious man for reciting psalms in the privy, whereupon Gregory defends himself, echoing the memorable line, "Ventrem meum purgo, et deum meum laudo," "I empty my bowels and I praise my God." Peter the Venerable, abbot of Cluny in the twelfth century, tells the story of monk who was able to expel a demon into a privy: "immundum spiritum per condignum ejus immunditiae locum a domo sua expulit," "he expelled the foul spirit from his dwelling via the place befitting his foulness."⁷ The biographer of Peter told another story in which a monk who had not confessed all his sins was oppressed by a demon; when he completed his confession, casting out his sins, the demon fled to the privy.⁸ Another story, retailed by Thietmar of Merseburg in the thirteenth century, tells of seven demons who emerged from a privy.⁹ The Prose Rule of the Céli Dé, an Irish rule preserved in a twelfth- or thirteenth-century manuscript, confirms that "the privy-houses and the urine-houses they are the abode of demons," and prescribes the blessings to be performed before entering, as well as the prayers permitted in the privy.[10] The *Cent nouvelles nouvelles*, a fifteenth-century French collection of stories, tells of a knight who met the devil in the latrine and struggled physically with him for an hour, and was only able to vanquish him by maintaining a steadfast faith in baptism.[11] The Icelandic tale *þáttr þorsteins skelks* describes the ordeal of Þorsteinn, who defies the king's orders that no one should visit the privy alone at night, and finds himself confronted in the privy by a demon. After describing hell, the demon advances on Þorsteinn until vanquished by the ringing of church bells.[12] In the early twelfth century, Guibert of Nogent tells the story of a man who witnessed the Devil creeping amongst the sleeping associates of a bishop and finally retiring into the latrine.[13] Elsewhere he describes a monk accosted by the Devil in the latrine.[14] The *Passion of St. Juliana* recounts Juliana's encounter with the Devil. Though he appeared to her disguised as an angel, she was able to discern his true identity and cast him into a latrine or dungheap.[15] The *Life* of the fifteenth-century holy woman Francisca or Francesca of Rome tells of the time she was accosted by two demons, who attempted to abduct her to the latrine; she resisted only by keeping a strong faith and by angelic intervention.[16] The fifteenth-century theologian Johannes Nider tells the story of a brother who cast out a demon and mockingly told it to repair to the latrine; when the brother later went to use the latrine at night, the devil tormented him so much there that he barely survived.[17] The very popular thirteenth-century *Dialogue on Miracles* of Caesarius of Heisterbach recounts the story of a lay-brother named Albero, who suffered eight days of illness after spotting a devil lurking by the latrine.[18] He also tells the story of a priest who encountered the devil in the privy and nearly succumbed to the devil's urgings to hang himself there; finally he purified himself through confession and hence was able to cast the devil out.[19]

A latent theme runs through all of these stories, most clearly articulated in the version of Caesarius of Heisterbach. The latrine is the realm of filth and danger both material and spiritual. When the man purifies himself—through confession, as in Caesarius, or through faith in baptism, as in the *Cent nouvelles nouvelles*—the devil is cast out of the privy. Both the latrine and the man undergo purification: it is as if the man himself *is* a latrine, full of corruption and vulnerable to the devil.

The motif extended past the close of the Middle Ages, appearing in the works of some of the most notable figures of the sixteenth century. The Protestant reformer Philipp Melanchthon is witness to a tradition that assigned the encounter to St. Bernard:

> Dicitur de sancto Bernhardo, qui cum aliquando in latrina oraret Psalmos, venit ad eum Diabolus et obiurgavit eum dicens: Quare tu in latrina oras sanctos Psalmos? Respondit ei S. Bernhardus: Illud, quod ex ore exit, Deo offero; sed id, quod infra ex ventre eiicio, tu comedas.[20]

4   *Sin and Filth in Medieval Culture*

Figure 1 The Devil appears to the hapless man in the latrine. As the latrine is the domain of the rear, and the Devil is its champion, the Devil is backing in and presents himself rear foremost. Illustration of the poem "A godly father sitting on a draught," from *A New Discourse of a Stale Subject, called The Metamorphosis of Ajax* (London, 1596), p. 18. "Ajax" is a pun on the contemporary word for a privy, "a jakes."

It is told of St. Bernard that once when he was praying the psalms in the latrine, the Devil came to him and reproached him, saying, "Why do you pray the holy psalms in the latrine?" St. Bernard answered him saying, "That which comes out of my mouth, I offer to God; but that which I cast down below from my belly, eat it!"

Even more prominently, the *Tischreden* or *Table-Talk* of Martin Luther offers another example, most likely an echo of a Latin jingle on the subject. Curiously, Luther proffers the verse shortly after mentioning Melanchthon, though his formulation differs from the version Melanchthon attributes to St. Bernard. The multiple recensions of Luther's version show how widespread the story had become. The rhyme is clear in the first version, in which Luther is said to have cited the following:

> Monachus super latrinam non debet orare primam. Deo, quod supra; tibi, quod cadit infra. Ita quidam respondit Diabolo.[21]

> [*The Devil*]: A monk on the latrine should not pray the hour of prime.
> [*The Monk:*] To God what is above, to you what drops below.
>   Thus a certain man responded to the Devil.

The motif of God/high, Devil/low is equally clear in the alternate version:

> Monachus quidam sedens super latrinam legebat horas canonicas; ad hunc accessit Diabolus dicens: Monachus non debet legere primam super latrinam! Respondit monachus: Purgo meum ventrem et colo Deum omnipotentem. Tibi, quod infra; Deo omnipotenti, quod supra.

> A certain monk sitting on the latrine was reading the canonical hours. The Devil came to him saying, "A monk should not read prime on the latrine!" The monk responded: "I purge my belly and I worship omnipotent God. To you, what is below; to omnipotent God what is above."[22]

An elaborated version is found in Sir John Harington's *Metamorphosis of Ajax*, published in 1596 and quoted above as the epigraph to this chapter.[23] As we shall see, from the medieval period there are dozens, perhaps hundreds, more serious theological stories centered on this least dignified of human necessities, stories in which the latrine is the focus of evil, a breeding-ground for sin or a locus of damnation.

St. Augustine himself wrote about the issue of whether the latrine was too filthy a place for God's presence. The question arose while he was staying in the country with his mother and friends. His mother had heard his friend Licentius singing a psalm in the latrine and expressed the familiar sentiment that the latrine was too sordid to be associated with God. As Augustine tells the story:

audio Licentium succinentem illud propheticum laete atque garrule: *Deus uirtutum, conuerte nos et ostende faciem tuam, et salui erimus.* Quod pridie post cenam cum ad requisita naturae foras exisset, paulo clarius cecinit, quam ut mater nostra ferre posset, quod illo loco talia continuo repetita canerentur. Nihil enim aliud dicebat, quoniam ipsum cantilenae modum nuper hauserat et amabat, ut fit, melos inusitatum. Obiurgauit eum religiossima, ut scis, femina ob hoc ipsum, quod inconueniens locus cantico esset. Tunc ille dixerat iocans: Quasi uero, si quis hic me inimicus includeret, non erat deus exauditurus uocem meam.[24]

I heard Licentius singing, joyfully and loudly, the verse of the prophet: *God of virtues, turn to us and show us your face, and we will be saved* [Ps 79:8]. The day before, when he had gone outdoors after dinner to satisfy the necessities of nature, he had sung this verse a bit more loudly than my mother was able to bear such things to be sung time and again in such a place. For he gave voice to nothing else, since he had recently learned the way the song went and, as usual, he loved a new melody. That woman, who is most pious, as you know, chastised him for this reason: that it was an inappropriate place for singing. Then he said, jokingly, "As if, truly, were any enemy to shut me in there, God would not hear my voice!"

Augustine goes on to interpret the episode symbolically: the latrine represents the bodily vices, which those who love God must rise above. He explains to Licentius:

Nam illi cantico et locum ipsum, quo illa offensa est, et noctem congruere uideo. A quibus enim rebus putas nos orare ut conuertamur ad deum eiusque faciem uideamus, nisi a quodam ceno corporis atque sordibus et item tenebris, quibus nos error inuoluit? Aut quid est aliud conuerti nisi ab immoderatione uitiorum uirtute ac temperantia in sese attolli? Quidue aliud est dei facies quam ipsa, cui suspiramus et cui nos amatae mundos pulchrosque reddimus, ueritas?[25]

"For I see that place at which she was offended, and the night as well, as relevant to the song. For what things do you think we pray that we may be converted to God and see his face, if not from a certain filth of the body and its ordures, and also from the darkness in which error has enveloped us? And what else is conversion but to raise oneself up from the excess of vice by means of virtue and restraint? And what else is the face of God but that truth for which we yearn, and that beloved thing which we repay with our own selves made clean and beautiful?"

Here Augustine lays out the essential dichotomies that make up the medieval system of thought about purity and pollution, and that will inform this book. God is associated with cleanliness, rising and the face; sin with excrement, the backside and the latrine. Like many another medieval author, Augustine is quick to use an essential aversion to the latrine as an occasion to think about these matters.

Although Licentius asserted that God would hear him from the latrine, it is significant that he did not claim the latrine as part of the realm of God. The unsuitability of this claim is the subject of a passage in Abelard's *Theologia "Summi Boni,"* in which Abelard discusses appropriateness in language, and particularly in discussing the divine. His lengthiest example concerns the essential incompatibility of filth and the divine:

> Vnde cum deum ubique esse et credamus et predicemus, nemo tamen dicere presumat eum in inmundo loco esse, ita ut locum ipsum aut latrinam nominet aut alioquo nomine alio determinate spurcitie ipsum assignet.[26]
>
> Hence although we believe and instruct that God is everywhere, nevertheless no one should presume to say that he is in an unclean place, either designating that place a latrine or defining it by any other term of filth.

Here Abelard too identifies filth as the antithetical to the divine and the latrine as the apotheosis of filth. He is hence witness to a long tradition of theologians, clerics and storytellers who told serious tales about the perils of visiting the latrine.

Faced with these examples, we might well ask what sensibility gave rise to such an abundance of pious scatology and how such sensational passages came to be invested with serious questions of religion. It is my contention that if we explore the popular and theological context of these stories, we will find them central to larger issues of medieval thought. For, like the devil in Salimbene's story, man was created to live, if not in heaven, at least in Paradise; but now, like the devil, he seeks out and goes visiting latrines. The need to attend to the "necessities of nature" has been a token of the sinful corporeality that has afflicted humankind since the Devil first tempted Adam and Eve to sin. Since that day, man has striven to deny and control his flesh—as vulnerable to corruption and odor as the privy itself—but, however abstinent he may be, he cannot abstain from the demands of the body. In the privy, he must acknowledge the flesh; there the lofty spirituality of the head must give way to the earthly concerns of the unthinking and unruly lower body. Thus the excrement that drove men to the latrine is both the emblem and the actual embodiment of the sin that made that flesh impure and corrupt.

This book, then, will examine the medieval understanding of material corruption and bodily impurity: the ways in which spiritual corruption was thought to take material form. The material corruption of the body was regarded as a tangible, unavoidable presence, an inescapable part of the human condition, like original sin—and indeed not just *like* original sin, but as the actual material embodiment of original sin. To recognize this is to make sense of the abundance of references to excrement, decay, illness and other afflictions of the flesh in medieval texts. In particular the Middle Ages found meaning in the effusions of the body and in the arrangement of the human body, topics that now tend to produce laughter or nervous embarrassment in modern observers. These are abundant in medieval culture, not only in the comic genres we might expect, but in serious realms: moral tales, sermons, saints' lives, theology, exegesis, historical chronicles and epics, accounts of the interrogation of heretics, royal decrees, church carvings and paintings and a dozen other forms. Far from serving as testimony to the crudeness of medieval taste, these appearances show the ways in which medieval writers and storytellers were alive to the significance of what they regarded as the shameful aspects of existence and used the full range of human experience as a subject for continued meditation.

THE UNCLEAN IN SCHOLARLY THOUGHT

It has long been recognized that biology and behavior are always overlaid with meaning by the culture in which they are expressed. As early as 1936, the anthropologist Marcel Mauss recognized that purely natural human behavior cannot exist: it is always modified and interpreted by its cultural matrix.[27] Mary Douglas pioneered the work of studying the unclean and its cultural meanings in her influential work *Purity and Danger: An Analysis of the Concepts of Pollution and Taboo*, in 1966.[28] In *Purity and Danger*, Douglas stressed the importance of the symbolic structures of meaning to traditional cultures and, in particular, the ways in which the polarity of purity and impurity provided a structure with which to organize an understanding of the world, arguing that pollution symbols reveal "elaborate cosmologies."[29] As she said, "Reflection on dirt involves reflection on the relation of order to disorder, being to non-being, form to formlessness, life to death."[30] Further, "dirt," she observes, "is essentially disorder,"[31] a definition that is particularly important for the Middle Ages, where formlessness, decay and sin are closely intertwined. Douglas inaugurated an important way of looking at such issues when she argued that the purity laws of the ancient Jews, codified in Leviticus, were formulated specifically to make conceptual distinctions between clean and unclean categories of things—not, as had been presumed, merely as a method of enforcing proper hygiene and food sanitation. The separation of the clean and unclean, in other words, is a fundamental of human thought and not a side effect of practical efforts to insure good health.

Douglas also looked at ways in which the body and its margins can serve as a source of symbols for larger society, and public rituals involving the body can have a social focus rather than a purely individual one.[32] In the course of this argument she articulates an important analysis of the power of bodily waste and the margins of the body. "Why should bodily refuse be a symbol of danger and of power?" she asks. She answers:

> all margins are dangerous. If they are pulled this way or that the shape of fundamental experience is altered. Any structure of ideas is vulnerable at its margins. We should expect the orifices of the body to symbolise its specially vulnerable points. Matter issuing from them is marginal stuff of the most obvious kind. Spittle, blood, milk, urine, faeces or tears by simply issuing forth have traversed the boundary of the body. So also have bodily parings, skin, nail, hair clippings and sweat.[33]

As she points out, the degree to which each of these is considered dangerous varies by culture. Nevertheless, even across cultures some have a greater tendency to be identified as "unclean" or dangerous, based on further distinctions, such as odor, susceptibility to decay, opaqueness and relation to procreation or digestion. Those regarded as most impure become the focus of rules and rituals that mirror larger anxieties about the body politic, as Douglas analyzes them—or about the place of humans in relation to God, as I will examine here.

Douglas's arguments have been influential in anthropology, and her work has proven useful to medievalists studying similar issues.[34] The nature of the topic—impurity, with its related fields of social and cultural unacceptability, transgression, the taboo, filth and so forth—has attracted a small number of other scholars, on the whole blustery and defensive. Most of these have tended to be interested in the more postmodern aspects of filth, in tacit acknowledgement of the fact that traditional forms of scholarship have regarded the field as ignoble and *infra dignitatem*, except in the more unshockable field of anthropology.[35] In recent years, with the growth of the idea that all culture is worthy of examination, attention to the field has increased. The majority of literary and cultural scholars have been most interested in the idea that all viewpoints, texts or substances embody their own contradiction and, thus, that filth is most interesting in the fact that it can be transformed into fecundity. This point of view was championed in Mikhail Bakhtin's landmark study of Rabelais and the scatological carnivalesque, *Rabelais and His World*, and elaborated by many scholars since.[36] Bakhtin saw the "lower bodily stratum" as simultaneously transgressive and fruitful and linked the realm of the lower body to modes and intervals of subversion that served to destabilize more seemly and repressive "official" culture.

Other critics have offered developmental models in which filth plays an essential part in personal psychological history or in human history, or in the two together. Freud regarded aspects of adult human culture as a sublimation of what he identified as a child's attachment to feces; in particular he associated feces with money, both, according to him, seemingly useless objects invested with value.[37] This interpretation of money, even if accepted uncritically, obviously would be less relevant to cultures in which money is unknown or scarce. A Freudian approach to scatological folklore is taken by folklorist Alan Dundes in *Life is Like a Chicken Coop Ladder: A Portrait of German Culture Through Folklore*.[38] Freudianism also informs Dominique Laporte's intentionally transgressive *Histoire de la merde*, which incorporates Marxist analysis in his reading of the development of subjectivity and privacy.[39] According to Laporte, a key development in the history of civilization came when laws prohibited the throwing of household excrement in the street but instead required that it be kept, or "hoarded," inside, thus transforming it into private accumulation, akin to the hoarding of money. Laporte cites a French edict of 1539 on the subject, in effect identifying the Renaissance as the turning point in the history of human development and of the sanitary practices that mirror it. Apart from the problem in logic in equating money hoarding with waste disposal, the history of waste disposal is much more complex than Laporte allows, as we shall see.

Psychoanalytic theory is also central to Julia Kristeva's *Powers of Horror: An Essay on Abjection*, which identifies the abject as fundamental to human life, in its familiar form as simultaneously despised and fruitful.[40] Abjection, according to Kristeva, is the condition of infants very early in their psychological development (pre-oedipal, in Kristeva's terms); it is also closely identified with bodies and especially with boundary violations such as excretion; and is intertwined with a rejection of the mother and hence the feminine. Thus the abject is repudiated, but also becomes a position from which misogyny can be critiqued, arriving once again at the recurring paradox that the reviled can be both filthy and fruitful. This paradox is perhaps most fully explored by Georges Bataille, who theorizes filth, waste and the despicable as elements of liberation.[41] The toilet is further identified as a site of ideological revelation by Slavoj Žižek's Lacanian *Plague of Fantasies*.[42] Much of the more theoretical work on the topics of excretion, filth, shame and the lower body has centered on the early modern period and on texts from that era that addressed such issues, such as Sir John Harington's pseudo-classical dialogue on sanitation systems, *The Metamorphosis of Ajax*.[43]

The most text-centered and up-to-date exploration of medieval thought on the unclean is Susan Signe Morrison's *Excrement in the Late Middle Ages: Sacred Filth and Chaucer's Fecopoetics*.[44] The study that most resembles the present one, in its combination of theological/exegetical analysis and anthropological dimension, is Jonathan Wyn Shofer's study of rabbinic literature in its cultural context, *Confronting Vulnerability: The Body and the Divine in Rabbinic Ethics*.[45] Historically informed literary analysis has also appeared in recent years, most notably in Albrecht Classen's studies of comic tales. Classen remarks, for instance, that in the late Middle Ages and sixteenth century "the body and its base functions were increasingly thematized for a wide range of epistemological functions."[46] These studies have recently been joined by a more historically focused examination of the issues of cleanliness, filth and contamination, such as Douglas Biow's *The Culture of Cleanliness in Renaissance Italy* (1300–1600), Emily Cockayne's *Hubbub: Filth, Noise and Stench in England, 1600–1770* and Alain Corbin's *The Foul and the Fragrant: Odor and the French Social Imagination* (on the eighteenth century). Modern sociological aspects have been examined in Rose George's *The Big Necessity*, on modern worldwide sanitation, and *Toilet: Public Restrooms and the Politics of Sharing*, an account of the politics of public latrines from ancient Rome to the present day.[47]

The study of impurity associated with the body draws on scholarship on bodily issues, although body scholarship has been focused more on areas such as gender, sex and identity.[48] Here the Middle Ages had two not entirely consonant traditions. One held that, of the sexes, women were governed less by reason and more by the flesh; they were, in short, more bodily, and by extension more shameful.[49] The other, the tradition that will be examined in this book, is non-gendered and held that all humans, regardless of sex, were equally subject to bodily corruption: excrement and putrefaction, the penalties of original sin, afflicted all alike. The great majority of the characters in medieval narratives and images concerning filth are men, in part most likely specifically so filth could not be dismissed as endemic only to women. Medieval religion was careful not to absolve men from the responsibility of having bodies subject to corruption.

This understanding of the world, mediated by the body, is medieval in its details, but recent thought in philosophy and cognition has provided support for the conceptual framework of such a system. Several works have identified the basis of human thought not as abstract reasoning, accomplished via the manipulation of symbols, but as a more fundamental reliance on metaphor and patterns.[50] What is more, it has been argued that all human understanding is crucially determined by the body, so that both philosophical and cognitive systems ("embodied cognition") are inseparable from their embodied origins.[51] "The mind is not merely embodied," Lakoff and Johnson state in *Philosophy in the Flesh*, "but embodied in such a way that our conceptual systems draw largely upon the commonalities of our bodies and of the environments we live in. The result is that much of a person's conceptual system is either universal or widespread across languages and cultures."[52] The medieval understanding of the meaning of bodily corruption is testimony to this. As the medieval world understood, "Because our ideas are framed in terms of our unconscious embodied conceptual systems, truth and knowledge depend on embodied understanding."[53]

In the medieval period, the precise structure and interpretation of such issues came from Christian theology, an amalgam of Scripture and pre-existing views about the body and its place in the universe. L. William Countryman explored these issues in *Dirt, Greed and Sex*, which looks at the way the rules for sexual behavior formed part of a larger network of purity issues in the New Testament.[54] Peter Brown's magisterial *The Body*

12 *Sin and Filth in Medieval Culture*

and Society: Men, Women, and Sexual Renunciation in Early Christianity* and *The Cult of the Saints: Its Rise and Function in Latin Christianity* examined the ways in which early Christianity regarded the body and its purification.⁵⁵ Caroline Walker Bynum has done related work in such books as *Fragmentation and Redemption*, which looked at the relation between ideas of wholeness and purity in medieval Christianity.⁵⁶ And considerable work has been done on such medieval phenomena as *contemptus mundi* literature, which sought to bring home the vileness of the corrupt body and world as a way of redirecting the sinner's affections to the spiritual.⁵⁷ The body was a particular focus of *contemptus mundi* treatises, since it formed one of the sinner's chief attachments, and its desires and responses mediated his or her experience of the world. Perhaps the most widely circulating medieval passage of this kind used the popular strategy of comparing the human body to a dungheap—a variant of the equivalence between the sinner and the latrine proffered by the tales discussed previously. A typical example of the passage, from the *Ancrene Wisse*, a thirteenth-century English treatise for anchoresses, reads:

> I þe licome is fulðe 7 unstrengðe. . . . Þi flesch, hwet frut bereð hit in alle his openunges? Amid te menske of þi neb, þat is þe fehereste deal, bitweonen muðes smech 7 neases smeal, ne berest tu as twa priue þurles? Nart tu icumen of ful slim? Nart tu fulðe fette? Ne bist tu wurme fode? Philosophus: Sperma es fluidum, vas stercorum, esca uermium.⁵⁸

> In the body is filth and weakness. . . . Your flesh, what fruit does it bear in all its openings? Amid the nobility of your face, which is the fairest part, between the taste of the mouth and the smell of the nose, do you not bear as it were two privy holes? Are you not come from foul slime? Are you not a carrier of filth? Are you not worm's food? The philosopher: "You are an ooze of sperm, a vessel of dung, the food of worms."

A related passage is found in a fourteenth-century English preachers' handbook:

> O esca vermium, o massa pulveris, o vapor vanitatis, cur sic extolleris? . . . Si ergo consideres, o homo, quid per os, quid per nares, quid per ceteros meatus corporis egreditur, numquid vilius sterquilinio invenies te?⁵⁹

> O food for worms, O lump of dirt, wisp of vanity, why do you exalt yourself in this way? . . . Therefore if you consider, O man, what comes out through your mouth, through your nose, through the other passages of the body, will you not find that you are viler than a dungheap?

The body as dung is a commonplace of such literature, which aims to reveal the true nature of the body so that the human, a "cloud of vanity," will no longer prize the things of the flesh. One of the most rhetorically impressive examples of the theme appears in the fifteenth-century dialogue *Der Ackermann aus Böhmen*. Here Death, the ultimate exemplification of the corruptibility of the earthly body, characterizes the body as

> ein besmiret binstock, ein ganzer unflat, ein unreiner mist, ein kotvaß, ein wurmspeis, ein stankhaus, ein unlustiger spulzuber, ein vaules aß, ein schimelkast, ein bodenloser sack, ein locheret tasch, ein blasbalk, ein geitiger slunt, ein stinkender leimtigel, ein ubelriechender harmkrug, ein ubelsmeckender eimer, ein betriegender tockenschein, ein leimen raubhaus, ein unsetig leschtrog und ein gemalte begrebnuß. Es merk wer da welle: ein jeglichs ganz gewurktes mensch hat neun locher in seinem leib, aus den allen so unlustiger und unreiner unflat fleußet, das nicht unreiners gewesen mag. So schones mensch gesahestu nie, hettestu eins linzen augen und kundest es inwendig durchsehen, dir wurde darabe grauen.[60]

> an abomination, a veritable spawn, an offal tun, a wormwood, a stench house, a filthy swill tub, a putrid carcass, a mildewed canister, a sack without bottom, a poke full of holes, a flatulent bellows, a voracious gullet, a stinking glue-pot, an evil-smelling puncheon, a deceitful straw-puppet, an earthen still-room, a bottomless firebucket and an alluringly painted tenement of clay. May it be heard by whomsoever: Every roundly made man hath nine orifices in his body from which exudeth such loathsome and filthy dirt, the like of which can scarce be found elsewhere. Thou never layest eyes upon a man ever so handsome, that thou wouldst not shudder if thou hadst the eyes of a lynx and couldst see through his insides.[61]

Such characterizations, likening the body to an array of worthless and repellent material objects, are designed to provoke disgust in the reader: and not only disgust for others, but disgust for one's own body. Like corruption itself, this disgust is twofold, with both a material and a moral dimension.

THE USES OF DISGUST

Moral disgust was a key emotion in the medieval cultivation of virtue and piety, the vehicle by which medieval sinners were taught to shun the body and the world. As an emotional and moral response with a biological underpinning, disgust has certain fundamental features which were used and manipulated to transform it into a medium of moral improvement.[62]

Although disgust is in origin a biological feature, its connection with morality made it a source of pride to medieval moralists. In particular, disgust separates humans from animals, who often exhibit a tolerance for smells, effusions and conditions that typically repel humans.[63] The Bible made note of this distinction in Proverbs 26:11, a passage widely quoted in the Middle Ages: "Sicut canis qui revertitur ad vomitum suum sic inprudens qui iterat stultitiam suam" ("As a dog returneth to his vomit, so a fool returneth to his folly"). The dog fails to be disgusted by its own bodily effusion; the fool has crossed the human/animal divide, becoming no better than the dog by failing to be disgusted by his own offenses. The fool's folly, moreover, is portrayed as the moral equivalent of bodily effusion, a scriptural example of the use of bodily waste as an essential sign of moral failing. Bodily effusion is animalistic; to feel disgust at that bodily effusion was to cultivate the non-animal—the human, and above that the spiritual—aspects of the self.

The biological roots of disgust helped shape the basic categories of material things that provoke the disgust response, and thus the things to which moral failings are likened. Disgust probably first evolved as a protection against illness. Humans seem to be hard-wired to recoil from certain things that may transmit disease or infection, such as the bodily secretions of others, decaying food or creatures such as lice, maggots or worms. In Steven Pinker's words, "Disgust is intuitive microbiology."[64] The responses to these things are more or less purely reactive, but these are then overlaid with a substantial ideational component: in other words, things that resemble disgusting substances, or are associated with them, can also provoke disgust. In this sense disgust has much in common with sympathetic magic; the two share ways of generalizing about the world. Disgust follows, for instance, what anthropologists of magic call the "law of contagion," meaning that disgust often operates at one remove from the disgusting object, inhering in things that have come into contact with disgusting substances. For instance, in experiments a salad in which an insect was placed and then removed were regarded as disgusting, even though the insect was no longer in evidence. In another experiment, a dried, sterilized cockroach was dipped in a glass of juice and then removed; people found the glass of juice disgusting, even though the subjects were assured that the cockroach and the juice it had touched posed absolutely no biological threat.[65] Bedsheets used by others were also judged disgusting, presumably because of their contact with others' bodies in a private setting, as well as the anxiety that they might have absorbed bodily secretions.[66] What is called "the law of similarity" also applies, so that things that resemble disgusting things also elicit a disgust response. Thus earthworms, which are harmless to humans, typically evoke disgust, perhaps because they resemble intestinal helminths.[67] The commercial market in fake disgusting objects, such as rubber dog excrement and fake vomit, shows the reactions that can be aroused by innocuous materials designed to resemble objects of disgust. Similarly the "mouth-feel" of certain foods such as tomatoes, undercooked eggs or okra arouses disgust in some people, presumably because their slipperiness resembles the sliminess of decaying food.

Ideational components also enter into the interpretation of the disgusting substance. One social psychologist tells a story about his own experience:

> I was walking through a field and passed by a shack from which a strong odor, which I took for that of some decaying dead animal, penetrated my nostrils. My first reaction was that of an intense disgust. In the next moment I discovered that I had made a mistake and recognized the odor as that of glue. The feeling of disgust immediately disappeared and the odor now seemed quite agreeable, probably because of some rather pleasant associations with carpentry.[68]

Thus interpretation is overlaid on basic reactions; similarly, the smell of a stable might have pleasant associations to a rider, while the same person would find the smell repellent in a restaurant.

Although disgust evolved in humans to distance a person from a dangerous substance, the actual relationship of danger to disgust is imperfect, and it is here that ideational elements become especially important. Some things which transmit disease to humans, such as mosquitoes, do not arouse a strong disgust response. What is more, the sensory qualities of an object are not necessarily the determining factors in disgust. People will willingly eat a deep-fried shrimp, but not a sterilized and deep-fried cockroach, even though the physical attributes of the shrimp are similar to the cockroach. In fact the two are such close biological relations that people allergic to shrimp are usually also allergic to cockroaches. Similarly, people will refuse to lick a lollipop if they know it has been licked by a healthy stranger, though the licked lollipop may look identical to a pristine lollipop. It is ideational attributes that qualify the cockroach and the lollipop as contaminating or disgusting.[69] Thus disgust is not a straightforward biological response, but involves ideas about likeness and association. The "law of contamination" has not been observed in any non-human species, or even in feral, unsocialized humans, and so it may be that biological survival is not the sole "aim" of disgust; it may also have important social functions.[70] The example of the lollipop, for instance, requires the person to make a distinction between intimate and stranger. The example of the cockroach and the shrimp depends on ideas of which foods are deemed edible, a cultural decision inculcated in childhood. Disgust, then, is one mechanism by which members of a group distinguish between themselves and outsiders. They may, for instance, be disgusted by outsiders but not by intimates. Or they may define people who share the same disgust as members of their group: "Our kind" is disgusted by something (eating dogs or snails, for instance, or certain sexual practices), but "their kind" is not.

Culture, then, both uses and determines many aspects of the disgust response. That said, certain things have been found to evoke disgust more reliably than others. Above all, the most disgusting things are death and excrement, which are both variants of carnal decay. The long list includes certain kinds of food, animals, bodily products, poor hygiene, certain sexual activities, body envelope violations and contact with death.[71] Bodily excretions in particular are universally regarded as potentially disgusting,[72] although the level of response tends to differ between cultures, and for that matter between different people in the same culture.

The unifying factor is all these categories involve carnality: bodiliness or fleshliness. The most fundamental disgust reaction, the reaction based on biology, is a horror of putting disgusting things in one's mouth. This essential disgust relating to ingestion has been termed "core disgust," and it is clear that the substances that evoke this disgust are usually carnal, that is, derived from animals. Decaying meat, decomposing bodies, wounds, pus and bodily excretions are all flesh-based. Although plant matter can become disgusting, the attributes that make it so (such as sliminess) overlap with signs of animal decay; in other words, plants are rarely disgusting in themselves, but only to the degree that they resemble disgusting animal attributes.

Just as disgust makes the leap from potentially dangerous substances to harmless things that resemble them, it makes a second ideological leap, noting the similarities between flesh and the body of the onlooker—the decay of flesh reminds the observer that his or her own flesh will also inevitably decompose. This is central to medieval thought about the body, and key also to modern scholarship on disgust. Paul Rozin has termed the response that abhors this evidence of fleshliness "animal reminder disgust" or "animal-nature disgust": "We fear recognising our animality because we fear that, like animals, we are mortal."[73] Rozin and his colleagues confirm that mortality is the fear underlying ideational disgust. (In this it is related to "core disgust," which operates to dissuade people to ingest decaying and hence dangerous substances, and thus has avoidance of death at its heart as well.) Death was the "chief elicitor" of disgust in the disgust-sensitivity scale established by Rozin and colleagues:

> Human consciousness, as it were, accesses the pre-existing distaste system, and all its involuntary mechanisms of revulsion physically force us to avoid contemplating our undeniable predicament: we are animals that must die.[74]

That denial of death is a primary motivating factor in human psychology has been the theme of a school of thought inaugurated by cultural anthropologist Ernest Becker, who argued that fear of death, rather than thought about sex, was at the foundation of the human condition.[75] Disgust would, then, be another of the manifold ways that humans react to reminders of mortality.

The fact that disgust is essentially a reaction to corrupt carnality has been confirmed by other studies. Valerie Curtis and Adam Biran devised a disgust experiment in which subjects viewed photos and assessed their disgusting qualities.[76] The experiment verified that animal-nature disgust is an important factor. For instance, participants reported disgust at pictures of people with acne or skin problems, conditions that disrupt the smooth, uniform and optimally healthy appearance of the skin. Similarly a small pool of yellow fluid on a white cloth was deemed disgusting, resembling, as it does, urine or pus. It was even more disgusting if it had a dark red spot at its center, resembling effluvia from a suppurating wound. By contrast, a small pool of clear blue fluid on a white cloth was not deemed disgusting; it does not remind the viewer of any body-envelope violations because the body never produces clear blue fluid. (The reactions produced by this range of colors are, incidentally, the reason that liquid laundry detergent is usually a clear blue color and never yellow or red.)

Animal-nature disgust also operates at one remove, following the law of contagion. In experiments, people viewed objects that had come into contact with physical corruption as contaminated: for instance, a significant proportion of subjects regarded a laundered sweater, a used car and a hotel bed with clean linen as disgusting when told they had been used by a person with an amputated leg.[77] Even more significant is the fact that moral contamination evoked the same response: The subjects were disgusted by the objects when told they had been used by a healthy convicted murderer.[78] However, it should be noted that although responses to the murderer might seem to be a case of pure moral revulsion, it is possible that the subjects were equally repelled by the physical nature of his crime—murder is an inescapable reminder that bodies are mortal and can be butchered. One wonders if the disgust response would have been as strong for a non-physical crime, such as insider trading. In fact experiments have found that, in the modern U.S., socio-moral behavior only elicits disgust reliably if it involves sexual behavior. Stealing from a blind beggar, although it may have been considered reprehensible, did not elicit disgust, but humans having sexual interaction with animals did.[79] The bodily nature of sexual behavior here seems to make the difference and push the behavior into the category of disgusting. This is confirmed by an experiment that found that inducing people to reflect on their mortality caused them to regard sexuality as more disgusting than they would otherwise.[80] Disgust here serves as a revolt against one's animal nature, a reaction that attempts to assert that the important aspect of humans is spiritual rather than corporeal.

The disgust response is not restricted to the material realm but is often generalized to include deviant morality of other sorts. Disgust is the characteristic and prototypical response to violations of essential social and moral codes. Here too the body is involved. This disgust often takes the form of a feeling of uncleanness—what has been termed the "Lady Macbeth effect." In one modern experiment, after recalling a deed of a certain type, subjects were offered a choice of a free pencil or an antiseptic wipe, independently established to be equal in appeal. The subjects who recalled an unethical deed took the antiseptic wipe 75% of the time; those who recalled an ethical deed chose the wipe only 37.5% of the time. The researchers concluded that "Exposure to one's own and even to others' moral indiscretions poses a moral threat and stimulates a need for physical cleansing."[81]

It is important to note that this disgust is not simply metaphorical, although metaphors themselves run deep and are not merely rhetorical associations.[82] Experiments show that direct experience of disgusting tastes, viewing photographs of disgusting things and moral disgust elicit the same physical responses.[83] However strongly felt in the body, disgust remains an emotional response, as much visceral as intellectual.

What is more, researchers have determined that disgust magnifies the severity of moral condemnation. In experiments, subjects were asked to levy moral judgments, and a subset simultaneously had disgust provoked by, for instance, being exposed to a disgusting smell. The disgusted subset were more condemnatory toward moral lapses than the control sample.[84] This artificial evoking of disgust merely duplicates what medieval preachers, churchmen and storytellers accomplished by larding their narratives with the details of filth, corruption and decay. This intensifying reaction can be provoked through repetition, as the study's authors say:

> Feelings of disgust fit particularly well into approachs that see emotion and cognition as fundamentally embodied. . . . More than any other emotion, disgust feels like a "gut" feeling, and because of its link to nausea, disgust may be the most effective emotion at triggering the gastroenteric nervous system. It also fits well into theories such as Damasio's (1994) somatic marker hypothesis. In this view, bodily reactions to real events (e.g., nausea, arousal) come to be so well learned that whenever people merely think about a similar situation, they get an "as-if" reaction in the parts of their brains that control or sense those reactions. These flashes of affect then guide behavior and judgment.[85]

Recent work has distinguished three ethics employed by cultures to interpret and resolve moral violations, what are called the "Big Three" of morality. These are the ethic of community, the ethic of autonomy and the ethic of divinity.[86] The ethic of community involves interpersonal relations and interdependence, including hierarchy, and evaluates behavior by how well it observes these codes. The second of the Big Three, the ethic of autonomy, stresses the agency of the individual and issues of justice and rights. The third, the ethic of divinity, focuses on sanctity, sacred order, sin and pollution, and hence violations of purity and holiness. Medieval ecclesiastical and theological culture interpreted human activity through the ethic of divinity and championed this ethic as the preeminent mode of interpretation, although the other realms were also present in medieval life. Paul Rozin and his associates have, furthermore, proposed that each of the three moral codes is associated with a particular emotional response.[87]

Violations of community are met with contempt; so, for instance, a person who disregards the official hierarchy will be treated contemptuously, which is a reassertion of superiority on the part of those reacting to the violator. Violations of autonomy evoke anger.[88] Most importantly for these purposes, violations to the realm of divinity evoke disgust. Researchers devised experiments to test responses to violations of an ethic of divinity (set, in this instance, in India). As it happened, the examples of violations to divinity used in the study all involved corporeality, such as eating a piece of rotten meat, shaking hands with someone who had an incestuous relationship or touching a corpse. Thus the most significant part of the experiment may not be that divinity violations elicit disgust—this is predictable as soon as the examples are proffered. The more important part of the experiment may be the underlying recognition that the corporeal and material are antithetical to the divine. The anti-divine will thus always involve the corporeal and material, and the only appropriate moral reaction will be disgust. This results in a dilemma for humans, who are inescapably corporeal, who must regard themselves as both spiritual and material, and whose only adequate moral response to their corporeal failings must be disgust at their own impurity.

The quandary of moral self-disgust is a defining feature of medieval Christianity. Although medieval Christianity may seem to have served as the font of a Cartesian dualism that separated spirit and body, in fact it integrated spirit and flesh. The corruptible, corporeal, material elements of being human were not incidental, but absolutely fundamental, the continuing testimony to original sin, and hence to human history and humans' relation to God. The corruption of the flesh was not to be denied or disguised, but served as a sign; disgust was to be cultivated because it propelled one away from the corrupt material world and moved one toward the realm of the divine, where corruption would no longer rule. Thus the attention to the matters of the flesh that merely appear crude and undignified in later periods. Medieval humans felt it essential to dwell on their full embodiment, not despite the fact that it was disgusting, but precisely because of that fact. It was only later eras that came to regard the flesh as an incidental and unfortunate container for the mind, as flesh whose lowliness was an offense to human dignity.[89]

Thus the continuing cultural attention to what might appear to be at first an unseemly problem of hygiene. As one recent commentator put it, with reference to Ernest Becker:

> If filth is so unpleasant, why . . . does it deserve our notice at all, other than as a straightforward technical problem? Becker's is an existential answer: much of the matter called filth is the inescapable emblem of our biologicality. Our fixation with it is part of our futile effort to exclude it from our identity. "Excreting is a curse that threatens madness because it shows man his abject finitude," Becker writes.[90]

To repudiate and distance oneself from any suggestion that we are mere animals, and hence mortal, is part of what has been called "Terror Management Theory."[91] Jonathan Haidt and his associates explain:

> But the most fearful aspect of being an animal may be mortality. Humans are like other animals in having fragile body envelopes that, when breached, reveal blood and soft viscera. For all our efforts to distinguish humans from animals (e.g. language, morality, two-legs-no-feathers), on the inside we are almost indiscriminable from other mammals. Body envelope violations may therefore be disgusting because they are direct reminders of the fragility and animality of our bodies. Similarly, death and contact with corpses are powerful disgust elicitors because a human corpse is the clearest evidence of human mortality. This analysis may explain our unexpected finding that death and body envelope violations loaded on the same factor of our factor analysis. This analysis is also consistent with theorizing by Becker ([*The Denial of Death*], 1973), who has argued that the fear of death is the great fear haunting human societies and shaping human cultures. The greatest threat and insult to the human soul or self may be the possibility that humans die just like animals, with nothing continuing after death.[92]

Religion, with its powerful insistence that humans are distinct from animals and that human death is not final, can be regarded as the ultimate terror management theory. As we shall see, medieval thought invested such attributes as body posture and orientation with religious significance and pointedly distinguished human posture from that of animals. Other aspects of carnality, such as excretion, death and decay, were common to both animals and humans, but it was emphasized that in the case of humans, these were all temporary attributes of the sinful earthly world. It was critical to assign excretion a temporary status, because excretion was *antithetical to the divine and hence to the life everlasting*—not only because of its disgusting physical attributes, disagreeable as those may be, but because excretion is an unavoidable reminder and correlate of the inevitability of "the greatest fear haunting human societies": mortality.

To the modern secular mind, then, excretion is repugnant first of all because of the biological disgust response, but this is also overlaid by the essential horror of bodiliness, death and the irreversible corruption and dissolution of the flesh. The same was true for the medieval Christian mind, except that the dissolution of the flesh was never final. Excretion, and the sin it emblematized and embodied, signified the impurity that distanced humans from the purity and stability of God—from a final rescue from corrupt fleshliness. Thus death was still the looming fear associated with excretion, but it was a spiritual death as well as a corporeal one.

The moral aspects of embodiment and corruption gave rise to medieval interpretations that stressed issues of divinity over what might seem to be more pragmatic aspects of a situation. This is exemplified, for instance, by a complaint of 1330 from Barcelona, when a scribe complained of a sewer from the Jews' quarter that passed through a Christian neighborhood.[93] No doubt the people of the neighborhood found the smell noxious, but the scribe did not mention the community aspects of the problem; instead the focus of his complaint was that the smell offended the Virgin of the Pine, patron of the parish church. The Virgin Mary, the spotless exemplar of sanctity, was here contrasted with the unbelieving Jews, exemplars of unrighteousness, and the excrement that symbolized and embodied that unrighteousness: the violation was in the commingling of the separate spheres of purity and impurity.[94] Thus the situation was framed in terms of the ethics of divinity: purity versus impurity, sanctity versus sin. Even the most seemingly straightforward matters of public hygiene, it is clear, form part of a discourse of purity. Of course, not every single violation of sanitation laws became the occasion for moral reflection: sometimes a sewer is just a sewer, particularly when it poses an immediate problem. When chamber pots from the upper floors of houses were emptied on the heads of passers-by, the passers-by did not need symbolic reasons to object. But moral interpretation was never far from the surface, even in the most concrete of circumstances. For instance, Ernest Sabine describes one particularly filthy street in medieval London: "a wardmote inquest for Basinghall Ward in 1421 reported that all the little rents of the Swan, belonging to Richard Clark, were without privies, so that all the tenants threw their ordure and other horrible liquids before their doors, to the great nuisance of holy church and of passers-by."[95] The fact that holy church is included in the list of those offended—as well as the fact that it takes precedence over passers-by—is a reflection of the lens of divinity through which such violations are viewed.

It is also no accident that stories such as these involve the sewer and the latrine. It was easy to impose issues of moral disgust on the substances that most easily provoked physical disgust, and the disgust aroused by the effluvia of the body is almost overdetermined. Effluvia violate the boundaries and assumed wholeness of the body, and they are frequently slippery, which is similar to the sliminess of decaying food or flesh. Excrement in particular has good cause to be deemed the most disgusting of bodily products and appears to elicit disgust almost universally.[96] On the physical level, it is constituted of decomposing formerly living things (whether animal or vegetable), reduced to a formless mass; on a conceptual level, the fact that the human body, to which we devote so much attention to keep pure and clean, can and must produce such a substance makes people appalled. On the physical level, the smell of excrement arouses disgust; on the existential level, it is an inescapable reminder that humans are bodily and that the body is subject to corruption: in a word, mortal. Excretion, like other bodily functions, reminds humans that they are inescapably animalistic— and, once again, hence mortal. As recent scholars have noted, "Human beings are suspended between God (or Gods) above and animals below, and we rise and fall as a function of our success in concealing or overcoming our animality."[97] The war between the animal and the divine, the material and the spiritual, the debased and the lofty, takes shape in places such as the latrine, where the necessities of the body make their demands.

In medieval culture, such demands inevitably had a theological dimension. Christianity held that humans were pure in origin but sinful in the earthly world, contaminated by the original sin committed in Eden. The behavioral expression of this was sin; the physical expression was bodily corruption. Augustine's commentary on Psalm 37:6, "My sores are putrefied and corrupted," exemplifies medieval thought on the essential relation between sin and bodily corruption:

> *Computruerunt et putuerunt liuores mei.* Iam qui liuores habet, non est sanus. Adde quia ipsi liuores computruerunt et putuerunt. Vnde putuerunt? Quia computruerunt. Iam quomodo hoc explicetur in uita humana quis hoc non nouit? Habeat aliquis sanum olfactum animae, sentit quomodo puteant peccata. Cui putori peccatorum contrarius erat odor ille, de quo dicit apostolus: *Christi bonus odor sumus Deo, in omni loco, iis qui salui fiunt.* Sed unde, nisi de spe? Vnde, nisi de recordatione sabbati? Aliud enim plangimus in hac uita, aliud praesumimus in illa uita. Quod plangitur, putet; quod praesumitur, fragrat. Ergo nisi esset ille talis odor qui nos inuitaret, numquam sabbatum recordaremur. Sed quia habemus per Spiritum ipsum odorem, ut dicamus sponso nostro: *Post odorem unguentorum tuorum curremus,* auertimus a putoribus nostris olfactum, et conuertentes nos ad ipsum aliquantum respiramus. Sed nisi ad nos oleant et mala nostra, numquam istis gemitibus confitemur: *Computruerunt et putuerunt liuores mei.*[98]

> *My sores are putrefied and corrupted.* Indeed, he who has sores is unhealthy. What is more, these sores are putrefied and corrupted. Whence the corruption? Because they have putrefied. Indeed, who does not know how this may be interpreted in human life? Anyone who has a healthy spiritual sense of smell can sense how sins fester. That festering of sin is opposite to that fragrance of which the apostle speaks: *We are unto God a sweet savor of Christ in every place, in them that are saved* [2 Cor. 2:15]. But whence that, if not from hope? Whence, if not from the remembrance of the Sabbath? We complain of one thing in this life, we anticipate another thing in that other life. What we complain of, festers; what we anticipate smells sweet. Therefore if there were no such fragrance to entice us, we would never remember the Sabbath. But because we sense such a fragrance through the Spirit, so that we say to our betrothed, *We will run after the fragrance of your ointments* [Cant. 1:3], we turn our nose away from our own corruption, and turning to him, we breathe more easily. But unless our own

evil also stinks to us, we will never confess with these lamentations: *My sores are putrefied and corrupted.*

Taking its cue from such passages, the imagery of sin and bodily corruption is widespread in the Middle Ages, often taking the form of disfiguring disease. Leprosy is a prominent case of this. Considered a venereal disease transmitted by certain kinds of sinful sexual behavior, the skin lesions and decay displayed by lepers was considered an accelerated form of the decay that affected all bodies after death. The shunning and isolation decreed for lepers illustrates the degree of disgust aroused by such corruption.

Death, of course, was the ultimate reflection of original sin, as recounted in Genesis 3:17–19:

> Ad Adam vero dixit, "Quia audisti vocem uxoris tuae, et comedisti de ligno ex quo praeceperam tibi 'Ne comederes,' . . . In sudore vultus tui vesceris pane donec revertaris in terram, de qua sumptus es; quia pulvis es, et in pulverem reverteris.
>
> And to Adam he said, "Because you have listened to the voice of your wife, and have eaten of the tree of which I commanded you, 'You shall not eat of it,' . . . in the sweat of your face you shall eat bread till you return to the ground, for out of it you were taken; you are dust, and to dust you shall return."

The corruption of the body after death was the physical reflection of the moral corruption to which all sinners were heir. While alive, the body produced excrement, as if in prefigurement of the body's ultimate decay; after death, the body became entirely corrupt. Thus excrement and death are two sides of the same coin: physical reflections of moral corruption. The use of death as a motif in medieval writing is clear and abundant. What has been less clear is that excrement is also used widely—nearly ubiquitously—as an emblem of corruption, and not only as an emblem, but as the embodiment of corruption itself—as the *literal* manifestation of the sin continually generated by the living, corrupt and earthly body. Excrement did not just *mean* sin; in medieval thought, it *was* sin, the material embodiment of corporeal corruptibility.

The association of dung and sinful, earthly corruption had its scriptural *locus classicus* in Job 2:8, in which Job takes his place on the dunghill. This was related to the corrupt earthly condition of the flesh by Gregory the Great, whose association of dung and the death of the corruptible flesh, articulated in the *Moralia*, became standard:

> In sterquilinio ponebat corpus ut ex terra sumpta quae esset carnis substantia, bene proficiens perpenderet animus. In sterquilinio ponebat corpus ut etiam ex loci fetore caperet, quod festine corpus ad fetorem rediret.[99]

> He set his body on a dunghill so that the mind, profiting well, should consider what the substance of the flesh was, taken from the earth. He set his body on a dunghill so that likewise he might apprehend from the stench of that place that the body quickly returns to stench.

The dunghill here becomes a metonym for the flesh, and Gregory emphasizes that the just man must remember, as Job does, that he is abject and sinful, afflicted by the sin of which dung is his constant reminder:

> *Sedens in sterquilinio.* In sterquilinio quippe sedere est uilia de se quempiam et abiecta sentire. In sterquilinio nobis sedere est ad ea quae illicite gessimus mentis oculos paenitendo reducere, ut cum ante nos peccatorum stercora cernimus, omne quod in animo de elatione surgit inclinemus. In sterquilinio sedet qui infirmitatem suam sollicitus respicit, et sese de bonis quae per gratiam perceperit, non extollit. An non apud se in sterquilinio Abraham sederet qui dicebat: *Loquar ad Dominum meum, cum sim puluis et cinis*? [Gen. 18:27]¹⁰⁰

> *Sitting on a dunghill.* To "sit on a dunghill" obviously is to perceive base and abject things about oneself. For us "to sit on a dunghill" is to bring the eyes of the mind in penitence back to those things that we committed unrighteously, so that when we see the dung of our sins before us, we may bend down everything that arises from haughtiness in the mind. He sits on a dunghill who is troubled in scrutinizing his weaknesses, and does not lift himself up because of those good things that he gains through grace. Did not Abraham sit by himself on a dunghill, who said *I will speak to my Lord, who am dust and ashes*?

Here again the abject condition of humanity is characterized by association with dung, the emblem and embodiment of loathsome corruption, and the whole is inextricably bound up with imagery of lowliness and rising. These themes characterize a vast quantity of medieval literature on the body and on sin.

CORRUPTION AS A CENTRAL THEME OF THE LITERATURE ON SIN

In the following chapters I will examine medieval thought on moral corruption and its manifestation in the material and cultural realms. Such thought was expressed in a variety of media, forming the subject matter of genres as diverse as popular tales, Biblical exegesis, judicial decisions, ecclesiastical ceremonies and illustrations. As a subject of theological explication, it was principally addressed as it related to particular scriptural or academic questions, such as why Jesus ate after his resurrection. The modern age, retaining the conviction that eating, food, digestion, excretion and "undignified" bodily practices are lowly, regards such questions as trivial and comic; but we should beware of devaluing the medieval attempt to understand the role of the body in the world. Being invested with bodies, as we are, and those bodies being inescapably corrupt, as they are, the questions of the relationship of the pure to the earthly body in all its necessities was of the utmost importance. Indeed, the medieval understanding of bodily corruption and purity issues is rarely formally articulated in its completeness precisely because the system was so pervasive and, by medieval lights, so obvious: not because it was inconsequential, but because it was self-evident. And although theology did not remain static over the course of the Middle Ages, either in scholarly understanding or in the emphases of popular religion, this is one aspect of religious understanding that for the most part holds constant. Hence the understanding of bodily corruption is not so much a point of religious doctrine as an aspect of *mentalité*.

Of course, attitudes toward the body were never monolithic in medieval culture, any more than they are in modern culture, and even attitudes toward excrement—one of the most universal elicitors of "core disgust"—were not rigidly invariable. Caroline Bynum has sought to complicate notions of a single medieval attitude toward the body, showing the variety and contradictions of different kinds of medieval discourse on the body.[101] Although it is important to recognize contending voices in medieval culture, there is nevertheless significant unity on issues of bodily purity, sometimes merely the result of fundamental disgust responses, more often overlaid with more or less sophisticated Christian interpretation. Bynum argues, "*Pissing* and *farting* did not have the same valence in the grim monastic preaching of the years around 1100 and in the cheerfully scatological, although still misogynistic, fabliaux of two centuries later."[102] But although sermons and fabliaux are different genres, in fact both share the conviction that the emissions of the lower body are lowly, undignified and repellent. Sermons invest this response with a lesson about the repugnance of the sinful body. The fabliaux leach any moral lesson from the narrative by framing it as comedy, and recruit the disgust response to give the reader a stimulating jolt of revulsion. But the sermons and the fabliaux are in perfect agreement that pissing and farting are disgusting; the only point of contention is the proper use of that disgust. Thus although the medieval discourses on the body are various according to genre and intent, at the most fundamental level they are unified. And most of the medieval world agreed in seeing, as Bynum says, "the cultivation of bodily experience as a place for encounter with meaning, a locus of redemption."[103] The particular forms of the emphasis could be different in different periods: so, for instance, *contemptus mundi* literature came to full flower in the later Middle Ages, and images of the devil expressed his monstrosity and sinful nature in different ways across the span of the centuries. But the underlying dichotomy of pure and impure, and the consonance of the material and the immaterial, remained constant and gave rise to this multiplicity of expressions in an abundance of witnesses.

We find these witnesses scattered throughout medieval culture. So, for example, in the thirteenth century Thomas Aquinas took up the question of the resurrection of the body, in particular its entrails, which are necessarily associated with impurities. His explanation makes it clear that resurrection involves physical purity as well as spiritual purity, and thus his unspoken assumption that the spiritual and the material are one and the same. The post-resurrection body will be fully fleshed and can eat, but its recovered purity means that it will no longer produce corruption, and it will not be subject to the process of digestion and the production of excrement.[104] In the Supplement to the *Summa Theologica*, Aquinas asks:

> Utrum omnia membra corporis humani resurrectura sint
> 2. Praeterea, intestina quaedam membra sunt. Sed non resurgent. Plena enim resurgere non possunt: quia immunditias continent. Nec vacua: quia nihil est vacuum in natura. Ergo non omnia membra resurgent. . . ..
> Sed contra: . . . intestina resurgent in corpore, sicut et alia membra. Et plena erunt, non quidem turpibus superfluitatibus, sed nobilibus humiditatibus. (Suppl. q. 80, a. 1)[105]

> Whether all the members of the human body will be resurrected
> 2. Further, the intestines are members, but they will not rise again. For they cannot rise full, because they contain impurities, nor empty, since nothing is empty in nature. Therefore not every member will rise again. . . .
> But against that: . . . the intestines will rise again in the body, just like the other members. And they will be full, not, certainly, of shameful superfluities, but of noble humors.

Further:

> Est autem in homine triplex humiditas. Quaedam enim humiditas est in recedendo a perfectione huius individui: vel quia est in via corruptionis, et a natura abiicitur, sicut urina, sudor et sanies et huiusmodi; vel quia a natura ordinatur ad conservationem specie in alio individuo, sive per actum genervativae, sicut semen, sive per actum nutritivae, sicut lac. Et nulla talium humiditatem resurget: eo quod non est de perfectione individui resurgentis. (Suppl. q. 80 a.3)[106]

There is, moreover, a triple humidity in man. One humidity is a lessening of the perfection of the individual, either because it is on the path to corruption, and is evacuated by nature, as urine, sweat, discharge, and things of this kind, or because it is established in an individual for the preservation of the kind, whether by an act of generation, like semen, or an act of nutrition, like milk. And none of these kinds of humidities will rise again, because they are not part of the perfection of the individual rising again.

Why does Aquinas assume that his audience will naturally understand that material impurity has moral valence? And why would Aquinas worry about whether a certain part of the body will be resurrected—why does he assume that not all parts of the body are equivalent and amoral?

A similar question might be asked of Francesc Eiximenis, a Franciscan of the mid-fourteenth century and advisor to the city councilors of Valencia. Francesc followed the Bishop of Amiens in believing that the Bible required every house to have a latrine, and wrote:

> si Adam no hagués peccat . . . axî com de pa e de cuyna; axí mateix lavors no hagera mester privada per amagar sa turpitut, car jatsia que llavors l'om porgàs per lo ses, emperò la purgació aquella no fóra pudent ne haguera ab si la turpitut de què parla la dita auctoritat al·legada.[107]

> if Adam had not sinned . . . also then he would not have the need to hide his shamefulness, because even though man would still have to empty his bowels through the natural opening, it would not stink nor would it have that shamefulness of which the aforementioned authority speaks.

These are ordinary, rather than extraordinary, expressions of the medieval understanding of the universe, and to turn a blind eye to them does violence to our comprehension of the medieval world. Yet such expressions have predictably been censored from modern texts. In the *Little Flowers of St. Francis*, for instance, Brother Rufino is tormented by a demon in disguise. Francis advises the brother to reply to the demon in his own mode:

> "ma quando il demonio ti dicesse più: Tu se' dannato, sì gli rispondi: Apri la bocca; mo' vi ti caco. E questo ti sia segnale, ch'egli è il demonio e non Cristo, ché dato tu gli arai tale risposta, immantanente fuggirà."[108]

> "But the next time the demon tells you, 'You are damned,' you tell him, 'Open your mouth and I'll shit in it.' This will be a sign for you that he is the devil and not Christ, that once you give this reply, he will flee immediately."[109]

Post-medieval devotional copies of this passage have often bowdlerized the text to "Open your mouth!", eliminating all reference to dung, and not incidentally making nonsense of the injunction.[110] Though this passage finally appears more graphically and authentically in modern editions, the topic itself has remained largely beyond the pale of scholarship: as if we can accept the crudities of medieval expression as crudities, but fall short of being able to apprehend them as meaningful.

These disparate kinds of expression are not inexplicable vulgarities, but witnesses to a common understanding of the essential relation of physical realities to abstract moral qualities, and of corruption, sin and excrement as important witnesses to the human condition. The many ways in which that understanding pervaded medieval culture is the subject of this book.

2 Pollution and Filth in the Middle Ages
Material Realities

Experience, even in the absence of authority, was enough to show that material corruption was the hallmark of the earthly world. Although the theological implications occasioned much commentary, direct experience had a more immediate effect: corruption and pollution had to be managed on a daily basis. The response to filth in the medieval world was thus a combination of theological interpretation and cultural attitudes determined in part by context and the exigencies of technology. The intersection of the symbolic and the material can be amply demonstrated in the management of excrement, particularly that most charged of substances, human excrement.

Although it is a truism that excrement is considered noxious in all cultures, in fact the degree of noxiousness and attitudes toward the practical value of dung varied widely in medieval Europe. They may thus serve to illuminate the ways in which material conditions and cultural context influenced the understanding of even one of the most fundamental and unavoidable of substances.

An examination of the realities of dung management in the Middle Ages also shows why it was so prominent in theology, art and literature. Dung was ubiquitous, unavoidable in the environment as well as in private life. In the modern West, excrement has been confined to a private reality; it is a transgression to import the topic into the public sphere. In the Middle Ages excrement was a public reality and hence a staple of public discourse. Human excrement, animal dung, latrines and dungheaps were common topics; there was no call to pretend that humans do not defecate and indeed great motivation, both theological and comic, to dwell upon the fact that they do. Hence scatology was a staple of comedy—then as now—making use of the humorous possibilities of the lowly undignified body. It is the theological uses of the topic that strike the modern reader as most unfamiliar. But all public discourse about excrement drew from the everyday realities of experience, experience that differed greatly from that of modern developed-world practices.

Modern snickering attention to medieval hygiene frequently focuses on the latrine, but what may be most distinctive about medieval latrines is how few there were of them. By far the vast majority of people made do without any formal provisions for excretion at all, and even the wealthiest aristocrat or traveler might expect to find him- or herself away from home and unable to resort to any formal privy when the need arose. All of these people—peasants, workers, many city dwellers, monastics in poorer monasteries, travelers or visitors, armies, warriors on the battlefield—simply "went" outdoors, making free use of the fields, ditches or streets. Excrement remained shameful and embarrassing, but common and often unconcealed rather than hidden and taboo—an ineluctable reminder of the scourge of the body. This chapter will examine the presence of dung as the material, public reality it was, the underlying actuality upon which systems of thought were overlaid.

But to begin at first principles, why is dung regarded as filth in the first place? The answer may seem obvious; in many ways the identity of dung as the apotheosis of filth is overdetermined. Both medieval and modern culture consider dung noxious for two chief reasons: it has an offensive smell that provokes disgust, and this magnifies the horror that it is produced by the body and violates its boundaries. The human reaction to the smell of dung— what we term a stench—is a fundamentally biological response. Indeed, it is clear that the human brain evolved an innate aversion to the smell of dung specifically to serve as a warning signal against it and the danger that it may contaminate one's environment and imperil health. This does not make the disgust reaction a constant, however: the human sense of smell has great variability and is blunted by repeated exposure to a substance. Through a phenomenon known as olfactory adaptation, in humans the nasal receptors to a smell cease responding to an airborne chemical after around twenty minutes. Thus those who are constantly exposed to a smell cease to find it bothersome. Those who are intermittently exposed, as was undoubtedly the case in the Middle Ages, will still find it offensive. In cases of prolonged exposure to dung, medieval people sought to damp down the smell by drying the dung or mixing it with other substances such as peat. When the situation warranted, medieval people were also not shy to use the odiferous properties of dung to shock, titillate or play tricks on others.

The second reason for the abhorrence of dung—because it violates the bounds of the body—is related to "animal-nature" disgust, a disgust that has the fear of death at its heart. Like other violations of the body envelope, excretion exposes the corruptible, mortal animality of the body even as it violates essential categories, transgressing the boundaries between inside and outside, whole and fragmented, pure and foul.

The reasons to find dung repellent both physically and conceptually are great enough that it may be surprising that they are not universal. Attitudes differ across the animal kingdom; some animals carefully avoid excreting near their sleeping place, while others seek out excrement deliberately. Dogs, pigs and chickens are among species that eat dung, a trait that can have positive survival value, as the process of digestion can leave significant nutrients unabsorbed and hence available in excrement. Rather than expending energy seeking out food, such animals could augment their nutrition by the simpler strategy of consuming the dung of animals who had already found the food, with the advantage that dung, unlike many forms of food, does not run away. This liking for dung did not go unnoticed by medieval authors, who often used animals' interest in dung as a metaphor or comparison to sinners' attraction to sin.

In the human realm, children under the age of around three do not find excrement repellent; disgust, like language, is an instinct that needs to be cultivated in line with the surrounding culture.[1] Among adults, the degree to which dung is either unwholesome or precious—life-threatening or life-giving—also determines attitudes. In some contexts dung is a valuable commodity, and hence hoarded carefully and used regularly; in such situations it will inevitably be regarded with less disdain than in those contexts in which it is a useless nuisance. The people who hoard and value dung, and who correspondingly are not repelled by it, are the object of frequent comment, both serious and humorous, by the more sensitive, in the Middle Ages and other periods. Peasants became so casual about the uses of dung that it was a staple of comic narrative: for instance, in the tale of a farmer who fainted when smelling a perfumery in town and who could only be revived when someone held dung under his nose.[2]

The limitations of organization and technology also meant that excrement was a familiar substance even in urban areas. The greater utility and ubiquity of dung meant that on a purely practical level, medieval people typically displayed less squeamishness than modern people. Chaucer singled out Absolon in the Miller's Tale, the clerk who was "somewhat squeamish of farting," precisely because he was laughably dainty and fastidious. In day-to-day life, the demands of the lower body called for pragmatism. But on a conceptual level, excrement always held the role as the lowliest and most disgusting of substances. In addition to stench and problems of contamination, it was considered abhorrent for theological reasons—because it corresponded to moral uncleanliness. Modern aversion to dung would involve biomedical explanations: it smells bad, but above all it is contaminating because it produces infection and illness. But in the absence of a bacterial model of illness, any medieval insistence on cleanliness was less scientific. Instead, theological or magical explanations were overlaid on a biological substratum. Where modern explanations would ascribe the cultural abhorrence of dung to ultimately pragmatic concerns about physical health, medieval explanations would grant equal primacy to moral issues. In the medieval view, the stench of dung was a symptom, not a cause, of its repellent nature. Thus the medieval revulsion to dung was, if anything, more conceptual than the modern.

In the moral and theological realm, then, dung was always regarded as disgusting. It loses this valence only in categories where the moral and theological do not apply: practical matters such as farming, or in the framework of comic narrative, which is amoral. The exception to this is satire, in which excrement retained its narrative force as an agent of the moral order, focusing opprobrium on sinners and wrongdoers. Whether in moral or amoral contexts, the disgusting nature of dung did not mean that it was omitted from public discourse—on the contrary, its nature gave it power. The jolt of reaction produced by disgusting experiences can be appealing; modern horror movies, television crime shows, "gross-out" comedies and forensic novels all use similar effects that simultaneously repel and gratify their audience. This was certainly the case in the Renaissance, as described by one disapproving commentator:

> Ist auch eben umb derselbigen ursach willen kein feine gewohnheit, wenn einem auf der Gassen etwas abscheuliches, wie es sich wol bisweilen zuträgt, fürkommet, statim ad comitem se convertat eique illam monstrat. Multo minus decebit alteri re foetidam, ut olfaciat porrigere, quod nonnumquam facere aliqui solent atque adeo urgere, quum etiam naribus aliorum rem illam grave olentem admovent et inquiunt: Odorare amabo quantopere hoec foetat.

> For the same reason it is not a refined habit, when coming across something disgusting in the street, as sometimes happens, to turn at once to one's companion and point it out to him. It is far less proper to hold out the stinking thing for the other to smell, as some are wont, who even urge the other to do so, lifting the foul-smelling thing to his nostrils and saying, "I should like to know how much that stinks."[3]

However repellent dung was held to be in official sources, it is also clear that its very repulsiveness made it an object of interest and invested it, as we shall see, with symbolic potency.

In sum, the degree to which human beings regard dung as noxious varies, and their response to that noxiousness are also various. Although customs varied somewhat from place to place in the medieval period, the practical differences were those between the habits of the rich and those of the poor, between those of country dwellers and city dwellers, with monasteries and convents forming yet another category. Despite this variety, all practices were subject to the constraints of technology and resources; and on the conceptual level, all were informed by a larger scheme of interpretation that translated basic categories of waste and pollution into an explicitly Christian ordering. Thus the practical arrangements for dealing with excretion were much more variable than the medieval understanding of the place of excretion in the symbolic order.

WASTE IN URBAN SETTINGS: NUISANCE AND DANGER

In the early Middle Ages, cities were small enough to afford many people a plot of land on which to establish a privy, as well as a garden to be fertilized with dung. As the size and density of cities increased, these opportunities were lessened. The growth of urban areas meant an increasing concentration of people, as well as the livestock kept in cities throughout the Middle Ages: horses, cattle, sheep, goats, pigs and poultry. All of these produced dung, but there were no large agricultural enterprises nearby that might be able to use the manure as fertilizer. Accordingly, sources from the later Middle Ages show growing concern about arrangements for managing dung in urban centers.

In many cities, human waste management was dealt with to some extent by local authorities, who established municipal latrines. In England there were municipal latrines in London, Leicester, Winchester, Hull, Southampton and Exeter, and possibly elsewhere.[4] The public facilities in London dated from as early as the twelfth century, when Queen Matilda ordered the "necessary house" built at Queenhithe, enlarged in 1237.[5] In time London came to have perhaps sixteen public latrines. Some of these were substantial: the one on London Bridge had two entrances, as witnessed by the fact that in 1306 a man escaped a creditor by going out one door while the creditor waited at the other.[6] At least some had separate areas for men and women, as was most likely true of the Postern latrine in Winchester.[7] An elaborate establishment along these lines was Whittington's Longhouse, built from a bequest by Richard (Dick) Whittington, the former Lord Mayor of London, who died in 1423. This latrine had separate sides for men and women, each consisting of sixty-four seats.[8]

But the establishment of municipal latrines did not mean satisfactory management of all city waste. By the end of the twelfth century London had bylaws governing waste disposal, but there were repeated complaints about citizens who built private latrines over the city's waterways, disposed of dung in the waterways, or dumped it in unauthorized places both inside and outside the city.[9] There were also numerous complaints about dungheaps, from stables and other sources, that blocked thoroughfares.[10] Although there were workers to clean out latrines, tumbrils and dungboats to carry away the dung and laystalls, or public dumping places, where people could take their refuse, these arrangements seem to have been too expensive or troublesome for many inhabitants. Motivation to dispose of dung illegally was exacerbated by the fact that many landlords supplied only a common latrine for a number of tenements, rather than an individual privy for each household, and so tenants had to walk a distance even to empty their chamber pots legally.[11] Many households, moreover, had no access to private latrines whatsoever and had to walk to public facilities if they wanted to use a formal privy. Complaints suggest that instead they often chose to excrete directly onto the street. This was especially likely of vagrants and the poor. A glimpse into the practice is provided by the London coroner's rolls of 1399, which report the death of a seven-year-old pauper, John le Stolere, crushed by a cart while squatting to defecate (*secreta nature faciendo sedentem*) in a London street.[12]

At home, when privies were inconvenient or unavailable, householders used chamber pots, which they tended to dump into street gutters or simply out of the window.[13] Fines were levied against this: the increasing strictness of the fines suggests that the problem continued unabated.[14] Some people even tried to turn such habits to their own advantage. Ernest Sabine describes the connivances of citizens who attempted to claim certain London thoroughfares as their own by using dung as a deterrent: "Both Ebbegate and Dowgate Lanes had been unlawfully closed to the public by certain citizens who, in order the more effectively to prevent citizens using them, had constructed divers latrines, in Ebbegate upon gratings, and in Dowgate projecting beyond the pathway, so that in each lane the filth fell upon persons passing through."[15] In another instance, "a wardmote inquest for Basinghall Ward in 1421 reported that all the little rents of the Swan, belonging to Richard Clark, were without privies, so that all the tenants threw their ordure and other horrible liquids before their doors, to the great nuisance of holy church and of passers-by."[16] Even in this matter-of-fact report we see an incursion of the symbolic system of which dung formed a part: the dung was not only a practical nuisance to passers-by, but offensive to "holy church," which above all other places ought not to be sullied by dung. Thus religious meanings creep even into secular reports of dung. In the past, an order of 1357 maintained that the city had been kept clean of refuse and material corruption, "whereby no small honour accrued to the city and those dwelling therein."[17] The cleanliness of the city was also in the interest of the king and indeed reflected on his ability to order and preserve his kingdom and to keep pestilence and diseases at bay. As Paul Strohm has observed, "Good plumbing, to put it baldly, is death-denying, and asserts the continuity of the social order."[18] Thus we see the consonance of spiritual order and material order—salvation and life—and their opposites, spiritual and material pollution, with their consequence of death.

In France, holy church and other institutions of wealth—monasteries, convents, palaces and the houses of prosperous citizens—had their own privies by the thirteenth century, but the houses of common people generally remained without privies as late as the fifteenth century. Some of the dung produced might be employed in fertilizing the household vegetable gardens, still common in the thirteenth century, but as the land was paved over in later centuries, the dung became superfluous and consequently a greater problem.[19] In the south of France, citizens used the roofs rather than the streets as open privies. André Guillerme reports: "This practice, suited to dry climates, offered the advantage of avoiding anaerobic fermentation, and thus the formation of obnoxious smells; but it also had the disadvantage of washing excrement into the street whenever it rained."[20] In France, laws requiring that all new houses be provided with privies were promulgated from 1522 onward, but the numbers of already established houses without privies ensured that sanitation remained a problem for centuries.

Tenants who had few legitimate or easy ways to dispose of waste, whether dung or other household refuse, tended to dump it elsewhere in the city, and to prevent this, lanes might be closed with locked gates at night.[21] Certain other streets, whether endowed with public latrines or not, became known as sites of defecation. By the middle of the fourteenth century, most French towns had a rue Orde ("ordure street"), a rue Basse-Fesse ("lower backside street"), or a rue des Aisances ("easement street"). The rue des Aisances was usually near the market, presumably for the convenience of marketgoers. It typically featured a tavern and had a reputation for the illicit behavior that accompanied both tavern-going and the baring of the body. Thus latrines tended to be sited as part of a conceptual cluster, a grouping of places associated with bodily needs, license and disgust. In addition the easement streets were often located near the steam baths, also places of license and censure.

The situation of latrines is exemplified by the Augsburg civic code of 1276, which defined the role of the public executioner.[22] The executioner had a monopoly on executions and corporal punishment: "The hangman has the right to carry out all punishments to the body." He was also entitled to all the possessions of the criminal worn below the belt, as if the executioner was the king of the lower body. In keeping with his rule over the corrupt and unruly body, he was also charged with supervising public prostitutes, driving lepers out of town and, most pertinently, cleaning the public latrines, a role which he held until the eighteenth century.[23]

Like bathhouses, public latrines were associated in the public mind with prostitution, many times apparently rightfully so. Troyes had a particularly apt conjunction of prostitution and dung: the Saint-Abraham Hospital, founded for reformed prostitutes, was charged with the duty of clearing dung from the marketplace, the Place du Marché-aux-Blés.[24]

Most private urban privies seem to have been merely seats over a cesspool, but both private citizens and the municipal authorities used running water to carry away the filth when they could.[25] The simplest way to accomplish this was to use already existing watercourses. In London, as in many other cities, gutters ran down the middle of many streets, collecting rainwater run-off, wastewater from wells, and household waste. Laws required householders to bring the chamber pots down and empty them into the gutters directly.[26] On occasion, private citizens also attempted to use water in the house to flush out their privies. The most ingenious of these may have been a citizen of London, one Alice Wade, charged in 1314–15 with creating a public nuisance with her latrine arrangements. She had run a wooden pipe from her upper storey privy down to the common gutter that washed away rainwater and ran beneath the houses on the street.[27] She had thus rigged up something of an informal sewer system, but the flow proved insufficient to carry away all the waste; the arrangement came to light when effluent from Wade's house clogged the common gutter. There are also records of at least two London citizens arranging for water to be piped down from cisterns into privies, where the water would wash the filth down into the street gutter—forerunners of modern valve toilets flushed with water.[28] An unusual situation pertained in Winchester, where the public streams had been diverted into channels of water that ran, first, in front of rows of houses and later actually through the front rooms of the houses. Since the water had to be used by householders farther down the channel, citizens were enjoined not to put various kinds of waste products such as dung in the water and not to wash their babies' dirty diapers (*panni puerorum cum sordidibus*) in the channel.[29]

Figure 2 A man sits in a privy. Note the moon on the outer wall of the privy: this is the earliest illustration of this emblem, still characteristic of modern outhouses (privies) in the U.S. Being small and enclosed, the privy is dark even in the daytime; the moon illuminates the darkness of the inside, as if the occupant is excreting under cover of night—a contrast to the open, well-lit, communal latrines of the Romans. Late fourteenth-century illustration of the *Decameron*. Vienna, Österreichische Nationalbibliothek 2561, fol. 307r.

Although systems that diverted water to flush out privies seem to have been rare in private houses, it was not uncommon for privies to be emptied through pipes, which allowed a greater distance between the privy and the cesspool and may have lessened the smell to some degree. Unfortunately, without extra water to flush the waste along, it was also common for the pipes to become clogged with excrement.[30]

Once a privy with a cesspit had been set up, there had to be arrangements for emptying the cesspit from time to time, a task which was accomplished by professional workers. In Paris a royal ordinance of 1350 made it illegal to insult such workers, a prohibition that gives witness to the fact that insulting them must have been frequent.[31] Such a law was apparently part of an effort to recruit new cesspit-cleaners in the dearth of laborers that followed the Plague. The ordinance terms such workers "ouvriers des basses oeuvres," "workers in low tasks," and opens the field to workers of all occupations, testimony to the low status of the job and—along with the promise that such workers will not be insulted—to the difficulty of finding cleaners when workers had their choice of other jobs. This may also be testimony to the undesirability of the occupation, despite the fact that many documents show that cesspit-cleaners were well paid.[32] In the later Middle Ages, the inhabitants of Paris also had the option of placing their chamber pots outside their doors, whereupon the cesspit cleaners would come by on regular rounds and empty them. The dung and other rubbish was carried to dumps outside the city walls, which had grown so high by the reign of Louis XIII (1610–43) that the fortifications of the city had to be extended beyond the dumps, to prevent enemies from using them as gun emplacements.[33]

The necessity of emptying the cesspit could be avoided if the privy emptied into a waterway, and we see abundant evidence that both private citizens and municipal authorities favored this convenience. In twelfth-century Exeter a stream called the Shitbrook served as a sewer carrying waste to the River Exe. Later the Exeter authorities set up municipal latrines; by 1467 there was a common latrine on Exe Island that emptied into the Exe, and another, called the Pixey or Fairy House, apparently served the same function on the Exe Bridge.[34] Another waterway called Scitebroc seems to have been used for such a purpose in Lincolnshire as early as 1202, when a man called Randulfus Bla de Scitebroc turns up in the records.[35] In London, several streams and waterways served as dumps for waste, among them the Thames; Walbrook, which flowed through the middle of the city; Fleet Stream; and the city ditch that surrounded the city wall.[36] The citizens living along Walbrook vented their household wastes into the stream through pipes, but were required to have grates on the pipes to prevent the passage of solid waste which might choke the waterway. Despite these requirements, in 1313–14 and 1345–46 several people were found guilty of constructing latrines directly over the stream. By 1374, the city had apparently bowed to the inevitable and instituted an annual fee of twelve pence to householders who had latrines over the stream.[37] In 1477, however, a new ordinance came into effect, once more forbidding the establishment of latrines over Walbrook or any city ditch.[38] The Fleet Stream suffered a similar fate. An inquest in 1355 established that the stream had been clogged and corrupted by thirteen privies that emptied into it, as well as by three tanneries and three small streams that also carried filth into the waterway.[39]

Despite the ordinances controlling the latrines of private citizens over the city waterways, many of the municipal latrines were built in such positions, over the city ditch, Walbrook or Fleet Stream.[40] Sabine describes one of the most ambitious of these, cleared by water from a stream: "In 1401–11 the wardens of London Bridge built what were doubtless large public latrines in their new Stocks Market in the east end of Cheap Street, bordering on Walbrook. They made an excavation of no less than one hundred and thirty-nine loads of earth, probably so as to pass sluices of water beneath the latrines from the nearby flowing stream."[41]

The Thames served as the largest remover of waste, and from the mid-thirteenth to the early fourteenth century, laws required citizens to take their refuse and waste to the river. Large rivers with a strong current might serve as relatively effective methods of waste removal. In France, Beauvais, Caen and Evreux were able to use their rivers to similar effect. Where the river was smaller or slow moving, as in the French cities of Troyes, Châlons and Noyon, or in the cases of Walbrook or Fleet Stream in London, the channel could become clogged and stagnant. Authorities often tried to remedy the situation by excavating and widening the ditches, resulting in what amounted to open-air water-treatment facilities. Guillerme explains this:

> It could easily be thought that all the excrement, together with the spent water of workshops, irremediably polluted the canals. But this would be to forget a role played by the hydric ecosystem: the slowness of the current, plus the widening of the ditches, encouraged anaerobic purification, and the ditches turned into high-yield decantation basins. This technique, utilized by the *merdereau* [filth-drainage ditches] of the thirteenth century and today called lagooning, could eliminate 70–90 percent of the organic pollution in four or five months.[42]

This inadvertent but surprisingly effective method of processing waste was most efficient in the summer; in the winter temperatures in northern Europe would not have been warm enough to enable the organisms to break down the effluent.[43] And even the success of large rivers like the Thames in abating pollution depended on people actually depositing their wastes in the water as required. Frequently, however, citizens left their filth in the streets and lanes leading to the waterway, a practice testified to by a gathering thicket of prohibitions and ordinances against such action in the late thirteenth and early fourteenth centuries.[44]

The situation in northern France was similar to that of England. Many cities had been ringed by defensive ditches in the late Roman Empire; since then the cities had expanded beyond the bounds of the ditches, and in the high and late Middle Ages the ditches came to serve as open sewers for the city that had come to surround them. Such ditches came to be known by the names Merderon, Merdron and Merdançon, their function apparent from their names, derived from the French *merde*. Troyes had ditches with such names as early as 1208, and other cities in northern France had followed suit by the middle of the fourteenth century. As in London, latrines were often built above the waterways. In contrast to London, however, these latrines had the sanction of the authorities, undoubtedly because they were almost exclusively the preserve of the wealthy and powerful, principally counts' and bishops' palaces and religious houses. In Reims, the Augustinians were housed next to the drainage ditch, ensuring sanitary drainage; in Sens, the Dominicans were similarly situated; and in Rouen, Auxerre and Provins it was the Franciscans. The mendicant orders even constructed aqueducts to ensure their water supply. Elsewhere in the cities, it appears that the nobility were behind the effort to ensure that slaughterhouses and butchers practiced sanitary habits and used the sewers, and the transformation of the outmoded defensive moats into drainage ditches may have been their undertaking. There is also cause to think that the counts of several cities which instigated these practices modelled their reforms on the more advanced sanitary practices of the local Jewish communities.[45] The reforms do not seem to have been the responsibility of the municipal authorities, who were under the sway of business interests such as butchers, who disliked regulation that interfered with their enterprises.[46] In Paris, it was up to the individual *prêvots de marchands* (city fathers) to take the initiative toward instituting systematic drainage systems. The earliest *prêvot* to undertake this was Hugues Aubriot, who built the first covered sewer in the city at the rue Montmartre in 1370.[47] The sewer emptied into a city brook, the Ménilmontant, and ultimately into the Seine. In subsequent years François I deplored the smell of the sewer and to escape it bought the Tuileries, which proved in turn to be tainted by the stench from the sewer at the Porte Sainte-Honoré.[48]

In Italy, many cities preserved the sturdily constructed Roman sewer systems for centuries, in Classe into the eighth century and in Pavia into the tenth.[49] In Pavia the Roman drains were still in use as late as the fourteenth century, and in fact they are still clear and working in the present day. Their houses had a prototype of the flush toilet in the form of latrine-chutes, flushed by rain into underground channels.[50] Municipal laws were full of the predictable measures forbidding the discharge of waste directly into waterways.[51] Verona prohibited the discharge of wastes into the river by day but allowed it at night.[52] Laws also sought to prevent industrial wastes passing into the water supply.

The authorities' desire to clear the streets of waste was not impeded only by the poverty or slovenliness of the people, but also by the need of some urban industries for dung. The manufacture of saltpeter required human and animal dung. Dung was also used in many regions to tan leather, especially when other tanning agents such as lime or fermented wheat were unavailable. In England pigeon droppings were used to tan leather; in western France, dog, chicken or pigeon droppings were added to broom flowers.[53] Hides were normally cured with alum, but when this was unavailable or too costly, dog droppings were employed instead. Guillerme describes the importance of dung in the medieval economy:

> The use of animal excrement was common; it was even indispensable during periods of crisis. The nuances of colors, the velvety smoothness of cloth, the suppleness of leather were the direct result of the quantity and degree of fermentation of the digestive juices contained in animal droppings.... This meant that wastes had to be stocked, both to allow their fermentation, and to cater to variations in demand. Hence the pits for droppings and urine along the waterways, and the manure deposits in front of house entrances, against which the municipalities and the king railed unceasingly, threatening repressive measures.... But piles of refuse and filth were sources of income for manual workers.[54]

City streets thus might be clogged by citizens deliberately hoarding dung. Others might collect dung to sell for use as fertilizer outside the city. In Winchester, for example, the bishop's officers bought muck for such a purpose.[55]

Dung might also be useful on the domestic level. In some locales it was used as a cleansing agent for laundry in the post-medieval period and very probably in the medieval period as well. A visitor to Edinburgh in 1705 reported that the Scots "put their cloaths with a little cow dung into a large tubb of water, and then plucking their pettycoats up to their bellyes, get into the Tubb, and dance about it to tread the cloaths."[56] The "neater sort" of Welsh peasant reportedly used swine's dung to clean clothes in the eighteenth century, and in the early nineteenth century the custom was reported in Ireland and Scotland.[57] It should be noted that the laundry was rinsed after this procedure, so that the dung was used as an agent and did not, presumably, soil the clothes further. It was not even as filthy a practice as it might appear, as the ammonia in the urine/dung mixture had the same cleansing properties as the ammonia in modern cleaning products.

Despite the utility of dung in trades, gardens and laundry, not everyone worked in occupations for which dung was useful; animal dung seems to have been preferred over human dung for most such enterprises; and dung-buyers preferred to buy from large producers such as stables, leaving the problem of the disposal of the excrement of thousands of city dwellers.

Thus urban arrangements were characterized by repeated attempts to manage and dispose of the great quantities of dung generated in such dense conditions, as well as by the frequent failure of these systems to contend with the scale of the problem.

The drive to find ways to manage the disposal of dung was not the consequence of any sophisticated theories of contagion or pollution, but the result of its stench and an intuition that this stench rendered the air unhealthy.[58] Until the plague of 1347–51, municipal efforts to deal with dung were largely concerned with its physical nuisance value: dungheaps encroaching on streets, cesspools eating away at walls, the dung from privies clogging up waterways and so forth.[59] As the plagues of the fourteenth and fifteenth centuries swept through cities, there was increased concern about sources of pollution and corruption of the air.[60] Health Boards were first set up in the cities of northern Italy, to be followed in subsequent centuries by Health Boards in the other major countries of Europe.[61] Although such Boards were concerned with pollution and hygiene, the sheer scale of the problem and the lack of resources meant that cities remained unsanitary by modern Western standards.

Problems with waste management in the urban environment outlasted the medieval period by centuries. Erasmus complained about the filthiness of English houses in which the bottom layer of rushes on the floor remained unchanged:

> the bottom layer is left undisturbed, sometimes for twenty years, harbouring expectorations, vomitings, the leakage of dogs and men, ale-droppings, scraps of fish, and other abominations not fit to be mentioned.[62]

This testimony is unusual in that its mention of the "leakage" of men suggests that men (and dogs) were wont to urinate inside buildings. Indeed there is cause to conclude that domestic animals typically remained unhousebroken. Complaints about the domestic "leakage of dogs and men" are rarely found in the Middle Ages, perhaps because such behavior was rare, but more likely because it was so commonplace as to be not worth mentioning. As civilization became more particular about such behavior, more complaints arose, although apparently not enough actually to put a stop to such practices. We can see another Renaissance witness of such problems in Leonardo da Vinci's plans for a city of utopian design. His outline called for spiral stairways in public places, "because in the corners of square ones nuisances are apt to be committed."[63] Similar testimony appears in the Brunswick Court Regulations of 1589: "Let no one, whoever he may be, before, at, or after meals, early or late, foul the staircases, corridors, or closets with urine or other filth, but go to suitable, prescribed places for such relief."[64] Illicit excretion was still a problem three hundred years later, when the Duchess of Orléans wrote:

Paris is a dreadful place. The streets smell so badly that you cannot go out. The extreme heat is causing large quantities of meat and fish to rot in them, and this, coupled to the multitude of people who . . . in the street, produces a smell so detestable that it cannot be endured.[65]

The resources of such cities were simply not adequate to accommodate the numbers of people and animals. It is unsurprising, then, that dung remained a nuisance and a danger to city dwellers throughout the medieval period.

THE PRACTICES OF THE COUNTRYSIDE: FERTILITY, HEAT AND WEALTH

In agricultural settings dung was first and foremost a useful commodity, essential in fertilizing the fields. Agricultural treatises emphasized the importance of manuring, and the evidence shows that country dwellers recognized this importance. The value of dung is, for instance, demonstrated by the eleventh-century English *Rectitudines Singularum Personarum*, which spells out the rights of estate workers. Among these is the shepherd, who is entitled to, among other things, twelve nights' dung at Christmas, presumably for the use of his personal garden.[66] Larger landowners were also sensitive to the value of manuring fields and hence increasing yield. English landlords often required their tenants to keep their sheep overnight on demesne land and held cattle fairs on their property, so as to claim the dung produced.[67] One vital reason that dung was not regarded with the distaste accorded to it in the city was not only that it was useful, but that it was in short supply. The amount available was usually not great enough to fertilize all the fields. Animals had to be rotated between fields to produce useful dung, since the soil is enriched only by animals who have eaten fodder grown elsewhere. Moreover, the value of dung dropped directly on the fields was limited; the most valuable fertilizer was dung from the stable yard, where the potassium and nitrogen from the animal's urine had been absorbed by straw. Keeping animals in a stable was much more demanding, however, than grazing them in the fields.[68] Most unfortunate was the paradox that most tenants could not produce the grain necessary to keep large amounts of livestock, but their limited livestock meant that they could not manure their fields enough to produce a good yield of grain.[69] In particular, the scarcity of grain limited the amount of stall-feeding a farmer could do, and thus the amount of the more valuable stable-manure that could be produced. Such high-yield manure usually went to the kitchen gardens rather than to the outer fields.[70]

Although advanced farming practices increased yields as the medieval period progressed, manure remained scarce and valuable. One thirteenth-century lease of land near Paris required the farmer to fertilize the land with manure "once in nine years, in the fifth year."[71] As Marc Bloch has noted, "Manure was by no means plentiful, in fact quite scarce and therefore valuable: so much so indeed that some lords demanded 'pots of excrement' as part of their dues, to the great indignation of some over-sensitive scholars who have mistaken what was merely prudent husbandry for a gross and calculated insult."[72]

Country dwellers also used dung for heating and cooking.[73] As fuel, dung is surprisingly efficient: air-dried dung has a calorific value of 4.0, the same as that for peat, higher than that of air-dried firewood (3.5), and more than half that of bituminous coal (6.9).[74] Although it was as efficient as firewood, because of its smell the use of dung was restricted to those without easy access to other fuels. It was still in use as fuel for the poor in the post-medieval period. In 1698 Celia Fiennes visited the town of Peterborough, near Cambridge, and "saw upon the walls of the ordinary peoples houses and walls of their out houses the cow dung plaister'd up to drie in cakes which they use for fireing." Fiennes thought dung "a very offensive fewell" but added that "the country people use little else in these parts."[75] Similar habits are reported in Yorkshire and northern Wales at the same period.[76] In 1791, Edward Daniel Clarke, on a trip through Cornwall and Devon, reported the sad sight of "an old woman hobbling after our horses in hopes of a little fuel from their excrement."[77] Dung was still in use as fuel among the poor in Cornwall and Wales in the late nineteenth century and in the Aran Islands in the 1930s.[78]

Dung on the roads or scattered around the countryside also served as fodder for pigs, chickens and geese. The everyday nature of dung was assured by the fact that in many areas of Europe rural people lived in longhouses, sharing their cottages with their livestock in the winter months, a practice that saved effort and resources in a number of regards.[79] It meant that the cottagers had to build only one structure, instead of a cottage and a stable or barn, and in case of inclement weather, the stock could be tended without leaving the house. In addition, the body heat of the animals could be an important source of warmth, and their dung could be easily retrieved and used for fuel as soon as it was dry enough to burn. It also meant that in times of scarcity, the dung was secure from the predations of other needy householders.

Nevertheless, the storage and management of dung was still often a problem in rural villages. A case study of these problems has been attempted for the English village of Prescot, east of Liverpool, in the seventeenth century.[80] At the time Prescot had a population of around six hundred. Records show that the villagers were repeatedly fined and admonished for much the same problems as occurred in medieval London: keeping dungheaps that blocked roads and disposing of dung in a way that clogged the village ditches. In contrast to those of London, however, the records also reflect the intrinsic value of dung in the local economy. Residents could be charged a fee for depositing dung in illicit locations, but also for laying claim to dung when they had "noe right or property thereto." If residents had dung for which they had no use, they were entitled to deposit it at a common pasture, for a fee; the village then sold the dung or left it to fertilize the pasture. Dung was, moreover, valuable enough to form part of a villager's estate. The study relates, "Thomas Parr, innkeeper, had £3 13s. 4d. worth of dung when he died in 1680, or four percent of his total worth. Another eleven inventories of inhabitants of Stuart Prescot mentioned between 6d. and 20s. in dung and muck."[81] The value of even small amount of dung is revealed by the situation at the nearby village of Ormskirk, where a carter was paid 5s. a year to come once weekly and cart away the "small heaps and Cobbs of Dung" that littered the streets—that, in other words, did not form a part of someone's established dungheap. Local authorities even anticipated that the villagers might find themselves in dispute with the carter about who had the right to certain deposits of dung, and prescribes the course of action that should be followed.[82] Though sources suggest that the management of dung in villages was not as formally regulated in the medieval period, the value of the dung reflected in these regulations must have been just as substantial.

Thus, in contrast to the situation in cities, in the countryside the scarcity and usefulness of dung outweighed its inherent noxiousness, and so it did not seem to provoke the disgust it did among city folk. We see this reflected in medieval sources: where city documents mention dung almost exclusively as a nuisance or with distaste, texts depicting dung in a country context are markedly more casual. Raymonde Testanière, an inhabitant of the French village of Montaillou in the early fourteenth century, reported matter-of-factly that she had climbed on top of a tall dungheap in order to spy into her neighbor's top-floor room.[83] Perhaps more surprisingly, it was on a dungheap that Arnaud de Verniolles, from the nearby village of Pamiers, sometimes seduced his young male partners.[84] Though the dung may have been mixed with straw, as illustrations commonly depict, the heap must have nevertheless been odorous as well as soft. But perhaps the dungheap as a bed of ease was not as unthinkable as one might suppose: the comic poem *Satyra contra Moriuht* also accuses the hapless Irishman Moriuht of seduction on a dungheap, comparing him to a goat.[85] In the fabliau *Le Sacristain*, a thief steals a side of bacon and hides it, in a sack, in a dungheap.[86] Although the story is comic, it is not suggested that a dungheap is an unthinkable place to hide stolen food. Chaucer describes his worthy Plowman as a man "that hadde ylad of dong ful many a fother"—a passage that both reflects dung as emblematic of humble farmwork and demonstrates how an association with dung can, given the right context, even be a virtue.[87]

WASTE MANAGEMENT AMONG THE WEALTHY: THE DEVELOPMENT OF PRIVACY

Throughout the Middle Ages, indoor privies were the province of the wealthier members of society. In the earlier period, indeed, even the wealthiest may not always have had access to indoor privies, or even the outdoor variety. As one example, kings on circuit must have had to contend with a range of types of facility. One piece of evidence in this regard is given by Notker Balbulus, writing around 884 about Charlemagne's dislike of the newly introduced short cloaks. Notker writes that Charlemagne complained:

> "Quid prosunt illa pittaciola? In lecto non possum eis cooperiri; caballicans contras ventos et pluvias nequeo defendi; ad necessaria naturae secedens, tibiarum congelatione deficio."[88]

> "What good are these little patches? In bed I can't cover myself with them; riding horseback I'm not protected from the winds and the rains; withdrawing for the necessities of nature, I'm tormented by freezing my shanks."

The passage suggests that the emperor is going, at the very least, to an unheated place, probably an outside privy or even possibly, as on circuit, the outside without a privy. Yet conventional latrines were certainly known at the time: just beforehand, Notker has related a story of a the palace steward, one Liutfrid, who died when he had gone *in latrinam*.[89]

By the end of the Middle Ages, indoor privies were within the reach of many ordinary town dwellers above the poverty level. (From at least the fourteenth century, French and English sources commonly refer to these indoor privies by the euphemism "garderobe.") By the thirteenth century many of the wealthier English townhouses had purpose-built garderobes, constructed with cesspits as part of the planned structure of the house. The garderobes are found in various locations: they could be situated near the solar (the upper level chamber), in the cellar, in the garret, off the kitchen or elsewhere; often they were located at a remove from the main living quarters. In succeeding centuries houses might have more than one garderobe. In 1543 one London house had three garderobes, one serving the owner's room, one the maidens' chamber and one the manservants' chamber, each with a pipe leading to a central cesspit.[90] The cesspit might serve not only for the necessities of nature, but as rubbish pits for the household. An excavation of a latrine pit in Cuckoo Lane, Southampton, most likely belonging to an affluent citizen named Richard of Southwick, who died in 1290, turned up a variety of refuse. "It was filled with the debris of a prosperous household, including kitchen wastes, dead domestic animals (cats, dogs, sparrow hawks, a ferret, and a monkey), pottery, wooden bowls, old shoes, metal objects, rope, and baskets."[91] With the practice of relegating dead domestic animals to the latrine, it is no wonder that the corpses of human sinners might be thought of in Biblical terms, as "dung for the land."

Larger houses and castles had indoor privies from an earlier date. Garderobe construction was well advanced by the eleventh century in England, for example, as the extensive remains in Richmond Castle demonstrate.[92] Greater wealth meant that the lord or householder had the resources to build indoor facilities, and the size of such large dwellings meant that indoor privies were vastly more convenient than requiring the inhabitants to walk to an outdoor privy or rely on chamber pots alone. The common arrangement seems to have been to build a chamber with both a fireplace and a garderobe.[93] In stone castles and houses, the garderobes were commonly constructed in the thickness of the exterior wall; where the walls were not thick enough to allow for this, the garderobe could be corbelled out from the exterior wall. Sometimes these garderobes discharged directly over rivers or moats, with the incidental consequence that trails of excrement might be seen down the face of the outside wall. By the fourteenth century, castles were well supplied with amenities. Middleham Castle, Yorkshire, for instance, had garderobes on three stories, all accessible from both adjoining rooms and, via a gallery or bridge, from the great chamber in the keep. Langley Castle had twelve privies on three levels.[94] By the fifteenth century, castles were being constructed with a garderobe for every chamber.[95]

WASTE MANAGEMENT IN MONASTERIES: SOPHISTICATION AND SHAME

As planned communities, monasteries provide singular testimony to medieval thought on the disposition of waste. Moreover, as a whole, monasteries were wealthier and more powerful than the average village or collection of townspeople, and thus had greater access to waterways and the wealth to take advantage of them. Monastic houses were therefore able to develop sophisticated systems of water management far in advance of most other communities. The impressive twelfth-century conduit system of Canterbury Cathedral Priory may serve as an example of the heights to which water-supply systems could rise. The system was installed in the time of Prior Wilbert (1151–67). It began at a spring a kilometer and a half outside Canterbury, where water was piped through an aqueduct, through five settling tanks to remove silt and sand and on to a variety of locations in the monastery, including the two *lavatoria*, or monastic washing-basins, the bathhouse, the brewhouse, the bakehouse, the great kitchen and the infirmary kitchen and so forth. The sytem was designed so that the water came to the latrines last, where it was joined by used water from the other buildings "upsteam" in the conduit. After serving the latrines, the water entered a sewer, which emptied ultimately into the town ditch.[96]

Many monasteries made use of wells or springs in similar ways and devised complicated conduit systems. In the fifteenth century, the London Charterhouse constructed such an ingenious system that water was piped to the individual monks' cells, providing a sanitary system for cleansing individual privies.[97] In other instances, a monastery might make simpler use of a stream or river, diverting water to run through the latrine building. A sluice gate was often set up to regulate the flow of water and make possible a periodic flushing of the latrine sewer, particularly in areas where there was not enough water to keep the sewer continuously supplied.[98] Poorer monasteries could avoid the expense of constructing such a system by simply building the latrines over a stream or river. Occasionally monasteries resorted to cesspits. The Carthusian Priory of Mount Grace, in Yorkshire, employed both cesspits and flushable sewers. Each "cell" at Mount Grace was a small two-story building with its own garden, running water supply and privy. Many of these privies were "flushable" by the water supply, piped in from a spring.[99]

One of the most detailed witnesses to monastic thought about sanitary arrangements is the Plan of St. Gall. The plan was drawn up at the request of Abbot Gozbert (816–36), who apparently hoped to reconstruct the entire monastery according to the plan.[100] Although the planned monastic buildings were never actually erected, the plan provides insights that can be absent in the archeological excavations of actual monasteries, in that it specifies the uses of each building and the rank and status of those who were appointed to them. In this instance, there is a direct correlation between rank and the provision of sanitary facilities. Those of the highest station had the greatest number of privies designated for their use. In the House for Distinguished Guests, for instance, the plan specifies bedrooms for eight noblemen and eighteen servants; each of the noblemen's bedrooms has its own privy, and there is in addition a communal outhouse with eighteen seats, presumably for the eighteen servants. One wonders if each was assigned his own seat or if all eighteen were expected to be in the privy at the same time. Similarly, the Guest House at Cluny, built by Abbot Odilo (994–1048), had seventy beds and seventy privy seats.[101] Going down the social scale at St. Gall, there was a reduction in the proportionate number of seats. The Outer School was designed to have around twenty-four students in residence, and its outhouse had fifteen seats; the House for Bloodletting had a capacity of perhaps twelve and had seven seats; the Abbot's House had a bedding capacity of eight and had six seats; and the Dormitories of the Novitiate and the Infirmary, which appear to have been designed to hold twelve people each, each have an outhouse with six seats. By contrast, the latrines of the regular monks were to have nine seats to serve seventy-seven monks. But there is a feature that induces surprise in modern observers:

One of the puzzling aspects of the Plan of St. Gall is the fact that although its author is scrupulously precise in the specifications of the privies that answer the needs of the monks and their noble visitors, the question of privies is not even raised on the level of the serfs, the workmen, and the paupers. The absence of privies (or even the provision of space for such) is most strongly felt in the case of the Great Collective Workshop and the Hospice for Pilgrims and Paupers. This is not an oversight, in my opinion, but a case of social discrimination. From a certain level downward the designer of the scheme left the solution of the individual privy to the ingenuity of the builder. In the case of those structures housing both humans and animals this poses no problem, as the sanitation of the human occupants is subject to the same order of cleanliness that governs good animal husbandry and can be met with the greatest of ease by an infinite variety of ingenious improvisations.[102]

One wishes the modern author had been a little more explicit as to what the "infinite variety of ingenious improvisations" might include. He continues:

But in the case of the Great Collective Workshop and the Hospice for Pilgrims and Paupers, the absence of privies—or even of the provision of space for them—is more disquieting. The designer simply chose not to express himself on this issue.[103]

With a planner of such precision, it would be curious indeed if he were to leave out sanitary facilities for a whole class of workers. Instead, it is almost certain that the plan is silent on the provision of built latrines for the lower classes because they had no formal latrines: like most ordinary medieval people, as we shall see in the next section, they were expected to use the great outdoors.

Monastic rules and similar documents allow us a view into official attitudes to the privy. The arrangements of the monastery also form the most dramatic contrast to their Roman predecessors. In Roman history, an early preference for portable chamber pots, favored in the Republican and early imperial periods, gave way to an ideological preference for public latrine blocks, culminating in the establishment of luxury latrines in the second and third centuries C.E. Excretion came to be regarded as a crucial part of a proper attention to health and digestion, and the whole was integrated into the idea of *urbanitas* and an emphasis on the social and civic aspects of life.[104] Roman communal latrines were usually square, but sometimes semicircular or of other shapes, with seats along all the walls, and with no internal partitions, giving the latrine a social aspect. This was to undergo wholesale change under the influence of medieval Christianity.

The standard design of the monastery was based in part on the Roman villa: hence also the popularity of the cloister, which was a feature of prosperous houses in the warm Italian countryside. The cloister remained unchanged since its origin in Roman custom, but the design of the latrines had undergone dramatic alteration. In contrast with the public, more open and social arrangement of communal Roman latrine seats, medieval monastic latrines arranged the seats in a long row, with partitions between the seats for greater privacy.[105] Indeed, Cistercian rules called for the monks to draw their cowls over their heads so they could not be recognized when visiting the latrines.[106] The latrines were identified not just as a site of supernatural danger but of practical spiritual danger. As the editors of the Plan of St. Gall say:

> The needs to which he attends in the privy were not only the lowest of all activities in which a monk was bound to engage, but were also a source of mortal danger. The light shown on the Plan of St. Gall as an obligatory piece of equipment in the Monks' Privy is a precautionary measure aimed at more than merely protecting the monks from stumbling in a physical sense. Besides his bed and his bath, this was the only other place where, by no fault of his own, he could not avoid bodily contact with himself. Like the temptations of the dormitory and of the bathhouse, the temptations of the privy could only be met with the most stringent of directives for conditions and time of use—especially strict in the case of the younger monks.[107]

The identity of the latrine as an occasion for sin is witnessed in Ekkehard's *Casus Sancti Galli*. Ekkehart relates how Ruodman, the abbot of the nearby monastery of Reichenau (972–86), attempted to catch the monks of St. Gall in the commission of sin by sneaking in the monastery late at night and hiding in the latrines. One of the monks heard him and woke others, and they processed to the latrine and scornfully offered him a lantern and a twist of straw—the two items necessary for legitimate use of the latrine.[108]

The spiritual dangers of the latrines called for strict regulation, and the times for visiting it were scheduled in rules and customaries. The Rule of St. Benedict, for example, makes a provision for the brothers to attend to the necessities of nature in a short interval. For the months between Easter and November 1, the interval was between Vigils and Lauds.[109] The monk Hildemar, writing in 845, specifies that the boys in the monastery should visit the privy after the late evening service in the company of their master; any boy who needs to go to the privy in the middle of the night must wake the master, who will light a lamp, accompany the boy and keep the lamp alight until they return to the dormitory.[110]

Such stringent restrictions on the times and conditions of visiting the latrines meant that the monks had to resort to other means to take care of their needs during the day. These means took the form of portable urinals, known as "jordans" in England, which are frequently excavated by archeologists in the area of monastic dormitories and latrines.[111] The fact that the monks had jordans at their disposal meant that the latrines must have principally been a place for defecation. When literature specifies what a monk is doing in the latrines—which it does with surprising frequency—this is indeed the case. As will now be clear, however, the norm in non-monastic medieval life was outdoor excretion; and so the practice of carrying jordans around, rather than merely resorting to the outdoors, is extraordinary, not to mention cumbersome. Monastic life demanded restraint not only in speech, the consumption of food, sexuality, sleep and other forms of bodily expression, but even in excretion—a chastity of excretion.

THE REALITIES OF MEDIEVAL WASTE MANAGEMENT

It is usually the more formal arrangements that have left traces, and evidence of other arrangements has to be gleaned from brief references and possible parallels from other times and cultures. With that in view, it should be noted that the mere existence of privies or latrines is not a given in all times and places or at all levels of society. It is erroneous to assume, as scholars have assumed about the plan of St. Gall, that all cultures have felt the need to provide privies for everyone, even if resources are available. Lack of formal latrines is certainly the case in contemporary traditional cultures, such as those of the South American rainforest, rural Papua New Guinea or isolated villages in Afghanistan. Even in modern countries with considerable development, privies are far from universal: it was reported in India in 1995, for example, that six hundred million of the country's nine hundred million people engaged in "open defecation."[112] In 2006 it was estimated that 2.6 billion of the world's people have no access to latrines.[113]

Open defecation was indubitably common in medieval Europe and persisted further into the modern era than many might suppose. In her memoir of the fens of East Anglia, Sybil Marshall recalls that in the childhood of her father, William Edwards, who born in 1870, privies were not yet standard:

> There was no such thing as a "toilet" or a "w.c."! *Water*-closet? In my Dad's childhood, there was no provision at all but the great outdoors, where one "went broadcast."[114]

As recently as 1960, the isolated villages of southern Spain, accessible only by donkey, had no privies, and the villagers used the outdoors.[115] Even in 2001, at a Finnish summer house, "toilet facilities consisted of the forest out back."[116]

In the areas of Europe that had been under Roman occupation, privies or latrines would have been introduced by the Romans if they had not been known beforehand, and it is a matter of reasonable supposition that the wealthier or more established householders would have continued to use privies through the Dark Ages and into the period when written records recommence. It is worth noting, however, that there is no archeological or other evidence for privies in Germania before the Carolingian era, and no ancient Germanic word for *privy*.[117] It has been suggested that the earliest sheltered places for excretion may have been the livestock byres that formed part of longhouses in that and later periods.[118] Another path for the institution of formal latrines would have been the construction of monasteries, which borrowed from Roman designs and thus may have contained latrine blocks as a matter of course. It is clear that these had arrived by the sixth century, when Gregory of Tours tells the story of a priest who died in the latrine, using the phrase "super sellula secessi defunctum," "dead on the seat of the privy," as witness to the fact that the priest was in a formal latrine when he died.[119] A formal latrine is likewise implied by Alcuin's poem on the subject, written in the later years of the eighth century.[120] There appears to be no evidence of a native Anglo-Saxon tradition of formal latrines, but if the Anglo-Saxons did not inherit them from the Romanized Celts, the knowledge of them certainly would have appeared with the arrival of missionaries and the monastic system, perhaps as early as the mission of Augustine to the English in 597.

The more informal arrangement of "going broadcast" in the countryside naturally leaves no archeological record, but there are medieval literary confirmations of the practice. In the eleventh-century satirical text *Unibos*, the peasant Unibos is defecating in the forest when he finds a hoard of coins:

> Omen habens argenteum   intrat lucum frondiferum;
> Qui dum ventris purgat lacum,   nummatum trahit meritum.
> Anum dum certat tergere,   herbam festinat rumpere,
> Sed herbam vellens repperit,   quod gens avara diligit.[121]

> Chance smiles on him as he enters a thick wood: while relieving himself, he discovers a treasure of coins. In fact, as he seeks to wipe himself, tearing handfuls of grass, under a tuft he finds what greedy people love.[122]

The text is making a point about the similarities between money and dung, but as it does so it casts light on an unexceptional peasant practice. There is also evidence that people of higher ranks used the countryside at times, even if they were accustomed to formal latrines as well. The *Urbanus Magnus* of Daniel of Beccles, a manual of conduct written around 1180, is addressed to young men who can read Latin well enough to follow its sometimes thorny hexameters. These educated young men are clearly familiar with latrines, as the poem mentions the *gumphus*, or privy, in several passages. It seems to take for granted, however, that its audience will also find themselves out of reach of a privy when the need strikes and exhorts the person answering the call of nature to keep his activities as unoffensive as possible:

> Si luco uel agro uentris purgatio fiat,
> Flamina sint uenti uentrem purgantis in ore,
> Et crupet in latebris dum fit purgatio uentris.[123]

> If the belly-purging should be performed in the woods or field,
> Let the gusts of wind be in the face of the one purging his belly,
> And let him squat in the shadows while the belly-purging takes place.

The practice of defecating on the ground also receives confirmation in its survival, in modified form, in many parts of Europe even to the present day, in the form of squatting latrines. Formal squatting latrines, made of stone or wood and emptying into cesspits, as analogues to seated latrines, appear not to occur in the archeological record, although the evidence is difficult to interpret since most latrines only survive below ground level. A number of wooden seats do survive, as well as the stone seats in buildings such as castles; these all appear to come from sitting rather than squatting latrines. There is also a very small amount of evidence for a third type of latrine, a bar or plank over a cesspit, upon which a person might perch. Though such latrines are known in other cultures—as among the Maori—there is only the scarcest of evidence that they were widespread in medieval Europe.[124]

The variability in attitudes towards domestic excrement is perhaps most dramatically demonstrated by two contrasting practices, that of medieval Iceland and that of certain areas of Celtic settlement. The attitude of medieval Iceland is attested in *Laxdæla saga*, in which hostilities between two groups are escalated by one group, headed by a man named Kjartan, which surrounds the other group and prevents them from leaving their farmhouse. The saga says:

> Hann biðr menn stíga af baki ok mælti, at sumir skyldu geyma hesta þeira, en suma biðr hann reisa tjǫld. Í þann tíma var þat mikil tizka, at úti var salerni ok eigi allskammt frá bœnum, ok svá var at Laugum. . . . Þeim Laugamǫnnum líkar illa ok þótti þetta miklu meiri svívirðing ok verri en þott Kjartan hefði drepit mann eða tvá fyrir þeim.[125]

> It was customary at that time to have an outdoor privy, some distance from the house, and so it was at Laugar. Kjartan stationed guards at all the doors of the farmhouse and barred the exit of all persons, so that they had to relieve themselves indoors for three days and nights. . . .The Laugar folk were ill-content and felt this to be more of a disgrace and a far worse one than if Kjartan had outright killed a man or two of them.[126]

Such horror at unheroic disgrace may seem reassuringly modern. Yet other examples show that overcoming such horror may be even more practical. There is considerable testimony to a practice of hoarding dung *inside* the living quarters of the house in several districts of the British isles, all of them cold, spartan and without ready access to firewood. The most extensively attested of these are the traditional practices on the Scottish island of St. Kilda, in force into the 1830s. Although these practices originated at an unknown date, it is implausible that they were devised only in the early modern period: there is every reason to suppose they were practiced throughout the medieval period, and were very possibly even pre-medieval in origin.

The St. Kildans, above all, should serve as witness that dung is not universally reviled, but that cultural practices are richly variable. On St. Kilda, villagers saved dung on the floor of their cottages throughout the winter.[127] The householders first burnt peat in fires on the earthen floor of their cottages, then spread the peat ashes on the floor, followed by dung, and then by peat dust. The layers were then watered and trodden upon to make a hard floor, upon which they lit new fires. They repeated this operation until the spring, by which time the height of the floor had been raised four or five feet. In the spring they used the mixture of dung and peat ashes as invaluable fertilizer for their poor and rocky fields. One observer of this practice, the Rev. Kenneth Macaulay, reported that they considered the manure "a commodity inestimably precious," although it "proves that they are very indelicate."[128] The Rev. Neil MacKenzie, who lived on St. Kilda from 1829 to 1843, gave a vivid description of the living conditions this practice engendered:

> The cattle occupied the half of the house next the door, and the manure was not removed till it was taken to the fields in spring. In the other portion dwelt the family, and there all the ashes, and the dirty water, and many things far worse, were daily spread over the floor. This was covered every few days with a layer of dry peat dust. Before the time for removal to the fields in spring the mixture was often higher than the side walls, so that at times a visit to a parishioner was quite an adventure. Owing to the great thickness of the wall the house door was at the end of a tunnel, and owing to the lowness of the door space one could not stand upright. In front of the doorway, and extending well into the tunnel, was a hollow into which were thrown all the portions of the bird not used for food, the entire carcases of those not edible, and all and every abomination you can think of. Stooping low, you groped your way over this till you reached the door. Inside the door you had to climb over the manure to among the cattle, which, on account of the presence of a stranger, and the barking of dogs, and the shouting of your friends above, soon got very excited. Amidst great confusion and excitement you got helped along and over the dividing *fallan* [wall].

Here you had to creep along on hands and feet, and it was only near the centre of the space that you could even sit upright. Carefully creeping along in almost total darkness, you made your way to the top of the steep slope which led down to the bed opening. Down this you went head foremost, nothing visible above but your legs, while you spoke and prayed. They wonder themselves why it is that they are not so strong as they believe their forefathers to have been. The wonder rather is that under such conditions of living they survive at all.[129]

These practices were also followed elsewhere in the most impoverished areas of the region. In the 1780s, a missionary to the Western Hebrides, John Lanne Buchanan, reported the same custom. The inhabitants lived in their cottages with cows, goats, sheep, ducks, hens and dogs and were cleanly enough to be "attending on their cows with large vessels" to collect and dispose of the urine but were steadfastly resistant to the idea of cleaning out the dung more than once a year: "the whole of them, whether rich or poor, keep the cow-houses without cleaning them till Spring."[130] Collecting the urine separately would have kept the smell down, as a large part of the stench of dungheaps is due to the ammonia, a component of urine. As on St. Kilda, in the spring they used the dung as fertilizer for their crops. The same custom was practiced in parts of Ireland, where a schoolteacher named Patrick McKye deplored the practice in an 1837 letter to the Lord Lieutenant of Ireland; a document of 1857–58 reports that "heaps of manure could still be seen at the bedside."[131]

Even if the cottagers' sense of smell had been eroded by continual exposure to dung and decay, this is a startlingly inconvenient way to live, particularly in the manner practiced on St. Kilda, and the reason for so doing is not explored extensively by outside observers. On the Scottish islands in particular, rocky island soil was so poor that the prosperity, and even the actual survival, of each family must have depended on the supply of fertilizer, and so one of the reasons they hoarded it so carefully may have been for fear others would steal it. Buchanan reports, "In the heart of Lewis, where many of the farms are far from the sea, they are necessitated not only to use all manner of cow dung, but even to strip the house of its thatch every Spring, to make an addition to their manure for the land."[132] But this is not the sole reason. Both the dung and the straw produce heat when decomposing. This reaction is so strong that when not carefully mixed with agents such as peat dust, spontaneous combustion can occur. Even in the present day, the spontaneous combustion of dungheaps and haystacks are the leading cause of barn fires. St. Kilda is an island with no trees, and consequently the only fuel for fires was peat and dung. The hoarding of dung on the cottage floors meant that they need not have used up these valuable fertilizers in heating their cottages: The natural fermentation of the mounds of dung and straw would have heated their houses throughout the winter. What seemed to be appalling hygiene begins to look like remarkable ingenuity.

The practices of these countryfolk, thrifty and ingenious with dung as with other contrivances for living, show that there is no "innate" and invariable practical reaction to excrement. It can be shameful, contaminating and disgusting, or in other circumstances it can be life-giving.

POLLUTION AS A SOURCE OF POWER AND SHAME

Whether regarded as noxious material or beneficent fertilizer, excrement was charged with power. It was a matter utterly unlike other substances: animal matter, yet not alive or consumable; repellant and yet fruitful. It had all the properties of carnality: it was corrupt, malodorous, decaying, and yet earthly, fecund, powerful and unavoidable. Alone among physical necessities, it required humans to disrobe, at least partially, and to bare their essential animal natures. It served as a daily reminder that, however much they deplored the fact, humans were not disembodied, pure and wholly spiritual. It was an entirely corporeal act, which could not be refined, restrained or abjured, as could such other corporeal acts as eating, sleeping, washing or sex. The body, which pious humans strove so mightily to tame, performed unthinkable acts of digestion and transmuted dainties into filth. Defecation had the power to make humans undignified at best and ungodly at worst.

Excrement itself, a substance produced in the body by invisible means, could be regarded as an efficacious substance, on par with other substances produced by nature. Godfrid Storms has observed about "excrements," "Their very repulsiveness lent them power, just as old and ugly women were taken for witches."[133] Dung accordingly sometimes appears as an ingredient in medical remedies, often in the form of bird or livestock droppings. Anglo-Saxon remedies might call for goat's dung, goose dung, sheep's dung, horse dung, calf or ox dung or pigeon dung mixed with various household ingredients.[134] One fifteenth-century recipe calls for pigeon dung, incense, wheat flour and an egg white to be made into a poultice, which will then allegedly cure headache; another preparation containing pigeon dung is touted to cure aching bones and bruises.[135] A cure for toothache calls for a raven's "tord" or turd, dyed so that the sick person "knaw it not ne wote not what it be."[136] Horse dung is called for in a recipe to make a poultice for bruises or wens.[137] Human dung in remedies is rare, though not unknown. One thirteenth-century English text calls for human dung in a concoction to cure disease of the eye.[138] Another recipe calls for human dung among seven products of the human body (tears, blood, earwax, etc.), not to bestow health, but as part of a supernatural process to create a magic mirror. The author of this preparation, as of other magical treatises, regards heat as an important process in such chemistry; as the practitioner might heat ingredients with fire, so the body heated ingredients in digestion, a reasoning that goes some way toward explaining why the medical profession might regard dung as potentially efficacious.[139]

Notwithstanding the sanitary arrangements of St. Kilda, most medieval Europeans displayed some unease with the human necessity for defecation, and the more dignified the context, the greater the unease. The response ran the gamut from embarrassment to shame. The embarrassment gave impetus to many comic tales, the shame to many pious admonitions about the corruptions of the flesh. This mixture of embarrassment and shame can be discerned in the use of euphemisms to describe the call of nature. Deuteronomy 23:12 had used the phrase *ad requisita naturae*. The Benedictine Rule employed a variant on the phrase: *ad necessaria naturae exeant*.[140] The phrase turns up in a number of similar locutions such as *necessitas fratrum, corporis necessaria, corporea necessitas naturae* and *necessitas naturae*.[141] The vocabulary for the latrine itself is also often euphemistic, typically employing some variation on "going out," "seat" or "small enclosure." Latin referred to the *secessus, exitus, necessarium, latrina* and *gumphus*. Old English had terms for "going," *gang* and *genge, utgang, forthgang, earsgang* ("arse-go"), *gangpytt*, sometimes with a term for "seat" or location, *gangsetl, gangstol, gangtun, feltun* (from "feld-tun," "field-place"), *grep/grype/grop* (ditch), *niedhus* and *longhus*. The French went to the *garderobe, chambre privée, retrait, fosse à retrait, chambre basse, chambre de pierre, chambre courtoise* or *longaigne* ("far-away place"). Middle English referred to the *gong, garderobe, warderobe, chaumbre foreine* and *prive*.[142] Old Irish had the *fialtech*, "veil house," perhaps derived or euphemized from *fualtech*, "urine house." Old Norse words for the outhouse include *heimilishús, nádahús, hysken, lillehus, salerni, (úti)kamarr, annathús, gardhús* and *gangr*. Two of these many terms are particularly apt. *Necessarium* sums up the inescapability of the need to defecate as if it were the single, lamentable, necessity of life. *Priue* or "privy" reveals the degree to which the latrine has become a place of individual retreat and shame—a contrast to the communal latrines of Roman days.

Medical texts, the texts most straightforwardly devoted to the description of the body, provide further witnesses of medieval expressions. One instructs that a plaster should be applied to a person's stomach "till he do to prevey," "until he goes to the privy."[143] Another prescribes a remedy "ʒif he may noʒt go to sege onys a day," "if he does not 'go to the seat' once a day."[144] An unusual variant manuscript of the same text is more explicit and replaces "go to sege" with the franker "schite."[145] Middle Dutch medical texts resort to the same roundabout wording, referring to *gang* (going), *ter cameren gaen* (going to the room) and *ten stoel gaen* (go to the stool). Allan and Burridge, who have studied such texts, note, "In a text devoted almost exclusively to enemas and suppositories, the lack of a single direct mention of feces indicates a topic about which the medievals felt uncomfortable."[146] The texts also use terms like *materie*, "matter," and *(be) roeringhe*, "movement," and speak of *die ripe materi . . . uut te seynden*, "sending out the ripe matter," and *die lede beneden sachten*, "softening the parts underneath." One text, the "Circa Instans," is distinctive in using the word *aers(gat)*, "arse(hole)" throughout, but in a second version the offensive term has been replaced by *fundmant*.[147]

Narrative texts allow us glimpses of more elaborate vernacular euphemisms, such as the husband in a Flemish tale who, finding his wife absent from their bed at night, concludes that she has gone out "to pick flowers."[148] This particular turn of phrase is interesting in its attempt to deodorize as well as disguise what the woman is actually doing. The Scandinavians went out to "ganga til trés," "go to the wood," or "ganga álfreka," "chase the elves away."[149] Some of the expressions are not so much euphemisms as circumlocutions. In Chaucer's Merchant's Tale, May pretends she needs to go to the privy, or, in Chaucer's phrasing, "she moste gon / Ther as ye woot that every wight moot neede," "she had to go where as you know every person needs to go."[150] In John Barbour's poem on Robert the Bruce, the king goes to "a cowert yat wes prewe, / Quhar ye king oft wes wont to ga / His prewe nedys for to ma," "a covert that was privy, where the king often was accustomed to go to take care of his privy needs."[151] The idea is also reflected in later texts. In the early sixteenth-century *Heptameron* of Marguerite de Navarre, a lady "eut une grande necessité d'aller au lieu où on ne peult envoyer sa chamberiere," "had a great need to go where you can't send your chambermaid for you."[152] In *Don Quijote*, Sancho feels the need "de hacer lo que otro no pudiera hacer por él," "to do that which no one could do for him."[153] Such locutions underscore the intimate nature of excretion: required of each person, who must confront corporeality directly, without any intermediaries, a *necessarium* that even the wealthy cannot delegate.

There are also numerous witnesses to the fact that the need to clean oneself after defecating was standard and practiced all the way down the social scale. The means for doing this varied by region and context. The text *Unibos*, cited previously, depicts a peasant using grass. The *Casus S. Galli* shows monks using straw. Straw is also used in the fabliau *Le Sacristain*, where the characters disguise the murder of a monk by propping his body on a seat in the monastic latrine with a wisp of straw in his hand. In 1180, Daniel of Beccles instructs the servant to wait by his lord at the privy, holding straw and wisps of hay (*busiae*) for his lord's use.[154] The intimacy of this arrangement had diminished by the fifteenth century, when John Russell, who describes himself as usher and marshall to Humphrey, Duke of Gloucester, wrote his *Boke of Nurture*. Russell outlines the duties of the chamberlain and shows that privy conditions have improved considerably for the wealthy:

> Se þe privehouse for esement be fayre, soote, & clene,
> & þat þe bordes þer vppon / be keuered withe clothe feyre & grene,
> and þe hoole / hym self, looke þer no borde be sene,
> þeron a feire quoschyn / þe ordoure no man to tene

looke þer be blanket / cotyn / or lynyn to wipe þe neþur ende;
and euer when he clepithe, wayte redy & entende,
basoun and ewere, & on your shuldur a towelle, my frende;
In þis wise worship shall ye wyn / where þat euer ye wende.¹⁵⁵

See that the privy-house for easement is fair, sweet, and clean,
And that the boards thereupon be covered with cloth fair and green,
And the hole itself, be sure that no board is seen,
(Put) thereon a fair cushion, so that the ordure bothers no one.
Make sure there is wool, cotton, or linen to wipe the nether end;
And always when he calls, attend and make ready
Basin and ewer, and on your shoulder a towel, my friend;
In this way you shall win praise wherever you go.

Archeological excavations of monastic cesspits have turned up bits of cloth, presumably worn-out robes; the contents of other cesspits suggest the use of moss.¹⁵⁶ William of Malmesbury is said to have provided testimony to the use of water for such cleansing.¹⁵⁷ Finally, a riddle from the fifteenth-century *Demaundes Joyous* testifies to the use of leaves:

Demaunde. Whiche is the moost cleynlyest lefe amonge all other leues.
Rx. it is holly leues / for noo body wyll not wype his arse with them.¹⁵⁸

Question. What is the cleanest leaf of all leaves?
Response. It is holly leaves, for no one will wipe his arse with them.

Although as a whole excretion was the subject of open discussion in the Middle Ages, the period was not monolithic. The degree to which such topics were permissible varied from region to region and from period to period. This may be particularly visible in non-religious discourse, where no theological purpose underlay the text. What is most noticeable about the period, however, is its comparative openness about such matters: what might be regarded by Norbert Elias as a want of refinement or what might conversely be called authenticity and an acknowledgement of the full range of human experience. The remainder of this chapter will survey the evidence for medieval openness and evasiveness about matters of excretion.

Again, the precise degree to which latrines and excretion were taboo varied from place to place and period to period. Thomas W. Ross suggests that the fifteenth-century Scottish poets were less fastidious in vocabulary than the fourteenth-century English had been, feeling free to use variants of *schit,* as well as frank terms for sex.¹⁵⁹ He concludes that in the fourteenth and fifteenth centuries *donge* was unexceptional but *toorde* had a "lingering taboo," as indicated, for instance, by one late–fifteenth-century scribe's omission of any vernacular translation for *merdula* in a list of glosses.¹⁶⁰ In addition to *merdula*, which is glossed only by *parua merda*, the scribe also omits vernacular glosses for *extercoro* (glossed *stercora auferre*) and *vrino* (glossed *vrinam facere, mingere*), as well as a number of sexual terms such as *defloro, mentula (uirga virilis), scortor (meretricor)* and so forth.[161] That the English were particularly "squaymous" about excretion is also evident from more literary sources. The English fabliaux, for example, never reached the level of scatological frankness that characterizes the French in such tales as *Jouglet* or *La Crote*.[162]

The greater fastidiousness of the English is clearly revealed in the English translation of the late fifteeth-century French riddle collection, the *Demandes joyeuses*.[163] The French versions are abundant in scatological and sexual jokes; the English version, the *Demaundes Joyous*, is decidedly tamer. In the French version, for instance, we get:

> Pour quoy chasse on les chiens hors du moustier?
> Pour tant que point ne vont a l'offrande, et se chient sur les mors.[164]

> Why do they chase dogs out of the church?
> Because they don't go to the offering, and they shit on the dead.

The English version has been bowdlerized:

> Demaunde. Why dryue men dogges out of the chyrche.
> Rx. Bycause they come not vp and offre.[165]

> Question. Why do men drive dogs out of the church?
> Response. Because they don't come up and make offering.

Later in the jestbook, such hesitation is less apparent, as in:

> Demaunde. Whiche is the cleynlyest occupacyon that is.
> Rx. That is a dauber / for he may neyther shyte nor ete tyll he hath wasshed his handes.[166]

> Question: What is the cleanliest occupation there is?
> Response. That is a dauber [plasterer/caulker], for he may neither shit nor eat till he has washed his hands.

In other matter-of-fact contexts, the English were as frank as other nations, as place names reveal. Streets known for their privies, or for the dumping of excrement, were called by unvarnished names. Shitteborwelane turns up in London as early as 1272–73; there was similarly a Schiteburne Lane in Romford (1272), a "Schitebur' lan'" in Oxford (c. 1290), a Shitelane in Winchester (late fourteenth century), a stream called Shitebroc in Lincoln (thirteenth century), another in Exeter and another called Shitewelle in Warwickshire, among others.[167] In later years, however, such names garnered euphemisms. Shitteborwelane in London had been transmuted to Shirbbouruelane by 1467 and to Shirborne Lane by 1540; it is now known as Sherborne Lane, the origins of its name obscured entirely.[168] Warwickshire's Shitewell is now Shutwell Farm, and Lincolnshire's Scitebroc is now Skidbrook. In an even more telling conversion, Winchester's Shiteburn Lane has become Paternoster Row.

In Dublin, one millpond into which effluent drained was known as Schyttclapp Mill, while another was called Muileann a Chacca (Shitty Mill).[169] The French rivalled the Irish and English in the straightforwardness of their geographic names. We have already noted the abundance of waterways with names like Merdron or Merdançon. Streets had similar names: Merdeux, Merdelet, Merdusson, Merdière and so forth. Other streets associated with dung might be named Rue Sale (Dirty Street) or Rue Foireuse (Runny-crap Street), as at Angoulême. In Châlons-sur-Marne there was even a ruelle du Pipi.[170]

French literature uses scatology as a font of humor in the fabliaux and in other types of literature, notably in the mock-epic scatological tour de force *Audigier*, the story of an inverted dung-world in which the hero, Turgibus, is seduced by his beloved after she has just eaten prunes and invites him to defecate with her.[171] The scatological heights of the English are much more modest. The thirteenth-century poem *The Owl and the Nightingale* frames its rather basic scatology in an animal setting. Most other English scatology occurs in a religious, albeit comic, context often associated with the devil, as in the play *Mankind* or in a number of religious plays that associate scatologic taunts with the devil. Chaucer's Summoner's Prologue and Tale, which hinge on what lurks under the devil's tail and the division of a fart, also qualify as religious satire; it is only his Miller's Tale in which the farting is arguably secular, although it is still a man of religion, the unsuitably dandified cleric Absolon, who bears the brunt of it.

The diffidence with which excretion was regarded is not confined to secular literary texts, but appears in descriptions of everyday life. We have already seen the Cistercian admonition that monks should raise their cowls so as not to be recognized when visiting the latrines. At Redburn Priory, the Abbot Thomas (1349–96) constructed a private latrine for himself, "quia prius una domus tantum capiebat eum et fratres ibidem, unde ipsi quandoque pro sui praesentia ad necessaria erubescebant accedere," "because formerly a single house had served him and the brothers in that one place, whence they where ashamed whenever they had to go to the necessary in his presence."[172] There is also evidence that the owners of castles became embarrassed by the trails of excrement visible on the walls under the garderobes corbelled out from the side of the building. In 1313, for instance, Sir William de Norwico ordered a wall built to hide the trail of excrement on the Tower of London.[173]

Baring the buttocks was a well-known insult, as the many examples in Chapter 3 demonstrate. This could even be used blasphemously against

God, as in the case of the notorious Alberigo da Romano, who blamed God for the loss of his falcon and in revenge defecated on the altar and pulled down his pants and bared his bottom to God.[174] The many images of sinners doing the same to Christ or to holy figures, as detailed in Chapter 3, participate in the same symbolic system. Excretion was powerful, though appropriate to the Devil rather than to God. The scatological strategy for defeating the Devil is significant: both St. Francis and St. Bernard were said to have countered the Devil by telling him variations on "Open your mouth and I'll shit in it!"[175]

At the same time, we should note that history is full of people violating etiquette and taboos about excretion. The London mayor's court rolls record the trial of Thomas Scott, the prince's groom, who had become embroiled in a violent altercation with two men who had reprimanded him for stopping in a lane when it would have been "more decent" to have used one of the city latrines.[176] Both the objections of the bystanders and the determination of the offender were vehement. As noted previously, Da Vinci deplored the use of stairways as latrines, but his plans to prevent it are testimony to how commonplace it must have been. Manuals of conduct likewise testify to both the degree to which the genteel deplored certain habits and the degree to which these habits were practiced. In the twelfth century, Daniel of Beccles laid down the rules for polite behavior:

> Illico non surgas post prandia mingere, uentrem
> Nec purgare tuum, nisi sit natura coacta.
> Hospes, legatus, famulans non mingat in aula.
> Urinare licet domino domui dominanti;
> Urinet noctu post sompnum, si uelit, hospes.
> A te mingentis uestes non sustineantur;
> Promere sepe solet inimica silentia mingens.[177]

> You should not get up immediately after the meal to urinate, nor to purge your belly, unless nature compels it. The guest, the envoy, the servant, should not urinate in the hall. The presiding lord may urinate in the household; let the guest urinate after sleep at night, if he likes. You should not hold up the clothes of a urinating man. A urinating man should habitually project a chilly silence.

Daniel also warns against loud farting, even in fun, and against all intestinal noises. Distinguishing the clean from the unclean, symbolically as well as practically, he also admonishes his readers to employ the left hand when using the straw to clean themselves.[178] The fact that these strictures needed to be spelled out suggests that such delicacy was not already ubiquitous.

Excrement's power to offend animates dozens of comic tales, and the popularity of such tales betrays the fact that such offenses are finely balanced: just offensive enough to bring comic disgrace upon characters' heads, but not so offensive as to preclude others' enjoyment of that shame. Thus every scatological tale is both a testament to the impropriety of dung and to the triviality of that taboo. A case in point is the German *Veilchenschwank*, or "Violet Trick," a widespread tale that first appears in the fourteenth century. The stock character Neidhart, a court entertainer, goes out to search for the first violet of spring; when he finds it, he puts his camp over it and runs back to tell the court. Having observed this, a local peasant lifts the cap, plucks the violet, defecates in its place and replaces the cap. Neidhart returns, leading the court, who perform a dance around the cap and eventually lift it up to great dismay when they find not the violet but a pile of dung. The story was clearly extremely popular: it is found in prose tales, drama and songs, as well as in wall paintings, on stone tablets and in woodcuts.[179] The Augustinian monk Gottschalk Hollen (d. 1481) even complained that the laudable habit of painting scenes from the lives of the saints on the walls of houses was being replaced by painting scenes from the dance of Neidhart.[180] The taboo and shameful nature of the trick made it scandalous, and its scandalousness made it popular.

The fact that unrefined habits were still prevalent in later, supposedly more civilized centuries shows how endemic they tended to be. Erasmus's manual of conduct for boys serves as a useful example:

> Incivile est eum salutare, qui reddit urinam aut alvum exonerat. . . . Membra quibus natura pudorem addidit retegere citra necessitatem procul abesse debet ab indole liberali. Quin ubi necessitas huc cogit, tamen id quoque decente verecundia faciendum est, etiam si nemo testis adsit. Nunquam enim non adsunt angeli, quibus in pueris gratissimus est pudicitiae comes custosque pudor.
>
> It is impolite to greet someone who is urinating or defecating. . . . A well-bred person should always avoid exposing without necessity the parts to which nature has attached modesty. If necessity compels this, it should be done with decency and reserve, even if no witness is present. For angels are always present, and nothing is more welcome to them in a boy than modesty, the companion and guardian of decency.[181]

Erasmus's instructions might serve as a summary of all anxieties present in the regulation of excretion. The person so doing must be disregarded, so the act can be segregated from daily life: it is a marked act which must not be treated casually, as if it held no shame. Excretion is not only shameful in itself, but doubly shameful in the bodily parts it engages (which in turn derive their shame from the fact that they give rise to such bodily effluvia). To be mindful of this shame is the "guardian of decency," restraining the willfulness and shamelessness of the uncontrolled body; to expose them offends the angels. In particular one should not display any interest in said parts or in anything connected with them, as if they were not shameful—much less display an interest in them specifically *because* they are disgusting, like the Renaissance man "lifting the foul-smelling thing to his nostrils and saying, 'I should like to know how much that stinks.'"[182]

Although excrement could be fruitful as well as abhorred, the actual act of excretion was inevitably the subject of disdain. Men's habit of urinating in public particularly excited the disapproval of authorities. One such was Don Antonio de Beatis, who accompanied Luigi d'Aragon, a Neapolitan cardinal, on a tour through Europe in 1517–18. Don Antonio wrote:

> Yet whereas in Germany there are one or two tin chamber-pots to every bed (in Flanders they are made of brass and very clean), in France for want of any alternative one has to urinate on the fire. They do this everywhere, by night and day; and indeed, the greater the nobleman or lord, the more readily and openly will he do it.[183]

A manual of conduct shows the practice prevalent in 1558:

> Moreover, it does not befit a modest, honorable man to prepare to relieve nature in the presence of other people, nor to do up his clothes afterwards in their presence. Similarly, he will not wash his hands on returning to decent society from private places, as the reason for his washing will arouse disagreeable thoughts in people.[184]

The Wernigerode Court Regulations of 1570 echo this sentiment:

> One should not, like rustics who have not been to court or lived among refined and honorable people, relieve oneself without shame or reserve in front of ladies, or before the doors or windows of court chambers or other rooms.[185]

Despite such admonitions, there remained cause for reproof two centuries later, in 1731:

> If you pass a person who is relieving himself you should act as if you had not seen him, and so it is impolite to greet him.[186]

Such lack of decorum was still in evidence in early nineteenth-century England. Louis Simond, an American born in France, deplored certain habits at English dinner parties:

> Drinking much and long leads to unavoidable consequences. Will it be credited that, in a corner of the very dining-room, there is a certain convenient piece of furniture, to be used by any body who wants it. The operation is performed very deliberately and undisguisedly, as a matter of course, and occasions no interruption of the conversation....

I have seen the article in question regularly provided in houses where there was [sic] no men, that is, no master of the house; the mistress, therefore, must be understood to have given the necessary orders to her servants,—a supposition rather alarming for the delicacy of an English lady. Yet I find these very people up in arms against some uncleanly practices of the French; for instance, spitting on the floor, the carpet, &c. &c. . . .[187]

Scandalized though Simond may have been, the English evidently found it trivial and comic. Such a casual attitude is echoed by John Keats in a letter to his brother, in which he described an incident of an overfull chamber pot in a cupboard at a dinner party and the *bons mots* which the incident occasioned.[188]

It should be clear from the varieties of conditions, practices and ideas of propriety that the management of the body's waste matter was an imperfect science at best. For every person with strict standards of hygiene or behavior there was someone with different priorities, and for everyone who felt such things were best ignored there was someone with a prurient interest in such matters. Speech and actions could be controlled; a person could abstain from sex; but in matters of excretion, the body and its products were irrepressible and unruly. It was upon this foundation that medieval culture mapped an understanding of the place of the body, and of humankind, in the larger world.

3 The Symbolic Order of the Body

In medieval Christian thought the body conveyed far more than issues of identity and location: it literally embodied vital evidence of humankind's relationship to God. Corporeal corruptibility was testimony to sacred history and the Fall of Man, the moment in which sin had entered the world and the reason for Christ's sacrifice. As a living testament to divine history, the body could be read and interpreted no less than scripture or other components of the universe. Indeed, the body took center stage in medieval thought, for although scripture described sacred history, the body lived it and literally died for it. This explains in part what Caroline Bynum has called the "radical physicality" of medieval religion, with its emphasis on physical suffering and corruption.[1]

Divine truth was equally embodied and revealed by the universe, forming a symbolic system in which aspects such as location and position were theologically meaningful. The larger universe and the body were not discrete systems, but parallel reflections of truth on different scales. The macrocosm of the universe was reflected in the microcosm of the body, an understanding inherited from Plato and widespread throughout the medieval period. Thus the orientation of both the body and the universe had specific theological significance in the Middle Ages.

In fact, the idea that orientation has meaning is universal rather than culture-specific. The work of George Lakoff and Mark Johnson has demonstrated that the specifics of our physical existence are central to thought or, as they say, that the mind is "embodied in such a way that our conceptual systems draw largely upon the commonalities of our bodies and of the environments we live in."[2] Meaning derives from the relationship of the world to the body, and these relationships structure thought and the metaphors with which thought is conveyed. Thus, for instance, concepts like *front* and *back* reflect our own bodies, which are not front/back symmetrical but always oriented in a particular direction; and the fronts and backs of other objects are defined by their orientation to our own fronts. These "body-based image schemas" also lend their structures to more abstract thought.[3] Much conceptual metaphor relies on the body to structure and orient it. The idea that Christmas "comes a week ahead of" New Year's

Day, for instance, conceptualizes the two days in terms of motion and orientation.[4] In addition, the concept employs the term *ahead*, which orients time in terms of bodily orientation, the head being the primary part, a "top-down" way of regarding the world. The body gives rise to structures of thought, and structures of thought give rise to culture. Thus "The most fundamental values in a culture will be coherent with the metaphorical structure of the most fundamental concepts in the culture."[5]

Although Lakoff and Johnson argue that all human thought procceds from an embodied stance, medieval thought regarded the matter differently. Of the human body and the physical universe, neither had primacy: rather, both were oriented toward God and defined by that orientation. The key factor was *likeness*, which was conceived of in both physical/spatial and moral/spiritual terms. Essential to this was that the two dimensions were identical: morality was mapped onto space or, to put it another way, the physical and spatial possessed moral valence. Physical uprightness embodied likeness to God and reflected moral uprightness, not merely metaphorically, but literally.

The "phenomenological embodiment" of Lakoff and Johnson sees the way in which embodiment structures thought; but the Middle Ages went one further. Medieval thought used not only the structure of the body, but also its processes and products, as a way of structuring thought about the cosmos, encompassing both the physical universe and time.

THE MORAL ORGANIZATION OF THE UNIVERSE

The common medieval understanding of the cosmos mapped a hierarchy of virtue and sin, or likeness and unlikeness to God, on the Ptolemaic universe. This, combined with ideas inherited from Neoplatonism, gave rise to an understanding of the universe as a hierarchy in both a concrete and a moral sense. God was literally at the top, the embodiment of ineffable purity and goodness, and from there the purity of the cosmos declined through the heavens down to earth, through the tainted goodness of man, and so on down to hell, the realm of pure evil.[6] The key to this cosmic order was that each moral element had its spatial counterpart: had, in short, a location, a natural association, and a likeness.[7] By and large medieval thinkers agreed in reading that physical universe, and in particular the human body, in specific moral ways. In this way the physical and moral universes overlap, and the structure of both can be expressed in polarities:

God ⟷ the Devil

good ⟷ evil

light ⟷ darkness

purity ←——→ corruption

integrity ←——→ lack of wholeness, commingling

forward ←——→ backward

right ←——→ left[8]

high ←——→ low

In some senses these can be regarded as opposites, but these are opposites with moral value, and hence are better understood as opposite levels in a hierarchy. True opposites or polarities might be equally worthy or valid and thereby reveal truth, as Abelard's treatise of contradictory arguments, *Sic et Non*, sought to demonstrate.[9] By contrast, these polarities are fundamental and definitional; in a word, constitutive, constituting the terms by which the universe is ordered and defined. What is most significant is that, in the medieval view, the moral dimension is mapped onto the spatial dimension, not metaphorically, not by human understanding, but as a basic property of the universe. Thus in a very real sense integrity *is* God, corruption *is* Evil, purity *is* loftiness, and there is an absolute orientation to the universe. *High* and *low* were not relative, but real locations in an absolute sense—relative only to God. Forward, up and towards purity and God are no mere metaphorical concepts, but partake of this fundamental orientation, which is essential for the medieval understanding of the human body.

In its most abstract form, this could mean that spatial imagery was used to express moral concepts. Spatial imagery is vital, for instance, to an influential passage from Augustine:

> intraui in intima mea duce te . . . . et uidi qualicumque oculo animae meae supra eundem oculum animae meae, supra mentem meam lucem incommutabilem, non hanc uulgarem et conspicuam omni carni nec quasi ex eodem genere grandior erat. . . . Nec ita erat supra mentem meam, sicut oleum super aquam nec sicut caelum super terram, sed superior, quia ipsa fecit me, et ego inferior, quia factus ab ea. . . . et inueni longe me esse a te in regione dissimilitudinis, tamquam audirem uocem tuam de excelso.[10]

> With you as guide, I entered into my innermost self . . . . and with the eye of my soul, of whatever kind, I saw an unchanging light, above the eye of my soul and above my mind—not this light which is common and apparent to all flesh, nor as if it were a greater light of the same kind. . . . Nor was it above my mind as oil is on top of water, or as heaven is above the earth, but superior, because it made me, and I

inferior, because I was made by it. . . . And I found myself far from you in a land of unlikeness, as if I heard your voice from on high.

Even as Augustine affirms that these terms are conceptual, he maps out likeness and unlikeness to God in terms of geographical and locational dimensions, using images of the body. He reiterates that literal geographical distance is irrelevant here:

> Non enim locorum interuallis sed similitudine acceditur ad deum, et dissimilitudine receditur ab eo.
>
> One draws closer to God not through intervals of space but through likeness, and is distanced from him through unlikeness.[11]

Although he emphasizes that spiritual movement is more significant than geographical movement, even he imbues his descriptions with spatial metaphors. Other traditions of medieval piety show that geographical space could indeed be assigned spiritual value. This is apparent in the consecration of churches and graveyards, the cults attached to sites related to saints, the tradition of pilgrimage and even the cult of relics, which functioned as portable sites of holiness. In all of these, physical location and proximity could confer holiness. Contact with relics could transfer holiness in the form of material stability and healing; proximity to the church could promote holy burial; visits to sites related to holy figures, saints and miracles could confer material wholeness and spiritual growth. The spiritual world was oriented toward the physical location of the holy on earth. What is more, Augustine's assertion involves the spiritual journey on earth. In the afterlife, one would indeed journey away from the mortal world towards God, whose land was unlike the corrupt human world in location as well as in purity.

Augustine and formal theologians of his ilk were concerned to point out the spiritual path to God, not to provide an overview of the universe. Yet even in works of official theology such as these, the spiritual dimension is outlined in spatial terms, a practice that both reflected and contributed to the continued understanding of the moral dimensions of three-dimensional space. Thus it was widely understood that the universe had a vertical orientation in an absolute sense, not merely in metaphor. Above was God, purity and light; below was the Devil, corruption and darkness. The moral valence of high and low was both reflected in and determined by vocabulary, which, due to its descendants in English, still works in the present day: *superior* denotes both higher and more worthy, and *inferior* denotes lower and less worthy. These qualities mirrored other hierarches, so that the soul was loftier than the flesh in the same way that the heavens were loftier than the earth. The earth and flesh were lowly in both spatial and spiritual terms, burdened by their heavy and corrupt nature. As Wisdom

9:15 taught, "The corruptible body weighs down the soul." In the twelfth century Hugh of St. Victor explained:

> Sicut ergo hic mundus visibilis habet terram suam et coelum suum, sic homo habet terram suam, et coelum suum. Nam et ipse homo mundus est et minor mundus dictus est homo. Hujus terra est caro ejus, et coelum ejus anima ejus. Sed in hoc mundo majore intra coelum terra est, in mundo autem minore coelum intra terram.... Quid est coelum in terra? Anima in corpore. Anima coelum, corpus terra. Anima in corpore; coelum in terra. Et tamen semper coelum sursum, terra deorsum.... Spiritus enim concupiscit sursum et caro concupiscit deorsum.[12]

> Therefore just as this visible world has its earth and its heavens, so a person has his earth and his heavens. For this person is also a world and a person is said to constitute a lesser world. His earth is his flesh, and his heavens are his soul. But in this greater world the earth is underneath the heavens, but in the lesser world the heavens are within the earth.... What is the heavens in the earth? The soul in the body. The soul is the heavens, the body is the earth. The soul is in the body; the heavens are in the earth. And yet the heavens are always above, the earth below.... The spirit desires the lofty and the flesh desires the lowly.

The human body, in short, mirrored the universe, and in both the lofty spiritual realms properly surmounted the lowly and impure. But as part of their sinful nature, humans invert the right order of the universe, having their loftier parts hidden rather than paramount, an image of inversion which will be repeated in more explicit terms by other authors.

Although much of this schema of spatial and moral superiority was taken for granted, and therefore must be gathered from chance remarks, it is often explicitly outlined in descriptions of the heavens. These distant realms could only be known by hearsay, and so were described in a more detailed fashion than more familiar elements. The heavens were commonly envisioned as a series of spheres nested inside each other in an orderly hierarchy, with those highest and farthest from earth being the purest and holiest. The celestial realms as a whole were the realm of angels and lighter spirits, and incorrupt.[13] Specifics of the scheme differed in detail but not in concept. Thomas Aquinas envisioned the third heaven (*tertium coelum*) as a non-physical realm inhabited by the saints, angels and God, eliminating the material from the realm of the spiritual entirely. More popular thought continued to regard the highest realm as still within the material universe but identified it as the most rarified of the realms. In his twelfth-century *Elucidarium*, for example, Honorius of Autun described three heavens. The bottommost was the physical heaven (*coelum corporale*), the realm of the celestial bodies; above that was the spiritual (*coelum spirituale*), home of the angels; and the highest was transcendental (*coelum intellectuale*),

70 Sin and Filth in Medieval Culture

where the Trinity dwell. Thus holiness corresponds to a physical location; to, in effect, degree of materiality. The system was summarized in the thirteenth century by Bartholomaeus Anglicus. The translation made by John de Trevisa reads:

> And þey heuen be *principium* and welle of generacioun, ȝit in hitsilf hit fongiþ no generacioun noþir corrupcioun, noþir decresinge noþir incresinge. For heuen in his substance haþ most simplicite and liknesse, clennes and purenesse, and haþ no departinge noþir contrarines in þe parties of þe whiche hit is compowned; and þerfore of hitsilf hit haþ no myȝt to corrupcioun. And as Aristotle arguyþ *in libro de celo et mundo*: al corrupcioun, he seiþ, comeþ of contraries, and noþing is ifounde contrarie to heuen, wherfore heuen is nouȝt corrupt.[14]

> And though heaven is the origin and well of generation, yet in itself it takes on no generation or corruption, neither decreasing nor increasing. For heaven in its substance has most simplicity and likeness, cleanness and purity, and has no division nor other contrariness in the parts of which it is compounded; and therefore of itself it has no force of corruption. And as Aristotle argues in *Libro de celo et mundo*: all corruption, he says, comes from contraries, and nothing is found contrary to heaven, and because of that heaven is not corrupt.

Here the qualities of the divine are enumerated: immutability, integrity and wholeness and the concomitant imperishability and absence of "force of corruption," which means that, in a kind of medieval physics, eternal life is possible and indeed the *proprium* of such a realm. It is free of its opposites and contraries. But purity declined as one descended in the universe. The highest realms were the purest, the lower realms diminished in purity, so that position and moral valence correlated. This is explained further by Bartholomaeus Anglicus, in John de Trevisa's translation:

> Also me takeþ hede of þe nobiltee of þe worlde by þe more nobil and worþi parties þerof, and also by þe more noble worchinges and doynges. And þerfore þe ouer parties of þe world is icountid more noble and worthi, for þere þe mater is more clere and pure, and schappe is fairere, and vertu is more, in þe ouer parties þan in þe neþere. For þe world at al is þe more faire and semeliche by as moche as þe neþir foul partye of þe worle is ihiȝt wiþ þe more fairnes and blis of þe ouer partye.[15]

> Also I take notice of the nobility of the world by the more noble and worthy parts of it, and also by the more noble workings and doings. And therefore the higher parts of the world are considered more noble and worthy, for there the matter is more clear and pure, and shape is fairer, and virtue is greater, in the higher parts than in the lower. For

the world as a whole is the more fair and seemly by as much as the lower foul part of the world is adorned with the more fairness and bliss of the higher part.

The assertion that in the higher realms "matter is more clean and pure, and shape is fairer, and virtue is more" sums up the equivalence of the material and the spiritual dimension. In such a system it was inevitable that hell should be commonly regarded as the lowest realm in physical location as well as in moral terms. Isidore's *Etymologies* summarizes this understanding:

> Inferus appellatur eo quod infra sit. Sicut autem secundum corpus, si ponderis sui ordinem teneant, inferiora sunt omnia graviora, ita secundum spiritum inferiora sunt omnia tristiora.[16]

> The underworld is termed thus because it is underneath. Thus also as with the body, if things take their order according to weight, the heaviest of all is the lowest, so it is with the spirit: the most wretched of all is the lowest.

A more extended summary of the scheme was offered by the thirteenth-century author Gossuin or Gossouin of Metz, whose *L'image du monde* summarized widespread views about the order of the universe:

> car sa bontez est toute pure et saintisme et sainne et nete, sanz nul mal. Car li mal li sont contraire, et pour ce couvient il qu'i se traient en sus de lui et de touz ses biens. Car ce n'est fors que fiens et ordure. Si le couvient descendre en parfont. Et li biens couvient aler contremont devant Dieu, qui est cler et purs et nez. Et li maus, qui est obscurs et laiz et tenebreus seur toute rien, laist le bien et descent aval. Car ce couvient il par nature, ausi comme l'en voit de l'ordure du vin qui est mis el vaissel, que li laiz se depart du bel, si que li bons demeure en haut et la lie demeure au fonz, qui est mauvaise.[17]

> for [God's] bounty is all pure and holy and whole and clean, without any evil. For evil is his contrary, and therefore by necessity it is withdrawn beneath him and all his goodness. For it is nothing but dung and ordure, which must descend into the depths. And good things must go in the opposite direction, before God, who is clear and pure and clean. And sin, which is obscure and foul and dark more than anything else, drops off from the good and descends. For so it must be by nature, as also when we see the ordure of the wine that is put in the vessel, when the foul drops out from the pure, so that the good stays at the top and the dregs stay at the base, which is bad.

The theory of gravitational pull being unknown, weight and falling were ascribed not to gravity but to morality. God was in effect a source of gravity, things like him (good, which was equivalent to whole, clean and pure) being drawn upwards to him, and the bad—sin—being dung and ordure, "obscure and foul and dark," dropping away, pulled away from God by its own weight of corruption. Thus spatial and physical position alone were moral signs.

THE HUMAN BODY AS A MORAL SYSTEM

The human body forms a microcosm of the moral polarities of the cosmos, and so, in the medieval understanding, shares this orientation. The upper half, crowned by the head, is the realm of reason, elevation and purity; the lower half of the body is the realm of animal desire, baseness and filth. The upright Christian will insure that he stands in right relation to God, with his head toward heaven.[18] In support of this understanding exegetes cited Ecclesiastes 7:30: "God created man upright" ("fecerit Deus hominum rectum"). In the fourth century, Basil affirmed:

> Man, the heavenly plant, excels as much in the shape of his body as he does in the worthiness of his soul. Of what sort is the shape of quadrupeds? Their head droops to earth, looks to the belly, and the belly's pleasure is in every way pursued. Your head is raised to heaven; your eyes look to those things above.[19]

Augustine confirmed that the uprightness of the body was intended to correlate with the rationality of the soul:

> corpus nostrum sic fabricatum sit, ut indicet nos meliores esse quam bestias, et propterea Deo similes. Omnium enim animalium corpora, sive quae in aquis, sive quae in terra vivunt, sive quae in aere volitant, inclinata sunt ad terram, et non sunt erecta sicut hominis corpus. Quo significatur, etiam animum nostrum in superna sua, id est in aeterna spiritualia, erectum esse debere. Ita intelligitur per animum maxime, attestante etiam erecta corporis forma, homo factus ad imaginem et similitudinem Dei.[20]

> our body is made in such a way that it denotes that we are better than beasts, and because of that, similar to God. For the bodies of all the animals, whether they live in the waters or on the earth, or fly in the air, are bent down toward the earth and not upright like the human body. By this it is shown that our mind should be raised up towards the lofty, that is to the eternal spiritual. Thus it is understood especially by the mind, with the upright form of the body also as testimony, that man is made in the image and likeness of God.

The Symbolic Order of the Body 73

Thus the *orientation* of the human body was a signal of moral importance and ought to serve as, so to speak, a design for living. Bernard of Clairvaux was particularly interested in this correlation between posture and righteousness:[21]

> Legimus quia Deus hominem rectum fecit, quod et magnum: capacitas, ut dictum est, probat. Oportet namque id, quod ad imaginem est, cum imagine convenire, et non in vacuum participare nomen imaginis...[22]

> We read that God made man upright, and great: his capacity, as it is said, demonstrates it. For it is right that what is made in the image should be appropriate to the image, and not partake of the name of the image insubstantially.

In one of many similar passages, he elaborates this:

> Quamquam et corporis staturam dedit homini Deus rectam, forsan ut ista corporea exterioris viliorisque rectitudo figmenti hominem interiorem illum, qui ad imaginem Dei factus est, spiritualis suae rectitudinis servandae admoneret, et decor limi deformitatem argueret animi. Quid enim indecentius, quam curvum recto corpore genere animum? Perversa res est et foeda, luteum vas, quod est corpus de terra, oculos habere sursum, caelos libere suspicere caelorumque luminaribus oblectare aspectus, spiritualem vero caelestem creaturam suos e contrario oculos, id est internos sensus atque affectus, trahere in terrma deorsum, et quae debuit nutriri in croceis, haerere luto, tamquam unam de suibus, amplexarique stercora. "Erubesce, anima mea," ait corpus, "in mei consideratione. Erubesce, anima mea, divina pecorinam commutasse similitudinem; erubesce volutari in caeno, quae de caelo es. Creata Creanti similis recta, me quoque accepisti adiutorium simile tibi, utique secundum lineamenta corporeae rectitudinis."[23]

> God indeed gave man an upright stance of body, it may be in order that this corporeal uprightness, exterior and of little account, might prompt the inward man, made to the image of God, to cherish his spiritual uprightness; that the beauty of the body of clay might rebuke the deformity of the mind. What is more unbecoming than to bear a warped mind in an upright body? It is wrong and shameful that this body shaped from the dust of the earth should have its eyes raised on high, scanning the heavens at its pleasure and thrilled by the sight of the sun and moon and stars, while, on the contrary, the heavenly and spiritual creature lives with its eyes, its inward vision and affections centered on the earth beneath; the mind that should be feasting on dainties is wallowing in the mire, rolling in the dung like a pig. [Lam. 4:5] ... Blush, my soul, that you have exchanged

the divine for a bestial likeness; blush that despite your heavenly origin you now wallow in filth. Created upright and in your Creator's likeness, you received me as a helper like to yourself, at least in bodily uprightness.[24]

This reiterates the now conventional exhortation that humans have a duty to ensure that the moral world conforms to the spatial world. Uprightness of posture and of morals are similarly equated in a sermon attributed to Hildebert of Lavardin (c. 1056–1133). The exposition begins by outlining the four positions of man: lying down, sitting, standing or walking:

> Cum jacet, omnes corporis ejus partes quiescunt; cum vero sedet, inferiores quidem partes quiescunt, superiores vero in sui erectione laborant; cum autem stat, totus laborat homo, erigens se, quia naturaliter pondere suo ad ima refertur [s. defertur]. . . . Ad hunc modum, quatuor sunt hominum status in Ecclesia Dei. . . . Mali ergo sunt jacentes, id est in mundo quiescentes, qui totam spem et jucunditatem ponunt in mundo divitiarum; quorum deus venter est.[25]

> When he lies down, all the parts of his body are at rest; when he sits, the inferior parts are at rest, and the superior work to keep him upright; when he stands, the whole person labors, raising himself up, because by nature he is brought down to the lowest point by his weight. . . . In these ways there are four states of man in the Church of God. . . . The bad are those lying down, that is, resting in the world, who put their whole faith and delight in worldly riches, whose god is their stomach.

This formulation, the correlation between human spatial orientation and moral demands, was echoed by others, including Peter Comestor and Anselm.[26] It also underlies other religious narratives, such as an account of a crippled man in the *Life of St. Kenelm*, an English text of the eleventh century. The crippled man's lack of uprightness is correlated explicitly with his sinful nature:

> Debilem quoque repentem per humum quis digne referet erectum? . . . Ligneas soleas cauatis truncis alligauerat genibus pro corturnis pedalibus, et calciatis ligno poplitibus, nitebatur pro gressibus. Scabellula pro bacillis suppeditabant manibus et egre sustentabant labile corpus. Videres hominem ad celestia contemplanda sublimatum, *peccati conditione* in reptile conuersum. [my emphasis]

> Also, who can properly restore to uprightness a crippled man who crawls through the dust? . . . He had bound wooden soles to his hollow disfigured knees in place of shoes, and, his knees shod with wood, he struggled forwards instead of walking. Little stools in his hands served

as walking sticks and scarcely held up his limp body. Here you may see a human being who had been raised up to contemplate heaven, turned *by his sinful state* into a crawling creature. [my emphasis][27]

The poor man has been reduced to an animal posture by his sinful, animalistic rejection of God. His cure further illustrates the schema: the purity of the saint soon restores the man to full uprightness, underscoring the fact that physical position can serve as a natural correlate of a moral condition.[28]

A related description of the Devil was used by Guibert of Nogent, whose description of a "chief devil" reported that he moved "exili capite, turgentibus scapulis," "with a puny head and a hunched back"—the physical signifiers we would expect of a creature whose reason has atrophied and whose upright nature has been crippled.[29]

The head, in short, had the heavens as its proper object of contemplation; the lower body, that nearest hell, was the province of corruption and sin. This dichotomy is nicely reflected in a widely circulating folktale of the later Middle Ages, in which Good and Evil share the same wife: Good has her top half and Evil her lower half.[30] In a sense good had the top half and evil the lower half of every human body. It was in the top half that reason resided; the lower half was the province of the belly, defecation, filth and the cravings of gluttonous and lustful corporeality. The Christian struggle was the struggle to keep the head paramount; to sin was to give way to the lower body. In the sinful, the lower body rules; sinners have confounded their moral polarities and have given their inferior parts the ascendancy. These inferior parts ought rightly to be hidden from God, and the body is designed accordingly, as Jerome describes:

> Quomodo posterior pars corporis et meatus per quem alvi stercora egeruntur relegatus est ab oculis, et quasi post tergum positus, ita et hic qui sub ventre est, ad digerendos humores et potus, quibus venae corporis irrigantur, a Deo conditus est.[31]

> In the way that the hindermost part of the body, and the passageway by which the dung of the stomach is discharged, is distanced from the eyes and positioned at the back, so also that which is below the stomach, to carry off the humors and drink, by which the veins of the body are irrigated, is hidden from God.

God is clearly envisioned as being situated above and in front of the human figure, and the human body was designed so that its shameful parts are, in a sense, out of view of the Lord. It is as much to say that the lower parts are shameful by nature, displeasing to God and, in being contrary to him, pertain instead to that inhabitant of the lower and hindermost realms, the Devil.

76 *Sin and Filth in Medieval Culture*

Figure 3 An ape, representing sinful, degraded man, worshipping a bottom with no head: all carnality, no reason. The image is both comical and serious. Early 14th century. New York, Pierpont Morgan Library William S. Glazier Collection 24, fol. 78. Photographic credit: The Pierpont Morgan Library, New York.

This system of moral polarities was widely reflected in images of the Devil and demons. The Devil is in fact the *locus classicus* of this infernal inversion, having given his lower body the ascendancy and thus ceding the place of the head as paramount. In the iconography of the Devil this scrambling of the right order of the body took visual form: as the Devil fell from heaven, so his face fell from its rightful ascendancy and finds itself a part of the sinful body. This accounts for the fact that medieval art often depicts him with faces on his bottom, his groin or his stomach, sometimes even as far down as his knees.[32] A prominent example is Michael Pacher's fifteenth-century illustration of the Devil, in which the Devil's rear constitutes a face, with his tail as its nose and his anus as his mouth.[33] At times such depictions are accompanied by other signs of inversion. In many cases the upper head, the one that remains up top, is almost wholly beast-like, signifying the lowly animalistic desires that have supplanted reason. Other images are ingenious in their method

The Symbolic Order of the Body 77

Figure 4 The Devil, the epitome of sinful inversion, is ruled by his sinful lower half, and thus has faces on his bottom. 14th century, English. Illustration from the Queen Mary Psalter. © The British Library Board: London, British Library Royal 2.B.Vii, fol. 1v.

of envisioning the lower body as the significant element of the demons' character, as the visual and physical correlate to their evil. In the medieval stained glass in the cathedrals in Bourges and Troyes, for instance, the devils' wings are attached not to their upper bodies but lower down, to their buttocks.[34]

INVERSION AS AN EMBLEM OF SIN

This same system of polarities and correspondences is found in the literature of sin. Here too sinners have confounded the head and the lower body, but this confusion is depicted not in visual terms but in functional ones. The two orifices form a polarity between the spiritual and animal parts of the body. The upper orifice, the mouth, is associated with reason, elevation and purity, the corresponding lower orifices with animal desire, baseness and filth. In the most common exemplification of sinful inversion, the anus—the opening on the lower body—was regarded as the topsy-turvy equivalent of the mouth, the opening on the upper half. As sinners confounded the spiritually lowly with the spiritually lofty, following sin where they should follow reason, their behavior had a physical manifestation, confounding their upper orifices with their lower. A passage from the Middle English devotional tract *Jacob's Well* reflects this system:

> whan þou flatryst an-oþer in his synne & in his euyl dede. Þou faryst as an hounde, þat lyckyth an-oþer hound, whanne he metyth hym, be-hynde in þe ers, in þat vnclene membre. vertewys arn be-forn, synne is be-hynde, & foulere þan þe ers, & þere þou, wyth þi flateryng, kyssest hym þat is in his synne.³⁵

> when you flatter another in his sin and his evil deeds, you behave like a dog that licks another dog, when he meets him, behind in the arse, in the unclean parts. Virtues are in front, sin is in the rear, and fouler than the arse; and there you, with your flattering, kiss him that is in his sin.

Here the sinner and the one who fails to rebuke him both have the status of animals, bent over with no uprightness and, like animals, undeterred by disgust either moral or material. Where uprightness would require meeting a fellow human at the level of the head, and perhaps offering the kiss of peace, the lack of uprightness substitutes the rear for the head. To lead a sinful life is to give way to the lower body, and the degenerate are depicted with these parts interchanged.

These correspondences became a common motif in medieval narratives, some serious, some comic. Among the serious is an episode from the *Life* of St. Alban, in which a blasphemer is punished for his dismissal of the remains of St. Alban. As the remains are being translated,

> Diues quidam, in translatione sancti Albani, ad agrum cum messoribus iuit, et uidens multos ad ecclesiam currens, dixit: "Quare ad Albanum pergerem ego, qui rusticus quidam fuit vt ego, per posteriora stercora egerens vt ego." Dixit, et cibum quo refectus fuerat, per os blasphemum euomuit et sub forma stercorum egessit. Per septem annos quibus vixit, numquam, nisi per oris blasphemi officinam, ventrem pergauit.³⁶

> A certain wealthy man was going to the fields with the farmworkers during the translation of St. Alban. And seeing many people hastening to the church, he said: "Why should I go to Alban, who was a peasant like me, expelling crap from his behind just like me?" He spoke, and vomited out the food with which he had been refreshed from his blasphemous mouth, and it came out in the form of dung. Throughout the seven years he lived, he never emptied his belly except through his blasphemous mouth.

It is clear that here excrement is the material equivalent of sin; what is more, in his sin, the sinner was inverted and his mouth assumed the functions of the anus. His assumption that no one who defecates can be holy is a theme reiterated in many other places, enumerated in Chapter 4. In this instance, though, his scepticism is blasphemous and answered by his own irruption of dung: he has not kept dung where it belongs, below the realm of the holy and the head, and it literally rises to take over his own mouth.

Another example appears in a story told of Julian the Apostate and his servant, found in the fourteenth-century *Polychronicon* of Ranulph Higden and thence borrowed by the exempla collection the *Alphabetum Narrationum*.[37] Julian the Apostate, a sinner by definition, confounded the polarities of the mouth and anus by using a communion vessel as a chamber pot. Thus what should be holy was inverted to lowliness, and what was meant to be used by the mouth was inverted to use by the lower orifice. The equivalence of spiritual and physical debasement is striking. The punishment for this blasphemy was physical as well: the text recounts that "mox vermes inde scaturientes posteriora Juliani adeo corroserunt ut quoad viveret liberari non posset," or in the medieval translation, "anon wormes sprang out þerof, and frate so Iulianus his neþer ende þat he myȝte nevere be delivered þerof while he was on lyve," "straightaway worms sprang out from it, and tormented Julian's rear end so much that he could never be relieved of it as long as he lived."[38]

Julian's servant engaged in a parallel blasphemy which resulted in an even more overtly symbolic punishment. His sin consisted of urinating into the vessel while swearing an oath against Christ, and for this he was afflicted with the clear confounding of polarities: "repente os ejus versum est in anum ejus, et egestionis organum effectus est," "anon his mouþ bycom his ers, and servede aftirward in stede of his neþer ende," "straightaway his mouth became his arse, and served afterwards instead of his rear end."[39] The English *Alphabet of Tales* makes this even more explicit: "sodanlie his mouthe was turnyd into his ars, & efter euer whils he liffid, all þe filthe and þe degestion of his bodie come out at his mouthe, & noght at his nache,"[40] "suddenly his mouth was turned into his arse, and ever after while he lived, all the filth and the digestion of his body came out from his mouth, and none from his anus."

The same collection describes a similar fate overcoming a woman who has murdered her husband. When the townsfolk want to declare him a saint, she objects that he should be considered a saint as much as her arse should sing. The text concludes:

> And onone hur ars made ane vglie noyse, and wolde not lefe for noght sho cuth do. And evur after, opon þe fryday at hur husband suffred martyrdom on, wekelie when sho spakk any wurd, hur ars began to syng & make ane vglie noyse, & wold neuer lefe it on þe fryday whils at sho liffid.[41]

> And straightaway her arse made an ugly noise, and would not stop for anything she could do. And ever after, on the Friday that her husband suffered martyrdom on, every week when she spoke any word, her arse

began to sing and make an ugly noise, and would never stop on the Friday as long as she lived.

It is important to note that the woman was also a confirmed adulteress and so had given her lower body the ascendancy in her affairs. On the anniversaries of the murder, the woman's true nature is revealed, and her nether regions expose this reversal by taking on the role of the higher regions. The image even appears in an excoriation of sinners:

> Qui enim non timet coinquinare linguam suam plus quam alia membra pocius porcus uidetur quam homo. Porcus enim ita cito ponit rostrum suum in luto. sicut pedem. Item porcus semper habet os apertum ad stercora et non ad flores. sic mali ad stercora peccatorum non ad flores uirtutum. Ex habundancia cordis os loquitur. de ore latrine et sepulcri non egreditur nisi fetor.

> He who does not fear to foul his tongue more than other members seems to be a pig rather than a human being, for a pig puts his snout in filth as readily as his foot. Likewise a pig always has his mouth open to dung but not to flowers, just as the mouths of the evil are open to the dung of sins and not to the flowers of virtues. "Out of the abundance of the heart the mouth speaketh" (Mt. 12:34). Nothing passes out of the mouth of a latrine or sepulchre except a stink.[42]

These equivalences were noted in everyday life, not merely in flights of rhetoric. The Cathar inquisitions also made note of a conversation between Bernard Massanas and Pierre Sabatier, a conventional Catholic from Varilhes, in 1318. Massanas has asked why a candle was customarily held over the mouth of the dying:

> et tunc idem Petrus respondit eidem Bernardo, quod ad significandum quod sicut lumen clarum erat anime moriencium qui confessi sunt et contriti de peccatis suis, clare ibant ad Deum, et si non essent de peccatis suis confessi et contriti, tantum valeret eis quod candela poneretur in ano eorum sicut in os.[43]

> and then Peter answered Bernard that it signified that the souls of the dying who have confessed and repented of their sins are as bright as light and will go to God shining, but if they have not confessed and repented of their sins, they might as well have a candle in their anus as in their mouth.

Sabatier showed an instinctual understanding of the anus as the sinful correlate of the mouth, as well as reflecting the popular belief that in the holy, at least, the soul exits through the mouth.

The correspondence between the mouth and the anus also comes into play in the classical insult in which the offending person is told to kiss the other's bottom. This was often, no doubt, used merely as a formulaic insult. But the symbolic value of such an interchange always lay behind such a formulation, and sanctions its appearance in contexts which modern sensibilities might find merely crude. It appears, for example, in the story about St. Francis already quoted, from the *Little Flowers*, or *I Fioretti*. Brother Rufino of Assisi is troubled by an appearance of a demon in the form of Jesus, who tries to proclaim that both Brother Rufino and St. Francis are predestined to hell. St. Francis advises the brother to reply to the demon in terms befitting his baseness:

> "ma quando il demonio ti dicesse più: Tu se' damnato, sì gli rispondi: Apri la bocca; mo' vi ti caco. E questo ti sia segnale, ch'egli è il demonio e non Cristo, ché dato tu gli arai tale risposta, immantenente fuggirà."[44]

> "But the next time the demon tells you, 'You are damned,' you tell him, 'Open your mouth and I'll shit in it.' This will be a sign for you that he is the devil and not Christ, that once you give this reply, he will flee immediately."[45]

The devil does reappear, and the brother does indeed tell him "Open your mouth and I'll shit in it!" sending the devil away in fury and consternation. St. Francis has implied that the Devil's mouth is on a par with another's anus, more fit for filth than for holiness. The Devil here embodies diabolical inversion, and St. Francis's easy use of the motif shows the degree to which it was a religious commonplace—not merely an imprecation, but theologically significant. To be identified rightfully as the exemplification of shameful lowliness robs the Devil of his power. Unfortunately St. Francis does not specify what Christ would do if Brother Rufino mistakenly aimed the imprecation at him, which would seem to be a possibility the text does not envision.

Another display of sinful inversion takes place in *Unguentarius* (*The Ointment Seller*), a Czech play from the 1340s. In the play, the disbelief of the Jews is represented by the Jew Abraham who buys a pot of dung, believing claims that it will revive his son Izák from the dead. Rather than anointing Izák's head, hands and feet in the usual practice, he smears the dung on the dead son's buttocks, a lowering and inversion of the sacred rites of believers.[46]

Similar formulations also appeared in humorous texts. Although comic literature tends to regard moral transgression as trivial rather than mortal, humor should not be excluded from reckoning as a serious cultural force. As John D. Niles has observed, "Cultural activities that are keenly expressive of the underlying spirit of an era have commonly been viewed as mere entertainment, and it is paradoxically this ludic quality that enables them to bear effortlessly a heavy cargo of meaning."⁴⁷ Thus transgressors' reversal of high and low, back and front, and pure and profane is a popular feature of satirical and comic literature. In the French tale *Du Con qui fu fez a la besche*, the irreligious chatter of women is explained by the fact that the Devil, in completing the creation of woman, made a fart on her tongue; hence women's speech is really a regurgitation of demonic farting.⁴⁸ The story essentially defines all women as transgressive, as if the Devil has transferred his upper/lower body interchange to women and hence decreed that every woman's mouth is equivalent to an anus and every word equivalent to breaking wind. *Le Pet au villain* makes a similar point, here about the lowliness of peasants, but in this instance the Devil gets the bad end of the deal. The story plays on the widespread belief that the soul was supposed to exit through the mouth of the dying. Peasants, however, are so base that the Devil assumes their souls emerge from the anus rather than their mouth. The Devil hence waits with a sack by the rear end of a peasant for his soul to emerge. When the peasant farts, the Devil mistakes this for the emission of the soul and is hence fooled into taking the peasant's fart to hell.⁴⁹ The story presents it as logical for the Devil to regard the anus as the lowly equivalent of the mouth, since the two are correlates and since the Devil's work consists of making lowly those things that should be exalted.

Fools in particular partook of such exchanges. The banner of the Dijon Fool Society depicted two fools inverting themselves in ways both comic and symbolic. The upright fool is holding the other upside-down; both are twisted around so that the face of the upright one appears at the other's backside, and the face of the upside-down fool appears at the bottom of the upright fool. Thus both uprightness and forwardness have been inverted; and both fools wear parti-colored clothing.⁵⁰ The implication that fools place their bottoms at the same level as their heads could not be clearer.

In a more somber mode, *contemptus mundi* literature used the same structure of debasement to emphasize that the mortal flesh of earthly life was not to be exalted, but to be regarded as corrupt and despicable. The thirteenth-century *Ancrene Wisse*, a rule for anchoresses, sought to drive home the despicable nature of the earthly body, to urge its audience to prize the spiritual rather than the earthly. The text echoed a popular formulation when, as quoted in Chapter 1, it exhorted its readers about the true nature of the body:

Þi flesch, hwet frut bereð hit in alle his openunges? Amid te menske of þi neb, þat is þe fehereste deal, bitweonen muðes smech 7 neases smeal, ne berest tu as twa priue þurles?⁵¹

Your flesh, what fruit does it bear in all its openings? Amid the nobility of your face, which is the fairest part, between the taste of the mouth and the smell of the nose, do you not bear as it were two privy holes?

Here it is as if sinners—all earthly inhabitants—live in an inverted state. They mistake their bodies for sinless matter when even the highest and fairest part of the body, the face, is low and corrupt in relation to God. The orifices reveal the corrupt truth behind the fair front: the body is made entirely of corruptible matter, as corrupt as the privy, and thus in valuing even the highest and fairest part their values are inverted.

The inversion of head and bottom can also be combined with conventional "mooning" practices: the practice of exposing the buttocks in insult, such as that performed by the obscene trickster Marcolf.[52] Tales of Solomon and Marcolf were immensely popular, appearing in Latin and most of the vernacular languages from at least the early thirteenth century.[53] After being exposed to Marcolf's vulgar foolery, the wise king Solomon admonishes Marcolf that he never wants to look between his eyes again. Marcolf goes away and positions himself in an oven so that when Solomon looks in, he does not see between his eyes, but between his buttocks and into his anus, as Marcolf triumphantly points out.[54]

Displaying the buttocks was the insulting gesture that it remains today, but its offensiveness was buttressed by theology. It was not just a social requirement, but a theological one, to keep one's head paramount and one's bottom concealed, above all in the presence of the holy. A story told by the twelfth-century British courtier Walter Map illustrates this. A monk named Dom Reric was out riding with King Henry II when they saw a monk walking along the road trip over a stone:

> nec portabatur ab angelis tunc, et coram pedibus equi regii corruit; uentus autem uestes eius in collum propulit, ut domini regis et Rerici oculis inuitis manifesta fieret misera ueritas pudendorum. Rex, ut omnis facecie thesaurus, dissimulans uultum auertit, et tacuit. Rericus autem intulit secreto "Maledicta religio que deuelat anum!"[55]

> nor was he borne up by angels [Psalm 90:11–12], but fell before the feet of the king's horse. The wind forced his clothing up around his neck, so that the abject reality of his shameful parts was accidentally revealed to the lord king and Reric. The king, that treasurehouse of all courtesy, pretending not to notice, turned his face away and said nothing. Reric, however, said under his breath, "Accursed the religion that unveils the backside!"

The episode serves as a miniature allegory of position and bodily righteousness. Unless borne up by angels, the stumbling man loses his uprightness and exposes the shameful body. To fall and to reveal one's shameful body are commensurate. Religion in particular is charged with enjoining humans to suppress and control their shameful backsides; the religion that makes the backside preeminent is more properly a religion of the Devil. In a particularly symbolic and illuminating coda, Map adds, "Monachus tamen qui cecidit honestius surrexisset, si corporaliter clausus fuisset," "Still, the monk who fell might have risen more honorably if his body had been concealed." Humans are shamed by their lower bodies, and the more these are exposed, the greater the shame when trying to rise.

Misplaced regard for the sinful, lower or hindermost portions of the body served as an identifying feature of unbelievers, satanists and heretics. Such sinners were regularly portrayed as honoring the bottom as a central point of their sinful ceremonies. Their misplaced attention to the sinful, diabolical part of the anatomy confirmed their status as sinful unbelievers who reversed the right order of things and who honored not just the sinful body, but the part of the anatomy that embodied shame. Examples of this occur throughout the second half of the Middle Ages. They take perhaps their strongest form in claims that Jews ate the dung of sows: dung being not just reprehensible in itself, but pigs being a notoriously filthy animal that ate dung themselves.[56] The rumor thus associated Jews inextricably with an animalistic love of filth and an inability to confine filth to the lower half of the body.

Other explicit accounts survive in abundance. In the early twelfth century, Guibert of Nogent told the story of an assembly of heretics who performed a ritual in which a recumbent woman with naked buttocks was approached from behind with a candle—a story with interesting similarities to the dialogue about the candle between the two citizens of Montaillou.[57] Later in the same century, Walter Map complained of a group of heretics whose rituals called for initiates to kiss the hind end of a cat, which was, of course, the Devil in feline form.[58] This was sometimes termed the *osculum infame*, the shameful kiss. At the same period Alan of Lille railed against a similar practice, deriving the term "Cathar" from "catus," and specifying that the cat whose backside was kissed was Lucifer in disguise.[59] In 1234, Pope Gregory IX described a similar ceremony. The heretics were said to convene assemblies at which a black cat might appear with tail erect, descending backwards to meet the worshippers, whereupon "the novice kisses the rear anatomy of the cat, after which he salutes in a similar manner those who preside at the feast, and others worthy of the honor."[60] They also had a practice whereby they took communion every Sunday, kept it in their mouths and returned home to spit the Host into the privy.

In the same period Guillaume d'Auvergne, Bishop of Paris from 1228 to 1249, claimed that devotees of Lucifer had a ritual in which they kissed a toad on the mouth and a black cat under its tail.[61] An account of a trial of the Templars from around 1310 suggests that inquisitors had as a standard item of inquisition a similar scenario involving a cat. Seventeen of the twenty-five men whose depositions survive confessed to worshipping the cat, and ten said that they had kissed its backside.[62] This does not suggest that such a ceremony actually existed, but that the charge was a standard item of questioning when suspected heretics were interrogated; under intense pressure, some of the accused agreed to the charge. Jews were also charged with kissing the hind end of a cat as part of sinful ceremonies.[63] Other charges had them kissing the hind end of a sow.[64] In another instance, the inquisition of one Lepzet, a man charged with witchcraft, revealed that the witches had, he claimed, a practice of inserting a silver spoon into the backside of their bishop, a practice that underlines the identity of the anus as a debased and sinful substitute for the mouth. Later the assembled blasphemers kiss the master's backside.[65] In a related charge, the late fourteenth-century *Malleus Maleficarum* cited the example of a wicked woman who added sinful words to the blessing bestowed in Mass: "Kehr mir die Zung im Arss umb," "Give me the tongue in the arse."[66]

Further examples of this iconography are legion, and the motif appears in images as well as in texts. Three images of the *osculum infame*, made in Flanders for the court of Burgundy in the 1460s, appeared in manuscripts of Jean Taincture's treatise against Waldensian witchcraft, the *Tractatus contra sectam vaudensium*. The images are not direct copies of each other, but in each example Satan-worshipers are shown paying homage to the Devil, who appears in the form of a goat. More witches fly on brooms in the background of the picture; in the foreground, a worshiper brings his or her face to the hind end of the goat, which has raised its tail to receive a kiss (Figure 5).[67] These illustrated the claim of the fifteenth-century Dominican Pierre de Broussart, who asserted that the Waldensians and diabolists in Arras kissed the backside of the Devil, who took the form of a goat.[68] The charges against witches in Arras, levied in 1459, were disputed by the chronicler Enguerrand de Monstrelet, who recognized them as trumped up; he records, nevertheless, the familiar accusation that as part of their ceremony of homage the witches kissed the Devil's backside.[69]

Claude Tholosan's fifteenth-century treatise *Ut magnorum et maleficiorum errores* claimed that to reject faith in Christ, witches spat three times and trampled on the cross—again a ceremony that debases that which should be lofty—and exposed their rears to heaven, a contemptuous inversion of the rightful orientation of the body, as well as unveiling that which should be concealed.[70] The anonymous *Errores Gazariorum*, a text of around 1437 from Savoy, also claimed that witches were required to kiss the Devil on the buttocks or anus.[71]

In these imagined scenarios the inversion of right order is complete: the kiss, belonging to the head, is displaced to the rear; humans debased themselves to an animal, inverting the proper hierarchy of reason over the animalistic; and the animal in question is, of course, bent over rather than upright—a meaningful characteristic of most animals but particularly meaningful in that the initiate has to bend over to complete the debasing ritual.

Sinners were also rumored to kiss the human backside. A man named Richard Berard reported that the Templars had been called "anus kissers" by someone familiar with their practices, a charge that may combine the motif of inverted worship with charges of sinful sexual practices.[72]

Figure 5 The *osculum infame*. Here the devil takes the form of a goat, regarded as one of the most carnal and filthy of animals, and would-be witches approach to kiss his rear, an inversion of front and back. Illustration of Jean Taincture's *Tractatus contra sectam vaudensium*, Flemish, late 15th century. Oxford, Bodleian Library, Rawlinson D.410, fol. 1.

The reputation of the Templars as sinful anus-kissers has other witnesses, among them one Andrew Armanni, who testified against errant Templars who denied the divinity of Christ. After being forced to take part in the ceremony of unbelievers, Andrew claimed, he complied in spitting on the cross and trampling it, and then observed the unbelievers exchanging kisses "in ano."[73] Templars under the scrutiny of the inquisition often claimed that they had been coerced to kiss other Templars on the navel and the "base of the spine," anus or "vile lower part." The charge once again seems to have been a standard item of questioning, reflecting not so much the practices of the Templars as the bias of the questioners, who assumed that sin and irreligion must involve commerce with the lower parts of the body.[74]

A similar inversion appears in the story of a sinful Templar whose body was examined after death by his sister. According to a certain Thomas de Redemer, she examined her brother's body thinking she would find evidence of sanctity but instead discovered a crucifix next to his anus.[75]

A sinful orientation was also the basis of Tertullian's complaint against unbelievers in the *Adversus Iudaeos*. Here the disbelief is literally embodied in the miscreants' orientation, affirming that position and righteousness are identical:

> Et introduxit me in aedem domus domini interiorem, et ecce in liminibus domus domini, inter medium elam et inter medium altaris, quasi uiginti et quinque uiri, qui posteriora sua dederant ad templum domini et facies suas contra Orientem; hi adorabant solem.[76]

> And he led me into the inner room of the house of the Lord, and within the boundaries of the house of the Lord, between the middle of the porch and the middle of the altar, there were some twenty-five men, who presented their backsides to the temple of the Lord and their faces to the east; they were adoring the sun.

The unbelievers' errant orientation towards the sun entails presenting their backsides to the temple of the Lord: their heads and their bottoms are reversed in sinful idolatry.

The importance of the lower body is emphasized in other ways as well, typically in emphasis on the lower body and backside of the sinner. Such portrayals had the support of Scripture, where three passages depicted God punishing miscreants by afflicting their posteriors. Psalm 77:66 has "Et percussit inimicos eos in posteriora, opprobrium sempiternum dedit illis," "He smote his enemies on the hinder parts: he put them to an everlasting reproach." 1 Samuel 5:6 recounts the fate of the Azotians: "Adgravata autem est manus Domini super Azotios, et demolitus est eos, et percussit in secretiori parte natium Azotum," "And the hand of the Lord was heavy upon the Azotians [Gazans], and he destroyed them, and smote the Azotians in the most secret part of their buttocks." Finally, Deuteronomy 28:27 exhorts: "Percutiat te Dominus ulcere Aegypti, et parte corporis per quam stercora digeruntur scabie quoque et prurigine ita, ut curari nequeas," "The Lord strike thee with the ulcer of Egypt, and the part of thy body, by which the dung is cast out, with the scab and with the itch: so that thou canst not be healed." The bottom and in particular the anus were hence not only sites of sin, but of retribution. In part, this was assigned to the idea that the Gazans had committed sodomy, but this charge was not always part of the indictment. Since the bottom was the bodily area most consonant with sin, it was entirely consonant that penalties for sin would be visited upon that area.

THE ICONOGRAPHY OF THE SINFUL BODY

Religious images of the fifteenth and early sixteenth centuries used the iconography of the immoral body to convey truths about sin and holiness. Such images often demarcated sinners by means of clothing, position, physiognomy and carnal repulsiveness.[77] Many of these have been assessed widely in modern scholarship, but the prominence of the bottom has largely escaped notice. With unmistakable emphasis, religious images of this period often highlight the buttocks of sinners. This serves to convey the extent to which sinners have given way to lower bodily desires, rather than being ruled by the spirituality and reason associated with the head. In addition, it depicts the sinners' contempt for holiness as they display their bottoms in the presence of the holy.

Such images draw upon an extensive history of literary examples: stories in which sinners express their sinful natures by baring their buttocks. The motif was in use as early as the late sixth century, when a sinful woman in the *Vita* of St. Paternus raises her clothing and displays her bottom to the saint (*eos pudore afficeret elatis a tergo vestimentis posteriora illis sua monstravit*).[78] In the twelfth century, a man possessed by the Devil was similarly punished for lowering his pants and farting at the relics of St. Aldhelm.[79] In the *Gesta Herwardi*, a twelfth-century tale of Hereward the Wake, an evil witch casts spells by muttering incantations and baring her rear at her opponents three times.[80] The thirteenth-century chronicler Salimbene de Adam told the story of the sinner, Alberigo da Romano, who was so enraged at the loss of his falcon that he defecated on an altar and "extraxit sibi bracas et culum ostendit Deo in signum opprobrii et convitii atque derisionis, credens se ex hoc de Deo ulcisci," "pulled down his pants and showed his bottom to God as a sign of reproach, insult, and mockery, thinking to take vengeance on God from this."[81] The charges against the Templars in the early fourteenth century also included the claim that they pointed their buttocks at the cross. It was reported that a certain Templar, Patrick de Ripon, had told another man that as part of his initiation he was ordered "to pull down his breeches [and] turn his back to the crucifix."[82] In all these examples, sinners are characterized by the scornful exposure of that shameful part that should stay hidden. It is incumbent upon the godly to be represented by their head and face; in a further example of sinful inversion, these sinners have substituted their buttocks for their faces.

Another common gesture involved displaying the rear with one hand on one cheek of the buttocks—often the left hand—completing the iconography of the sinful body. The hand may originally been meant to pull the buttocks apart and expose the anus, but it also serves to add visual emphasis to the gesture. A classic example of the gesture is found in an illustration of *Der Ritter vom Türn*, problematically attributed to Dürer, in which a demon graphically turns his backside to a vain young woman, his hand on the cheek of his buttock (see Figure 6). Another instance appears as a sculpture on a building in Goslar, Germany, from 1494: a naked man emphasizes his buttocks to the viewer in an unmistakably rude gesture, his left hand in the characteristic position upon the cheek.[83]

Figure 6 This scene from an incident in *Der Ritter vom Türn* illustrates the diabolical nature of vanity. The devil displays his rear to the vain young woman, with characteristic hand position and the details of his anus graphically displayed. She looks in the mirror, which displays not her face but the rear of the devil, as if the proper order of her body had been inverted by her sinful attention to the physical. 1493.

90 *Sin and Filth in Medieval Culture*

This iconography became especially widespread in images of the late fifteenth and early sixteenth centuries. In these, the same position of the hand on the hip or rear, pulling back or emphasizing the buttock, is also used when the clothed bottom is displayed and helps confirm that the identical gesture of insult is intended. It is unmistakable in the Herzogenburg Crowning with Thorns by Jörg Breu the Elder (*c.* 1501), in which a fool crouches before Christ, a jeering expression on his face and his hand pulling at his clothed, jutting rear.[84] It similarly appears in an image of the Crucifixion by the Hamburg Master from around 1500, in which a kneeling man in green and yellow in the forefront of the picture displays his clothed bottom to the viewer, his left hand prominently on his rear.[85] It is also found in an image of the beheading of John the Baptist by the Master of the Freising Neustift (*c.* 1480–90).[86] The Baptist's executioner emphasizes his backside, clad in prominent white hose, with the familiar hand gesture. He stands with his back to the viewer, in a posture that emphasizes his rear. The gesture is seen yet again in an image of the Last Supper by Thierry Bouts, where Judas's left hand is held behind him.[87]

In other instances the bottom is glimpsed or fully exposed. An example is provided by the Carrying of the Cross, from *c.* 1400–30, by the Austrian Master of the Worcester Panel (see Figure 7). A soldier stands in front of Christ, his rear to the viewer, and the back of his trousers sag down to reveal partially bare buttock cheeks, highlighted by the white of his underwear. The exposed buttocks are so prominent that they form a counterpoint to the nobility of Christ: the holy versus the sinful. A second striking example is found in a painting of the Mocking of Christ by Jörg Breu the Elder (*c.* 1534), in which a man directly behind Christ has his trousers lowered and his buttocks graphically exposed (see Figure 8). The man's head is not in view, so that he is defined by his bottom.

The motif makes another appearance in a Flagellation of Christ, painted by a Northern German artist, the Master of the View of St. Gudule, in the second half of the fifteenth century.[88] The soldier to the left of Christ again has trousers gaping open, revealing his shirt and what appears to be the white lining of the trousers themselves, drawing attention to the man's imminently exposed bottom. A very similar idea appears in a painting of the Crowning with Thorns by Wolfgang Katzenheimer the Elder (*c.* 1485): the persecutor's trousers are only barely held on by the straining ties to his upper garment, and his white underwear is conspicuously on view, exposing that which should be concealed.[89]

The bottom is emphasized even more dramatically in a depiction of the Crowning with Thorns from the Stundenbuch der Sophia van Bylant, painted in Cologne in 1475 (see Figure 9). Here the fool kneels with his hand emphasizing his mooning position, his bottom before Jesus. His blasphemous pose is highlighted by an enormous wad of fabric gathered

Figure 7 One of the soldiers at the carrying of the cross displays his backside through gaps in his leggings, emphasized by the whiteness of the lining or underclothes. *c.* 1400–30. Austrian Master of the Worcester Panel. Chicago, Art Institute, Charles H. and Mary F. S. Worcester Collection. Photography © The Art Institute of Chicago.

at his rear. Although his backside is pointed toward Christ, his top half has turned around so that he can jeer and strike Jesus with a stick. His position, anatomically impossible, embodies a literal instance of sinful reversal.

92   *Sin and Filth in Medieval Culture*

Figure 8 The Mocking of Christ, in which the man directly behind Christ has his trousers lowered and his buttocks graphically exposed. The blowing of the trumpet suggests that the man is breaking wind, and the garlic below suggests an offensive smell. To taunt divinity is to abandon rationality, and the man's head has disappeared from sight, leaving only his shameful bottom. Jörg Breu the Elder, *c.* 1534. Innsbruck, Tiroler Landesmuseum Ferdinandeum.

A further instance of such emphasis is displayed in the *Ecce homo* of Jörg Ratgeb (1514). The soldier in the middle of the picture wears leggings exhibiting a high gloss, with the prominent buttock highlighted so that the soldier's bottom appears naked.[90] The soldier is much lower in the picture, with the tormented Christ on a stair above, but the highlighted globe of the buttock is so prominent that it is central to the image both literally and figuratively. It forms a contrast with the similarly shaped and colored cap of the soldier; although the cap has a pattern that distinguishes it from the globe of the buttock, the two are alike enough that the similarities between the head and the bottom of the sinner are suggested.

The Crucifixion by Maarten Van Heemskerck (1543) exhibits the same effect.[91] A sinner at the foot of the cross, distinct from the devout on the other side, is in a semi-recumbent, sinful position, grasping the base of the thief's cross. His top half is adumbrated, as is appropriate for those who have forsaken the holier upper half of the body. His lower half is

The Symbolic Order of the Body 93

Figure 9 An unbelieving fool character points his rear to Jesus, with the characteristic hand position emphasizing his backside. His position, so twisted that it is anatomically impossible in reality, makes it look as if his lower backside really has been switched with his front. The inverted figure, buttocks displayed, in the frame to the left of the central image underscores the theme. Illustration of the Crowning with Thorns, Stundenbuch der Sophia van Bylant (formerly known as the Homoet Hours), 1475. Cologne, Wallraf-Richartz-Museum, Graphische Sammlung, Inv.-Nr. 1961/32, p. 102.

brightly lit, his buttocks emphasized in brightness and visibility as if he is naked, exposing his sinful flesh and abjuring holiness even as the savior redeems the fallen. A similar fifteenth-century illumination depicts Christ surrounded by Roman soldiers, two of them sans trousers. One raises his leg to kick Christ, exposing his white underwear, in a striking example in which symbolic aims produce an image very peculiar from a modern point of view.[92]

Other instances abound. Images with sinners emphasized by their buttocks include the Crowning with Thorns, a panel of the altarpiece at Melk Monastery, painted by Jörg Breu the Elder around 1502;[93] the Crucifixion by the Kempten Master (c. 1460–70);[94] the Mocking of Christ (c. 1504–05) by Matthias Grünewald;[95] the Betrayal and Arrest of Christ (c. 1490) by Fernando Gallego;[96] Dürer's Execution of St. Catherine (c. 1498);[97] the Flagellation of Christ (c. 1530–38) by the Master of the Messkirch;[98] Balthasar Berger's Crucifixion (c. 1532);[99] and Jan Baegert's Crowning with Thorns and Flagellation of Christ (first quarter of the sixteenth century).[100]

Other religious subjects use the same motifs, underscoring the figure's sinful nature by displaying the barely concealed prominence of his buttocks. In Rogier van der Weyden's Beheading of John the Baptist (the right wing of the St. John the Baptist altarpiece, c. 1454), the sinful bottom of the executioner sports a jaunty scarlet wrapper, coming open as the sinner thrusts his bottom out. In a painting of the martyrdom of St. Veit (c. 1480), a persecutor in the center of the image has his bottom thrust toward the viewer, his trousers parting to provide a view of black underwear and a glimpse of his bottom.[101] In a depiction of St. George raised on a cross and scraped with combs, from an altarpiece in Valencia (c. 1410), one of the saint's tormentors has no trousers but underwear, which reveal the crack of his buttocks.[102] The Martyrdom of St. Leodgar of Autun (c. 1510–15) also features a central tormentor leaning over the saint, his rear clad in an eye-arresting pale color and prominently displayed.[103] The martyrdom of John the Baptist foregrounds the executioner's rear in Rogier van de Weyden's Martyrdom of St. John the Baptist and Hans Memlic's Triptych of John the Baptist and St. John the Evangelist.[104]

Whether it was to emphasize the lower at the expense of the higher or to privilege the back over the front, to have the body oriented in the wrongful direction was contrary to the right order of things. One historical manifestation of this understanding of inversion was the so-called "Jewish execution," in which Jewish criminals were hanged head downwards, their inverted physical position intended to denote their inverted moral status.[105] The "Jewish execution" was practiced in Germany by the late thirteenth century and appeared elsewhere as well; it was known, for instance, in early fourteenth-century Beauvais and appears in illustrations from the fourteenth, fifteenth and even eighteenth centuries.[106] The symbolic impact of the judgment was heightened by hanging animals (usually dogs) along with the condemned man. The dogs were sometimes alive and attacked the man, and so the punishment may have been intended to intensify the agony; but in other cases the dogs were already dead. In these cases, the staging had a purely symbolic motivation, undoubtedly intended to signify the animalistic character of the unbelieving Jews, drawing parallels between Jewish and beastly lack of uprightness and reason, a parallel that was also frequently drawn in literature.[107] Inverted hanging was also the conventional method of execution for homicidal animals, for the same reasons: their baseness and lack of reason meant that they could not occupy a position similar to humans.[108] Thus executing Jews in the same way served to liken them to animals and to draw attention to the moral inversion that differentiated them from the allegedly more rational believers.

Inverted execution played a symbolic role in literature as well. Bernard of Cluny used the iconography of inversion to describe the punishment in hell, in which sinners were hanged both upside-down and backwards. He adds the detail that the filth clinging to their feet is now above their heads, a description that underlines the inversion of purity and impurity and emphasizes the inversion of the sinful:

> Stat cruce triplice gens rea, vertice mersa deorsum,
> Ora tenet sua, dorsa simul sua versa retrorsum,
> Sunt superhorrida, nam lue sordida, crura, pedesque,
> Inferius caput. Haec mala sunt apud infera certe.[109]

> The guilty folk are placed on the cross in three ways: their heads plunged downwards, their faces and backs reversed; for their legs and feet are above, foul with filth. Certainly these are the punishments of hell.

A similar punishment is levied upon sinners in the fourteenth-century English poem *The Siege of Jerusalem*. In the narrative, during the conquest of Jerusalem the Christians avenge the insults suffered by Christ by hanging Caiaphas and other Jews upside-down.[110]

The dichotomy of high and low was most prominent in medieval orientational morality, but forward/backward and before/behind also played a significant role. As the tract *Jacob's Well* (cited previously) stated, "Virtues are in front, sin is in the rear," and this echoed similar Biblical formulations. *Before* and *behind* could denote directions in time as well as in space, but the basic understanding of the concept took its orientation from the body: *before* is in the direction of the face, *behind* of the rear. This division, originating in the body, was essential to orientation and was exemplified by God in Exodus, where God speaks of showing himself to Moses. God says, "non poteris videre faciem meam: non enim videbit me homo et vivet," "You shall not see my face, for no man shall see my face and live" (Ex. 33:20), but instead states that he will conceal Moses in a hole and protect him with his right hand, "et videbis posteriora mea; faciem autem meam videre not poteris," "and you shall see my back parts; but my face you cannot see"

(Ex. 33:23). Exegetes commented that the vision of God's face was reserved for the saved in the afterlife, so that the face represented both the good and forward motion in time.[111] In the thirteenth century Hugh of Saint-Cher confirmed this dichtomomy between face/divinity and behind/earthliness, glossing the passage at Matthew 17:1, "et resplenduit facies eius," "and his face did shine":

> idest, divinitas. Exod. 33 videbis posteriora mea, idest, humanitatem meam, faciem autem meam videre not potest, idest, divinitam.
>
> that is, [his] divinity. Exodus 33, *thou shalt see my back parts*, that is my humanity, *thou canst not see my face*, that is [his] divinity.[112]

In accordance with this schema, sinners and criminals could be punished in a way that exemplified their moral backwardness in physical ways. This often took the form of forcing the guilty to ride backwards, a motif that also appears widely in illustrations. Such punishments were most often levied for religious offenses, a fact that emphasizes that the sinner's misdeeds were crimes against a universal order rather than merely against human law. In 967, for example, the antipope during the time of Pope John XIII was forced to parade through Rome riding backwards on an ass.[113] In the late tenth century Pope Gregory V punished the antipope John XVI by making him ride backwards on an ass with his vestments turned inside out.[114] In 1121, Pope Calixtus II imposed a similar fate on antipope Gregory VIII, compelling him to ride a camel backwards and to hold its tail instead of reins. In 1184, anti-papal forces compelled some of Pope Lucius III's clerics to ride backwards on asses.[115] Records of similar punishments are found in many sources. Caesarius of Heisterback tells the story of one Pandolph, who saw a ghostly procession of men, headed by Pandolph's master, an avaricious Cistercian cardinal, seated backwards on animals, with the animals' tails in the men's mouths, being led away to divine judgment.[116]

In some cases moral backwardness is portrayed as a desire to ride backwards, for instance in depictions of Jews riding sows or goats—both emblems of moral uncleanliness—backwards.[117] In an image from the Stowe Missal, around 1300, we see the iconography of backwardness accompanied by the iconography of animal nature: an ape, symbolizing degraded man, seated backwards on a goat, the emblem of sinful carnal desire (see Figure 10). The diabolical nature of this physical and moral inversion is confirmed by an image in a twelfth-century manuscript depicting the fourth rider of the Apocalypse, Death, as the Devil seated backwards on his horse.[118] Similar punishments involved making miscreants face and pay homage to the degraded rear end, as in the case of troublemakers who forced Henry of Donington and another cleric to kiss the rear end of a horse in 1292.[119]

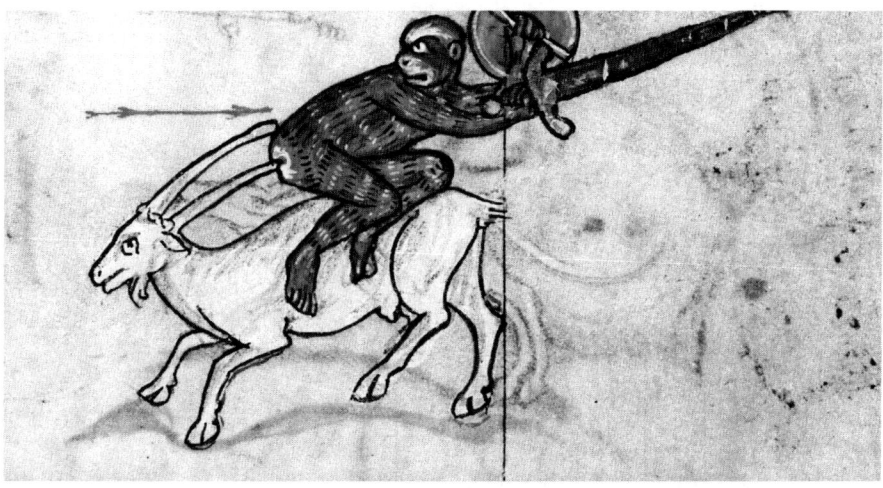

Figure 10 Sinful reversal: an ape, representing sinful, degraded man rides backwards on a goat, the most carnal of animals. The goat's horn in the ape's anus further draws attention to the importance of the bottom. 13th–14th centuries, Flemish. © The British Library Board: London, British Library Stowe 17 (the Stowe Missal), fol. 214r.

The body was a moral entity, even when not engaged in action. It reflected the moral orientation of the universe, and it was vitally important that the body should be kept in physical and moral alignment with that orientation. Yet the unruly lower body, like sin, continued to make its desires known.

4 The Realm of Corruption

Across the period, and across different levels of culture—clerical, popular, secular, theological, monitory and sensational—excrement was a powerful element of narrative, image and life. To use an ironically appropriate term, it was the apotheosis of earthly corruption. It provoked a visceral reaction of disgust. Whether in daily life or in literature, it commanded attention, even if that attention was to distance oneself as far as possible from the offending substance. And most critically, these instinctive reactions were imbued with theological meaning. In the medieval understanding, excrement did not just serve as a symbol or analogue for sin, it *was* sin. It was a day-to-day embodiment of the results of the Fall of Man: inescapable, foul, shameful. It was crucial testimony to the sinful earthly predicament of humans. Thus the status of excrement in the Middle Ages was radically different from that of the present day, where it is abhorrent and trivial; in the medieval view it was abhorrent and of the utmost importance.

As outlined in previous chapters, a number of factors positioned excrement as a manifestation of sin. The consonance of the moral and the material meant that material substances were easily understood as having moral valence. The disgust provoked by excrement, a biologically determined reaction, had ideational components and could easily be translated into moral disgust. Excrement was, moreover, closely allied with death. Both were characterized by corruption and decay. Both were carnal. Both were understood as afflictions of the body that had become impure as a result of sin. Excretion was associated with the shame that was regarded as a natural consequence of having sinful bodies: carnal, daily shame that emphasized the distance between the sinner and the purity of God. What is more, excrement embodied corruption, which was an emblem and exemplar of the mutability that characterized the entire sinful world. Heaven was incorrupt and therefore eternal, associated with jewels and gold: beautiful and imperishable. Hell, by contrast, was the place of movement, agitation, admixture, disintegration and decay. The process that mirrored these most greatly was digestion and the substance excrement.[1]

It was thus inevitable that excrement should be important in medieval religious thought, concerned as it was with purity, sin and order. Questions of purity and impurity, sanctity and sin, were paramount to the medieval understanding of order. Every human action occupied a place on a scale of moral value ranging from holy to sinful, and this hierarchy of values was not abstract and distinct from the material realm, but applied to matter as well. Some places, objects and materials were holy, others corrupt. Churches were among the holy sites, regarded as outposts of heaven, the pure realm of God. Thus arose the concern to inter the faithful in churchyards, where the proximity to holiness would counter the corrupting dissolution of death and prefigure the ultimate restoration of bodily integrity at the resurrection. Saints' relics also formed sites of holiness and purity, valued as emblems of human sanctity and of incorruption. A sweet "odor of sanctity" might be emitted by the corpses of the holy, evidence that sinful corruption could be overcome and that the saints were, in a sense, already denizens of incorrupt heaven.[2] The consecrated Host, being literally the body of Christ, was the most incorrupt and salvific matter on earth.

It is no accident that sites of earthly sanctity were those that resisted or countered material corruption, particularly corporeal corruption. Relics were often called upon to restore health; churches attempted to foster the faith and holiness that might allow the pious to transcend death and be restored to incorruption in the afterlife. The horror of material corruption was fundamental to this schema. The body was the seat and focus of corruption: the wages of sin were the corruptibility of the body, which was in turn the source of death. The purest and holiest of places and matter were those that prefigured the end of bodily corruption, the incorruptibility and stability of heaven. Conversely, those substances that most reflected or involved material corruption were the least holy, the most sinful. Moreover, of all forms of material corruption, bodily corruption was both the most significant and the most reviled. This theological system dovetails with the modern findings of Rozin and others that disgust is invoked most strongly in response to carnal stimuli such as corporeal decay, body-envelope violations and corporeal disfigurement. Mortality and the horror of death are at the heart of both systems.

On this spectrum of the holy and the corrupt, the body was not a neutral site, but a meeting-ground of purity and impurity, and a battleground upon which the central struggle against sin and corruption always had to be fought. For all these reasons, it was inevitable that the body would be a focal point in questions of impurity both moral and material, and its processes and products the subject of moral scrutiny.

DIVINITY AS INCORRUPTIBILITY

The inclination toward sin had inhered in the body since the Fall. The flesh, in its post-lapsarian corruptible earthly form, gives rise to manifold sins, as expounded in Galatians 5:16–25:

> Dico autem spiritu ambulate et desiderium carnis non perficietis. Caro enim concupiscit adversus spiritum, spiritus autem adversus carnem. Haec enim invicem adversantur ut non quaecumque vultis illa faciatis. . . . Manifesta autem sunt opera carnis quae sunt fornicatio, inmunditia, luxuria, idolorum servitus, veneficia, inimicitiae, contentiones, aemulationes, irae, rixae, dissensiones, sectae, invidiae, homicidia, ebrietates, comesationes et his similia. . . . Qui autem sunt Christi carnem crucifixerunt cum vitiis et concupiscentiis.
>
> I say then, walk in the spirit, and you shall not fulfil the lusts of the flesh. For the flesh lusteth against the spirit; and the spirit against the flesh; for these are contrary one to another: so that you do not the things that you would. . . . Now the works of the flesh are manifold, which are fornication, uncleanness, immodesty, luxury, idolatry, witchcraft, enmities, contentions, emulations, wraths, quarrels, dissensions, sects, envies, murders, drunkenness, revellings, and such like. . . . And they that are Christ's, have crucified their flesh, with the vices and concupiscences.

Christianity hence held that the corrupt material body was antithetical to purity and divinity. In extreme cases, this distrust of materiality gave rise to organized heretical sects, such as the Bogomils, a group espousing a dualist belief system that spread across eastern Europe in the tenth, eleventh and twelfth centuries. Bogomil belief held that all matter was base and corrupt, originating in the fall of Lucifer, and that corporeal acts such as marriage and reproduction were to be abjured. This dualist mistrust of matter in turn appears to have influenced the Cathars, the heretical sect arising in eleventh-century France.

The Bogomils and Cathars espoused formalized beliefs that the divine and immaterial were antithetical to the sinful and material, but more informal belief in the same antitheses tended to characterize popular mainstream Christianity as well. This understanding shows up most visibly in accounts of blasphemy, in which people imputed an excess of materiality to God, and especially imputed to God the particulars of the sinful lower body. However blasphemous the official church might decree the thought, in many people's minds it stood to reason that if man was created in God's image, God should have the same bodily orifices as man. This remained a question with regard to God the Father, and became even more tempting in the case of Christ, whose fleshly incarnation was central to the entire theological structure. If God the Father provided the model for the design of man, and if Christ was created fully human, did this not mean that they would have the same lowly orifices as ordinary men? In humans, these orifices were clearly designed for excretion, which raised the question of whether God too excreted through these orifices.

The very question was a forbidden melding of conceptual opposites, the divine and the corrupt. It was the province of heretics and sinners to suggest it. The problem attracted the commentary of Augustine, who attempted to refute charges of divine bodiliness in arguing against the Manicheans:

> *Et dixit Deus: Faciamus hominem ad imaginem et similitudinem nostram.* . . . Istam maxime quaestionem solent Manichaei loquaciter agitare, et insultare nobis quod hominem credamus factum ad imaginem et similitudinem Dei. Attendunt enim figuram corporis nostri, et infeliciter quaerunt utrum habeat Deus nares et dentes et barbam, et membra etiam interiora, et caetera quae in nobis sunt necessaria. In Deo autem talia ridiculum est, imo impium credere, et ideo negant hominem factum esse ad imaginem et similitudinem Dei. Quibus respondemus, membra quidem ista in Scripturis plerumque nominari, cum Deus insinuatur audientibus parvulis; et hoc non solum in Veteris Testamenti libris, sed etiam in Novi. Nam et oculi Dei commemorantur, et aures, et labia, et pedes, et ad dexteram Dei Patris sedere evangelizatur Filius. . . . Sed omnes qui spiritualiter intelligunt Scripturas, non membra corporea per ista nomina, sed spirituales potentias accipere didicerunt, sicut galeas, et scutum, et gladium (*Ephes.* VI, 16, 17), et alia multa.³

> *And God said: Let us make man to our image and similitude.* This question especially the Manichees continue to pursue with their jabbering, and they jeer at us because we believe that man was made in the image and similitude of God. For they observe the shape of our body and ask infelicitously whether God might have a nose and teeth and beard, and even inner organs, and the rest of the things that are necessary in us. It is ridiculous, however, or rather, unholy to believe such things of God, and therefore they deny that man was made in the image and likeness of God. To which we respond that these parts are mostly mentioned in the Scriptures when God is introduced carefully to an audience of little ones, and not only in the books of the Old Testament, but also in the New. For in addition God's eyes are mentioned, and ears, and lips, and feet, and the Son is proclaimed to sit at the right hand of God the Father. . . . But all those who understand the Scriptures spiritually have learned to understand by these terms not bodily parts but spiritual powers, as they do helmets and shield and sword and many other things.

Despite Augustine's arguments, the idea that these features might be literal continued to trouble ordinary Christians. The question became most tempting in the case of Jesus because of his incarnation and tenure on earth in earthly flesh. It was clear to commentators that because Jesus embodied divinity and unfallen flesh, his earthly body should be pure and free from corrupt materiality and its attendant pollutions. But what did this imply about Jesus and excretion? The very question meant envisioning the unthinkable, even blasphemous notion of Jesus defecating in an earthly, disgusting manner.

It was a point of orthodoxy that Jesus had been incarnated fully human, which included human digestion. The standard interpretation of Luke 24:43, in which Jesus ate fish after the resurrection, held that he had eaten to demonstrate that he was resurrected in the flesh, not merely as an immaterial presence.[4] Yet despite substantial exegesis on this point, the question of whether this meant that the fish was digested and excreted is the subject of an enormous silence, as if excretion is so inherently corrupt, foul and undignified that Jesus could not have done it, and as if even to broach the question taints the purity of the divine. The absence of these discussions, in a theological culture that discussed nearly every other question avidly, is testimony to the unassailable valence of excrement. In orthodox Christianity the topic arises solely in characterizing the blasphemous questioning of heretics and unbelievers. These we can see as early as the second-century gnostic theologian Valentinus, who wrote that Christ's body was too pure to admit of defecation.[5] Through such witnesses we can see that the question came to mind, but the very idea was a topic of vigorous contempt and suppression. Nevertheless theology allows us to form the medieval answer to the question, though to dwell on it at all would be regarded as abhorrent in medieval terms. We shall return to this topic after outlining the medieval understanding of purity and corruption in greater detail.

In the earthly world, corruption inhered in materiality and fleshliness. Though Christ was present on earth in the flesh, when issues of his purity arise he is depicted as effectively virtually immaterial. The theme surfaces, for instance, in the apocryphal Latin infancy gospels, which appear in manuscripts of the thirteenth and fourteenth centuries, based on earlier sources. In this passage from the shorter, fourteenth-century infancy gospel, the midwife who delivered the baby Jesus describes him as practically weightless. She narrates the moments after Jesus' birth:

> et assumpsi audaciam et inclinaui me et tetigi eum, leuauique eum in manibus meis cum magno timore, et perterrita sum quod non erat pondus in eo sicut hominis nati. et inspexi eum, et non erat in eo aliqua coinquinatio, sed erat quasi in rore dei altissimi totus nitidus corpore, leuis ad portandum, splendidus ad respiciendum. . . . et subito [r]egressa est lux magna de oculis eius tanquam choruscus magnus.

> and I put on boldness and bowed myself and touched him and lifted him up in my hands with great fear and I was smitten with fear for there was no weight in him as of a man that is born. [A]nd I looked upon him, and there was not in him any defilement, but he was as it were all shining (*or* washed) with the dew of the most high God, light in body to bear, and bright to look upon.[6]

Though in human form, the infant Jesus partakes of the qualities of the divine: bright and nearly weightless. The physics of gravity as laid out by Gossuin of Metz and others are exemplified here: the pure are light, drawn upward to God, while the sinful are weighted down by impurity. What is more, in keeping with the sinless painlessness and purity of the birth, the baby and Mary both were free of the bodily mess that characterizes normal, sinful births:

> Illa igitur hora qua tuli infantem <in> manus meas [r]espiciens uidi eum corpus habere mundissimum et nulla parte coinquinatum sicut solent alii infantes cum inmundicia nasci. . . . Accessi ad eam et pertrectans manibus meis inueni eam penitus ab omni non solum sanguine sed etiam aliqua corporis pollucione uel macula omni genere esse mundissimam.[7]

> In that hour therefore when I took the baby into my hands, I looked and saw that he had a body most pure and in no part defiled with the uncleanness of birth as other infants have. . . . I approached [Mary] and, feeling her thoroughly with my hands, I found her entirely clean, free from not only blood but also any impurity of the body or stain of any kind.

Here the sinless, painless labor of Mary, as well as the purity of Jesus, are expressed by the preservation of bodily integrity and lack of effusions. The sinless incarnation is expressed in material incorruptibility, and the material and the moral are once again identical.

The concern that God should not be subject to the filth of human childbirth makes an appearance in popular Christian testimony. Aude Fauré, a young wife who had recently given birth near the French village of Montaillou, reported that she found it difficult to believe in Christ's incarnation in the Eucharist because of her own experience of the messiness and defilement of human incarnation, in the form of childbirth:

> cogitavit turpitudinem quam emittunt mulieres pariendo, et cum videret elevari in altari corpus Domini, habuit cogitationem ex illa turpitudine quod esset infectum corpus Domini.[8]

> she thought of the filth that women expel in childbirth, and when she saw the body of Christ raised up at the altar, she had the thought that the body of the Lord was corrupted by that filth.

Another form of this was voiced by the sceptic Raymond Delaire, who expressed disbelief in most of the tenets of Christianity and maintained that Jesus was not the result of Virgin Birth, but of Mary and Joseph having sexual relations. This took the form of claiming that Jesus was made by "foten e mardan," "fucking and shitting out" like any other human.[9] The characterization of childbirth as "shitting out" demonstrates that transgressing the boundaries of the lower body was in a sense always regarded as repellant and producing filth—in the case of childbirth, producing more flesh which would eventually die and become "as dung."

In a similar vein, Guibert of Nogent reported on the charges of Jewish debaters, who objected to the idea of the incarnation of God, finding it offensive that God might take form in "the corruption of a woman's womb" and would himself have endured the excretions of the body. As one example, the twelfth-century rabbi and scholar Joseph Kimhi protested:

> how shall I believe that this great inaccessible *Deus absconditus* needlessly entered the womb of a woman, the filthy, foul bowels of a female, compelling the living God to be born of a woman, a child without knowledge or understanding, senseless, unable to distinguish between his right hand and his left, defecating and urinating, sucking his mother's breasts from hunger and thirst. . . . Indeed, if she had not suckled him, he would have died of hunger like other people. If not, why should she have suckled him? He should have lived miraculously! Why should she have suckled him for nothing, that he should engage in all foul and miserable human practices?[10]

To Joseph all of the animalistic, unreasoning, excreting characteristics of the human body appear indisputably antithetical to the divine. The moral schema of the body is particularly visible in his argument that it is inconceivable that the divinity should not know the difference between the right hand and the left. In a similar vein, Guibert of Nogent's *De Incarnatione contra Judaeos* directed invective against Jewish unbelievers who tried to dismiss the incarnation by dwelling on the disgusting aspects of fleshly existence:[11]

> Interroga, putidissime et nequam, de Domino nostro, si spuerit, si nares emunxerit, si pituitas oculorum vel aurium digitis hauserit, et intellige quia qua honestate superiora haec fecerit, et residua peregerit. Aut dic mihi, ille tuus, qui Abrahae apparuit Deus, ea quae comedit in quem alium [f., alvum] deposuit? quomodo etiam, aut si factum est, quod consequens fuit?[12]

> Ask, most shameful and wicked one, about our Lord: if he spat, if he wiped his nose, if he picked the discharge from his eyes or ears with his fingers; and understand with what honor he did these things above, and carried out all the other things. Or tell me, that man of yours, that God who appeared to Abraham—the things he ate: in what gut did he deposit them? How also, if the function continued—what happened next?

Even in reporting on the blasphemous challenges of unbelievers, Guibert cannot bring himself to articulate explicitly the implicit charge of the last question:

if Christ ate food, does that mean that he defecated? Even to consider the question in objecting against it is profane. Guibert charges: "Contremisco dum de his disputo; sed vos, filii diaboli, me cogitis," "I tremble violently when I argue about these things; but you, sons of the devil, you compel me."[13]

The temptation to speculate about the physical processes of God could even creep into the conception of how other parts of the cosmos worked. In one example, a thirteenth-century man named Gausbert d'Aula claimed that believing in God who made the wind and the rain meant believing that God had an anus and a vagina.[14] This seems to mean that he imagined wind as God's farts. (He may also have believed that women urinate from the vagina; his logic is not clear.) The blasphemous imputation of lower bodily orifices to God predictably brought him to the attention of the authorities.

The sacrilege of questioning God's relationship to digestion found another form in heretical thought about the Eucharist. If Christ were physically present in the communion wafer, sceptics wondered, would his body not be subject to corruption in the processes of digestion—would he not be subject to being transformed into excrement? Thus purity would be vulnerable to sin and corruption, the most exalted of substances would be subject to disintegration, and the holiest of substances would be transformed into the basest. In our present formulation, it would also mean that the divine (the Host) would be transformed into sin (excrement), which would clearly be inconceivable.

To evade these implications, many concluded, in opposition to the doctrine of the official Church, that the Eucharist could not consist of the literal and material body and blood of Christ. This concern with the implications of literal transubstantiation appears as a heresy as early as Heriger of Lobbes (*c.* 925–1007), who mentions it in his *De corpore et sanguine domini*, and Alger of Liège (*c.* 1055–1132), whose *De sacramentis corporis et sanguinis domini* enumerated common Eucharistic heresies.[15] Doubt about the real presence of Christ in the Eucharist found focus in the Berengarian heresy of the eleventh century. Berengar, a teacher at the cathedral school at Tours, formally articulated the argument that the process of eating and digesting the wafer would bring about sacrilege and that therefore the Eucharistic materials must undergo a purely spiritual transformation. This assertion sparked controversy, and in 1059 Berengar was called to Rome by Pope Nicholas II. Ultimately he was induced to sign an oath drawn up by Humbert, the papal legate, avowing that the Eucharist was the genuine body and blood of Christ, broken by the priest and chewed by the communicant. The wording of this statement unintentionally drew further attention to the physical act of eating the wafer, provoking greater thoughts of unseemly corporeality by commentators. Subsequently Berengar recanted his avowal that the Eucharist literally consisted of Christ's body, and the controversy continued for centuries.

These doubts about the implications of the corporeal Eucharist became known as the stercoran heresy, the term deriving from *stercus*, "dung."

Orthodox commentary on the Eucharist solved the problem by stressing that although the wafer was the genuine physical body of Christ, the materials were not subject to physical digestion; pure flesh, by implication, was not vulnerable to disintegration. This was the position of Guitmund, a student of Lanfranc and monk of Bec, whose *De corporis et sanguinis Christi veritate in eucharista*, written between 1073 and 1075, argues that the true species of the Eucharist remains undigested. Those Church Fathers who may have lived on the Eucharist alone, Guitmund argues, did so only as a miracle, not because they were digesting the Host as food.[16]

The issue also arose in more popular form, in instructive miracle stories about the Eucharist. In the twelfth century, Roland Bandinelli (most likely the future Pope Alexander III) told the story of a man who tried to live on the Host alone, but who died after fourteen days. Bandinelli argues that even though the man excreted, which might suggest that the Host was digested, he was in fact digesting his own humors and not the Host.[17] Gerald of Wales recounts a story that demonstrated the same point. A woman was inhabited by a demon, and helpers attempted to exorcise her by feeding her the Eucharist. The demon ridiculed them, stating that the Host is the food of the soul, not of the body.[18] The implication is that the Host cannot affect physical processes (and by implication cannot be digested). It is interesting that the tale implies that demonic possession is a physical rather than spiritual condition: the Host is spiritual, but demons physical. The two states seem to be envisioned as overlapping but not converging. The Host, being entirely pure, is not subject to bodily processes, but similarly, in this tale, does not serve to dislodge the physical demon.

Gerald follows this with a similar tale of a sceptic who tested the Host's value as food by eating nothing else for three days. Here again the Host is too spiritual to be vulnerable to physical corruption. Gerald relates:

> Qui cum hostiis sacratis tribus diebus continue vesceretur, eisque solis, cotidie tanquam nihil comedisset esuriit, et quasi ventre vacuo prorsus in toto illo triduo ad egestionem non secessit. Corpus enim Christi cibus mentis est non ventris.[19]

> When he ate the sacred hosts, and them alone, continually for three days, he felt hungry every day as if he had eaten nothing, and, as if he had an empty stomach, he did not withdraw to evacuate for the entire three days. For the body of Christ is food for the mind, not for the stomach.

This undigestability or immateriality of the Host was not entirely consonant with the position articulated by Albertus Magnus in the thirteenth century, who pronounced of the consecrated wafer, "quamdiu valent discerni species tamdiu est ibi Christus,"[20] "as long as the form can be distinguished, it is Christ." But once the wafer had dissolved in the mouth, he implied, the purity of Christ had been absorbed by the sinner, and the Host reverted to its former material constituents. If this were the case, the sinner's excretions should indeed have been composed of the digested, desacralized Host. But a story in a Middle English sermon also claimed that the Host was indigestible, insisting it maintained its holiness and integrity in the body. In this tale, sinful Jews slice open a Christian cleric to get at the Eucharist he has just swallowed. The Host has wholly retained the shape of bread, undigested inside the cleric, and shines so brightly that it blinds the Jews.[21] The story, concerned with demonstrating the holiness of the Eucharist and the perfidy of unbelievers, does not explain what it envisions happens to the Host thereafter. If the Host is not subject to digestion and excretion, does it melt away into immateriality? This would seem to be the logical conclusion for something too pure to be subject to digestion; certainly it cannot be envisioned as remaining in the communicant's system perpetually, for a variety of reasons: too many Hosts would accumulate, and presumably even one undissolved Host would obviate the need for further Communion. Thus the implication is that the Host is essentially not only incorruptible but, once consecrated, in a sense inclines to immateriality.

The issue of the digestability of the Host also troubled Margery Baxter, a fifteenth-century Norwich Lollard woman charged with heresy. Baxter was unable to overcome her disquiet that the body of Christ would have to be multiplied endlessly to supply sufficient Eucharists, and that it would then inevitably be transformed into foulness and excrement. Asked whether she held to the belief that the consecrated bread was Christ's body, she responded, in the words of the report:

> "tu male credis quia si quodlibet tale sacramentum esset Deus et verum corpus Christi, infiniti sunt dii, quia mille sacerdotes et plures omni die conficiunt mille tales deos et postea tales deos comedunt et commestos emittunt per posteriora in sepibus turpiter fetentibus, ubi potestis tales deos sufficientes invenire si volueritis perscrutari."[22]

> "You believe wrongly, because if any such sacrament were God and the true body of Christ, gods would be innumerable, because a thousand priests and more make a thousand such gods every day, and afterwards eat such gods and discharge them eaten from their backsides repulsively in stinking enclosures, where you can find sufficient gods if you want to look carefully."

Baxter's conviction that the pure and the excremental were immutably antithetical underlay her disbelief. The antithetical nature of the divine and the earthly was quantifiable as impurity. Humans were weighed down by their corruptible flesh, and excrement was an ineluctable reminder of that corruptibility. The incompatibility of the divine and the corruptible, epitomized by excrement, also finds witness in one woman's rejection of Cathar belief. Raymonde Testanière, of Montaillou, had been discussing Cathar claims with her mother, including the belief that men could assume the power of God. Her mother rejected the notion that corruptible flesh could possess the power of God:

> "Non credas hoc, filia, quia nullus homo carnalis potest animas salvare qui egerit stercora, sed solum Deus et Beata Virgo Maria."[23]

> "You should not believe that, daughter, because no man of flesh, who produces excrement, can save souls; but only God and the Blessed Virgin Mary can."

Again, purity and excrement are antithetical, and the hallmark of humans is excrement, which exemplifies and indeed contributes to the gulf between humans and the divine. The passage is also interesting in that it appears to imply that Christ and the Virgin Mary are free from excrement, though whether Raymonde's mother meant this because they are in heaven, rather than because they were free from it on earth, is unclear.

SIN AS CORRUPTION

Although the earthly flesh of sinful humans was impure and corruptible, Christian belief held that it had not always been this way. God had created the body pure, but sin had engendered corruption. Guibert of Nogent articulated this in his argument against the Jews, who held that the human body was too impure to envelope the divine. Guibert responded:

> *Membra, cum abest peccatum, sancta sunt.*—Porro Dei Filius in carnem veniens, si competentia corpori membra habuit, membrorum compositio non nocuit. Frustraque non pudeat quod ipsum non puduit. Et quid eum puderet, ubi nihil non sanctum fuit! Si quidquid est, bonum est, nisi ubi peccatum est, membra quae per se bona sunt, cum peccatum non est, sancta sunt. Membra nostra imbecillitati nostrae sunt administratoria, et cum aures, ora vel nares superfluis capitum egerendis inserviunt, caetera quid mali faciunt, quae inferius intestinorum pondus exponunt?[24]

> *The parts of the body, when sin is absent, are holy.*—Further, the Son of God, as he came into the flesh: if he had parts suitable to his bodiliness, the composition of his parts was not harmful. For he should not be ashamed, to no purpose, of that which did not shame him. And what should have shamed him, where there was nothing that was not holy! If anything exists, it is good, except where there is sin, and the parts which are good in themselves, when there is no sin, are holy.

The Son of God represents the sinless condition of the flesh before corruption entered the world; he alone retains the sinless, incorrupt body. As Guibert emphasizes, it is not the body in itself that is sinful, but the corrupt body that is the result of sin. This was also articulated by Augustine:

> demonstrarem non corpus esse animae, sed corruptibile corpus onerosum. Unde illud est quod de scripturis nostris in superiore libro commemoravimus: *Corpus enim corruptibile adgravat animam* [Wisdom 9:15]. Addendo utique *corruptibile* non qualicumque corpore, sed quale factum est ex peccato consequente vindicta, animam perhibuit adgravari.[25]

> I have explained that it is not the body that is burdensome to the soul, but the corruptible body. Hence what we have cited from our Scriptures in the book above: *For the corruptible body weighs down the soul* [Wisdom 9:15]. Certainly by adding "corruptible," he means the soul is weighed down not by any kind of body, but by the kind it became as a consequence of sin and punishment.

Sin and the material corruption of the body were two sides of the same coin: this had been clear since mortality had been levied as the wages of sin in the Garden of Eden. At the simplest level, it was, after all, an act of eating that brought sin into the world, and so it was only natural that excrement, the corrupt results of digestion, should be the emblem of this original transgression.

Francesc Eiximenis (*c*. 1330–1409), the Franciscan priest quoted in Chapter 1 above, expresses most precisely the relation between excrement and the original sin of eating the apple. Francesc was advisor to the city councillors of Valencia, writing *Regiment de la cosa pública* (*Rule of the Commonweal*), which later formed the twelfth book of *Lo Crestià*. As part of his duties he recommended a latrine for every building, a directive with a theological as well as a practical mandate. In this he was explicitly following the Bishop of Amiens, who focused on the teachings found in Ecclesiasticus 29:28, "Initium vitae hominis aqua et panis et vestimentum et domus protegens turpitudinem," "The essentials of man's life are water and bread and clothing and a house to cover his shamefulness." The Bishop of Amiens interpreted this shamefulness as the need to excrete and understood the passage to mean that every dwelling should have a house to cover that shamefulness, or in other words a privy. Francesc elaborates on this in *Lo Crestià* (*The Christian*), his monumental encyclopedic work of the 1380s, intended to supply all important knowledge to a lay audience. In his explanation, Francesc makes explicit what much medieval commentary implies:

> E vol dir que en lo començament, quant nostre senyor Déu creà l'om, Ell volch dir que la sua vida estigués principalment en pa que menjàs, e en ayga que bagués, e en vestedures de què·s cobrís, e en haver loch separat en què porgàs son ventre. Açò, emperò, se deu entendre que fo ordonat

per nostre Senyor aprés lo peccat del primer pare, car, axí com dit és longament en lo VIII *libre*, si Adam no hagués peccat, natura humana usara solament de menjars naturals, axí com de fruytes, e no de artifficials, axî com de pa e de cuyna; axí mateix lavors no hagera mester privada per amagar sa turpitut, car jatsia que llavors l'om porgàs per lo ses, emperò la purgació aquella no fóra pudent ne haguera ab si la turpitut de què parla la dita auctoritat al·legada.[26]

And [this] means that in the beginning, when our Lord God created man, he intended that his life be principally in the bread he ate, and in the water he drank, and in the clothes with which he covered himself, and in having a separate place in which to purge his belly. That part, however, should be understood as having been ordered by our Lord after the sin of our first father, because, as is said at length in book VIII, if Adam had not sinned, human nature would use only natural foods such as fruits and not artificial ones like bread and cooked products; also then he would not have the need to hide his shamefulness, because even though man would still have to empty his bowels through the natural opening, it would not stink nor would it have that shamefulness of which the aforementioned authority speaks.

Unfortunately Francesc never wrote the promised book VIII, but his account of the identity of sin and the disgusting and shameful properties of excrement is clear enough. Although body processes are not impure by nature, sin has tainted them and made excretion disgusting. The idea that there was no defecation in the pre-lapsarian Paradise may seem comical to modern sensibilities, but it is very serious and absolutely central to medieval assumptions about divine history. Although the details of Martin Luther's theology and expression are beyond the scope of the present volume, it is worth noting that he articulated the same understanding. In his description of the earthly paradise in the *Lectures on Genesis* (1535), Luther commented on what would have happened if Original Sin had never been committed:

Hominis alia fuerat futura conditio: edisset, bibisset, fuisset mutatio ciborum in corporibus facta, sed non ita foeda, ut nunc.[27]

The situation of man would have been different. He would have eaten; he would have drunk; and the conversion of food in his body would have taken place, but not in such a disgusting manner as now.[28]

He is even more explicit later in the *Lectures*:

Mira autem hodie nobis res est, esse animalem vitam, sine morte et sine omnibus accidentibus mortis, qualia sunt morbi, pustulae, foetidae superfluitates in corporibus etc. Nulla enim pars corporis fuit sordida in statu innocentiae; non fuit foetor in excrementis, non aliae foeditates, sed omnia fuerunt pulcherrima, sine ulla offensione organorum sensuum, et tamen fuit animalis vita. Comedebat Adam, concoquebat, digerebat, fecisset alia, si sic permansisset, quae animalis vita exigit, donec tandem esset translatus ad spiritualem et aeternam vitam. . . . esset exutus inferioribus actionibus, quae tamen purae et non molestae fuissent, sicut nunc sunt post lapsum.[29]

For us today it is amazing that there could be a physical life without death and without all the incidentals of death, such as diseases, smallpox, stinking accumulations of fluids in the body, etc. In the state of innocence no part of the body was filthy. There was no stench in excrement, nor were there other execrable things. Everything was most beautiful, without any offense to the organs of sense; and yet there was physical life. Adam ate, he masticated, he digested; and if he had remained as he was, he would have done the other things physical life demands until at last he would have been translated to the spiritual and eternal life. . . . he would have been divested of his lower activities, which nevertheless would have been pure and not burdensome, as they are now after the Fall.[30]

The shame of man inheres in excrement: it is the enduring token of original sin.

The correspondence between excrement and original sin was also rehearsed in parables and exempla, such as that in Caesarius of Heisterbach's thirteenth-century *Dialogue on Miracles*, where the Fall is recast in explicitly excremental terms. The knight Henry of Wied, Caesarius reports, was debating the character of Eve with his wife. Henry took the position that sinful human nature always seeks to defy prohibitions. His wife disputed this and they made a bet on the subject, whereupon he forbade her to wade in the cesspool in their courtyard. She was thereupon "grievously tempted" to do just that, and finally plunged into the cesspool up to her knees, in emulation of Eve, who could not stay away from sin.[31] Here original sin is figured as dung, making the symbolic role of excrement in the Fall as explicit as possible.

Association with excrement was thus emblematic of the earthly and despicable condition of the sinful body. The Sienese Francesco di Giorgio Martini, writing on architecture in the fifteenth century, connected the filth of the latrine to human misery:

naturalmente l'omo non con piacere venendosi alla evacuazione del corpo perché rennova a molti la memoria della miseria umana, essendo a quella spurcizia sotto posta, con maggiore molestia a quello atto si conduce essendo el loco incomodo o per venti o per figura de esso loco.[32]

man, naturally coming not with pleasure to the evacuation of the body—because it renews for many the memory of human misery, being subjected to that filth—approaches that act with great trouble, the place being inconvenient, either because of winds or because of the appearance of that place.

Other disgusting bodily habits might be forbidden or forsworn, but the need to defecate was ineluctable, an unavoidable reminder of human sinful corporeality. It epitomized "human misery."

The corruption engendered by original sin took a number of other forms, all involving violations of the body envelope and the dissolution of bodily integrity. The most profound of these was the physical corruption and dissolution of the entire body, the decomposition that happens after death. Following the Fall, the body of the sinner became mortal and corruptible, leading inevitably to death, which was followed by the further decomposition, fragmentation and dissolution of the body.[33] The horrors of the dead body were evident, and considerable energy was expended in literature and art to keep these horrors vivid in the minds of those who might otherwise be seduced by the attractions of the living body. A case in point is the late medieval cadaver or transi tombs, featuring a sculpture of the decayed, repulsive body beneath a sculpture of the intact one: they served to remind every observer that the hideous corruption of death lay behind the temporary illusion of vigor and life.[34]

The decay that followed death, being a consequence of sin, could also be observed in living sinners. It was considered the hallmark of leprosy, a disease with a longstanding moral dimension, often thought to be the consequence of illicit sexual relations. The leper was regarded as having an accelerated and visible case of the decay and corruption that would bring down all sinners. The leper was, in a sense, pre-dead, exhibiting postmortem corruption while still alive, as a token of his or her sinful nature.[35] Lepers' identity as the living dead was such that in some places priests required them to stand in an open grave while burial rituals were performed. In other places, spadefuls of dirt were thrown over the head of the living leper, in imitation of burial. The status of the leper as protodead was such that in many places, after rituals declaring the still-living leper "dead," the uninfected spouse was free to remarry.[36] Whether walking the roads with their warning bells and identifying garb, isolated in hospitals or communities, or declared dead while still alive, lepers were segregated and shunned, their isolation testifying to the disgust provoked by such outward corruption.

In many instances it is clear that all material corruption was considered essentially identical: dung, excrement, fleshly decay and the corruption of death were alternate mainfestations of the same thing. In one sense, literally speaking, the body does not become dung; but here, as in many instances, dung was shorthand for all material corruption of the sinful body. This usage had the authority of Scripture, which described the body of the sinner Jezebel as "sicut stercus super faciem terrae," "like dung on the face of the land" (Vulgate 4 Kings 9:37), or other enemies of God as transformed into "stercus terrae," "dung of the land" (Vulgate Ps 82:11).

The corrupt nature of the physical body was also a staple of *contemptus mundi* literature, which used it as a metonym for the contemptibility of the earthly world.[37] The earthly realm was a realm of corruption and dung, and a realm in which humans inevitably contributed to both moral and material corruption. As the medieval meditation went, addressing God: "Ego de paradiso fugi; pro loco quem dederas cloacam inveni, et in ea me obvolvi," "I fled from Paradise; in exchange for the place you granted I found a sewer, and I wallowed in it."[38] The natural disgust engendered by decomposition and bodily effluvia could hence be recruited to encourage the devout to distance themselves from the sin represented by such corruption.

The effluvia of the body were incontrovertible signs of its corruptibility: spittle, vomit, urine and excrement revealed the body's earthliness and contemptibility. Accordingly, the decomposition of the dead body and the emissions of the live body were regarded as essentially equivalent. Pope Innocent III was one of many who made the comparison:

> Vivus, gignit pediculos et lumbricos; mortuus, generabit vermes et muscas. Vivus, producit stercus et vomitum; mortuus, producit putredinem et fetorem.
>
> Alive, he brings forth lice and tapeworms; dead, he will beget worms and flies. Alive, he produces dung and vomit; dead, he produces rottenness and stench.[39]

The disgusting aspects of excrement, in short, are like death, the result of original sin. Both odious forms of corruption, it is little wonder that the two are so equated so frequently in medieval literature. Both death and excrement provoke disgust; both are the unavoidable material consequences of spiritual corruption. Both are non-gendered, afflicting all sinners; and both are intimately related to carnality. If we step out of the medieval world and look at the paradigm through the theories of Lakoff and Johnson, we can see that the medieval understanding of corruption conforms to their argument that the human understanding of the world is embodied at the most essential level.[40] The body is the map upon which human history of sin has been inscribed and through which it is understood. The body is a testament to the legacy of sin, in an ultimate sense in its mortality, but in the daily sense by its generation of corruption.

We find innumerable examples of the correspondence between the corruption of death and the excremental corruption of sin, as in this Middle English sermon by Master Robert Rypon of Durham. In a sermon on Mary Magdelene, Rypon complains of those who pridefully seek to incite lust by adorning themselves in shameless garments, some of which are "fashioned from the entrails of worms":

> be they men or women, such as adorn themselves in their garments or by means of some other artificial decoration, to give wanton pleasure to each other, are well compared to a painted sepulchre in which lies a foul corpse, or to a dung-heap covered with a vine. So, for a surety, beneath such adornment of the body, whether artificial or even natural, there lurks the vilest filth, yea rather, a soul befouled with the vilest sins. . . .Wherefore, men and women adorning themselves to excite lust, without a doubt, in the eyes of God are more shameful and foul than the foulest corpses or dung-hills.[41]

Giving way to carnal concerns makes the body equivalent to a dungheap: utter corruption and foulness with no redeemable spiritual element. This was the danger inherent in the wayward body. At its most essential, scholars characterized the corruptible human body itself as excrement:

> O esca vermium, o massa pulveris, o vapor vanitatis, cur sic extolleris? . . . Si ergo consideres, o homo, quid per os, quid per nares, quid per ceteros meatus corporis egreditur, numquid vilius sterquilinio invenies te? . . . "Arbores ergo et herbas," dicit Bernardus, "investiga et considera, quia ille de se producunt frondes et flores, et tu de te lendes et pediculos et huiusmodi; illi eciam de se fundunt vinum, oleum et balsama, et tu de te stercus, urinam, et sputum."[42]

> O food for worms, O lump of dirt, O wisp of vanity, why you do exalt yourself like this? . . . Therefore if you consider, O man, what comes out through your mouth, through your nose, through the other passages of the body, will you not find that you are viler than a dungheap? "Study and consider the trees, therefore, and the plants," says Bernard, "for they bring forth leaves and flowers from themselves, and you bring forth fleas and lice and things of that kind; moreover they pour out wine, oil, and balm from themselves, and from yourself you pour out dung, urine, and spit."

Again, movement across the boundaries of the body envelope engenders disgust, and as Rozin and others have noted, disgust is attendant on the carnal, in marked contrast to the appealing fruitfulness of the plant world. Master Rypon describes the human condition as if bodily excretions were not by-products but the essential work of the body, positioning them as the body's defining characteritic—which for the Middle Ages they were. Thus the body consists of all things antithetical to the divine: corrupt, permeable, commingled, a breeding-ground for vermin and, in the comparison with the dungheap, already lifeless and abject. In addition to the repeated excremental images, it is worth noting the common description of the body as "food for worms," the food of corruption, which stands in marked contrast to Christ's body, a pure body which also serves as food, but as the food of salvation.

Religious literature called upon the sinner to abandon the realm of the body and live, in so far as possible, in the purer realm of heaven. Those few who were able to accomplish this were granted some of the characteristics of the pure and incorrupt body. A common example is those saints whose bodies were found incorrupt after death, or who, when exhumed, emitted the fragrant odor of sanctity. Where sinners' bodies were called vessels of dung, the bodies of virgins were likened to vessels of myrrh or balsam, substances that possessed a sweet odor and were used to embalm bodies. As corruption was the result of sin, the implication was that those bodies, innocent of fleshly sin, remained sweet and incorrupt. In the late tenth century the Anglo-Saxon abbot Ælfric used these images to describe the power of devotion to keep the body pure and incorrupt in the struggle against sin:

> Myrra deð, swa we ær cwædon, þæt þæt deade flæsc eaðelice ne rotað. Witodlice þæt deade flæsc rotað leahtorlice, þonne se deadlica lichama ðeowað þære flowendan galnysse, swa swa se witega be sumum cwæð, "ða nytenu forrotedon on heora meoxe" [Joel 1:17]. Þonne forrotiað þa nytenu on heora meoxe, þonne flæsclice men on stence heora galnysse geendiað heora dagas. Ac gif we ða myrran Gode gastlice geoffriað, þonne bið ure deadlica lichama fram galnysse stencum ðurh forhæfednysse gehealdan.

> Myrrh, acts, as we have said before, so that the dead flesh does not rot easily. Truly the dead flesh rots iniquitously when the mortal body is a servant to overflowing lust, as the sage said about certain ones, "The beasts rotted in their dung." Then the beasts rot in their dung, when fleshly men end their days in the stench of their lust. But if we offer myrrh to God sprirtually, then our mortal body will be preserved from the stench of lust through continence.

As myrrh preserves the dead body from becoming "as dung," so chastity preserves the live body from corruption. Bernard of Clairvaux elaborated on this:

> Vas interim fragile quod portamus...tenet castitas, ut monet Apostolus, in sanctificationem, et instar odoriferi balsami, quo condita cadavera incorrupta servantur.

> The fragile vessel which we carry for a time...contains chastity, as the apostle warns, in sanctification, and in the likeness of fragrant balsam, by which embalmed corpses are preserved incorrupt.

116 *Sin and Filth in Medieval Culture*

We must take care, warns Bernard, "ne dissolvantur otiis, ne corrumpantur desideriis, ne carnis voluptatibus computrescant, quemadmodum legitur de quibusdam quia *Computruerunt ut iumenta in stercore suo*,"[43] "lest we be dissolved by idle things, or corrupted by desires, or putrify in carnal indulgences, as it is read about certain people that *They rot like beasts in their dung* [Joel 1:17]." Once again carnal indulgence and material corruption are commensurate. *Holy Maidenhood*, a thirteenth-century English tract, elaborates on this:

> Þis is ȝet þe uertu þe halt ure bruchele ueat, þet is, ure feble flesch, as Seinte Pawel leareð, in hal halinesse; ant as þet swote smirles ant deorest of oþre þet is icleopet basme wit þet deade licome þet is þerwið ismiret from rotunge, alswa deð meidenhad meidenes cwike flesch wiðute wemmunge. Halt alse hire limen ant hire fif wittes—siðhe ant herunge, smechunge ant smellunge ant euch limes felunge—þet ha ne merren ne ne mealten þurh licomes lustes i fleschliche fulðen þe Godd haueð þurh his grace se muche luue ivnnen; þet ha ne beoð of þeo iliche, bi hwam hit is iwriten þus þurh þe prophete, þet ha in hare wurðinge as eaueres forroteden . . .[44]

> This is also the virtue that preserves our brittle vessel, that is, our feeble flesh, as Saint Paul teaches, in whole holiness; and as that sweet and most precious of all ointments that is called balm keeps the dead body that is smeared with it from rotting, so virginity keeps the virgin's living flesh without corruption. It also protects her limbs and her five senses—sight and hearing, tasting and smelling and the feeling of each limb—upon which God has bestowed so much love, through his grace, so that they are not marred nor dissolved through the body's lusts into fleshly filth; so that they will not be like those of whom it is written thus by means of the prophet, "They have rotted in their dung like beasts."

Death, corruption and the dung that exemplifies them are all consequences of sin.

A similar freedom from sinful corruption was supposedly available to those who rejected fleshly delights by fasting. Clement of Alexandria declared: "Fasting empties the soul of matter and makes it, with the body, clear and light for the reception of divine truth."[45] It is clear that the absence of impediments to salvation corresponds to the absence of excrement. Authorities frequently verified the purity of fasting-girls by the absence of excrement—a practical method of proof, but also a symbolic one.[46]

THE UNDERSTANDING OF SIN

Although every sin is associated with dung at some point, it is above all the carnal sins that were associated with excrement. This includes gluttony, which was commonly identified as Eve's sin when she ate the apple, the action that generated both excrement and sin in Eden. The link between excrement and carnal sin also coheres strongly with the observations of Paul Rozin and others, outlined in my Chapter 1, that disgust is intrinsically tied to bodily corruption and violations and that excrement is an ineluctable source of disgust. Bernard of Clairvaux expressed it in medieval terms:

> Nos vero qui jam de populo exivimus; qui mundi quaeque pretiosa ac speciosa pro Christo reliquimus . . . cuncta denique oblectamenta corporea arbitrati sumus ut stercora [Phil. 3:8].[47]

> Truly we who have retired from society, we who have relinquished all the precious and lovely things of the world for Christ . . . in the end, all bodily delights we regard as dung.

To regard corporeal delights—corporeal sins—as dung meant to regard them with disgust, and thereby to distance oneself from them. Dung hence becomes a way to think about the world. Worldly things are revealed in their true qualities as dung in relation to their contrary, God; thus in addition to characterizing the precious things of the world as empty delights, the statement establishes the antitheses upon which the moral and material universe is founded.

It is apposite that the human body should reflect and express truths about human history, since the image of the body is central to the relation between God and humankind. The body was, of course, made in God's image, as recounted by Genesis 1:27: "et creavit Deus hominem ad imaginem suam; ad imaginem Dei creavit illum" ("and God created man in his image; in the image of God he created him").

Above all, the body is the locus of God's contact with humankind, representing in its pure state the union of humankind with the divine and in its earthly state the corruption with which the earthly world has been afflicted. The body was essential to the understanding of sin, and excrement was essential to an understanding of the way sin afflicted the body.

Since the mortal body was a site of sin, any situation in which the body was unregulated was a source of danger. Clothing not only covered the body but contained it; thus the uncovered body was tantamount to the sinful body. This assumption was even inscribed in law: in later medieval England it was a commonplace of both culture and law that a couple seen naked and in bed together were guilty of sexual intercourse, so much so that there was a legal formula for the situation: *solus cum sola, nudus cum nuda*.[48] The phrase emphasizes the two principal occasions for sin: privacy and nudity. Even nudity alone was morally perilous, as suggested by Scripture. Genesis 3 made clear that original sin was intimately connected with the issue of nakedness: the eating of the forbidden fruit was followed by an awareness of nakedness and by the first feelings of shame about the naked body. In response Adam and Eve made the first covering, from fig leaves, and later God himself made clothes for them (Gen. 3:20). Thus the shame of nakedness, as well as the necessity for clothes to veil that nakedness, is rooted in sin. Removing those clothes exposed a person to shame; and the injunction of Erasmus may be repeated here:

> Membra quibus natura pudorem addidit retegere citra necessitatem procul abesse debet ab indole liberali. Quin ubi necessitas huc cogit, tamen id quoque decente verecundia faciendum est, etiam si nemo testis adsit. Nunquam enim non adsunt angeli, quibus in pueris gratissimus est pudicitae comes custosque pudor.
>
> A well-bred person should always avoid exposing without necessity the parts to which nature has attached modesty. If necessity compels this, it should be done with decency and reserve, even if no witness is present. For angels are always present, and nothing is more welcome to them in a boy than modesty, the companion and guardian of decency.[49]

Thus nudity is not merely an offense against human onlookers; even in their absence a freeness about the body may offend the spiritual. Certain parts of the body are ignoble by nature, and they must be dealt with not just with privacy, but with shame. Although Erasmus's own delicacy prevents him from identifying those parts specifically, it is clear that the shameful parts are those to do with excretion.

So the exposure of the body, alone or with another, was perilous, and the exposure of the lower parts most perilous. This made latrines a site of moral peril. Exposure, if only to the self and angels, was a necessary part of a latrine visit, and concern about this is expressed in both admonitions and in latrine design. Writing in 845, the monk Hildemar decreed that boys visiting the monastic privy at night had to be accompanied by three elders, one with a lamp—to light their way, but undoubtedly also to ensure that no sinful mischief took place in the latrine late at night.[50] Monastic latrines were often constructed in rows with partitions between the seats to ensure privacy and separation between latrine-goers. Indeed, the need for privacy was such that neighboring stalls were sometimes designed to be entered on opposite sides—for instance, the first from the east, the second from the west, the third from the east, the fourth from the west, and so on—an ingenious design that ensured a monk would not see the occupants entering the stalls immediately adjacent to his.

This arrangement contrasts with pre-Christian practices such as those of the Romans, who eased themselves in communal toilets without barriers. Rather than being arranged in rows like medieval latrines, Roman latrines were often designed as four sides of a square, forming communal spaces with a genuine community function. Medieval Christian latrines, by contrast, were constructed to ensure that elimination was a private and solitary practice. Although the Christian emphasis on privacy meant that there was less opportunity for interpersonal mischief, there was correspondingly greater opportunity for personal relaxation of the denial of the flesh. The individual was alone with the body, partially unclothed, and might let down his or her guard against sensual pleasure. The latrine was the kingdom of the lower body, especially that part of the lower body that was both *down* and *back*, and thus that part in which greater sin naturally inhered; and so it is no surprise that the latrine was a source of mortal danger. It was the site of the *requisita naturae*, not in the sense of the modern expression "nature calls," suggesting a benign physicality, but in the sense that it is in the nature of earthly, mortal, corrupt beings to generate corruption.

The peril and abominability of the body was underscored by its nature: in a kind of grotesque transubstantiation, it transforms the pure into the corrupt.[51] As Alcuin admonished in the eighth century,

> Quod commedisti et bibisti hesterno, hodie stercus est, quod non dico tangere, sed etiam horrescis videre. Tales sunt nostrae voluptates: stercus et putredo. Talia sunt corpora, in quae deperimus, omni putredine et inmunditia sordidiora, dum in sepulchro iacent.[52]

> What you ate and drank yesterday is dung today, which you find horrifying to look at, let alone touch. Such are our pleasures: dung and corruption. Such are the bodies in which we perish, in every putrefaction and the basest filth, when we lie in the tomb.

The body transmutes pleasures into dung, generates dung and becomes as dung. Pope Innocent III concurred, noting, "quanto sunt delicaciora cibaria, tanto fetidiora sunt stercora,"[53] "the more delicate are the foods, the more the excrement stinks." A fourteenth-century preachers' handbook elaborates on the theme:

> Nota eciam quod caro hominis potest dici terra pessima et fetidissima. Ceteris autem terris apponuntur stercora ut frucificent, set econtra terra corporis hominis appositis cibariis delicatissimis nichil fructificat nisi stercora, et quanto preciosiora sunt cibaria, tanto ad secessum perveniencia sunt viliora.[54]

> Note also that the flesh of man can be called the worst and most fetid kind of earth. For dung is put on other pieces of land so that they may be fruitful, but by contrast when the earth of the body of man is given the most delightful food, it bears no fruit but dung, and the more precious are the foods, so much more vile is that which goes down into the latrine.

The human body, producer of dung, becomes an engine of corruption. Sermons returned to the theme repeatedly to drive home the point that the body was to be despised for its corrupt nature. As the same handbook declared:

> Nam corpus corrumpit quicquid infunditur, sicut vas corruptum liquorem reddit fetidum aliquatenus ei infusum. . . . Inde enim est quod plus fetet os gulosi quam maximus fimarius.[55]

> For the body corrupts whatever is put into it, just as a bad vessel lends a stench to whatever is poured into it. . . . Hence for that reason the mouth of a glutton stinks more than the biggest dunghill.

Even when other images are proffered—the body as piece of land or bad container—the dungheap returns to the picture. Unlike pieces of land or bad containers, dung produces an immediate and visceral disgust response, and unlike other images, it is profoundly tied to the lived experience of the body. This too made it a more immediately potent illustration of corporeal foulness than the decay of the body after death. Although decomposition was the manifestation of that corruption that ultimately awaited the body, it was not experienced on a daily basis; but excretion was. Thus excrement became the more powerful reminder of man's sinful nature. In this way the disgust evoked by excrement could be turned to moral purposes, to provoke a reaction to sin equivalent to the disgust engendered by material corruption.

A widely circulating story from the *Vitae Patrum* illustrates the equivalence of moral and material disgust. An angel was helping a desert father bury the bodies of the dead:

> Nec de fetore illorum horrebat sicut senex, set transeunte quodam iuvene luxurioso, nares suas obturavit dicens quod in centuplum plus fetebat coram Deo et angelis quam quodcumque aliud cadaver corruptum. Set quod dolendum est, hunc fetorem ipsi luxuriosi non senciunt, eo quod naturaliter inter fetentes fetor non sentitur. Unde illud Ioelis: "Computruerunt iumenta in stercore suo." Unde dicit Gregorius: "Iumenta, inquit, in stercore putrescere est homines brutales in fetore luxurie vitam finire." Unde Psalmista: "Disperierunt in Endor, facti sunt ut stercus terre." Unde Gregorius: "Endor, inquit, est fons generacionis vel oculus naturalis," et bene significat voluntatem humanam que operi carnali et generacioni deservit, et non sequitur racionem set sensualitates. Et ideo tales propter sui vilitatem bene comparantur stercori terre, etc.[56]

> The angel was not as much stunned by their stench as the desert father was; but when a lecherous young man walked by, he stopped his nose saying that he stank a hundred times worse before God and his angels than any decomposing corpse. But it is to be feared that

> lechers themselves cannot smell this stench, because it is natural that an evil smell is not felt among people who produce it. Hence the words of Joel: "The beasts have rotted in their dung." On which Gregory comments: "Beasts rotting in their dung signify bestial people who end their lives in the stench of lechery." Hence the Psalmist: "They perished at Endor, they became like dung of the earth." And Gregory comments: "Endor means 'the fountain of procreation' or 'the natural eye,'" and signifies man's will that is busy about the work of the flesh and of procreation and does not follow reason but its sensual pleasure. Therefore, such people are, on account of their baseness, compared to the dung of the land.[57]

It is significant here that the sinner whose moral stench was so odious was one who desired the body. His sin was emphatically carnal, and the reader is reminded that the bodies desired by the lecher both stink in life (to the pure, if not to the sinful) and are destined to be decaying corpses thereafter. Thus sinners are like animals, acting from carnality without reason. The sinful body was nothing more than a perambulant cadaver or—since a decaying corpse was akin to dung—a perambulant dungheap.

To be pure, it was necessary to abjure the lower body and its temptations. Those who failed to do so were sinners, who dwelt in the lower realms of their bodies on earth and, after suffering the ultimate corruption, death, were doomed to dwell in the *infernus*, or depths, thereafter. The sexual and sensual sins inherent in the lower body were clear, and many succumbed to them.

If sinners were Christians giving way to the lower body, and being, in effect, taken over by excrement and sin, sinners' corpses, devoid of the spirit, were entirely corrupt and could be entirely compared to excrement. This identification had the authority of the often-quoted passage of Joel 1:17: "they shall rot like beasts in their dung." The thirteenth-century chronicler Salimbene de Adam tells a number of allegedly true stories with this motif. In one, a lecherous canon is strangled to death by the devil and buried in a cesspool near a pigpen.[58] Having become spiritually rotten through carnal desires, it was appropriate that the canon was buried in a place of dung; the proximity of the pigpen, the dwelling of animals renowned for their filth, underscores the theme of ordure. The canon's carnal sins have transmuted him into something entirely material and hence corrupt. In another story told by Salimbene, Lord Guido de Sesso, whom Salimbene identifies as a terrible enemy of the Church, perishes when his horse falls into the cesspool of the lepers at Modena.[59] It was a doubly symbolic fate in that Lord Guido died not just in a cesspool, already a locus of filth, but in the cesspool of lepers, those human exemplars of corruption.

Other narratives focused on the bowels as the vessels of excrement and sin alike. If excrement is corruption both moral and physical, it stands to reason that sin should arise in the bowels, and indeed this is how it was regarded. The idea that the bowels were the dwelling place of demons appears as early as Lactantius's fourth-century *Divinae Institutiones*. Lactantius explains that demons infiltrate the body, giving rise to both corporeal and moral maladies:

> qui quoniam spiritus sunt tenues et inconprehensibiles, insinuant se corporibus hominum et occulte in uisceribus operati ualetudinem uitiant, morbos citant, somniis animos terrent, mentes furoribus quatiunt.[60]

> And since spirits are slight and not to be grasped, they insinuate themselves into the bodies of men and, secretly working in their viscera, impair their well-being, hasten diseases, terrify their souls with dreams, harass their minds with turmoil.

Whether *viscera* here denotes the bowels or merely "innards," this is part of a long-lived tradition that envisioned demons as invading the body in the most material and literal sense. Caesarius of Heisterbach concurred in identifying the bowels as a dwelling place of demons, being careful to specify that by *viscera* he did mean the bowels:

Quomodo daemones sint in hominibus.

> NOVICIUS: ... Quidam asserunt, daemones non esse in hominibus, sed extra, eo quod castrum; non intus, sed extra dicatur obsideri. ...
> MONACHUS: ... Non potest esse diabolus in anima humana.... Illabi autem menti, illi soli possibile est qui creavit.... Mentem hominis iuxta substantiam nihil implere potest, nisi creatrix Trinitas.
> NOVICIUS: Quid est ergo quod diabolus dicitur cor hominis intrare, tentare vel immittere?
> MONACHUS: Non aliter intrat vel implet vel immittit, nisi quod animam decipiendo in affectum malitiae trahit. Et haec est differentia inter adventum Spiritus sancti et spiritus maligni, quod ille proprie dicitur illabi, iste immitti.... Cum diabolus dicitur esse in homine, non intelligendum est de anima, sed de corpore, quia in concavitatibus eius et in visceribus ubi stercora continentur, et ipse esse potest.[61]

How Demons Can Be Inside People:

> Novice: ... Some assert that demons cannot be inside people, only outside, just as a fortress may be said to be besieged not from inside, but from outside...

Monk: ... The devil cannot be in a human soul. ... For to move into the mind is possible only to he who created it. ... Nothing is able to fill the mind of a man, according to its substance, except the Creator Trinity.

Novice: Why therefore is the devil said to enter, tempt, or push into the heart of man?

Monk: He does not enter or fill or push into it in any way except that he draws the soul into a disposition to evil through deception. And this is the difference between the coming of the Holy Spirit and of an evil spirit, that the one is said to flow in, the other pushes in. ... When the devil is said to dwell in a man, this should not be understood as concerning the soul, but rather the body, because he is in its empty spaces and in its viscera where the dung is kept, and there he is able to dwell.[62]

Demons are thus understood as inhabitants on the physical realm, from where they may try to influence the soul. This understanding of demons as physical indwellers accords with the view espoused by Gerald of Wales, who told the story of the demon that could not be dislodged by the Eucharist because the Eucharist treats the soul and not the body. As demons are evil, they have a physical rather than a spiritual form, notwithstanding that they are apparently invisible; and their evil nature ensures that they should lodge in the bowels, the physical location of sin. In this context it is clear that it was no mere metaphor when Peter Damian condemned simony as "primam omnium haereseorum ex imis diaboli visceribus erumpentem,"[63] "the first of all the heresies to erupt from the deepest bowels of the devil."

Other sources echo this conception of the bowels. Roger of Wendover's thirteenth-century chronicle, the *Flores Historiarum*, applies this schema to Richard I. Roger reports that Richard ordered his body to be interred near the feet of his father at Font-Evrault and bequeathed his heart to the church at Rouen, with his *viscera* to Poictou. Richard then revealed his reasons: with his body he gave homage to his father, in reparation for the damage he had done to him; his heart he gave to Rouen in recognition of the inhabitants' loyalty; and to the citizens of Poictou "propter notam proditionis, stercora sua reliquit, quos non alia sui corporis portione dignos judicavit," "he left his dung, in accordance with their treachery, to those whom he judged unworthy of any other part of his body."[64]

The judicial process could also reflect this understanding of the innards as the breeding-ground for sin. In thirteenth- and fourteenth-century Britain, punishment was often related to the biological parts identified as the origin of the crimes. A prominent example is the sentence of the Scots rebel William Wallace, who was sentenced to be drawn, hanged, beheaded and disembowelled in 1305. The edict stated: "cor, hepar et pulmo et omnia interiora ipsius Willelmi, a quibus tam perversae cogitationes processerunt, in ignem mittantur et comburentur," "let the heart, liver, lungs and all the innards of this man William, from which his evil thoughts arose, be thrown in the fire and burnt up."[65] Similar sentences, specifically identifying the heart and entrails as the wellsprings of wickedness, were passed on a number of others. These included the Welsh prince Dafydd ap Gruffydd in 1282; the record specifies that his bowels (*viscera*) were burned because his blasphemy was committed on the day of the Lord's Passion.[66] Others who paid similar penalties included Andrew de Harclay, the earl of Carlisle, in 1323, whose "coer & bouels & ent[r]ailles" (heart and bowels and entrails) were burnt because they had given rise to his "treitrouses pensees" (treacherous thoughts); and a treacherous knight named Gilbert of Middleton in 1318.[67]

These men were charged with treason or related crimes, and their punishment recapitulates the understanding of the death of Judas, whose treachery was said to have been fomented in his bowels. This interpretation was buttressed by a pair of Biblical passages. Matthew 27:5 recorded that Judas hanged himself: "καὶ ριψας τα αργυρια εν τω ναω ανεχωρησεν και απελθων απηγξατο," "And [Judas] threw the money into the temple and left. And he went away and hanged himself." Acts 1:18 had an alternate version of his death: "καὶ πρηνὴς γενόμενος ἐλάκησεν μέσος, καὶ ἐξεχύθη πάντα τὰ σπλάγχνα αὐτοῦ," "and falling headlong, his body burst open and all his intestines spilled out." Jerome's translation of Acts 1:18 for the Vulgate conflated these accounts, rendering the Greek πρηνὴς γενόμενος ("falling headlong") as *suspensus*, "hanged." Thus the Vulgate Acts 1:18 reads "et suspensus crepuit medius, et diffusa sunt omnia viscera eius," "and, hanged, he burst in the middle, and his bowels gushed out."

Later commentators preserved this striking detail of the scene and supplied interpretation. The earliest retellings of Judas's death, such as those of Juvencus and Arator, had his bowels slipping out of his anus.[68] Subsequent formulations held that the bowels burst out of his belly. Whichever scenario was favored, both reflected and contributed to a popular understanding of the bowels as the seat of treachery.[69] Each aspect of the event held symbolic significance, as Bede's *Expositio Actuum Apostolorum* serves to illustrate:

> *Et suspensus crepuit medius* [Acts 1:18]. Dignam sibi poenam traditor amens inuenit, ut uidelicet guttur quo uox proditionis exierat laquei nodus necaret. Dignum etiam locum interitus quaesiuit, ut qui hominum angelorumque dominum morti tradiderat, caelo terraeque perosus, quasi aeriis tantummodo spiritibus sociandus [cf. Eph. 2:2], iuxta exemplum Achitophel et Absalon qui regem Dauid persecuti sunt, aeris medio periret, [cf. II Rg 17:23, 19:9]; cui utique satis digno exitu mors ipsa successit, ut uiscera quae dolum proditionis conceperant rupta caderent et uacuas euoluerentur in auras. Cuius simillima poenae mors Arrium heresiarchem damnasse refertur, ut quia ille humanitatem Christi, iste diuinitatem extinguere moliebatur, ambo sicut sensu inanes uixerant sic quoque uentre uacui perirent.[70]

"And being hanged, he burst asunder in the middle" [Acts 1:18]. The insane traitor found himself a worthy punishment, because the knot of the noose brought death to the throat from which the voice of betrayal had issued. He also found a place suitable for his destruction, for he who had delivered the Lord of men and angels to death, he who was hateful to heaven and earth, died in the middle of the air, as if he were a fit associate of the spirits of the air, as in the example of Achitophel and Absalon, who had persecuted King David. Death also came to him in a fitting way, as the viscera which had conceived the deceitful betrayal burst and fell open, and unrolled into the empty air. His punishment was very similar to the death to which Arius the archheretic is said to have been condemned, and so where the one sought to deny the humanity of Christ, and the other his divinity, both had lived as if devoid of sense, and thus died with bellies empty.

In this interpretation the bowels are identified as the source of treachery, but the emptiness of the body corresponds to a lack of sense, implying that some kind of reason or righteousness might have dwelt in their viscera if the men had only been virtuous. This tradition was echoed in Sedulius's *Carmen Paschale*. Later tradition connects the entrails more specifically with Satan, as in commentary found in Drogo and Bernard of Clairvaux:

Exterioris poenae qualitas, supplicii modum aperuit, quia *per quae peccaverit* homo, *per haec punietur* (Sap. xi). *Suspensus crepuit medius* (Act i), plenus erat venter, et ruptus est. Uter crepuit medius ubi sedes erat Satanae, crepuit ergo vas contumeliae.[71]

The kind of external punishment reveals the mode of the supplicant, for *the way in which a man sins, by that he shall be punished. Hanged, his bowels burst*, his belly was full, and it burst. The middle bag burst, where the seat of Satan was, and therefore the vessel of evil burst.

The passage makes it clear that the bowels and belly are the stronghold of Satan and are intimately connected with the evil and treachery of Judas. These connections took like forms in other commentators. In the ninth century Hincmar of Reims connected the manner of Judas's death to his sinful behavior at the Last Supper. Since Judas took this first communion in a state of wickedness, he was possessed by the devil when he swallowed the bread and wine. Hincmar explains that this led to the bursting of his bowels, because "cum intravit sanctus panis in plenum de iniquitate ventrem, intravit hostis antiquus, qui dicitur diabolus et Satanas, in crudelem et impiam mentem,"[72] "when the holy bread entered the belly full of wickedness, the old enemy, who is called the devil and Satan, entered his cruel and impious mind." It is as if Judas's greed and gluttony made his mind and his belly identical, so that the devil that entered

126 *Sin and Filth in Medieval Culture*

his mind did so by lodging in his bowels. Other texts had variants of this interpretation. The thirteenth-century *Legenda aurea*, for example, echoed Bede in identifying the bowels as the engine of evil: "Dignum etiam erat ut uiscera que proditionem conceperant rupta caderent," "It was also fitting that the bowels which had conceived the treachery should burst and fall out."[73]

A more elaborate interpretation of the bowels as a seat of evil involved the location of Judas's soul. When Judas died, his soul had to leave the body. As we have seen, souls conventionally exited the dying through the mouth, consonant with the understanding that the soul dwelt in the upper half of the body, in the brain or heart or both. But Judas had been kissed by Jesus, meaning that his mouth had been in contact with the divine and

Figure 11 It was his intestines that gave rise to Judas's treachery and so the devil takes his soul from his intestines, which have burst when he hanged himself. The soul is represented as a small human figure. English, second quarter of the 14th century. Holkham Bible Picture Book © The British Library Board: London, British Library Add. MS 47682 (Holkham 666), fol. 30r.

could not serve as an outlet for his sinful soul. Instead the soul was forced to break out directly from its place of habitation, the bowels, where his treachery had lodged. This was the explanation espoused by the *Glossa ordinaria* in the early twelfth century. The *Glossa* borrowed Hrabanus Maurus's account of Judas's death, but reverted to the earlier explanation that his bowels had come out through the anus rather than through the belly.[74] The *Glossa* also adds the significant explanation that evil had come *in* through the anus—whereupon, presumably, it had lodged in the bowels, just as others reported that the bowels were the dwelling place of Satan. The *Glossa* explains:

> Viscera igitur que sunt sedes fraudis: tanto scelere dirupta: se cohibere non valuerunt. Merito autem per sedem doli viscera funduntur non per locum osculi i. os quo osculatus est ihesum quamvis falsa superficie, sed per alium cui virus occultę malicię inerat.[75]

> The bowels, therefore, which are the seat of deceit, burst open by such a great crime, could not hold together. Fittingly, moreover, the bowels poured out through the seat of treachery, not through the site of the kiss, that is, the mouth where Jesus was kissed, albeit with deceitful insincerity; but through another place by which which the poison of hidden evil had entered.

Since the place by which the bowels poured out was clearly the anus, the *Glossa* is affirming that the anus is the entry point for treachery and evil, the site of the greatest bodily vulnerability to sin. If demons could lodge in the physical bowels, it made sense that they had to gain entry in a physical rather than immaterial way, and it was logical again that they should do so via the foulest orifice of the body.

This understanding of the bowels was rehearsed widely not just in theological treatises but on a more popular scale, in religious drama. The death of Judas was a popular topic of drama: devils were often depicted waiting, frustrated, because Judas's soul does not come out of his mouth. The play then has the bowels burst, which allows the devils to carry the soul away. The scene appears, for instance, in *Le Mystère de la Passion*, written in Angers in 1486, which shows the devils searching for Judas's soul after his suicide:

> Berith: L'ame est encor dedans ses trippes,
> qui de son ordure s'abreuve;
> et, si la pence ne luy creve,
> nous perdons cy nostre saison.
>
> Sathan: Berith a tres bonne raison,
> car, par sa bouche orde et maligne

qui baisa son maistre tant digne,
elle ne peult ne doit passer.

Ycy creve Judas par le ventre et les trippes saillent dehors et l'ame sort.[76]

Berith: The soul is still in his bowels,
which quenches its thirst from their ordure;
and if the soul does not burst the belly,
we're wasting our time.

Sathan: Berith has a good point,
for by his filthy and evil mouth
which kissed his master so worthy,
the soul couldn't come out.

Here Judas breaks open at the stomach and his intestines come out and the soul departs.

Here the sinful soul dwells in the bowels rather than in the upper body and consumes the dung ("de son ordure s'abreuve"), certainly a very material depiction of Judas's corrupt moral state. Shortly beforehand, in the play, Judas has spoken his last will and testament, which juxtaposes upper and lower in leaving his nose to smell the stench of ordure, so that even his head, the loftiest part of the body, will not escape the fetid lowliness of dung:

Item, j'abandonne mon nés
a sentire l'ordure punaise
de l'ort bourbier de la fournaise.[77]

Item: I leave my nose
to smell the fetid ordure
of the horrid place of fire.

The repetition of the term *ordure* draws a parallel between the filth of hell and that contained in Judas's bowels: dung, but also sin. It is as if his bowels, the dwelling place of sin, are an outpost of hell.

The association of Judas with the bowels was so strong that it even makes an appearance in apocryphal variants. In the Greek apocryphal tradition, transmitted by the second-century bishop Papias of Hierapolis, Judas is killed by being crushed by a chariot so that his bowels gush out.[78] His treachery is so great that it is as if it cannot be expressed without reference to an origin in the foulest part of the human body, the bowels.

As Bede noted, the heretic Arius was renowned as a victim of the lower body: he served in effect as a posttype of Judas. A priest of the late third century, Arius was responsible for the Arian heresy; the story of his shameful and scatalogical death was thought to be eminently suitable for a heretic, and the tale circulated widely. It is found in Athanasius's *De morte Arii* and *Ad episcopos Aegipti* and was promulgated to the Middle Ages through Eusebius's *Ecclesiastical History* (published in 325), which reached the West through Rufinus's translation and continuation (published in 402 or 403).[79] Rufinus's version reads:

> Arrius ad ecclesiam pergens episcoporum et populorum frequentia constipatus, humanae necessitatis causa ad publicum locum declinat. ubi cum sederet, intestina eius atque omnia viscera in secessus cuniculum defluxere; ita tali in loco dignam mortem blasfemae et foetidae mentis exsolvit.[80]

> Arius, cramped by a crowd of bishops and people, proceeded and went down to a public provision for reasons of human necessity. When he sat down there, his intestines and all of his innards slipped down into the hole of the privy; and so in such a place he discharged a death worthy of his blasphemous and fetid mind.

As Willis Johnson has pointed out, Rufinus's wordplay on *constipatus* (cramped/constipated), *pergens/purgans* (proceeding/excreting) and *exsolvit* (discharged/loosed dung) heightens the emphasis on the excremental nature of Arius's fate.[81] The term *declinat* (went down, lowered himself) adds to the symbolism of the narrative: he is moving to a literally and morally inferior state. It was as if Arius was infected by his corrupt lower body; his mind became fetid as if it too had moved to his bowels, and hence his entire body was transformed into corruption. His fate reenacts that of Judas as reported by the early writers such as Juvencus and Arator, in which the intestines slip out through the anus. In a sense the soul has become one with the dung-filled bowels, transmuted from what should be lofty and spiritual into something foul and material.

Commentators and exegetes were not slow to take up the significance of Arius's death and told a number of stories that illustrated the potential of the sinful body to be transformed into the stuff of sin, or dung. It is important to note that these narratives are not intended as literary fancies with excremental metaphors; they are written as religious history, both monitory and devotional, and above all factual. Composed in Latin, they were addressed to the most learned and theologically sophisticated sectors of society. Sinners' deaths in the privy were not positioned by exegetes as handy metaphors, but ordained by God as powerful indicators of the consonance of the moral and the material, and of the very real wages of sin. In the case of the first-hand or close-at-hand narratives, commentators shaped the narrative of actual deaths according to a larger understanding of the role of sin and dung in the world. How factually accurate these accounts were, we have no way of knowing: what we can view is how the writers felt the world worked, and in this we can see the powerful roles played by these elements.

In the sixth century, Arator tied Arius's fate to that of Judas, emphasizing the motion of falling. Unspoken but implied is the reminder that the first fall was that of the wayward angels; this is recapitulated as they lure the minds of men to fall, exemplified by the fall of their bowels:

> Qui criminis auctor
> Errorisque tui est, fusa ruit Arius alvo
> Infelix, plus mente cadens, letumque peremptus
> Cum Iuda commune tulit, qui gutture pendens,
> Visceribus vacuatus obit, nec poena sequestrat
> Quos per culpa ligat, qui maiestatis honori
> Vulnus ab ore parant; hic prodidit, ille diremit,
> Sacrilega de voce rei.[82]

Unlucky Arius, who is the author of your crime and of your error, tumbled down with his bowels poured out, [though] falling more in his mind, and in dying bore a common death with Judas, who, hanging by his neck, died emptied of his entrails, nor does the punishment separate those [two] whom an equal fault bound together, who fashioned a wound on the honor of the majesty [of the Holy Trinity] by their mouth; the one betrayed, the other divided, [each] guilty by a sacrilegious voice.[83]

A similar morality tale appears in Gregory of Tours's sixth-century *History of the Franks*, which recounts the story of a priest and enemy of the bishop Sidonius Apollinaris. Scheming to overthrow Sidonius, the priest withdraws to the privy to think over his plot, and in his sinful scheming is overcome by the literal foulness. Gregory relates:

> Ingressus autem in secessum suum, dum ventrem purgare nititur, spiritum exalavit. Expectat enim eum puer a foris cum cereo dominum egressurum. Iamque advenerat lux. . . . elevato puer velo ostii repperit dominum super sellula secessi defunctum. Unde indubitatum est, non minoris criminis hunc reum esse quam Arrium illum, cui similiter in secessum fuerunt interna deposita per partis inferioris egestum.[84]

He went into his privy, and while he strained to purge his belly he lost his soul. Indeed a boy was waiting for him outside with a candle, expecting his master to come out. Dawn had already come. . . . the boy, lifting up the curtain of the doorway, found his master dead on the seat of the privy. Whence it cannot be doubted that this man was guilty of no less a crime than that of Arius, who similarly poured out his innards by emptying his lower parts in the privy.

In both cases the sinner has given way to his corrupt nature entirely: he is entirely flesh, entirely corrupt. As in a number of other narratives, the soul seems to have been dwelling in the bowels, as if moral foulness had made it more like dung, material, corrupt and sinful, until finally it inhabited the place of dung and resulted in the ultimate triumph of corruption, death. Death converts the sinner entirely into corruption.

An even more striking example of the sinner as excrement is found in Walafrid Strabo's ninth-century *Life of St. Gall*, where an oppressive bishop pays for his sins by being overcome by the lower body:

> Nam intestina eius more sartaginis igni superpositae fervere coeperunt, et tam dirae viscerum tortiones illum invaserunt extemplo, ut sine aliorum adminiculo nequaquam egredi potuisset, sed, quod dicere pudet, egestio naturae turpi impetu prorumpens, cum asstantes nimio foetere gravaret, sine mora ab ecclesia eiectus, vehiculo, quo decedere monasterio posset, sicut rogaverat, est impositus. Sicque immoderato fluore, naturae consuetudine carens, vasi in quod egesta defluerent supersedens, egressus est. . . . Tali itaque poena multatus . . . post aliquot dies de cloaca corporis spiritum exhalavit.[85]

> For his intestines began to burn like a pan set on the fire, and such horrible twistings of his viscera penetrated him straightaway that he couldn't go out without support. But (as it is shameful to relate), when he oppressed the bystanders with a terrible stench, the evacuation of nature bursting open with a filthy onrush, and having been thrown out of the church without delay, he was laid, as he had requested, in the only conveyance by which he could leave the monastery. And thus he departed, sitting on a vessel into which his effusions flowed with immoderate force, not in the usual way of nature. . . . And thus with this reward for his deeds . . . after some days his spirit left the sewer of the body.

Here the agitation of his bowels represents the death throes of the sinner's soul, and his moral corruption has left his body a sewer. The same theme is found in other narratives, for instance that of a sinful oppressor named Radulphus who died when his bowels poured forth into a latrine. The man's son Hugo died in the same way, with, in addition, his mouth and tongue distended, "non ut homo, sed ut diabolus, moritur," "dying in the semblence not of a man, but of a devil."[86] In another story, told by Guibert of Nogent, a monk who had illicitly received and hidden money from a noblewoman failed to die with absolution because of an outpouring of diarrhea. The abbot had come to absolve him but found the monk sitting on a vessel to relieve himself, and the abbot withdrew from shame. Before absolution could be given, the Devil killed the monk. The account implies that absolution and defecation are at odds, almost contradictory; and it is as if the monk's sin took hold of his bowels, as in the case of Judas, and the Devil held sway as long as the monk continued to defecate.[87]

In other stories told by Guibert, sinners' refusal to repent becomes equivalent to soiling themselves with feces, so that they foul themselves on the spiritual and material level simultaneously. In one, a provost who persecutes the Church is called to repentence by the assembled clergy, in the name of Mary and patron saints. The provost refuses to repent but falls off his horse: "Sed inter ipsa verba, cum equo insideret, ruit, et sordidissimas bracas, quibus cingebatur, ventris profluvio mox sub se respersit," "But in the midst of these words, perched on the horse, he fell, and straightaway spattered the trousers he had girded on, most filthily beneath him with an overflow from his belly." A similar thing happened to a man who struck the reliquary of St. Just with his sword: he immediately fell to the ground and soiled himself.[88] Sin, in short, is homologous with defecation. In a third tale recounted by Guibert, it is as if the sinner, becoming excrement, has secreted himself in the latrine and slipped down the drop-slot to hell:

> praenominatam gloriosi domini Benedicti ecclesiam viro sanctissimo ac eruditissimo Abboni abbati praeripuit. Quem cum idem Abbo insecutus fuisset ut eum corripiens, oberrantem scilicet ovem, custodiae relegaret, eum forte Aurelianus offendit. Cujus adventu symoniacus ille comperto, nec effugium uspiam reperiens, ad latrinas, quasi alvi eum pondus urgeret, se contulit. Abbone itaque superveniente, requiritur, sed nusquam persona reperta, sola ejus cuculla unco appensa reperitur.[89]

> he seized the aforementioned church of our glorious lord Benedict from the most holy and learned abbot Abbo. When Abbo followed him so that, laying hold of him as of a straying sheep, he might take him into custody, he strove against him vigorously at Orléans. The simoniac, having heard of his arrival and not being able to find any way of escape, made for the latrine as if the heaviness of his bowels compelled him. When Abbo arrived he was sought after, but there was no person to be found; only his cowl was found hanging on a hook.

The latrine is perilous to sinners; as the realm of the Devil, it is there that the Devil claims his due. In this instance the simoniac has disappeared, apparently seized by the Devil; having shed his monastic role in the form of the cowl, he has vanished into the latrine, as if he has been taken down the privy hole into hell.

The authority of tradition stood behind such examples, as demonstrated in a story from the *Vita* of St. Gengulph, of the ninth or tenth century. Gengulph is a Burgundian nobleman whose wife has a wicked affair with a lustful cleric. The cleric, "diaboli vas effectus," "having been made a vessel of the Devil," murders Gengulph, and the murderer and the treacherous wife do a gleeful dance. Then:

> ut ventrem purgaret secessum petiit latrinarum: moxque ut diversorium petiit naturæ debitum persolvere, ad instar Judæ proditoris & Arii hæresiarchæ (quorum alter humanitatem Christi extinguere, alter inseparabilem Trinitatis unitatem nisus est dividere) *diffusa sunt viscera ejus* [Act 1:18]: & sicut erat vacuus sensu, sic vacuus quoque ventre remansit: sicque infelix . . . in cloacam descendit inferni.[90]
>
> he sought out the seat of the latrine so he could empty his belly; as soon as he sought out the private place to pay the debt of nature, in the likeness of Judas the traitor and Arius the archheretic (one of whom strove to deny the humanity of Christ, the other to split up the inseparable unity of the Trinity), his bowels poured out, and just as he was empty of sense, so he remained empty in his belly; and thus the wretched one . . . descended into the sewer of hell.

It was as if, becoming a vessel for the Devil, the Devil inhabited him and seized his soul, which appears to have migrated to his belly, as in so many other cases. With his belly emptied, his soul had departed, and the dung/soul dropped down the privy hole into hell. The wording betrays a knowledge of Bede's *Expositio Actuum Apostolorum* (quoted above), which compared Judas and Arius in nearly identical phrasing.[91] In the story of Gengulph, however, the wife also suffers a fitting punishment. Told that Gengulph's remains were giving rise to miracles, the wife responded, "Sic operatur virtutes Gengulphus quomodo anus meus," "Gengulph works miracles as much as my anus!"—whereupon a "vox nefanda" or wicked voice made an obscene sound from her bottom, and continued to do so on anniversaries of the murder for the rest of her life.[92] This is the motif of the "singing arse" found in other narratives: it was quoted from the Middle English *Alphabet of Tales*, written some five centuries later, in Chapter 3.[93] In the *Vita* of Gengulph it is particularly interesting, paired with the excremental fate of the partner in crime: they both have been reduced to carnal corruption, one by being effectively transformed into excrement in the privy, the other by inverting her upper and lower body. The wording in this instance implies that both have been possessed and literally inhabited by the Devil: he becomes a "diaboli vas," she emits a diabolic voice from her rear.

As should be clear from the abundance of examples, the moral peril of the latrine was widely understood. The theme is especially explicit in the story of a sinful twelfth-century monk named William Pigun, related in the *Gesta abbatum monasterii Sancti Albani*. Neglectful of the divine office, having given way to gluttony and love of drink, he has unrighteously entered the realm of the Devil in both a spiritual and a material sense. The narrative describes the scene:

> Contigit enim una noctium, ut idem flebilis memoriae Willelmus super sedile in secretiori dormitorio, Matutinarum oblitus, sederet, referto

ventre, potibus inebriatus, et cibariis ingurgitatus. Inclinato capite igitur, coepit dormitare, et dormitando strepitu stertere taedioso. Et sic de ebrietate in soporem, de sopore in mortem subitam, gradatim transmigravit; forte frigore correptus, sed potius, ut credi potest, divina percussus ultione. Nam cum cessasset per tracheam ebulliendo perstrepere, audita est in cloaca, ubi moriens sedebat, haec vox manifeste reboare,—"Cape, Sathan, cape, Sathan;" quod manifeste audierunt, qui tunc in dormitorio fratres extra chorum ob causam remanserunt. Sic igitur miser ille, simul cum stercore, animam turpiter egessit.[94]

For it happened one night that that William of doleful memory sat down on the seat in the dormitory privy, heedless of matins, belly stuffed, drunken with drinks and gorged with foods. Because of that his head grew lower and he began to sleep and, in sleeping, to snore in repugnant noisiness. And so he began to slip gradually from drunkenness to slumber, and from slumber to unexpected death; perhaps overcome by the cold, but more probably, as may be believed, stricken by divine retribution. For when he had ceased to sound out from his throat, this voice was heard resounding in the dungpit in which the dying man sat: "Seize him, Satan, seize him, Satan"; which those brothers who had then had cause to remain in the dormitory heard clearly. And in that way that wretch passed out his soul repulsively along with his dung.

The details of neglecting matins and subsequent carnal indulgence set up the scene, but the most telling indicator comes when the monk's head begins to grow lower. As he drifts into sleep and death, undefended by religious devotion, carnally dissolute, he has abandoned reason and lowers his head to become no better than an animal, bent-backed and ignorant of God. His lowering of the head is thus theologically significant, as outlined by Augustine, Bernard of Clairvaux and others in the previous chapter. The monk is asleep to God, and his snores obscure the demonic cry to Satan which might otherwise have been heeded and proven salvational. William's carnal deeds have reduced him to nothing but flesh and its attendant corruptions, excrement and death. His soul, like those of the previously described sinners, has clearly been moved to his belly by his carnality, and there, already in the realm of the Devil, it is vulnerable to seizure by Satan. This story hence forms a consummate paradigm of the way sin, excrement and death are allied, and the way they are employed in narrative to illuminate truths about damnation.

This idea of the bowels as the locus of sin also gives greater resonance to a popular story about a knight who sinned by dicing with the Devil. The Devil, winning, seizes the man, whose body bursts, leaving only his bowels, as if the sinner has been reduced to bowels alone. In the words of *An Alphabet of Tales*:

And his body breste & his bowels cleuyd on þe sclathe stonys. And on þe morn his bowels was fon, bod what at wurthed of þe bodie cuthe neuer man tell to þis day, & þai went & berid his bowels.[95]

And his body burst and his bowels split on the slate stones. And in the morning his bowels were found, but what had become of the body no one can tell to this day; and they went and buried his bowels.

As this narrative illustrates, the bowels were the danger zone of the body, the liminal space in which demons might always take up residence, seize the soul and overpower the sinner by force of corruption, transforming him into nothing more than bowels—sometimes literally, as in this case.

This transformation was most marked in the case of sinners who abandoned reason and let carnality rule their actions. But even the godly could be vulnerable through their bowels. In some narratives they are presented as the entryway of treachery. A prominent example of this is the legend of the death of King Edmund Ironside of England (d. 1016), who was said to have been murdered in the latrine, a victim of a traitor hiding symbolically in the pit of the privy.[96] Henry of Huntingdon recounted the most relevant version of the story in the early twelfth century. In this telling Edmund is so fearsome that the narrative implies that he would have vanquished any conventional assailant, but a traitor lowers himself to attack the king in his most secret and vulnerable parts:

Edmundus rex, post paucos exhinc dies, prodicione occisus est apud Oxineforde. Sic autem occisus est. Cum rex, hostibus suis terribilis et tremendissimus, in regno floreret, iuit nocte quadam in domum uacuationis ad requisita nature. Vbi filius Edrici ducis in fouea secretaria consilio patris delitescens, regem inter celanda cultello bis acuto percussit, et inter uiscera ferrum fugiens reliquit.

A few days after this, King Edmund was treacherously killed at Oxford. This is how he was killed. When the king, fearful and most formidable to his enemies, was prospering in his kingdom, he went one night to the lavatory to answer a call of nature. There the son of Ealdorman Eadric, who by his father's plan was concealed in the pit of the privy, struck the king twice with a sharp knife in the private parts, and leaving the weapon in his bowels, fled away.[97]

It was as if the only way treachery could find an entrance was through the lower body and the bowels and the latrine the only place that sin and mortality could prevail. The perfidy and cowardliness of the traitor are expressed through the choice of a latrine-pit as his hiding place. The narrative is constructed to give much greater weight to its symbolic elements than to the plausability of the plan as a method of assassination.

When the vulnerability of the bowels signifies the corrupt carnality of the sinner, opening the way for demons to enter his bowels, the demon and evil could sometimes be dislodged. In these instances the demon may be expelled not through the mouth but through the predictable carnal exit. This is the case in Sulpicius Severus's influential fifth-century life of St. Martin, in which the saint compels the devil to exit by means of a fetid "fluxu ventris," "discharge from the belly."[98] The same theme is elaborated in an account of an English youth by the name of Ædwin, contained in the twelfth-century *Liber Eliensis*. The youth was tempted away from compline by a demon and, consequently defenseless against demonic possession, fell into storms of madness and frenzy. He was healed at the tomb of the founding saint, whereupon he

> sensum reciperet et post paululum suum per fedos recessus vexatorem eiceret. Nam post sompnum iuvenis ad se reversus, nuntiavit custodibus suis se iam sanum sapere et de cetero penitus convaluisse, excepto quod ventris resolutio intestina torqueret et secreto exitu indigeret. Ductus ergo ad locum necessarium, tantam illico passus est effusionem ac si omnia viscera funderentur et post eiectum furorem mentis tantus eicitur fetor ventris, ut per omnes proximas officinas vix esset aer tolerabilis, corrupto flatu per omnes angulos se spargente, fumum eius vix aliquo evandente. Nec minor erat illa inmunditia, quam ante fuerat illa vesania, sed par sibi factus est uterque impetus, alter in excessu mentis horribilis, alter in fluxu ventris mirabilis, quasi nequissimus ille spiritus aut totus verteretur in stercus aut ipsas latrinas secum ferret eiectus.[99]

> recovered his reason and, shortly afterwards, ejected his tormentor through his foul orifices. For after his sleep, the young man, coming to his senses, gave word to his guards that he was now feeling well and had completely recovered in all other respects, except that the internal looseness of his stomach was torturing him, and was in need of evacuation in a privy. After being taken, therefore, to the necessary place, he experienced as great an efflux as if all his bowels were being poured out and, after the raving of his mind, such a stink of the stomach was ejected that the air throughout all the nearest domestic buildings was scarcely bearable, as the polluted exhalation spread itself through every nook and cranny, and scarcely anyone escaped its vapour. And this uncleanliness was no less extreme than the former madness, but rather, both attacks turned out equal, one to the other: one horrible because of his going out of his mind, the other astonishing, because of the effluvium of his stomach, as if that most evil spirit was either totally being changed into excrement or, on being ejected, was taking the latrines themselves with him.[100]

By modern standards this narrative is tasteless; it is only when we see it as a witness to a complex theological system that its exemplary value becomes clear. The legend is clearly a variant on a circulating monastic folk narrative, also exemplified by the previous story of William Pigun. In each, the victim imperils his soul by failing to attend the divine service, typically diverted by carnal cravings. This genre of admonitory tale—the terrible consequences of skipping services—must have been told frequently, particularly to truant young monastics.[101] The theme of the wayward monk was then often combined with the motif of diabolical death in the latrine, so that the death was understood as a consequence of the waywardness. The fact that these are widely circulating motifs does not mean they were regarded as fictitious; indeed, each time something approaching the legend happened it could be understood more easily by framing it as another instance of the already accepted mode of demonic justice. The examples of Sulpicius Severus and the *Liber Eliensis* are distinctive in emphasizing the correspondence of the spiritual and the physical: the demonic madness is explicitly paralled by physical effluvium, the demon seemingly able to take either form. Though this idea underlies the entire genre of wayward monk/deadly latrine tales, it is made nicely explicit here, with the equation of the devil and the latrine underscored in the final passage of the story of Ædwin.

Above all, then, to sin is to inhabit the lower body and to come to exist wholly as that corruption—excrement—which is its hallmark. It is no wonder that latrines constitute a danger to such people: as a locus of bodily corruption, they function as an outpost of hell, indeed, as a dropslot directly to the infernal realms. This accords with a common depiction of the entrance to hell in medieval iconography, the hellmouth, in which hell is depicted as an animal that swallows the sinner.[102] In many medieval depictions of hell, the sinners reach hell by becoming excrement in a literal sense and being excreted into hell. This appears, for instance, in Taddeo's late-fourteenth-century Last Judgment, as well as in Bosch's depiction of Hell, in which the Devil sits on a privy and excretes sinners into the pit.[103] A popular textual source for the idea was the *Vision of Tondal*, first written in 1149 and surviving in two hundred forty-three manuscripts, in Latin, German, French, Dutch, Italian, Icelandic and English. In hell, according to the *Vision*, the "beast that eats unchaste priests and nuns" consumes their souls and then defecates them out again.[104] The danger is then that in the latrine, attending to the corrupt body, sinners may lose sight of their spiritual nature, become transformed wholly into corruption and drop down into hell as if swallowed and excreted by the hell-beast.

Excrement can be an essential component of hell in other ways, as in a Middle English version of *St. Patrick's Purgatory*, in which the narrator describes his vision of hell: "and þan I saw the fendes turnyng here arses toward þe sowles, shytyng vppon hem, the whiche dirt stonk so fowle þat it was a passyng payn" "and then I saw the demons turning their arses toward the souls, shitting upon them, the filth from which stank so foully that it caused exceeding torment."[105] St. John explains that this is because the sinners were clerics whose fruit in life was "stinking sin and unclean living." Similar images abound: in Taddeo di Bartolo's depiction of Hell at the Collegiata di San Gimignano, for instance, a demon is defecating coins into the mouth of a swollen figure labeled USURIO, with AVARITIA inscribed underneath.[106] The punishment is not just foul, but symbolic: the sinners are repaid with the foulness that they loosed upon the world in their earthly existence.

If sinners were those who had given way to the lower body and, in effect, taken over by excrement and sin, sinners' corpses, devoid of the spirit, were entirely corrupt and could be entirely compared to excrement. This identification had the authority of the widely quoted passage from Joel 1:17: "they shall rot like beasts in their dung." Salimbene de Adam's stories, cited previously, utilize this motif. The lecherous canon buried in a cesspool near a pigpen is a prime example.[107] The cesspool as a burial site emphasizes the excessive corruption of the canon, while the detail of the pigs underscores the carnal nature of his sin, magnifying the fleshly aspects of the punishment. Pigs were known not only for being generally odorous and gluttonous, but especially to be despised because they ate dung. The tale of Lord Guido de Sesso, the sinner who died in the lepers' cesspool, is likewise overtly symbolic, with the lepers serving as the sinners whose corruption is most manifest and exaggerated. A similar fate was assigned to Theodoric, ruler of the Ostrogoths. Salimbene de Adam enumerates his wrongdoing: he was an Arian, he persecuted those of conventional faith, and he executed Boethius, Symmachus and Pope John. In response, Salimbene reports, Pope Gregory had Theodoric disinterred from his tomb in Ravenna and thrown into a pit of dung.[108]

These equations were to be found in all periods of the Middle Ages. Gregory the Great told another story in which a sinner's body is equated to dung. A monk has committed the sin of illicitly hiding three gold sous. When he dies, he is ordered to be buried in a dungheap with the sous, with everyone calling out "Pecunia tua tecum sit in perditione!", "May your money be with you in perdition!"[109] Since the monk's soul was corrupt, his body is deposited in a place of material corruption. The cry of the monks connects the dungheap to hell, suggesting that the dungheap is a prefiguration of hell on earth. The equation is drawn between the sinner's corrupt carnality, the filth of earthly life and money. This is not in any Freudian sense that dung is like money, but rather in the conviction that money is like dung: a material source of corruption.

However the body was reduced to its unspiritual state, the equation of the body and dung was shocking. This is the case in an eleventh-century Latin poem, *De marito ab uxore turpiter interempto*, in which an adulterous wife murders her husband and hides the body in a latrine.[110] The wife's sins of the body lead her to regard the body as wholly carnal. The result is that she regards her husband's body as disposable and relegates it to the realm of the corrupt. Death and corruption are conflated once again.

The Devil is the ruler of the lower body; just as he governs sin, he wields power through excretion and its related activities. In the Cornish *Ordinalia*, for instance, Lucifer exhorts his devils to counter Jesus by breaking wind—a ludicrous activity, but also one that illustrates the foulness and corporeality of demonic force. Lucifer urges:

"Push, O riffraff, strain, blast your tripes! or else you'll get it hot and heavy since the plain truth is, [Jesus] robs us of our power each passing instant and will leave us, I am convinced, without the strength even to break wind."[111]

This instance emphasizes the devils' ludicrous blasphemy and powerlesness in the face of the divine. Other texts illustrated more somber ways in which demons used their hallmark, dung, to afflict the world. As the Devil works his way in the world through sin, his power over sinners is exemplified by its material manifestation, excrement. This is clear in the many excremental punishments visited upon sinners, but also true in a more general sense. Jerome outlines this in a comment on Psalm 141, "a prayer when [David] was in the cave." The psalm is alluding to the episode from Vulgate 1 Kings 2:4, in which David flees from Saul and takes refuge in a cave. Saul comes in pursuit and, not realizing David is hiding there, enters the cave to defecate:

> eratque ibi spelunca quam ingressus est Saul ut purgaret ventrem. Porro David et viri eius in interiori parte speluncae latebant. . ..

> and there was a cave into which Saul went to empty his bowels. Now David and his men lay hidden in the inner part of the cave. . ..

This episode of the defecating persecutor led Jerome to comment on the Devil's presence in the world:

> Accipitur quidem et in Dominum uerum Dauid iste psalmus; et intellegitur Saul in diabolum, spelunca autem in hunc mundum, et quod diabolus non inmittit in hunc mundum aliquid boni, sed stercus, et si quid putridum.[112]

> In this psalm certainly David is understood as the true Lord, and Saul is interpreted as the devil, and the cave as this world, because the devil does not send into this world anything good, but dung and whatever is corrupt.

Again dung is the exemplar of all corruption, a shorthand signifying the Devil's place in the world, inscribed even in holy history.

THE EXEGETICAL TRADITION

The idea of the latrine as a place of evil and danger ultimately springs from the hard-wired disgust response to excrement documented by modern researchers such as Paul Rozin. Thus it was not specifically Judeo-Christian. The same concerns were reflected in the Roman Empire, which had a tradition of apotropaic imagery in latrines.[113] For instance, a wall painting from Pompei shows a person using the latrine, surrounded by figures of snakes and the goddess Fortuna, with the inscription *Cacator cave malum* ("Shitter, beware of bad things/evil.")[114]

The symbolic system that opposed excrement and the divine was also already in place in pre-Christian Judaism.[115] Excretion was associated with animality and humility. The wise followed certain precepts in the latrines: the body should not be in alignment with the Temple (presumably to distinguish excretion from the holy), nakedness should be minimized and the hand used for cleaning should be the one not used for holy activities.[116] In practice this meant the right hand was used for the holy, the left for the latrine. A parallel set of attitudes held that, like other bodily activities, excretion was life-giving. Jonathan Shofer sees this as contradictory to the view that separated the holy and the divine, but as in Christianity, this need not be the case. In the medieval Christian understanding, it was not defecating per se that was unholy, but excrement itself. Defecation was an occasion of peril because the person came into contact with dung, and because it could serve as a contact-point for the Devil or a risk of losing one's soul along with the dung. But the purgation of dung served to purify the body, albeit temporarily, and in that sense was life-giving. Thus these two views need not be contradictory in either Judaism or Christianity.

A prominent text of the rabbinic period also represented the human body as a microcosm, a tradition echoed in other texts, in 1 Corinthians 12:27 and ultimately in medieval reflections of the tradition, as surveyed in Chapter 3. Shofer summarizes the instructions of the rabbinic texts: "Rabbinic ethical instruction concerning excretion reveals intimate ways that bodily management is central to sagely behavior."[117]

Just as the themes surrounding filth in Christianity can be found in the rabbinic period, the profane and blasphemous associations of filth are clearly visible in the Old Testament. From an early period demons, for instance, were associated with ordure. A prominent example is Beelzebub, who originated as a foreign god but soon came to be interpreted as a demon. The ultimate derivation of his name is apparently irrecoverable—it may actually mean "lord of the flies" or a number of other things—but in the Rabbinic period it was interpreted as "lord of the dungheap." This was connected to the word *zabal*, meaning "to dung," which the rabbinical literature uses to refer to idolatry. Gehenna, which came to mean hell in both the Jewish and Christian traditions, was originally a valley outside Jerusalem which was used as a refuse dump and was filled with dung, refuse and fires.[118] It was reached through the dung-gate, mentioned in Esdras 2:13, 12:31 and elsewhere. From very early days, then, dung was intimately associated with hell.

The Old Testament describes a number of events in which sinners or the ungodly are threatened with or transformed into dung as a reflection of and punishment for their evil deeds. Authors and prophets understood dung as a way of conveying the ultimate corruption and unlikeness from God. An excremental fate is wreaked upon the godless in 4 Kings 10:27, when the house of the pagan idol Baal is overthrown and converted into a latrine. In Vulgate 3 Kings 14:10 the evil house of Jeroboam will be swept up like dung. In Isaiah 5:25, the Lord punished his wayward people and struck them, and "facta sunt morticina eorum quasi stercus in medio platearum," "their carcasses became as dung in the midst of the streets." At Jeremiah 8:2, 9:22 and 16:4, the Lord's enemies "in sterquilinium super faciem terrae erunt," "shall be as dung on the face of the earth." 2 Chronicles 21:15–19 depicts the story of the wrongdoing king Joram (Jehoroam), stricken by a fatal disease of the bowels in which they came out little by little and finally killed him.

The most straightforward Biblical text on excremental filth appears among the injunctions of Deuteronomy. This passage establishes that God and material filth are antithetical:

> Habebis locum extra castra ad quem egrediaris ad requisita naturae, gerens paxillum in balteo. Cumque sederis fodies per circuitum et egesta humo operies quo relevatus es. Dominus enim Deus tuus ambulat in medio castrorum ut eruat te. Et tradat tibi inimicos tuos ut sint castra tua sancta, et nihil in eis appareat foeditatis, nec derelinquat te. (Deut. 23:12–14)

> Thou shalt have a place without the camp, to which thou mayst go for the necessities of nature, carrying a paddle at thy girdle. And when thou sittest down, thou shalt dig round about, and with the earth that is dug up thou shalt cover that which thou art eased of. For the Lord thy God walketh in the midst of thy camp, to deliver thee, and to give up thy enemies to thee. And let thy camp be holy, and let no uncleanness appear therein, lest he go away from thee.

Medieval exegesis on the passage runs along predictable lines, interpreting "that which thou art eased of," the dung, as the corruptions of the sinful mind. A verbatim formulation of this was echoed by exegetes for most of the Middle Ages, beginning with Isidore and Gregory the Great, and continuing through Bede, Hrabanus Maurus, Hincmar of Reims, Rupert of Deutz and others.[119] Gregory the Great may serve as an example of this standard formulation:

> Naturae enim corruptibilis pondere grauati, a mentis nostrae utero quaedam cogitatio<n>um superflua quasi uentris grauamina erumpunt. Sed portare sub balteo paxillum debemus, ut uidelicet ad reprehendendos nosmetipsos semper accincti, acutum circa nos stimulum compunctionis habeamus, qui incessanter terram mentis nostrae paenitentiae dolore confodiat, et hoc quod a nobis fetidum erumpit abscondat.[120]

> For burdened by the weight of a corruptible nature, certain excesses of thought burst out from the guts of our mind like the weight of the

belly. But we ought to carry a paddle under our girdle so that, always girded to reprimand ourselves, we may have about us the sharp goad of compunction, which will ceaselessly dig at the soil of our mind with the pain of penitence and bury the fetid that bursts forth from us.

The conventional interpretation hence produced the unsurprising result that dung should be interpreted as sin. The mind that produces sin is envisioned as a body generating filth. Bruno of Segni (c. 1047–1123) provides an even more straightforward reading of the passage in Deuteronomy:

Stercora et egestiones vitia sunt, et peccata. Haec autem in castris fidelium fieri non licet. Quidquid igitur sordidum, quidquid fetidum, quidquid nefarium et vitiosum est a fidelium domibus et a sanctorum castris procul pellatur. Dominus enim ambulans, et habitans talium fetorem abhorrens commorari illic dedignabitur.[121]

The dung and effluvia are vices and sins. But these are not allowed in the camps of the faithful. Whatever is dirty, whatever is fetid, whatever is foul and full of vice should be expelled far from the dwellings of the faithful and the camps of the holy. For the Lord, walking about and dwelling there, despising the stench of such things, disdains to stay in such a place.

In both examples of exegesis, the sin of the mind is characterized as bodily dung, as if the mind is lowered and transformed into the material by sin—almost as if thoughts, digested by the body, are transformed into dung.

Similar interpretations are applied to a second fundamental passage in the Bible, the murder of Eglon, committed by Aoth (Ehud), in Judges 3:22. The preceding passages establish that Eglon is very fat, which means that the dagger sinks into the body:

nec eduxit gladium sed ita ut percusserat reliquit in corpore, statimque per secreta naturae alvi stercora proruperunt.

he did not draw out the dagger, but left it in the body as he had struck it in: and forthwith, by the secret parts of nature, the excrements of the belly came out.

The exegesis on the death of Eglon is not abundant, but what exists is fully in line with interpretations of other passages: the corpulence of the body represents fleshly evil; dung, sin; the dagger, that which purges sin, and so forth.[122]

After the murder Ehud closes the doors of the room so that the servants assume that Eglon "purgat alvum," "is purging his belly," until finally, suspicious, they break in and find him dead. The story hence has a number of parallels with tales of Arius and his aftertypes, and must have come to mind when later evildoers were found dead in the latrine.

Several such medieval accounts clearly drew on these Biblical precedents. One appears in two versions of the miracles in St. Salvius, recounted in the thirteenth-century *Cronicon* of Helinand of Froidmont and in the *Vita of St. Salvius*.[123] Two sisters have come to the king to complain of their brother, who has refused to give them money they are owed. The king asks the brother to swear to the truth on the body of St. Salvius, but the man swears falsely and is punished for his perjury. The man's fate is recounted in Biblical phrasing: "Qui cum jurasset laetus, statim *medius crepuit* [Acts 1:18], et *per secretum alvi stercora proruperunt* [Judges 3:22] . . . et post duas horas vitam finivit," "When he gaily took the oath, straightaway *he burst in the middle* and *by the secret parts the excrements of the belly came out* . . . and after two hours he ended his life."[124] Here the inclusion of Biblical phrasing emphasizes the association between sinners such as Eglon and Judas and those contemporary wrongdoers who sin in the face of the divine, whether by swearing falsely on saints' relics, by skipping the service or by fomenting heresy.

Exegesis was quick to interpret all such Biblical passages concerning dung in the obvious fashion. The *Allegoriae in sacram scripturam*, of the late eleventh or early twelfth century, has a typical roundup of the things excrement can signify:

> Stercus est humanitas, ut in Psalmis: "Et de stercore erigens pauperem," quod qui se humiliat, exaltabitur. Stercus, res mundialis inordinate contra Deum dilecta. . . . Stercus, fetor luxuriae, ut in Joele: "Computruerunt jumenta in stercore suo," quod carnales in fetore luxuriae terminaverunt terram. Per stercus occultae malitiae cordis, ut in libro Judicum: "Statimque per secreta naturae alvi stercora proruperunt," id est, in occulto fetidae cordis malitiae innotuerunt. . . . Per stercus peccata carnis, ut in Jeremia: "Et qui nutriebantur in circeis [sic], amplexabantur stercora" [Thren. 4:5], id est, qui in spiritualibus delectabantur bonis, peccata exercent carnalia. *Sterquilinium* est infirmitas hominis, ut in Job [2:8]: "Sedens in sterquilinio," id est, humilians se in cognitione infirmitatis suae. *Sterquilinium*, fetor internorum, ut in Job [20:7]: "Quasi sterquilinium in fine perdetur," quod reprobus quilibet vitiorum fetore plenus, ad extremum destruetur.[125]

> *Dung* is humanity, as in the Psalms: "And he lifts the poor man from the dungheap," for he who humbles himself will be exalted. *Dung*, worldly things cherished inordinately in opposition to God. . . . *Dung*, the stench of excess, as in Joel [1:17]: "The beasts have rotted in their dung," because the carnal bound the earth in the stench of their excess. By *dung* is meant the hidden wickedness of the heart, as in Judges [1:22]: "And straightaway, by the secret parts of nature, the excrement of the belly came out," that is, the stinking vices of the heart became known in secret. . . . By *dung* is meant the sins of the flesh, as in [Lamentations of]

Jeremiah: "And those who were brought up in circuses have embraced the dung," that is those who have delighted in spiritual goods cultivate carnal sins. A *dunghill* is the frailty of humanity, as in Job, "sitting on a dunghill," that is, debasing himself in the recognition of his frailty. *Dunghill*, the stench of the inner parts, as in Job: "In the end he shall be destroyed like a dunghill," because the base man, full of the stench of sins of any kind, will be destroyed at the last.

Thus dung represents carnal and worldly sins—and above all, humanity, which is both carnal and worldly, and which both produces and is constituted of dung. The sinfulness and instability of the world are depicted in a similar fashion. The Bible supplied several such images, a prominent example being Lamentations 4:5: "Qui vescebantur voluptuose interierunt in viis; qui nutriebantur in croceis amplexati sunt stercora," "Those who feasted on dainties perish in the streets; those who were brought up in purple lie in dungheaps."

Thus far the understanding of dung is predictable: it is a symbol of moral filth and an exemplar of loathesome material corruption, particularly that engendered by sin. More complex meanings arise from the Biblical passages in which dung is juxtaposed with the good, as when the righteous Job was reduced to sitting on a dungheap, or when dung is presented as a fruitful fertilizer. Equally telling analyses emerge when the discussion of dung arises when the term is not actually mentioned in the Bible, as in discussions of the sanitary arrangements on Noah's ark or elaborations on the progress of the Passion.

The most common Biblical image of the sinfulness and degradation of the world appeared at Job 2:7–8, in which Job, seemingly abandoned by God and suffering under the afflictions of Satan, is reduced to dwelling on a dungheap. Satan departs from the Lord, tellingly referred to as his "face," and afflicts Job with corruption until he is reduced to sitting on a dunghill, as if Job had become corruption itself:

> Egressus igitur Satan a facie Domini percussit Iob ulcere pessimo a planta pedis usque ad verticem eius, qui testa saniem deradebat sedens in sterquilinio.
>
> So Satan went forth from the face of the Lord and struck Job with a most terrible ulcer from the sole of the foot up to the top of his head; and he scraped the discharge with a potsherd, sitting on a dunghill.

The infliction of the ulcer subjects Job to corruption and foulness, and so it is entirely apt that this is the moment he is condemned to dwell on the dunghill, that apotheosis of foul corruption. It is also significant that it is the Devil, the lord of corruption and excrement, who brings this about. In this passage, as in so many, it is as if the Devil *is* decay.

The standard exegesis of the Book of Job was that of Gregory the Great, whose *Moralia in Job* was vastly influential. Gregory equates Job's dunghill with the flesh, both being corrupt and earthly:

> In sterquilinio ponebat corpus ut ex terra sumpta quae esset carnis substantia, bene proficiens perpenderet animus. In sterquilinio ponebat corpus ut etiam ex loci fetore caperet, quod festine corpus ad fetorem rediret.[126]

> He set his body on a dunghill so that the mind, profiting well, should consider what the substance of the flesh was, taken from the earth. He set his body on a dunghill so that likewise he might apprehend from the stench of that place that the body quickly returns to stench.

The dunghill, then, betokens the part of Job that can never be righteous. Gregory continues that the dunghill should bring to mind one's own earthly and sinful nature:

> *Sedens in sterquilinio.* In sterquilinio quippe sedere est uilia de se quempiam et abiecta sentire. In sterquilinio nobis sedere est ad ea quae illicite gessimus mentis oculos paenitendo reducere, ut cum ante nos peccatorum stercora cernimus, omne quod in animo de elatione surgit inclinemus. In sterquilinio sedet qui infirmitatem suam sollicitus respicit, et sese de bonis quae per gratiam perceperit, non extollit. An non apud se in sterquilinio Abraham sederet qui dicebat: *Loquar ad Dominum meum, cum sim puluis et cinis*? [Gen. 18:27][127]

> *Sitting on a dunghill.* To "sit on a dunghill" obviously is to perceive base and abject things about oneself. For us "to sit on a dunghill" is to bring the eyes of the mind in penitence back to those things that we committed unrighteously, so that when we see the dung of our sins before us, we may bend down everything that arises from haughtiness in the mind. He sits on a dunghill who is troubled in scrutinizing his weaknesses, and does not lift himself up because of those good things that he gains through grace. Did not Abraham sit by himself on a dunghill, who said *I will speak to my Lord, who am dust and ashes*?

The Book of Job pointed out explicitly the connection between the sinful, earthly human body and excrement, and the situation of even the righteous in the early realm, surrounded by corruption, dung and ultimately the decay of death. Medieval images of the scene conventionally depict the dungheap as a dark mound with wisps of straw in it, but at least one manuscript, a fifteenth-century French Book of Hours, makes the association with death more explicit by depicting bones in the heap.[128] The picture of Job on the dungheap is common in Books of Hours: to remind us of the implications of earthly corruption, the image often formed the illustration for the Office of the Dead.[129]

Job's humble endurance of his situation on the dungheap was a model of patience and humility. In his wake many saints were said to have endured afflictions of dung with humble minds as evidence of their sanctity. So they might minister to the sick and endure their bodily effusions or not be too proud to clean out monastic latrines. Such actions demonstrated that they had no illusions about their lowliness: they acknowledged that they were made of corruptible flesh, but their spiritual powers were such that their minds were not lowered by it. This became a theme in accounts of many medieval saints, among them Margaret of Hungary and John of Gorze.[130]

The dungheap was so prominent in the story of Job as to become the emblem of the entire book of the Bible. A less obvious discussion arose around other Biblical passages such as the accounts of Noah's ark and Jesus's birth in a stable. In both instances the presence of animals calls to mind the theme of dung: although excrement is human as well as animalistic, it is associated with animality.

This is clear in discussions of the sanitary arrangements on Noah's ark, a question unaddressed in Genesis. As the Flood was supposed to be a time of cleansing and purification on earth, and as dung embodies sin, we would expect dung to be out of place on the ark. Bede posed the question of why the dung accumulated by the animals rescued by Noah did not overwhelm the ark:

> Quomodo non stercus et urina tot animantium uel intolerabilem fetore ipsis animantibus locum faceret, uel fundum arcae quamuis optime bituminatum corrumperet? . . . Ipse ergo Dominus qui arcam cum eis quae gestabat omnibus incorruptam seruauit, quique hanc ne in mare dilaberetur gubernauit, sed tali in loco montium deposuit, ubi de ostio quod habebat facilis esset ac promptus ad terram egressus cunctis quae in illa continebantur animantibus. Prouidit etiam eisdem qualiter in arca uescerentur ac salua perdurarent. Nec ab re est credi, ut quidam astruunt, quod ingressuris arcam animantibus Noe uictum singulis qui unius diei usui sufficeret praeparauerit, et hoc refecta singula ob significandum mysterium quod in ecclesia cuncti pro modo propriae capacitatis uitae cibo reficimur deincepsque ad diem egressionis suae quieta diuino nutu uel etiam sopita manserint.[131]

How could the dung and urine of so many animals not have made the place unbearable to the animals because of the stench, or corroded the bottom of the ark, even if it was well covered with tar? . . . Therefore it was the Lord himself who kept the ark incorrupt, along with everything it carried, and who piloted it so that it did not perish in the sea, but set it in such a place in the mountains where, from the door it had, the exit to land was easy and clear for all the animals that were contained in it. He provided for them, moreover, such that they ate in the ark and remained healthy. Nor is it wrong to believe, as some say further, that for each one of the animals coming onto the ark Noah prepared food for use on a single day, and with each one refreshed, this was to signify mystically that we are all refreshed in the church with the food of life, according to our singular capacity. And from the beginning to the day they went out, by divine will they remained calmed or even sleeping.

It is not entirely clear that the issue of the dung on the ark needs such an elaborate explanation—one might have thought it would be easy enough to pitch the dung overboard. The exegetes seem to have worried about the passage "et inclusit eum Dominus de foris," "and God shut him in on the outside" (Gen. 7:16), and whether this means there was no access to the outside of the ark for those inside. A number of exegetes seem to be writing with this passage in mind, although later commentators did not feel it posed a hindrance: Martin Luther, for instance, asserted that the dung must have been thrown out of the window.[132] Those who avoid this solution may have been felt that pitching dung overboard would have sullied the purifying waters of the flood. During a time of purification, filth must not pollute the waters, and in Bede's view indeed filth was not produced by the animals. Their bodily functions, including eating, are effaced entirely, as if purification consists of eradicating all corporeal flux, and as if they can only be incorrupt without bodily processes. This conclusion is actually somewhat in contradiction to the evidence of Genesis 6:21–22, "Thou shalt take unto thee of all food that may be eaten, and thou shalt lay it up with thee: and it shall be food for thee and them. And Noah did all things which God commanded him." The logistical problem of where so much food might be stored is turned into a symbolic interpretation of the situation, to the point where a far from obvious answer is proffered in answer to the puzzle of how the animals fared.[133]

The place of dung aboard the ark was also raised by Hugh of St. Victor in the twelfth century, who could not keep from thinking about the problem and ordering the dung as it fit into the universal hierarchy. Hugh saw the ark as a symbol of the world, and in his interpretation the dung was stored aboard the ark:

Illi mansioni, quae fundo erat contigua, deputatus erat fimus animalium, qui recte vitam carnalium exprimit, quoniam ii qui carnis desideriis inserviunt, quid aliud quam putredo fiunt?[134]

To the quarters next to the bottom, the dung of the animals was consigned, which fittingly represents the life of the carnal, since they who serve the desires of the flesh, what do they produce except rottenness?

The conjunction of the corrupt and the lowly (in the most literal sense) is clear here. As in others' descriptions of the universe, Hugh positions lightness and incorruptibility higher than and opposed to dung and material carnality:

> Quintam mansionem homo tenet, et volatilia. Per hominem designatur vivacitas rationis, et intelligentiae in volatilli exprimitur agilitas incorruptibilis naturae. Quando ergo *mortale hoc induerit immortalitatem, et corruptibile hoc* vestierit *incorruptionem* (I Cor. xv[.45]), tunc mente pariter, et corpore spiritales effecti, secundum modulum nostrum, et per mentis illuminationem omnia sciemus, et per corporis incorruptibilis levitatem ubique esse poterimus. Volabimus mente per contemplationem, volabimus corpore per incorruptionem.[135]

> Man occupies the fifth level, along with the flying creatures. By man is meant the vigor of reason and intelligence; the flying creatures signify the activity of incorruptible nature. When, therefore, *this mortal has put on immortality, and this corruptible* has put on *incorruption*, then we, being made equally spiritual in mind and body in our small measure, will also understand everything through the illumination of our minds, and will be able to be everywhere through the lightness of the incorruptible body. We will take flight in mind through contemplation; we will take flight in body through incorruption.

The ark is hence a microcosm of the order of the body and the universe, with the foulest and most material and corrupt at the bottom, and the lightest and incorrupt at the top. The actual passages in Genesis say nothing about this other than that God commanded the ark to be constructed with several storeys and that both unclean and clean animals were to be saved. The rest of the familiar hierarchy, including the discussion of dung, is introduced by commentators who reproduce their understanding of universal hierarchy, with dung at its foundation, whenever discussions of the world arise.

The tenaciousness of the association between excrement, lowliness and sin is so strong that in theological contexts it tended to override contradictory examples. Even when dung appears to have a neutral or positive meaning in the Bible, medieval exegetes interpret it in line with the prevailing system of sin and corruption. Matthew 15:17–18, for instance, controverts the established interpretation of material filth, arguing that spiritual filth is the actual force of corruption and that, in effect, material filth is a comparatively unimportant metaphor:

> Non intellegitis quia omne quod in os intrat in ventrem vadit et in secessum emittitur? Quae autem procedunt de ore de corde exeunt et ea coinquinant hominem. (Cf. Mc. 7:19–20.)

Do you not observe that all that goes into the mouth travels to the belly, and is cast into the sewer? Whereas all that comes out of his mouth comes from the heart, and it is that which makes a man unclean.

But the influence of this passage is negligible in the face of the larger cultural understanding of material filth. Despite Matthew, exegetes will not relinquish excrement as the ultimate locus of sin. Thomas of Chobham, writing in the early thirteenth century, comments on this passage, bringing in the story of Saul defecating in the cave where David is hiding. Even though Jesus has said that evil lies in the heart rather than in the latrine, Thomas takes us back to the latrine:

> Diabolus, enim, habitans in corde humano facit ibi latrinam suam, quia diabolus, sicut bubo, semper inquinat nidum suum, quia scit quod in loco sordidato Dominus non habitabit. Facit enim diabolus sicut uulpes: cum numquam habeat domum propriam querit foueam animalis quod dicitur taxus siue melota, et ponit stercora sua ante ingressum fouee, propter quorum inmunditiam numquam reuertitur taxus in foueam illam, et ita liberam habet domum uulpecula. Horribile est tam inmundum hospitem suscipere qui lectum suum coinquinat. Quod significatur per hoc quod Saul speluncam intrauit ut ibi uentrem purgaret, ut Regum I°, XXIV°. Saul interpretatur *abutens* siue *abusiuus eorum*, et significat diabolum quia semper abutitur loco sibi concesso. Vnde si permiseris eum intrare in speluncam cordis tui, statim eam inquinabit.[136]

> For the devil, dwelling in the human heart, makes his latrine there, because the devil, like the owl, always fouls his nest, because he knows that the Lord will not dwell in a polluted place. The devil behaves like a wolf: if he should have no home of his own, he seeks out the den of an animal that is called the badger, and deposits his dung in front of the entrance of the den, and because of this uncleanness the badger will never return to his den, and thus the wolf has a free home. It is horrible to take in such an unclean guest, who defiles his own bed. This is what is signified when Saul entered the cave to purge his belly, as in 1 Kings 24: Saul is interpreted *abuser* or *abusive of them*, and signifies the devil who is always abusive of any place granted to him. Whence if you let him enter into the cave of your heart, immediately he will defile it.

Thus the exegete portrays anything defiling as material and excremental, whether spiritual in origin or not. Jesus says that filth originates in the heart not in the dung of the body, but Thomas characterizes the filthy heart as a site where the devil has defecated. The ultimate source of moral corruption is then not the sinner's bowels, but the Devil's. However immaterial

Jesus meant the origin of immorality to be, in practice the corrupt cannot be understood without reference to materiality—and to dung.

Indeed, filth and dung are so problematic to medieval culture and theology that the second half of Matthew 15:17–18 is almost effaced in some discussions of the matter. The introductory question, "Do you not observe that all that goes into the mouth travels to the belly, and is cast into the sewer?" only assumes its full meaning in contrast with the concluding statement, "Whereas all that comes out of his mouth comes from the heart, and it is that which makes a man unclean." Yet the introductory question is divested of the second passage and used as a proof-text in the stercoran controversy of the eleventh century and later, as discussed previously.[137] Jesus's statement was employed as medical evidence as to what digestion really entailed, to what extent food contributed to the substance of the body and whether all things, including the incorruptible body of Christ, could truly be subject to defecation. The corresponding passage from Mark was subject to similar inquiry. Mark 7:18–21 reports Jesus as saying:

> non intellegitis quia omne extrinsecus introiens in hominem non potest eum communicare quia non introit in cor eius sed in ventrem et in secessum exit, purgans omnes escas. Dicebat autem quoniam quae de homine exeunt illa communicant hominem. Ab intus enim de corde hominum cogitationes malae procedunt adulteria, fornicationes, homicidia . . .

> do you not understand that everything from without entering into a man cannot defile him, because it enters not into the heart but goes into the belly and goes out into the privy, purging all foods. But he said that the things which come out from a man, they defile a man. For from within out of the heart of men proceed adulteries, fornications, murders . . .

If outward things cannot defile a man because they are purged via defecation, it follows that the matter of defecation consists of that very corruption that must be purged. Thus, although the passage may seek to emphasize the wicked heart of man, it also defines excrement not as trivial but as pure corruption.

Dung also appears in Jerome's statement on Jesus's birthplace, a location in which no dung is mentioned in the original Biblical context. Jerome argued that Jesus was born in a stable because stables are full of dung, and this symbolizes the corrupt world Christ had come to cleanse:

> non nascitur inter aurum et diuitias, sed in stercore nascitur, hoc est, in stabulo (ubicumque enim stabulum, ibi et stercus est), ubi erant spurcitiora peccata nostra. Propterea in stercore nascitur, ut eos qui sunt de stercore subleuet. "Leuans de stercore inopem." In stercore nascitur, ubi et Job sedebat, et postea coronatus est.[138]

He is not born in among gold and riches, but he is born in dung, that is, in a stable (for wherever there is a stable, there is also dung), where the filth was our sins. For that reason he is born in dung, so that he may lift up those who come from dung. "Lifting up the poor from the dung" [Ps 113:7]. He is born in dung, where Job sat as well, and he is crowned thereafter.

The passage makes dung key to the story of salvation, defining sinful humans as "those who come from dung." It provides that which must be left behind, a polar opposite to the divine. In both these examples—Jerome on the stables and various commentators about the ark—the dung is not part of the Biblical account, but comes into the mind of the commentator through its association with animals, whether those of the ark or those in the stable. Without reason or knowledge of God, ruled by base appetites, animals bring dung into the picture, and dung, even human dung, brings the animalistic, "where the filth was our sins."

THE EXCREMENTAL BODY

The bowels are, then, the breeding-ground for sin, the part of the body that above all generates corruption. They are thus the ultimate exemplar of the corrupt nature of the earthly body. The question naturally arose of whether the entrails would be resurrected with the rest of the body in heaven. Thomas Aquinas took up this question in two forms, asking whether Christ's body, the ultimate embodiment of incorruption, would be resurrected with all its earthly attributes and whether the entrails had a place in the resurrected human body in heaven at all. He argued that Christ's body was fully human, and therefore had all the attributes of a human body. Following Augustine, he confirmed that this included fluids such as bile, but no flesh "which implies any corruption" (*cum secundum corruptionem intelligitur*),[139] since heaven is the realm free of both spiritual and material corruption. The same understanding is reflected in Aquinas's thoughts on the resurrection of the entrails, as quoted in Chapter 1. As usual, Aquinas presents a survey of the possibilities before supplying his conclusion.

> Utrum omnia membra corporis humani resurrectura sint
> 2. Praeterea, intestina quaedam membra sunt. Sed non resurgent. Plena enim resurgere non possunt: quia immunditias continent. Nec vacua: quia nihil est vacuum in natura. Ergo non omnia membra resurgent. . . .
> Sed contra: . . . . intestina resurgent in corpore, sicut ut alia membra. Et plena erunt, non quidem turpibus superfluitatibus, sed nobilibus humiditatibus. (Suppl. q. 80, a. 1)[140]

152 Sin and Filth in Medieval Culture

Whether all the members of the human body will be resurrected

2. Further, the intestines are members, but they will not rise again. For they cannot rise full, because they contain impurities, nor empty, since nothing is empty in nature. Therefore not every member will rise again. . . .

But against that: . . . the intestines will rise again in the body, just like the other members. And they will be full, not, certainly, of shameful superfluities, but of noble humors.

Est autem in homine triplex humiditas. Quaedam enim humiditas est in recedendo a perfectione huius individui: vel quia est in via corruptionis, et a natura abiicitur, sicut urina, sudor et sanies et huiusmodi; vel quia a natura ordinatur ad conservationem specie in alio individuo, sive per actum genervativae, sicut semen, sive per actum nutritivae, sicut lac. Et nulla talium humiditatem resurget: eo quod non est de perfectione individui resurgentis. (Suppl. q. 80 a.3)[141]

There is, moreover, a triple humidity in man. One humidity is a lessening of the perfection of the individual, either because it is on the path to corruption, and is evacuated by nature, as urine, sweat, discharge, and things of this kind, or because it is established in an individual for the preservation of the kind, whether by an act of generation, like semen, or an act of nutrition, like milk. And none of these kinds of humidities will rise again, because they are not part of the perfection of the individual rising again.

Since we are promised that the body will rise up intact and perfect, he concluded, we can be certain that the entrails will be present in heaven. But because the body will be free from sin, the entrails will be filled not with their usual contents—"turpibus superfluitatibus," "shameful superfluities"—but with "noble humors." Thus it is not the entrails per se that give rise to sin and blasphemy; it is their contents, excrement, that is the corrupt and corrupting element. After humankind is purified, the entrails will no longer generate the corruption (excrement, sin) which was their defining feature on earth.

With this understanding, we are in a position to venture an answer to the unspeakable question of the Middle Ages: whether Christ defecated. Guibert of Nogent skirted by the subject when addressing the Jews' doubts about the incarnation. As Guibert asserted, the sinless body is pure and without defilement, free of shame. To recapitulate Guibert's statement on the matter:

Membra, cum abest peccatum, sancta sunt.—Porro Dei Filius in carnem veniens, si competentia corpori membra habuit, membrorum compositio non nocuit. Frustraque non pudeat quod ipsum non puduit. Et quid eum puderet, ubi nihil non sanctum fuit! Si quidquid est, bonum est, nisi ubi peccatum est, membra quae per se bona sunt, cum peccatum non est, sancta sunt. Membra nostra imbecillitati nostrae sunt administratoria, et cum aures, ora vel nares superfluis capitum egerendis inserviunt, caetera quid mali faciunt, quae inferius intestinorum pondus exponunt?[142]

The parts of the body, when sin is absent, are holy.—Further, the Son of God, as he came into the flesh: if he had parts suitable to his bodiliness, the composition of his parts was not harmful. For he should not be ashamed, to no purpose, of that which did not shame him. And what should have shamed him, where there was nothing that was not holy! If anything exists, it is good, except where there is sin, and the parts that are good in themselves, when there is no sin, are holy.

Because Christ was pure, we should know that he "nihil hominis veritum praeter peccata fuisse," "feared nothing of humanity except sin."[143] In other words, being in the flesh per se was not humiliating. The potential for sin was there, but corruption was not an ineluctable consquence of incarnation. The wording of this passage is, unfortunately, not entirely explicit; no medieval authority wants to approach the question of whether Christ defecated in explicit terms. Thus Guibert's deliberate vagueness could possibly (but, I believe, wrongly) be interpreted as "Christ was not afraid of being incarnated as a body that defecated." However, the equation of sin and defecation suggests with overwhelming likelihood that Guibert's emphasis on Christ's sinlessness and lack of shame means that Guibert believed that Christ literally did not defecate as sinful humans do.

Whatever Christ's unspecified processes of digestion were, we can be sure that, in the medieval understanding, they were as shameless and holy as the rest of his earthly body. We know from Francesc Eiximenis that the pre-lapsarian human body did not suffer from shamefulness: "even though man would still have to empty his bowels through the natural opening, it would not stink nor would it have that shamefulness of which the aforementioned authority speaks."[144] By the testimony of Thomas Aquinas, pure excretion involves noble humors rather than shameful superfluities. Christ's own body was fully human, according to orthodox belief, but as a pure substance it might effectively incline to immateriality, just as did the Eucharist in miracle stories.

Thus it would be not only improper, but fallacious and sacrilegious, to maintain that Christ discharged shameful substances. A belief in his full human incarnation does not alter that, because his was a sinless and therefore incorrupt human incarnation. Many writers and artists in more recent eras have sought to depict Christ defecating or to associate him with dung, usually out of a desire to use the transgressive power of the association to lend force to their art. But we should not mistake this for the medieval view: these works are profoundly unmedieval. Those of the medieval period who worried at the subject were those who found it challenging to accept one of the fundamental assumptions of the equation: that the earthly human body could exist unshamed, or that Christ could be fully incarnated. Once those two beliefs, both of them points of faith, are accepted, the conclusion—that Christ lived on earth unshamed and incorrupt—is manifest. The fact that medieval art, literature and devotion focus on certain aspects of Christ's human life, such as his infant swaddling clothes or his eating, does not contradict this. For the earthly, post-lapsarian, sinful human body, swaddling clothes suggest diapers, and eating leads inevitably to fetid excretion. But in the medieval understanding, purity is material as well as moral. The pure, sinless body needs neither diapers or foul excretions.

The body and its shameful superfluities also served as vehicles for religious truths about the Church. In this case their role is not so much symbolic as mystical, as the Church was felt to constitute God's body in a mystical sense, not merely as a metaphor. As the Church had its corrupt elements, such corruption also had to appear in the description of the body of Christ, an image that was constructed with great delicacy. The image was explicated by Hugh of St. Victor, using the orientational aspects of the body:

> Si ergo caput Dei dicimus esse quod fuit ante constitutionem hujus mundi, et pedes ejus quod futurum est post consummationem saeculi, recte longitudinem corporis ejus accipimus, quod inter principium et finem medium est spatium temporis. Caput ergo et pedes teguntur, quia prima et novissima investigare non possumus. Corpus apparet, quia ea quae media in hoc praesenti saeculo geruntur, videmus. Hoc corpus est Ecclesia, quae coepit a principio mundi, et usque ad finem saeculi durabit. Haec est arca, de qua loqui proposuimus, quae a capite usque ad pedes pertingit, quia a principio usque ad finem per successionem generationum sancta Ecclesia se extendit. Sed sciendum est quod sicut in persona hominis alia sunt circa corpus ejus, et neque in corpore sunt, neque de corpore, ita etiam est in corpore Christi, id est Ecclesia, quae habitat in medio pravae nationis, et dum assuitus infidelium excipit, quasi quibusdam fluctibus procellosis foris arca tunditur; dum vero a falsis fratribus tribulationem sustinet, quasi quibusdam noxiis humoribus intus corpus torquetur. Quaecunque ergo corpori contraria sunt sive intus sive extra sint, non sunt de corpore.[145]

If we therefore say that the head of God is that which existed before the establishment of this world, and his feet that which will be after the consummation of the ages, we rightly interpret the expanse of his body as the period of time between the beginning and the end. The head and feet are covered, therefore, because we cannot discern the first things or the last. The body is visible because we can see those intermediate things that are carried out in this present age. That body is the Church, which began in the beginning of the world, and will endure to the end of the ages. That is the ark, on which we proposed to speak, which extends from the head to the feet, because holy Church extends from the beginning to the end through the succession of generations. But it should be understood that just as in a particular man there are outside things affecting the body, but which are neither in the body or from the body, so it is also in the body of Christ, that is the Church, which dwells in the midst of a corrupt people, and when an attack of unbelievers afflicts it, it is as if the ark is pounded from outside by stormy waves; when, in truth, it suffers troubles from false brethren, it is as if the body is tormented inwardly by noxious humors. Whatever things, therefore, are harmful to the body, whether they are inward or outward, do not belong to the body.

Although the body as hierarchy is a traditional image, the image here is temporal and unconventionally non-hierarchical. The body is also the ark, but the writer is not concerned with the dung of the animals, but of the threat to the ark from without, the "noxious humors" that afflict the body's interior. Hugh of St. Victor comes to conclusions similar to those of Thomas Aquinas: the noxious humors are not intrinsic to the body, but related to sin and impurity. The body of Christ and the ark are both vessels of purity afflicted by corruption. This ecclesiological metaphor is as close as medieval orthodox theology comes to imputing corrupt processes to Christ's body. It is of course stressed that these processes are not of the body; so Christ's is not afflicted by his own corruptions, but by those of earthly sinners. In this the image is more of the suffering of Christ under pain inflicted by sinners, as during the Passion and crucifixion. The noxious humors, moreover, might be any of a number of corporeal afflictions caused by an imbalance of humors; though if the ultimate origin is external, something that has been eaten and disrupts digestion would be the most apt metaphor. The exegete is skating distinctly close to an image of Christ's indigestion, a picture which only the stylized mysticism of the passage lets him avoid.

The image of the Church as Christ's body afflicted with corrupt workings is offered more graphically in Honorius of Autun's twelfth-century *Elucidarium*. The passage begins with the mystical body of Christ, proceeding down through the features of the body, and accounting for another objectionable excretion by defining heretics as mucus that must be wiped from the face of the Church. This occasions the last mention of the body of Christ; thereafter the features are mentioned solely as attributes of the Church, proceeding through mouth, teeth, hands and feet, until the author arrives at the excrement:

> D.—Quomodo est Ecclesia ejus corpus et electi membra?
> M.—Ut corpus capiti inhaeret et ab eo regitur, ita Ecclesia per sacramentum corporis Christi ei conjungitur; immo unum cum eo efficitur, a quo omnes justi in suo ordine, ut membra a capite, gubernantur. Cujus

capitis oculi sunt prophetae, qui futura praeviderunt; sunt et apostoli, qui alios de via erroris ad lumen justitiae deduxerunt. Aures sunt obedientes. Nares, discreti. Phlegma, quod per nares ejicitur, haeretici, qui judicio discretorum de capite Christo emunguntur. Os sunt doctores. Dentes, sacrae scripturae expositores. Manus, Ecclesiae defensores. Pedes, agricolae, Ecclesiam pascentes. Porro fimus, qui de ventre porcis egreditur, sunt immundi et alii infra Ecclesiam facinorosi, qui ventrem matris Ecclesiae onerant, quos per mortis egestionem daemones, ut porci, devorant.[146]

D.—How is the Church his [Christ's] body and the chosen his limbs? M.—As the body is joined to the head and is ruled by it, in the same way the Church is joined to him by the sacrament of the body of Christ; or rather it is made one with him by whom all the just are governed in his ordering, as the limbs are by the head. Of this head the prophets are the eyes, which foresaw the future; they are also the apostles, who led others from the way of error to the light of justice. The ears are the obedient. The nose is the discerning. Mucus, which is discharged by the nose, is heretics, who are wiped from the head of Christ by the judgment of the discerning. The mouth is the teachers. The teeth are those who explicate the holy scriptures. The hands are the defenders of the Church. The feet are the farmers feeding the Church. What is more, the dung that passes out of the belly to the pigs is the unclean and other evil-doers beneath the Church, who burden the belly of Mother Church, and whom, when purged by death, the demons devour like pigs.

By the point at which excrement is mentioned, the image has been distanced from the mystical image of Christ, and the body has been silently transformed into that of Mater Ecclesia, Mother Church. Although the Church has been the subject of the passage from the beginning, it has not been characterized as a body in any way distinct from Christ's until the mention of excrement, whereupon it becomes distinctively different by being characterized as female. This is most likely not a gendering of excrement—which clearly pertains to both sexes—as a strategy to avoid too graphic an identification of the body in the passage as Christ's body. The discomfort with the idea of Christ defecating is too powerful, and excretion, even symbolic excretion, is assigned to a more abstract image.

This image of corporeal desecration, both literal and symbolic, was often assigned to sinners of all types. It was, for instance, a commonplace in charges against Jews.[147] The widespread blood-libel legend held that Jews committed a ritual murder of a Christian boy as an annual rite, often at Eastertime. Many of these stories reported that the Jews cast the victim into a dungheap or cesspool after the murder, a desecration that emphasized the sinful denial of the divine potential of the body. A case in point is the blood-libel story of Adam of Bristol, a work most likely of the late thirteenth century.[148] Although the story was retailed as truth, it has strong allegorical aspects, doing double duty as an indictment of Jewish unbelief as a whole. The innocent Christian boy, with the symbolic name of Adam, is enticed into the power of an evil Jew by means of apples, so that the Jew functions as the Devil in the Garden of Eden, tempting humankind into the clutches of sin. The Jew then crucifies the boy Adam in the latrine and later buries him there, a parallel that serves to equate Jewish unbelief with the sins for which Christ died, both sins and unbelief being figured as excrement. The Jew is vanquished by an angel who appears at the entrance to the latrine and declares, "Miser, hic non purgabis ventrem!" "Wretch, you shall not empty your bowels here!" The Jew's sin is here explicitly equated with defecation. Last, the latrine is transformed into a sweet-smelling place by the presence of the martyr's sinless and purifying body. Thus the entire tale conflates the moral and the material, excrement serving a central role in the narrative of unbelief.

Discourse on Jewish unbelief often involved this understanding of excrement as the manifestation of sin, and similar charges were levelled in many times and places. These were purportedly factual, but each used excrement as a way of underscoring Jewish unbelief, which was viewed essentially as blasphemy. In these stories this blasphemous unbelief took the form of offenses against Christians or Christian holy objects, associating them with dung in a symbolic juxtaposition that characterized Jewish sacrilege. Examples are legion. In 1205 Pope Innocent III asserted that French Jews had murdered a Christian and disposed of the body in a latrine.[149] Jews were also accused of casting images of the Virgin Mary into latrines, a story in circulation as early as the seventh century, when it appears in Adamnán's *De locis sanctis*.[150] It appeared in more than a dozen other versions assigned to different perpetrators, purporting to recount genuine incidents.[151] A recurrent accusation held that Jews had abused the Host and thrown it onto a dungheap or cast it into a latrine.[152] One such accusation took place in the Austrian village of Pulkau in 1338.[153] It was said that the Host had been found on the dungheap, placed there by Jews; the presence of the Host was signalled by a miraculous light. The rumor fomented violence that resulted in the deaths of a hundred and fifty Jews.

In a striking example of the ways in which holiness might involve the body, Innocent III also levelled charges that Jewish women were compelling Christian wet-nurses who had taken communion to pour their milk into the latrine for three days.[154] The *Summa aurea* of the twelfth-century canonist Henry of Segusio echoes the charge.[155] This custom meant that the Host, incorporated into the women's bodies and hence into their milk, would be cast into the latrine. The scenario is an unusual variant on the theme of the inversion of the upper and lower body, where women are compelled to "lower" a substance proper to the upper body by treating it as if it emerged from the lower body and was hence polluted. The charges paralleled those levelled against Rhineland heretics, charged in 1233 by Pope Gregory IX with spitting the Host into latrines at Easter.[156]

These stories were accompanied by a widespread tale of Jewish intransigence, in which a Jew effectively chooses dung and is therefore condemned to die in it.[157] In the tale, a Jewish man falls into a latrine but implores his rescuers to delay in saving him, as it is his Sabbath. The next day is the Christian Sabbath and so his rescuers refuse to rescue him then; the story often ends with the Jew dying in the latrine. This narrative was in circulation by the twelfth century and survives in more than fifteen versions, many in multiple manuscripts, and was still circulating at the end of the seventeenth century. It was included in the widely popular *Gesta Romanorum* and also assigned to specific dates and persons: to 1257 or 1258 in the English town of Tewkesbury, with the Christian identified as Richard de Clare, Earl of Gloucester; in 1270, with the Christian identified as Bishop Conrad of Magdeburg; 1272, with the Christian identified as the Pope; thirteenth-century Paris, with the Christian identified as King Louis IX; and so forth. Though brief, it was thus perhaps the most pervasive anti-Semitic narrative of the Middle Ages, and in its definition of Jews as willful unbelievers, and hence sinners, whose religion condemns them to the dungpit of error, the story was central to the identification of excrement and Jewish sacrilege.

The charges associating Jewish sinful unbelief with excrement also appeared in the late medieval devotional tracts on the Passion, in which, in a concrete realization of the afflicted body described by writers such as Hugh and Honorius, the sinful unbelievers persecuted Jesus with dung. These accounts expanded on the Biblical account by drawing from the Psalms, which were understood to prefigure the incidents of the Passion. Thus Psalm 68:3, "I am stuck in the mire of the deep," combined with several other passages, gave rise to this incident:

> And thus they came to Jerusalem. And as some say, there was a foul deep pool just by the gates in which people used to cast all the filth and dirt of the city. There they rudely cast the blessed Jesus in, and repeatedly and cruelly dragged Him through so that He might well say, "I am stuck in the mire of the deep."[158]

Other passages were employed as well, among them Psalm 18:15, "Draw me out of the mire that I may not stick fast"; Psalm 87:5, "I am counted among them that go down to the pit"; and Psalm 87:7, "They have laid me in the lower pit." With these passages as authority, narratives described Jesus being led into a cellar in the house of Caiaphas and plunged into two privies. The episode illustrates the blasphemous behavior of unbelievers, whose unbelief is so egregious that it leads them to commingle those two irreconcilable opposites, divinity and dung. The *Heimelike Passie* narrates:

> Oh, they dragged our beloved Lord cruelly through the cellar to a stinking place with two privies, and there they plunged our beloved

Lord in, and maltreated Him so with the filth that His heart might have broken from the pain and agony He suffered from the stench. Oh, the evil folk rejoiced that they might treat the Lord so basely with filth. And after they had tormented Him in this manner, they dragged Him cruelly forth to a place that was full of water, rudely cast Him in, and sprinkled Him with all the filth.[159]

The sin of unbelief is expressed in a similar way in other narratives. In a fifteenth-century example, the Jews are depicted throwing dung on Christ's head:

> Dum Cristus filius meus precone clamante et Pilato imperante sibi baiulans crucem traheretur, factus est concursus populorum post ipsum euncium et conculcancium ipsum. Alij enim superridentes et illudentes ei, et alij proiciebant lutum et stercora et inmundiciam et in caput et in faciem eius.[160]

> When Christ my son was dragged along, bearing the cross, with the herald calling out and at Pilate's command, a great crowd of people rushed after him, running along and kicking him. For some mocked and ridiculed him, and others threw muck and dung and filth onto both his head and face.

To sin was to associate with dung; but the ultimate sin was to bring together those two opposites, divinity and dung. This was blasphemy and sacrilege, the ultimate disordering of the world God had set in order.

Other insults to divinity could also be expressed in excremental terms. A well-known satirical instance appears in Chaucer's Summoner's Prologue, in which the friars in hell make their habitation beneath the tail of the Devil.[161] Locating sinners in such a place was an easy way to make a satirical point. A fourteenth-century student song from Prague charges rebellious Germans with an origin in the anus of Pontius Pilate—a charge that incidentally implies that the anal passages of sinners are fouler than those of the virtuous.[162]

Thus excrement formed a natural marker of sin, and all sins are associated with excrement at some point in the period. Dante depicted flatterers immersed in human excrement in Canto XVIII of the *Inferno*.[163] But just as corruption is most potent when it afflicts the body, it is carnal sin that is most often associated with latrines and excrement. Thus sexual sin, being carnal, is often linked with excremental imagery. William of Malmesbury told the story of the sister of the Holy Roman Emperor Henry III. She was a nun, but Henry was so fond of her that he kept her in his household, oblivious to the fact that she was committing carnal sin with a cleric. The emperor's eyes were only opened to the sin when he went to satisfy the necessities of nature and caught a glimpse of her trying to smuggle the cleric out of the court after an amorous night.[164] It is as if only answering the needs of his own flesh allowed him to see the sins of the flesh in others.

The same is true for murder, which is a sin that violates the integrity of the victim's body and reduces it to corruption. In one medieval popular tale, a priest takes his mistress to stay at the house of a woman who reproves them both, declaring that the latrine is the only place in the house fit for them.[165] Lechery and murder were associated with excrement in *De marito ab uxore turpiter interempto*, in which the adulterous wife murders her husband and hides the body in a latrine.[166] The latrine is never incidental in such tales—it is always marked, a key emblem of sin and death. It is as if, in sinning, the subject brings a latrine into the story; the latrine contains the sin in material form.

Although latrines and dung had literary power in such stories, they also reflected practical realities and real-world habits of mind. Dungheaps were a natural place to hide bodies: strangers could be trusted not to chance upon the corpse, and refuse was often thrown on the dungheap or put down the privy, often to stay there indefinitely. We may recall the domestic latrine pit of late thirteenth-century Southampton, which contained the carcasses of a variety of domestic animals: five dogs, nine cats, two sparrow hawks, a ferret and a Barbary ape.[167] In one incident of violence in Bedfordshire in 1273, a man, Raymond le Tailur, aided by his son Robert and daughter Eve, murdered the children's stepmother, Emma, and buried her in a dung-pit by their door.[168] The incident, though factual, is also symbolic in the way in which the corpse was regarded as offal. A sexual example comes from early fourteenth-century France, where Arnaud de Verniolles sometimes had homosexual sex with young men on a dungheap.[169] Although this too is a genuinely historical, it is also acutely symbolic, with the dungheap appropriate to the supposed sinfulness of the transgression, and particularly important to its sodomical aspects.

Excrement was also associated with avarice. Medieval venality-satires often depict coins as excrement and purses as bladders, and illustrations show men or apes excreting coins into chamberpots.[170] The eleventh-century Latin comic tale *Unibos* is typical in its elaboration of this association between money and excrement. The clever peasant Unibos first discovers a hoard of coins while defecating in the forest, almost as if the coins themselves had been excreted. Later, as if acknowledging their excremental origin, he stuffs his treasure into the rear end of a mare and dupes three greedy people, one of them a priest, into paying a high price for her in the belief that she excretes coins. The climax of the story sees the three greedy fools waiting eagerly at her rear with sacks. In the economy of impurity, sin and dung are interchangeable.

In another instance, a priest named Alberic at the church of Fourgères in Brittany was found to be illicitly slipping coins from the collection money into his sleeves. Further investigation also revealed that he had smeared a cross on the altar with human excrement.[171] The sin of avarice and excremental blasphemy are seen as closely related. The association of dung and money was widespread, as has been noted. Similarly, an English sermon described a religious fine as a laxative for purses, and a Goliardic poem satirized Rome as medicine for constipated purses.[172]

The religious significance of the *requisita naturae*, the corrupt necessities of nature, is further demonstrated by what may be, to our eyes, the extraordinary rite of the *sedes stercoria* in the papal investiture. The rite of the stercory seat was described as early as the twelfth century and continued until 1560.[173] The twelfth-century *ordines* describing the ceremony say:

> Et postquam papa descenderit, faciunt eum ibi sedere in quadam sede marmorea que vocatur 'stercoraria', et veniunt omnes cardinales et 'honorifice' elevant eum, ut vere dicere possint "Suscitat de pulvere egenum et de stercore erigit pauperum, ut sedeat cum principibus et solium glorie teneat."[174] [1 Sm 2:8]

> And after the pope comes down, they have him sit in a certain marble seat that is called the "dung seat," and all the cardinals come and raise him up honorifically, so that it may be said truthfully: "He raises up the needy man from the dust and from the dung he lifts up the poor man, so that he may sit with princes and hold the throne of glory."

In becoming pope, the candidate is, as it were, rising to the purity of heaven and leaving behind the impurity of the flesh, a point that is conveyed by having him essentially rise from the toilet. After rising from the seat, the pope throws coins to the assembled crowd, vowing to undertake the protection of the people, and enters the Basilica of the Lateran palace, where he sits on a chair with a pierced seat. The chair, which exists to the present day in the chapel of San Silvestro, is an example of a type of chair with a pierced seat; it still puzzles modern scholars, who have suggested that it may have been a parturition chair used in childbirth or, in fact, a toilet.[175] The pierced seat of the chair played into rumors that the pope had to be checked by feeling from underneath to ascertain that he was not a woman. This was never actually part of the ceremony, though a legend to this effect persisted for centuries.

The pierced chair became confused with the stercory seat, also still in existence, now in the portico of the Basilica of St. John Lateran. A later writer, Platina (Bartolomeo Sacchi), identifies the pierced chair as the stercory seat in his *Life of the Popes*, a work commissioned by Sixtus IV and completed in 1474. In discussing the chair, he reiterates the understanding of the stercory seat as a symbol of lowliness and humility:

> Sunt qui haec duo scribant pontificem ipsum, quando ad Lateranensem basilicam proficiscitur, detestandi facinoris causa, et viam illam consulto declinare, et eiusdem vitandi erroris causa, dum primo in sede

Petri collocatur, ad eam rem perforata, genitalia ab ultimo diacono attectari. De primo non abnuerim; de secundo ita sentio, sedem illam ad id paratam esse, ut qui in tanto magistratu constituitur, sciat se non Deum, sed hominem esse: et necessitatibus naturae, utpote egerendi subiectum esse, unde merito stercoraria sedes vocatur.[176]

There are those who write two things about the pope on these matters: when he proceeds to the Lateran basilica, he purposely turns aside from that road, out of detestation of that crime; and to avoid that same error, when the pope is first seated on Peter's throne, perforated for this purpose, his genitals are touched by the least of the deacons. About the first, I will not contradict it; about the second, I understand it thus: that seat was prepared to this purpose, that he who is established in such a magisterial office should know that he is not God, but a man, as he is subject to the necessities of nature and defecation. Whence the seat is rightly called the "dung-seat."

Again the emblem of sin that distinguishes even the pope from the angels and the divine is excrement, the corruption that embodies human lowliness. In becoming pope he makes contact with human frailty and then rises up from corruption and the realm of the Devil. The inclusion of a ceremony involving the latrine in the papal consecration is powerful testimony to the significance of excrement in the religious understanding of the world.

* * *

With such an array of examples, which could be easily doubled or tripled in number, it should be clear why hapless sinners often encountered the Devil in the latrine. As the brother said to the Devil in Salimbene's story, "like rejoices in like."[177] Dung is not simply a metaphor for things that are despised; it is literally the substance belonging to the Devil, the result of sin, the corruption to which every human is subject. The question of whether it was proper to pray in the latrine is hence an important question involving the conjunction of the divine and the corrupt. Those who juxtapose the divine and the excremental in other contexts are accounted blasphemers, and the possibility clearly was of concern. But as we have seen, in a larger sense, every human, with his perishable, corruption-producing flesh, was a walking latrine, and prayer was not only advisable but critical to allying the devout with the divine rather than with the flesh that was trying to pull him down. Religious devotion reasserts purity and is the only thing that vanquishes the Devil in the latrine. Thus in the *Cent nouvelles nouvelles*, the knight triumphs over the Devil in the latrine only by maintaining his faith in baptism, the cleansing of sins.[178] In *Páttr Þorsteins skelks*, the demon in the latrine is put to flight by the ringing of church bells. In the story told by Caesarius of Heisterbach, the Devil in the latrine is overcome when the priest purifies himself by confession. As Augustine said when his mother reproved Licentius for singing a psalm in the latrine, "For what things do you think we pray that we may be converted to God and see his face, if not from a certain filth of the body and its ordures?" The fifteenth-century philosopher and theologian Gabriel Biel recounts the usual story of the man reproached by the devil for praising God in the latrine and takes pains to explain why this praise is not out of place:

> In domo, in foro, in mensa, in lecto, in latrina, in pallacio, nec aliquis locus turpis est orationi, dum orans mundus fuerit atque purus. . . . Opera enim nature perfectis turpia non videntur, nec infernus orationi non congrueret, si inesset qui orandi affectum haberet.[179]

> Neither in the house nor in the market, at the table, in bed, in the latrine, in the palace, no place is too base for prayer; while praying it will be clean and pure. . . . The works of perfect nature do not appear foul, nor is hell unsuitable for prayer, if there is someone with the disposition of prayer in it.

His very story of the devil appearing in the latrine affirms that the latrine is effectively an outpost of hell, a waystation to the inferno in which a Christian might be tempted to believe that God is no longer accessible. The virtue of prayer is that it purifies even the filthiest place, as it purifies even the filthiest of souls. Similarly, Salimbene de Adam finishes his account of the devil in the latrine with the pronouncement, "Deus enim non nisi sordes vitiorum abhorret," "For God abhors no filth except the filth of sin."[180] Although dung is not consonant with God, it does not serve as a threat to God, because God is incorruptible. Rather, dung is an emblem of *human* sin and corruption. Like sin, indeed *as* sin, it soils human purity and threatens human life; it embodies the corruption that threatens human imperishability. Its role in the earthly world is not to digust God, but to disgust humans. As both emblem and embodiment of mortal threat, it remained of compelling concern to the medieval world.

5 In Conclusion

THE MEANING OF FILTH

As we have seen, references to filth, and in particular to excrement, are pervasive in medieval culture. The arbiters of taste had not yet excluded this mark of the human condition from public discourse and restricted it to the realms of the medical or to the comedy of squeamishness. It was fully available to play its role in the examination of the entire range of human experience: to denote the inescapable corruptibility of earthly life and to signify the human distance from the divine.

Having laid out this scheme in its entirety, it is possible to evaluate more ambiguous, less explicitly moralized texts and images in which dung figures. In previous generations, any mention of dung or the lower body was typically effaced from scholarly editions; if left in, it was studiously ignored. Thus those who had no access to the primary manuscripts themselves had no way of knowing that, for instance, St. Francis advised his disciple to castigate the Devil in scatological terms, or that the Queen Mary Psalter contains prominent images of bottoms. Editions were simply expurgated, the subject deemed both worthless and vulgar.

In more recent times scholars have begun to reclaim and analyze these passages in their work, though often with apologies and some unease. Jonathan Wyn Shofer, who writes about rabbinic literature, comments on the reception of arguments about human waste:

> For audiences today, I have noticed through presentations that the topic of excretion and toilets in classical rabbinic texts often inspires one of two responses. Either people laugh, or they ask why one would study such an ignoble topic as part of rabbinic ethics. In these moments, I think we gain glimpses of contemporary anxieties about these very topics, perhaps anxieties that late ancient rabbis did not have.[1]

Many people certainly still regard the field as valueless, at best comical; this includes not only audiences but conference organizers as well as journal and book reviewers and editors. The result is that people working with materials that concern dung and filth have a limited range of comparative material and analysis. That is part of what I have sought to remedy. With the wealth of particulars and interpretations supplied in previous chapters, it may now be possible to refine, expand or controvert interpretations of some perplexing texts.

The wealth of examples related in this book should demonstrate that wherever dung makes an appearance in medieval writings or images, it participates in this theologically informed, popularly understood system of interpretation. Those witnesses that are explicit in their explanations are uniform in their understanding of such filth—dung is sin: corrupt, shameful and diabolical. The only significant variation is not a variation in meaning, but in valence: the difference between serious and comic texts. Serious texts are informed by a moral worldview, whether these texts are explicitly moral, like exempla and exegesis, or implicitly moral like chronicles and *gesta*. Comic or more playful works, by contrast, typically do not have overt moral or pedagogical aims; but this does not mean they participate in a different worldview. In comic texts the upper body is still superior and the lower body still unruly; dung is still humiliating and breaking wind is still coarse and improper. The essence of humor, however, is that consequences are trivial: no one we care about is killed, injuries and offenses are laughable rather than ruinous and the protagonist falls ludicrously into a dungheap rather than perishing shamefully in the latrine. The comic work does not disagree about the meaning of dung—dung is still filthy, earthly and unholy. It differs only in its assumptions about the magnitude of that significance.

Before we move to medieval views, however, we should return to a pervasive modern view. We have seen in Chapter 1 that the radical modern scholarly view of filth has become conventional: that filth embodies its own contradiction. In other words, the assertion holds that filth is reviled, offensive and repugnant, but also subversive, fertile and life-affirming. Mikhail Bakhtin regarded filth as an aspect of the lower bodily stratum that proves so fruitful in generating the carnivalesque, that popular, transgressive, festive dimension of life that opposes the more serious and constrained elements of society. Succeeding critics such as Julia Kristeva, Georges Bataille and Slavoj Žižek have articulated structurally similar analyses, arguing that the abject or filthy can serve as a fruitful site of resistance and redemption. More recently art historian Ruth Mellinokoff has argued for the apotropaic value of medieval scatological images, seeing them as protective against demons and malign influences.[2]

Although it provides an interesting paradox, especially useful for literary-critical theses, this seeming paradox is actually not unusual. Most things embody their own contradiction, if we understand that as meaning that a thing can be either good or bad depending on use and context. Among other things that embody their own contrary—that can be both good and bad—we could count regulation, science, chemotherapy, pesticides, frugality, market forces and literary criticism. The dictum that a thing embodies its own contradiction is only counterintuitive when applied to filth and dung, as these are generally regarded as trivial and without redeeming value (in the modern age) or as the embodiment of sin (in the medieval period). The fact that dung was a valuable fertilizer, an ingredient in some medicines and a popular agent in comedy, therefore, seems to put dung at the center of this interesting paradox. But do the useful aspects of dung really contradict its status as the embodiment of sin?

Although dung embodies sin, in the medieval understanding, this should be distinguished from any larger formulation. It embodies sin, but it does not embody *evil*. Evil is the cause; sin is the result. Dung is not evil; it is earthly and corrupt. As an earthly substance, it is no surprise that it has earthly uses: it fertilizes the earth, it can help the earthly body and it is an agent of laughable earthliness. These are not contradictions but part of its essential earthly nature. In the earthly realm, dung and filth are useful for earthly purposes. It is in heaven that they are out of place, useless and contradictory.

Ruth Mellinkoff goes one step further on the beneficent uses of scatology, averring that scatological images in the margins of manuscripts, and defecating gargoyles and the like in churches, are apotropaic, intended to frighten away demons and evil.[3] Mellinkoff writes:

> Like so many other motifs and themes, those of a sexual and scatological nature have a twofold significance: they are at once hostile and lucky. In the religious imagery of later periods they signified insult and mockery, a way to depict the depravity of the enemies of Christ and Christianity. But they also served as apotropaic protection, an ancient role that developed from their association with fertility, and hence the assurance of safety, good fortune, and abundance for humankind. As a kind of indecency associated with fertility magic, they conversely served to warn off malign influences. Remnants of pagan fertility cults, these powerful sexual symbols survived, embedded deep in Christian society.[4]

Mellinkoff cites a great deal of interesting evidence showing that the people of the Middle Ages were more interested in fertility and its associated motifs than has generally been recognized, whatever the ultimate origins of those motifs. However, fertility is irrelevant here. To conflate sexuality and scatology is to confuse the issues. Mellinkoff explains her choice to conflate the two: "[Sexuality and scatology] often overlap or appear in the same context, making individual discussion of them impractical."[5] As we have seen, however, the overwhelming proportion of scatology in medieval literature and art has no sexual associations whatsoever. In those few instances in which the two are associated, they are linked solely because of the sinful aspects of the sex rather than its erotic or pleasantly transgressive aspects. Of the wealth of examples of fertility motifs in medieval culture cited by Mellinkoff as context for her manuscript images, none is connected in any way with scatology. The only context in which sexual and scatological motifs are found together are in comic literature. The French fabliaux and their analogues in other languages are classic territory for such baring of the lower body. We are then more justified in classing manuscript and church marginalia as another manifestation of the genre of the playful.

This interpretation is supported by the other kinds of motifs found in manuscript marginalia, such as the tradition of the inverted world, where women rule men, animals hunt humans and so forth. Indeed, one of Mellinkoff's examples is actually a specimen of the inverted world. Speaking of a marginal image, in the Yolande of Soissons Psalter/Hours from late thirteenth-century France, Mellinkoff writes:

> A striking scatological portrayal occurs on folio 268 recto (Fig. VI.10), where just above the top margin a dog attacks the bare buttocks of a man on his hands and knees. Note the rabbit musician just to the right.[6]

This is in fact an instance of the inverted world. The dog is a hunting dog, urged onward by the rabbit, who is blowing a hunting horn. The man's tunic has slipped up to his waist, revealing his bare bottom, at which the hunting dogs nips. This is not a scatological motif but an instance of becoming animal: the man is on all fours, bent over, clothes slipping up to unveil his naked corporeality. As animal, he is flesh subject for hunting. Thus the image participates in the symbolism of bodily order as described in Chapter 3, but it does so as part of an established tradition of inverted-world comedy. The rabbit is hunting men with dogs, and the man is in a most humiliating position. Unless we are to say that all inverted-world images are apotropaic, however—a claim Mellinkoff does not make—we cannot identify this one as apotropaic.

Of course, many images of people displaying their buttocks and defecating into vessels do not participate in the inverted-world tradition. They occupy the same playful spaces as inverted-world images, however, in the margins of manuscripts and churches. As should be clear, these images do not contradict the larger understanding of the lower body and the backside as earthly, sinful and humiliating. They differ from more serious and didactic images merely by their more light-hearted and comic aspects. They say, in effect, *Aren't the things of the body ridiculous? They're all around you, in life as well as in godly places, and they're ridiculous. Keep in mind how ridiculous they are.* This message is both playful and serious at once.

A larger understanding of context may, then, help to interpret some of the issues posed by sources that treat the filth or purity of the lower body. What follows is a sample of case studies on a selection of disparate texts, all of which involve excrement and religion, and most of which have bemused or confounded scholars.

FOUR CASE STUDIES

i. Valentinus on the Incorruptibility of Jesus

The question of the implications of Christ's incarnation arose very early in the Christian era. The belief that Jesus was incarnated fully human provoked questions about whether this included the lowliest aspects of human existence; Biblical testimony that he ate and drank further precipitated thoughts of digestion. One strand of early thought on the subject is apparent in the writing of Valentinus (c. 100–175), an important early gnostic theologian. The works of Valentinus survive only in fragments; the passage in question is preserved as a quotation in the *Stromata* (also called *Stromateis*), or "Scraps," of Clement of Alexandria (c. 150–215). Examining the passage in light of subsequent discussion of Christ's materiality and digestion throws light on Valentinus's thinking. A survey of modern scholars on the subject similarly reveals modern difficulties with believing that such questions could be taken seriously.

Clement of Alexandria raises the issue of Christ's digestion in a discussion of abstaining from inadvisable or unrighteous things. He writes, "It is continence to despise money, softness, property, to hold in small esteem outward appearance, to control one's tongue, to master evil thoughts. In the past certain angels became incontinent and were seized by desire so that they fell from heaven to earth."[7] In support of this he then quotes an otherwise unknown letter from Valentinus to one Agathopus. Clement reports that Valentinus wrote, about Jesus:

> πάντα ὑπομείνας ἐγκρατὴς ἦν. θεότητα Ἰησοῦς εἰργάζετο, ἤσθιεν καὶ ἔπινεν ἰδίως οὐκ ἀποδιδοὺς τὰ βρώματα. τοσαύτη ἦν αὐτῷ ἐγκρατείας δύναμις, ὥστε καὶ μὴ φθαρῆναι τὴν τροφὴν ἐν αὐτῷ, ἐπεὶ τὸ φθείρεσθαι αὐτὸς οὐκ εἶχεν.[8]

> He was continent, enduring all things. Jesus digested [or: labored for] divinity: he ate and drank in a special way, without excreting his solids. He had such a great capacity for continence that the nourishment within him was not corrupted, for he did not experience corruption.[9]

Modern scholars have felt it necessary to apologize for this passage or to draw attention to the fact that it lies outside the norms of polite modern scholarship, using terms like "odd," (or "*at best* odd" [my emphasis]) "distasteful" and "exaggerated." Ismo Dunderberg writes, for instance, "From the modern perspe[c]tive, speculation about Christ's digestion may seem odd and Valentinus's solution that Christ ate and drank but did not defecate may even sound distasteful."[10] Piotr Ashwin-Siejkowski prefaces his defense of the statement with the acknowledgement, "To our modern sensitivity the whole argument about Christ's digestive system may seem at best odd."[11] Bentley Layton, the definitive translator of Valentinus, calls the passage an "exaggerated statement" about Jesus's digestion.[12] Indeed investigations of any conjunction of the divine and the bodily tend to provoke this nonplussed response, as witness the title of a study of medieval theology, Philip Lyndon Reynolds's *Food and the Body: Some Peculiar Questions in High Medieval Theology*.[13] To the modern mind, all such questions appear peculiar and must be prefaced with apologies and acknowledgements about the nature of the investigation.

Commentators have striven to puzzle out what could have given rise to Valentinus's apparently extraordinary statement. Layton suggests that it may be based on Jesus's command to the people of Tiberius in John 6:27, playing on a double meaning of the Greek verb ἐργάζομαι, "labor/digest."[14] The Biblical passage reads:

> ἐργάζεσθε μὴ τὴν βρῶσιν τὴν ἀπολλυμένην ἀλλὰ τὴν βρῶσιν τὴν μένουσαν εἰς ζωὴν αἰώνιον, ἣν ὁ υἱὸς τοῦ ἀνθρώπου ὑμῖν δώσει.
>
> Do not *labor for* [or *digest*] the food which perishes, but for the food which endures to eternal life, which the son of man will give to you.[15]

In this understanding thus the passage would be a literalization of Christ's metaphor-making. In a similar vein, Larry Hurtado proposes that Valentinus's passage may have grown out of a response to Psalm 16:10: "nor will you allow your holy one to see corruption," which Valentinus may have interpreted in a literal, digestive sense.[16]

These explanations see the idea arising from an understanding (or misunderstanding) of Biblical tradition. Alternate explanations suggest that the theme of the man exempt from defecation is a common Classical motif. As Dunderberg writes:

> Valentinus' claim that Christ did not defecate was less original in antiquity than it may sound now. The same claim was made in other sources of Pythagoras. It may be, thus, that Valentinus' idea of Christ's digestion was based upon earlier stories about this legendary Greek sage.[17]

Ashwin-Siejkowski echoes that the passage refers to the "classical *topos* of the sage or saint who does not need to defecate and acquires the special status of a hero," again citing Pythagoras, although without specifying any of the saints he mentions in addition.[18] Both Dunderberg and Ashwin-Siejkowski refer to Diogenes Laertius's *Lives of the Eminent Philosophers* (perhaps of the mid-third century B.C.E.) on both Pythagoras and Epimenides as evidence. These passages, however, do not serve as very substantial proof. The passage on Pythagoras (Diogenes Laertius 8.17) does not claim that Pythagoras never excreted but cites a number of enigmatic precepts of the philosopher. One of these involves defecation, with another two involving urination; the meaning is contested, but they appear to involve restrictions on excretion or, since Diogenes has reported that the precepts have hidden meanings, restrictions on excretion used as metaphors for other behavior.[19] They certainly do not claim that Pythagoras never excreted and so have no connection to Valentinus's passage.

Diogenes Laertius's account of Epimenides (1.114) is only slightly more useful. He reports that Demetrius recounted a story from others that Epimenides received a certain special food from the Nymphs, which he kept in a cow's hoof, and that by taking small amounts of this food "he expelled no kind of excrement and appeared never to eat."[20] This does not seem a very convincing parallel to the case of Jesus. Jesus's case required no special or magical food, there is no motif of peculiar storage, and not only was Jesus seen to eat, but his eating was understood as crucial testimony to his full humanity. Thus with Pythagoras eliminated and Epimenides dismissed as a useful parallel, evidence for the "classical *topos*" of the non-excreting sage is slim.

Among those who understand Valentinus's passage literally, the consensus has generally been that it means to indicate that Jesus was able to exercise a supernormal self-control over his desires and bodily processes. Ashwin-Siejkowski writes:

> Like Valentinus, Clement too believed that Christ's nature was unique, and one of the aspects and expressions of that uniqueness was his total control over the natural desires and needs of his body. The Saviour has the power of self-mastery ($απελθων$) which not only prioritises his activities, but also silences distracting, unnecessary desires such as sexual passions, ambitions, or pleasure in nourishment, since he did not experience any form of corruption.[21]

April DeConick concurs in this interpretation and analyzes it as a result of a balance of elements within the body. She compares this to two thirteenth-century women, one described by James of Vitry (Jacques de Vitry) and the other by Roger Bacon.[22] The woman in Bacon's example, Bacon argued, did not eat or excrete for twenty years on account of an extraordinary internal equilibrium.

It should be noted, however, that these examples are both women of a period that saw an explosion in somatic forms of female devotion, in the form of "fasting girls": women who were claimed to live solely from the Eucharist or from no food at all.[23] Bacon's intent is to explain physical phenomena by means of mechanical causes, but the fact that the fasting of the woman in question was verified by the bishop, as Bacon relates, shows that to the larger culture she was classed as a mystical phenomenon, neither eating nor drinking. The example of Jacques de Vitry is a straightforward account of a "fasting girl." The woman in question was a young recluse living in a cell in Vernon; Jacques testifies that for years she refrained from eating and drinking anything apart from the

Eucharist and that nothing came out from any exit on her body. Her sanctity was confirmed by the fact that she received the Eucharist from the mouth of a dove and that she heard angelic singing and saw a mystical light shine from heaven. In both cases the lack of excretion was likely not confined to an absence of defecation. Amenorrhea was also a typical consequence of fasting, and the accounts of both authors are worded so as to suggest it. Jacques de Vitry states that nothing came out "per alia nature instrumenta," "though any instruments of nature," and Roger Bacon that the woman was "nullam superfluitatem emittens," "emitting no superfluity," carefully leaves room for this conclusion.

Thus these examples differ from Valentinus's account in two important respects. They are focused not on an absence of defecation, but on a miraculous absence of eating, as confirmed by the lack of all types of bodily effusion. Moreover, they are products of a particular moment in the history of a specifically female sanctity, and their details conform to that model.

DeConick also locates an early witness to the idea of a natural internal balance that results in lack of defecation, although this passage also ascribes such purity to a golden age when the ancients "were born close to the gods." The passage appears in Porphyry (of the third century C.E.), who was describing the reports of Dicaearchus, some five centuries before. According to Porphyry, Dicaearchus was concerned to understand the tales of the lost golden age by reason, rather than accepting them uncritically as mythology. Thus Dicaearchus looked for natural explanations for the characteristics of the golden age.

The reports with which Dicaearchus was working seem to have represented a golden age much like that of the Garden of Eden, where humans did not have to farm or work for their food, enjoyed perfect health and were free of cares. Their perfect health and balance meant they were also free of "residues," or substances extruded from the body, residues being a concept articulated by Aristotle.[24] Residues might include not only excrement but such things as sweat, and even, according to some authors, hair. Thus when it comes time to address the question of defecation, Porphyry supplies a "scientific" explanation for the lack of defecation reported by his sources:

> Among the doctors' precepts, you could find none more important for health than not to make residues: and they kept their bodies pure from these at all times. They ate no food which was too strong for their nature to digest, but food with which their nature could cope; they took no more than a moderate amount, because of availability, and usually less than was sufficient, because of scarcity.[25]

In his formulation, then, the golden age was one of internal corporeal balance. We can see behind this interpretation, though, an original legend that much resembles the Christian understanding: in the lost golden age, the body was pure, and humans did not suffer from foul excretions. Dicaearchus and Porphyry take a different path in interpreting this imaginative nostalgia, but it originates in a similar view of the current human body as a decline in perfection from the excretion-free body of a lost age of purity.

Is Jesus's lack of bodily corruption, then, the result of an overliteral understanding of the Bible, a heroic folk-motif, or the consequence of digestive equilibrium? I hope the previous chapters have made clear that the lack of corporeal corruption is a logical consequence of bodily purity in a body unafflicted by original sin. As recounted in Chapters 3 and 4, medieval heretics broached the question repeatedly, and the orthodox, though reluctant to discuss Christ's body with unseemly explicitness, repeatedly affirmed that he was without stain, using "shamefulness" as a euphemism for defecation and excretion. As Guibert pronounced, "if [Christ] had parts suitable to his bodiliness, the composition of his parts was not harmful . . . what should have shamed him, where there was nothing that was not holy!"[26] As Francesc Eiximenis explained, "if Adam had not sinned . . . even though man would still have to empty his bowels through the natural opening, it would not stink nor would it have that shamefulness."[27] It follows, then, that the sinless divine would have no such shamefulness. Valentinus is not alone in articulating such things; he is only distinctive in articulating them so graphically. And he means literally what he says.

We should not understand "continence" (ἐγκράτεια), then, as "self-control," particularly self-control about eating and digestion, but more as an expression for sinlessness. This accords with Clement's argument, which held that certain angels were seized by "incontinence" and fell to earth. Surely this means that they were seized by a desire to sin. Thus Christ's bodily stainlessness is not the result of a wilful control over his organs of digestion, but a natural concomitant of divine purity.

ii. St. Francis in the Saint-Omer Psalter

An understanding of the system may also illuminate images as well as texts. A case in point is a manuscript image of St. Francis found in the Saint-Omer Psalter, a manuscript of the 1270s.[28] The relevance of the image was first brought to light by Susan Signe Morrison, who noticed a significant part of the image—the doings of the dog—overlooked by previous scholars. In Morrison's words:

> A Flemish psalter (MS. Douce 49, folio LXIII v) [*recte* 64v] shows a highly decorated initial with St. Francis preaching to at least four birds. In the foreground we see a crouching dog, concentrating mightily as it defecates.[29]

It is indicative of the way in which medieval defecation has been effaced from modern scholarship that the precise occupation of this dog had escaped identification. Even the description on the Bodleian Library website has only "On the end of the tail [of the letter Q] crouches a glowering brown dog."[30] Yet on closer inspection the dog does indeed seem to be glowering with the kind of concentration with which dogs defecate and in the same position, and a dropping the same color as the dog appears to be emitted from his rear (Figure 12).

Morrison has done valuable service in recognizing that the dog is defecating; her scholarship on the subject has alerted her to the possibility, indeed probability, that this is what is taking place. In recent years such images have started to appear in scholarship, though the field remains understudied, and thus the medieval popularity of such images remains hard to apprehend.[31] However, it may require a larger context to interpret the image in medieval terms. Morrison understands the image as a holy acceptance of bodily corruption:

> What could possibly be the religious content of such an image? While St. Francis preaches to birds, all God's creatures are worthy of His

Figure 12 St. Francis preaches to the animals. The birds are attentive; the dog appears to be disregarding the saint and concentrating on defecating. Is this a sign that even the foul are saved, or that sinners isolate themselves in their sin and disregard the word of God? Oxford, Bodleian Library Douce 49 (the Saint-Omer Psalter), fol. 64v (of the 1270s).

word, even a shitting dog. This animal symbolizes us in our earthly degradation, a state God can redeem only by becoming as degraded and material as we are.[32]

In the medieval understanding, Christ did indeed become as material and fleshly as we are, but his was a sinless, pure and incorrupt fleshliness, as we have seen. Morrison argues that certain facts of Jesus's infancy imply that he must have soiled his diapers, as do human babies born of sin: the fact that Jesus's swaddling clothes were venerated, for instance, or that human babies often soil themselves after nursing, a fact that might have been called to mind by medieval viewers of the infant Jesus and the Virgin Mary.[33] But as we have seen, when medieval writers such as the composer of the infancy gospels took up the question, they represented Jesus as stainless and entirely free from earthly pollution: an incarnated body that partakes of the characteristics of immateriality. God redeems us not by indulging in carnal pollution along with us, but by drawing us away from such corruption, toward his stainlessness and purity.

We can see these themes in the image of St. Francis. Few images in the Bible have only one kind of medieval interpretation—dung is unusual in that regard—but among the various interpretations, birds are often used to signify upper or superior things, the things of the spirit. We might recall the exegesis of Hugh of St. Victor on the animals in the ark: "the flying creatures signify the activity of incorruptible nature. We will take flight in mind through contemplation."[34] The compendium of symbolic meanings, the *Allegoriae in sacram scripturam*, concurs, among its positive meanings suggesting "spiritual men" and

> *Avis*, anima hominis, ut in Job [5:7]: "Et avis nascitur ad volandum," quod anima pura in contemplatione se extendit.[35]
>
> *Bird* [signifies] the soul of man, as in Job: "And the bird is born to fly," because the pure soul stretches itself in contemplation.

The extended necks of the two birds at St. Francis's feet, looking up to the saint and to heaven, would certainly exemplify this interpretation.

The dog, by contrast, is isolated, sitting apart from the animals, ignoring St. Francis, absorbed in its own bodily experience. Both Biblical and medieval tradition regarded the dog as an unclean animal; the proof text of dogs' uncleanliness was the widely cited Proverbs 26:11: "As a dog returneth to its vomit, a fool returneth to his folly." Revelations 22:15 has "Without are dogs, and sorcerers, and unchaste, and murderers, and servers of idols, and every one that loveth and maketh a lie." Most pertinently, Matthew 7:6 has "Give not that which is holy to dogs." The *Allegoriae* comments:

Canis est peccator impudens, ut in Parabolis: "Canis reversus ad vomitum suum" [Prov. 26:11], id est, peccator impudens redit ad peccatum suum. . . . Per *canes,* reprehensores, ut in Evangelio: "Nolite mittere sanctum canibus" [Matt. 7:6], id est, sacrae Scripturae mysterium illis qui mordaciter reprehendunt. Per *canes,* detractores, ut in Paulo: "Videte canes" [Phil. 3:2].³⁶

Dog is the shameless sinner, as in Proverbs: "The dog returns to his vomit," that is, the shameless sinner returns to his sin. . . . By *dogs,* critics, as in the Gospel: "Do not give what is holy to dogs," that is, the mystery of holy Scripture to those who condemn it bitingly. By *dogs,* detractors, as in Paul: "Watch out for dogs."

In this scene, then, we see a figure of the holy and the audience. The word of God is offered to all, even those whose mind is on their own corporeal concerns rather than on the divine. Some, like the birds, are attentive to the holy. Others, like defecating dogs, disregard it in favor of the filth of the flesh. The audience is invited to consider which they would rather emulate: the attentive, contemplative and flight-worthy birds or the isolated, ridiculous dog, concentrating on the bodily functions he does not realize are disgusting.

iii. The Torments of Christina of Stommeln

The *Life* of the thirteenth-century stigmatic Christina of Stommeln provides an even more graphic example of the way filth and the divine could be configured, a way radically out of step with modern conventions. Like Job on the dung heap, the holy could be tormented by dung, their humility and longsuffering tried by demonic scatology. Peter of Dacia's thirteenth-century *Life* of Christina of Stommeln exemplifies this, enumerating a long list of ways in which a demon tormented the saint with dung.³⁷ In the presence of Peter and several other clerics, he reports, a demon defiled Christina with human excrement in more than twenty ways, many of them graphically described. The demon covered her body or her head with dung, put dung between her eyelids and her pupils and filled her mouth with it so firmly that it could only be removed with difficulty. Peter reports that he helped remove the filth himself. On one occasion the demon also covered Christina's detractors with dung in church.³⁸ In a further episode, a Brother Gerardus made a joking request for the devil not to defecate on him, and the devil responded by appearing and literally covering him with human excrement. Peter comments that this is the way the devil treats his friends, making it clear that he understands excrement as the *proprium* of the devil.³⁹

The episodes in which Christina becomes covered in excrement, reported from first-hand testimony, certainly invite modern speculation as to her psychological condition, and it might be noted in this regard that she was also the first female stigmatic in Christian history (and that she voluntarily produced the nails with which she was wounded, which she had been keeping in her sleeves). Leaving aside modern questions about the origins of Christina's afflictions, we can see that her story is conventional in the medieval understanding of the workings of the Devil and filth. Like Job, Christina is humbled and tormented by dung; as in the story of Job, the afflictions are the work of the Devil; and Christina's patience in the face of those afflictions testifies to her humility.

Although these episodes fit neatly into the larger medieval schema, they are at odds with modern sensibilities. On the episode in which the demon douses Brother Gerard with human dung, Aviad Kleinberg comments: "it functions, if anything, like a comic relief. The devil is more a prankster than a threatening ag[g]ressor."[40] And on the episode in which the demon torments Christina's face with dung, Kleinberg remarks:

> There is something disconcerting about this passage for the modern reader. First, one finds it hard to overcome the repulsion that the author's detailed description arouses.... But worse still, Christina comes out of the episode looking ridiculous. There seems to be little or no danger in the demonic attack. Christina is simply made the victim of scatological slapstick. I cannot help feeling that there is something slightly comic about this episode.[41]

The repulsion, of course, was part of the effect the author must have hoped to evoke. I would suggest, too, that Christina's ordeal looks ridiculous only when emptied of meaning by the modern sensibility that regards dung as insignificantly repulsive and such episodes as implausible. Kleinberg explores the doubt of modern readers and adds:

> Can we assume that in contrast with their modern descendants, medieval readers would have accepted the veracity of such an account without further question and therefore immediately conceived it as tragic rather than comic? Although we are dealing with speculations, it is more probable that without supplementary data, a medieval reader would not be able to assign truth value to the episode.[42]

Kleinberg goes on to examine the unconventional aspects of the *Life*, looking at the possibilities of making sense of it from a modern point of view.

The scatology of the *Life* certainly seems extraordinary viewed from the modern perspective on saints and demons, but a comprehensive view of the literature demonstrates how commonplace demons and their scatological afflictions and associations were in the Middle Ages. A medieval audience would have recognized the devil's tricks immediately, and might not have merely connected such afflictions with Job, but with versions of the stories that formed the elaborated later medieval Passion narratives, in which unbelievers afflicted Christ with excrement. If we conclude medieval audiences disbelieved such tales, the wide circulation of the stories must have meant that they disbelieved a great deal of their own moral literature.

iv. Comic Corruption in *The Sacristan*

The thirteenth-century fabliau *The Sacristan* participates in the schema of medieval filth from a different direction: that of the comic. Here we see all the familiar equations: dung, corruptible earthliness, sinful flesh and the diabolical are all interchangeable. The only difference is that the story has comic rather than moral aims: it emphasizes the ludicrousness of earthly desires, rather than the deadliness.

The tale survives in three French versions.[43] The plot concerns a lecherous sacristan who propositions a respectable woman of the town, offering her money to surrender her favors. Poverty-stricken, the woman and her husband hatch a plan to lure the monk to their house, accept the money, but thwart him before the rest of his intent can be realized. The plan goes wrong and the monk is accidentally killed. The husband initially tries to hide the body by propping it up on a seat in the monastic latrine, a wisp of straw in its hand, as if the monk had died in the middle of his necessities of nature. The prior of the monastery finds the body, panics, worries that he will be accused of murder, and hauls the body into town, propping it up at the door of the husband and wife. When they discover it, the husband attempts to hide it a second time by concealing it in a dungheap. As the husband is rooting about in the dungheap he discovers a flitch of bacon hidden there in a sack, which he at first mistakes for another monk. The husband takes the bacon home and leaves the monk in the dung. There the monk is discovered by the thief who has hidden the bacon and has returned to retrieve it. Finding that his bacon has apparently been transformed into a dead monk, he sees it as a sign from God and repents, returning the dead monk to the house where he stole the bacon. The householder goes to cut off a slice of bacon in the dark and finds that the bacon is wearing shoes. Horrified, his household devises a plan to seat the dead sacristan on a pony and pretend he has stolen the pony and fled. With the sacristan atop, the pony blunders into the abbey kitchens, battering all the equipment, until it charges off and finally unseats the sacristan into a ditch, ending the story.

The monk's degradation into dung begins when he starts to regard others as carnal bodies. Sexual sin and gluttony are collapsed as he attempts to consummate his agreement with the wife:

> Il se leva, faire li vost
> Dejoste le foier en rost . . . (319–20)[44]

> he leaped and like a roast he tried
> to spit her by the fireside.[45]

The lecherousness of the monk renders him wholly carnal, and thus wholly corruptible; as such his virtual transformation into dung is in keeping with his sins. Once dead, he is first transported to the latrines, the site where so many other sinners get their due and are effectively transformed into pure corruption. This is a version of the motif applied to Arius, to Gregory of Tours's evil priest, to Walafrid Strabo's oppressive bishop, to Guibert of Nogent's sinful priest, to the sinful monk William Pigun and to other iniquitous men of the Church. The scene in which the corpse is exchanged for a stolen flitch of bacon (itself hidden in a dungheap), emphasizes his status as mere flesh, and the flesh of a notoriously filthy animal, the pig, at that. The tale shows the same network of associations as Salimbene de Adam's story of the lecherous canon buried in the cesspool near the pigpen.

So that there is no doubt about the ultimate author of carnal sin, at every point the finders of the body exclaim that the Devil is behind all of this. The thief cries:

> Or s'est dëable en guise mis
> de moine por nos enconbrer . . .

> Now it's the Devil in the guise
> of a monk to trouble us . . .

And the bacon's owner cries:

> N'est pas bacons, ainz est malfez
> Qui sanble moine coronez! (737–38)

> it isn't bacon, but a devil
> tonsured monkwise, on the level![46]

Dung is diabolical, the Devil the ultimate agent of the transformation of flesh into dung. Carnality thus converts the monk into corrupt flesh and finally into excrement. He is propped in the latrine, as if in the process of being transformed like the litany of other sinners who lose their souls in the privy. He is then deposited in the dungheap, interchangeable with flesh. Mistaken for food, he is transported into a kitchen and finally arrives at the *fosse*—as is clear in Chapter 2, the equivalent of an open sewer. Carnal desire turns even a man of the Church into mere corrupt flesh; he is at once sinful carnality, excrement and diabolical. The fabliau is fictional and comic, but in no way does this make its scheme of purity irrelevant; it is only comic in that it regards the downfall of the sacristan with an amused eye rather than with the horror of the Church.

SHAME AND SHAMELESSNESS—THE CIVILIZING PROCESS?

What, then, was the true nature of the civilized attitude toward filth in the Middle Ages, and how was this altered in later centuries? The stereotyped view of medieval bodily processes holds that in the medieval period, filth, vulgarity and the bawdy were rampant: chamber pots continually rained down their contents on the heads of passers-by, humor was coarse and tastes were so primitive that even sophisticated authors such as Chaucer reveled in lowly tales of lascivious wives and excremental friars. It was not until the Renaissance, according to this traditional view, that Western civilization recovered Classical purity, restraint and good taste. This model was articulated most fully by Norbert Elias in his influential two-volume study *The Civilizing Process* (*Über den Prozess der Zivilisation*), first published in 1939.[47] Elias's thesis held that the Middle Ages shared with "primitive" societies a lack of shame about excretion and other bodily matters, expressed by their ease in discussing and performing these things openly. In Elias's argument, the Renaissance inaugurated the development of civilization and refinement, characterized by the cultivation of bodily shame. His argument was buttressed by numerous examples from the growing abundance of conduct books and other manuals. Elias's outline of the development of manners is echoed in Dominique Laporte's *Histoire de la Merde*, which argues that the Renaissance first promulgated laws to regulate dung, providing a turning point in the history of the West and inaugurating modern ideas of individuality.[48]

Elias's picture of the development of self-restraint and shame has come under fire, most prominently by Hans-Peter Duerr's five-volume refutation of Elias, *Der Mythos vom Zivilisationsprozess* (1988–2002), which traces the development of sensibilities in more detail in a variety of realms.[49] A number of other objections have since been raised to Elias's work. Most of these are irrelevant to the present topic, having to do with querying the ideas of "civilizing" and "progress," as well as with Norbert's choice of manners as indicative of the degree of civilization in a society, as opposed to, for example, levels of violence.[50] Other objections concern Elias's analysis of the social forces underlying the developments he identified. More to the present point, critics have identified numerous indications of bodily shame in both "primitive" cultures and medieval culture, examples that undermine Elias's contention that shame took modern form only in the Renaissance.[51]

It should be clear from the abundant examples in the present work that excretion, excrement and bodily filth were potent sources of shame throughout the medieval period. What changed in the centuries following the medieval period was not the underlying response but the discourse on filth. In the Middle Ages, bodily shame had a recognized moral function—a function that in fact continued to be recognized for centuries afterward. Against Elias's assertions, for instance, is the fact that the writings of Martin Luther (1483–1546), all indubitably serious, are more pervasively scatological than those of any medieval theologian. We can see the identical system operating as late as the writings of the New England Puritan minister Cotton Mather (1663–1728), who, faced with the shame of his animalistic earthly body, used this as a prompt toward divine elevation:

> I was once emptying the cistern of nature, and making water at the wall. At the same time, there came a dog, who did so too, before me. Thought I; "What mean and vile things are the children of men ... How much do our natural necessities abase us, and place us ... on the same level with the very dogs! My thought proceeded. "Yet I will be a more noble creature; and at the very time when my natural necessities debase me into the condition of the beast, my spirit shall (I say *at that very time!*) rise and soar. ... Accordingly, I resolved that it should be my ordinary practice, whenever I step to answer the one or other necessity of nature to make it an opportunity of shaping in my mind some holy, noble, divine thought.[52]

This realization of his corrupt materiality, his carnal animality, tellingly resembles the examples of the medieval pious men who encountered the devil—the very spirit of corruption—in the latrine. Once again the subject is brought face to face with his animality and must make a conscious decision to rise above it—the metaphor of "up" versus "down" is intrinsically involved—whether, in the medieval examples, to pray, or in Cotton Mather's example, to "rise and soar."

In the medieval period, as well as into the Renaissance, excrement and bodily filth were popular subjects of public discourse specifically because they could drive home the need for shame and the abjuration of worldly pleasures. To associate excrement with the Devil, as did Luther, was no mere metaphor; similarly, to discuss religious opponents in scatological terms was not a simple-minded form of ridicule, but a forceful statement about demonic corruption.

The humiliating aspects of dung also meant that, in less moralistic genres, it was also a perennial staple of comedy. In humor, which tends to the amoral, bodily realities were agreeably disgusting and transgressive, pure and simple.

As the early modern period progressed, simple advances in wealth and technology meant that the upper reaches of society could successfully become more and more particular about hygiene and privies. This progress is visible by the later Middle Ages, with the water-flushed latrines in wealthier monasteries and even in the homes of ingenious citizens such as Alice Wade, as well as in the increasing number of garderobes built in to aristocratic residences such as Middleham and Langley castles. The change is not that people wanted to be more particular in their sanity arrangements than in early periods; the change is that they could be.

What this reveals is that when people had the resources to separate themselves, as much as possible, from the filthy reality of excretion, they did. With these developments in provisions came an increasing delicacy about referring to excretion in polite secular speech, so that what became more hidden in daily life did so in conversation as well. It is important to note that this happened only on the upper levels of conversation—there is ample evidence to demonstrate that excretion has remained a popular topic of humor and unrefined speech throughout the centuries. But as such topics were excluded from refined speech—indeed speech can be identified as "refined" simply because it excludes these topics—earthy humor itself became relegated to the lower levels of culture. It should be noted that this was nominally the case even as early as the fourteenth century, when Chaucer puts his scatology in the voice of humorous "low" characters such as the Miller and the Summoner. The idea that more sophisticated people do not tell or hear such tales is obviously a fiction, since both the author and his audience are relishing the spectacle. As the early modern period progressed, however, the fiction that only the unrefined countenanced such topics increasingly became a reality. As people were able to confine excretion to private, secret life, so it was increasingly masked and euphemized, so that, for instance, the frank street names of the Middle Ages were changed to efface their lowly associations. Thus, as we have seen in Chapter 2, Shiteburn Lane became Paternoster Row. The reluctance to acknowledge or mention such matters gathered pace as the centuries proceeded. John Ray's 1670 edition of the *Collection of English Proverbs* left out those which were regarded as "openly obscene," but even so his subsequent edition, published in 1678, omitted some which had been printed in the first edition. As he noted, those he had left out referred to excretions and "those actions and parts of the body by which they are expelled, and therefore the mention of them is uncivil and contrary to good manners."[53] Even in proverbs, excretion had lost its power to instruct.

Most importantly, as theology became more abstract and reason became paramount, as culture entered the Enlightenment, the emphasis on the bodily experience of shame diminished. The *necessaria naturae* remained shameful, but corporeal shame was effaced from public discourse. Excretion and bodily filth were no longer central to religious teaching. This was coupled with the rise of secular humanism and a deemphasis on religion in many areas of life. The exact progress of this is beyond the scope of this work: the main point is that bodily processes induced shame in equal measure throughout the Middle Ages and after, but the role of that shame in religious teaching lessened, and even more significantly, the hegemony of religious discourse in public life was lessened. That left humor as the only response to the degradation of excretion and bodily filth.

The decline of excretion as a serious topic of discussion is, then, directly related to the rise of the secular. It is no accident that the authors who continue to mention excrement in serious contexts, such as Martin Luther and Cotton Mather, are religious writers. As the hegemony of religion in public life waned, the serious view of excrement went into eclipse as well: it was downgraded to something trivial, comic, empty of meaning.

182 Sin and Filth in Medieval Culture

Figure 13 The sense that the toilet is a place of demonic peril has not died away. Here the story claims the woman's toilet began to belch flames and heat only after the woman "renewed her Christian vows" and began to attend church regularly, as if the toilet formed an entryway for the Devil to try to reclaim her soul. *Weekly World News,* August 4, 1998.

Notes

NOTES TO CHAPTER 1

1. Sir John Harington, *A New Discourse of a Stale Subject, Called the Metamorphosis of Ajax* (London, 1596), pp. 17–18. For copyright reasons this poem is quoted from the original; it is also reprinted in *Sir John Harington's A New Discourse of a Stale Subject, Called the Metamorphosis of Ajax*, ed. Elizabeth Story Donno (London: Routledge and Kegan Paul, 1962), p. 94.
2. Salimbene de Adam, *Cronica*, ed. Guiseppe Scalia, CCCM 125–125A, 2 vols. (Turnhout: Brepols, 1998–99), vol. II, p. 857 (s.v. 1285).
3. Salimbene de Adam, *The Chronicle of Salimbene de Adam*, trans. Joseph L. Baird et al. (Binghamton, NY: Medieval and Renaissance Texts and Studies, 1986), p. 577.
4. Salimbene de Adam, *Cronica*, II, p. 857.
5. Salimbene de Adam, *The Chronicle of Salimbene*, trans. Baird, pp. 577–78.
6. Gabriel Biel, *Gabrielis Biel Canonis Misse Expositio*, ed. Heiko A. Oberman and William J. Courtenay, 4 vols. (Wiesbaden: Franz Steiner, 1963–67), vol. III, p. 27 (lectio LXII.F). Gabriel Biel attributes the story to Alexander of Hales.
7. Peter the Venerable, *De Miraculis*, PL 189, col. 877 (lib. I, cap. XIII).
8. Rodulphus Cluniacensis, *Vita Domni Petri Abbatis*, PL 189, col. 24.
9. Thietmar of Merseberg, *Die Chronik des Bischofs Thietmar von Merseburg*, ed. Robert Holtzmann, MGH, Scriptores Rerum Germanicarum n.s. IX (Berlin: Weidman, 1955), p. 215.
10. "Let these houses be blessed by any one going thither, and let him bless himself when he enters them, and it is not lawful to say any prayers in them, except 'Deus in adjutorium' to 'festina.'" William Reeves, "On the Céli-dé, commonly called Culdees," *Transactions of the Royal Irish Academy* 24 (1873), 119–263 at p. 209.
11. *Les Cent nouvelles nouvelles*, ed. Franklin P. Sweetser (Geneva: Droz, 1966), tale 70, pp. 426–30.
12. *Flateyjarbók*, ed. S. Nordal et al., 4 vols ([n.p.], Prentverk Akraness,1944–45), I, pp. 462–64. On the tale see also Carolyne Larrington, "Diet, Defecation and the Devil: Disgust and the Pagan Past," in *Medieval Obscenities*, ed. Nicola McDonald (Woodbridge, Suffolk: Boydell and Brewer/York Medieval Press, 2006), pp. 138–55.
13. Guibert de Nogent, *Guibert de Nogent: Autobiographie*, ed. Edmond-René Labande (Paris: Société d'Edition 'Les Belles Lettres', 1981), p. 120 (book 1, ch. 15).
14. Ibid., p. 254 (book 2, ch. 5).

15. "Passio Sancte Iulianae Martyris" in Boninus Mombritius (Bonino Mombrizio), *Sanctuarium seu Vitae Sanctorum*, 2 vols. (Hildesheim: Georg Olms Verlag, 1978), vol. II, p. 79.
16. *Acta Sanctorum*, ed. J. Bollandus et al. (1643–), Mar. II, p. 156 (lib. III, cap. II).
17. The story is in Johannes Nider's *Formicarius* (1516 or 1517), quoted by Nancy Caciola, *Discerning Spirits: Divine and Demonic Possession in the Middle Ages* (Ithaca, NY: Cornell University Press, 2003), pp. 204–05.
18. Caesarius of Heisterbach, *Dialogus Miraculorum*, ed. Joseph Strange (Cologne, 1851; repr. Ridgewood, NJ: Gregg Press, 1966), book 5, ch. XXVIII, pp. 311–12; *The Dialogue on Miracles*, trans. H. von E. Scott and C. C. Swinton Bland, 2 vols. (London: Routledge, 1929), vol. I, pp. 355–56.
19. Caesarius of Heisterbach, *Dialogus Miraculorum*, vol. I, p. 129 (Dist. III, ch. xiv); *The Dialogue on Miracles*, vol. I, pp. 144–45.
20. From Melanchthon's *Historia quaedam recitatae inter publicas lectiones*, section X, printed in *Philippi Melanthonis Opera quae Supersunt Omnia*, ed. K. G. Bretschneider and H. E. Bindseil, Corpus Reformatorum 20 (Brunsviga, 1854), col. 523.
21. Martin Luther, *D. Martin Luthers Werke. Kritische Gesamtausgabe. Tischreden*, 6 vols. (Weimar: Hermann Böhlaus, 1912–21), vol. II, p. 413 (no. 2307 a and b).
22. An alternate version with German surrounding the narrative is supplied in the notes to this version, ibid.
23. Also in *Sir John Harington's a New Discourse*, ed. Donno, p. 94.
24. Augustine, "De ordine," in *Aurelii Augustini Opera pars II, 2*, CCSL 29 (Turnhout: Brepols, 1970), I, viii, 22, pp. 99–100.
25. Ibid., I, viii, 23; ed. p. 100.
26. Peter Abelard, "Theologia 'Summi Boni'," in *Petri Abaelardi Opera Theologica*, ed. E. M. Buytaert and C. J. Mews, CCCM 13 (Turnhout: Brepols, 1987), III, ch. 79, lines 1054–57, p. 191.
27. Marcel Mauss, "Les techniques du corps," *Journal de Psychologie normale et pathologique* 32 (1935), 271–93.
28. Mary Douglas, *Purity and Danger: An Analysis of Concepts of Pollution and Taboo* (London: Routledge, 1966). Douglas also discusses the subject in her *Natural Symbols: Explorations in Cosmology*, 2nd ed. (London: Routledge, 1996).
29. Douglas, *Purity and Danger*, p. 5
30. Ibid., p. 5.
31. Ibid., p. 2.
32. This is also central to the focus of Douglas Biow, *The Culture of Cleanliness in Renaissance Italy* (Ithaca, NY: Cornell University Press, 2006).
33. Douglas, *Purity and Danger*, p. 122.
34. Among those who have used Douglas's approach are Anthony Spearing, in his analysis of the Middle English poem *Purity* (or *Cleanness*), "Purity and Danger," *Essays in Criticism* 30 (1980), 293–310; Miri Rubin, "Europe Remade: Purity and Danger in Late Medieval Europe," *Transactions of the Royal Historical Society*, 6th series, 11 (2001), 101–124.
35. Anthropology came to the subject as early as 1891, with John G. Bourke's *Scatalogic Rites of All Nations* (Washington, D.C.: Lowdermilk and Co., 1891). Bourke's compendious but unanalytical round-up of evidence is provided with a Bakhtinian context by Stephen Greenblatt, "Filthy Rites," *Daedalus* 111 (1982), 1–16, and more on the subject is offered by Peter Stallybrass and Allon White, *The Politics and Poetics of Transgression* (Ithaca,

NY: Cornell University Press, 1986), pp. 125–48 and passim. General scholarship on the topic of "filth" is also outlined by William A. Cohen, "Introduction: Locating Filth," in *Filth: Dirt, Disgust, and Modern Life*, ed. William A. Cohen and Ryan Johnson (Minneapolis: University of Minnesota Press, 2005), pp. vii–xxxvii. An overview of the human relationship to excrement has also been provided by Claude Gaignebet and Marie-Claude Périer, "L'homme et l'excretum," in *Histoire des Moeurs* vol. I: *Les Coordinnées de l'homme et la culture matérielle*, ed. Jean Poirier (Paris: Gallimard, 1990), pp. 831–93.
36. Mikhail Bakhtin, *Rabelais and his World*, trans. Helene Iswolsky (Cambridge, MA: MIT Press, 1968).
37. Sigmund Freud, *Civilization and its Discontents*, trans. Joan Riviere, rev. and newly ed. James Strachey (London: Hogarth Press and the Institute of Psycho-Analysis, 1969); *Three Essays on the Theory of Sexuality*, trans. James Strachey (London: Hogarth Press and the Institute of Psycho-Analysis, 1962); "Character and Anal Eroticism," in *Standard Edition of the Complete Psychological Works of Sigmund Freud*, ed. James Strachey, 24 vols. (London: Hogarth Press, 1953–74), vol. 9, pp. 169–75; "On Transformations of Instinct as Exemplified in Anal Eroticism," in *Standard Edition of the Complete Psychological Works*, ed. James Strachey, 24 vols. (London: Hogarth Press, 1953–74), vol. 17, pp. 126–33.
38. Alan Dundes, *Life is Like a Chicken Coop Ladder: A Portrait of German Culture through Folklore* (New York: Columbia University Press, 1984).
39. Dominique Laporte, *Histoire de la Merde* (Paris: Christian Bourgois Éditeur, 1978). Translated as *History of Shit* [sic], trans. Nadia Benabid and Rodolphe el-Khoury (Cambridge, MA: MIT Press, 2000).
40. Julia Kristeva, *Powers of Horror: An Essay on Abjection*, trans. Leon S. Roudiez (New York: Columbia University Press, 1982).
41. Georges Bataille, *Visions of Excess: Selected Writings 1927–1939*, trans. Allan Stoekl with Carl R. Lovitt and Donald M. Leslie Jr. (Minneapolis: University of Minnesota Press, 1985).
42. Slavoj Žižek, *The Plague of Fantasies* (London: Verso, 1997).
43. See, for instance, Gail Kern Paster, "The Epistemology of the Water Closet: John Harington's *Metamorphosis of Ajax* and Elizabethan Technologies of Shame," in *Material Culture and Cultural Materialisms in the Middle Ages and Renaissance*, ed. Curtis Perry (Turnhout: Brepols, 2001), pp. 139–58, as well as her *The Body Embarrassed: Drama and the Disciples of Shame in Early Modern England* (Ithaca, NY: Cornell University Press, 1993); and Julian Yates, *Error, Misuse, Failure: Object Lessons from the English Renaissance* (Minneapolis: University of Minnesota Press, 2003), particularly the chapter titled "Under the Sign of (A)Jax; or, The Smell of History," pp. 67–100.
44. Susan Signe Morrison, *Excrement in the Late Middle Ages: Sacred Filth and Chaucer's Fecopoetics* (New York: Palgrave Macmillan, 2008). Susan Morrison's book was in preparation at the same time as the present volume, and I am grateful to her for the opportunity for cross-fertilization. These themes are also explored by John W. Velz, "Scatology and Moral Meaning in Two English Renaissance Plays," *South Central Review* 1 (1984), 4–21, with a substantial section on the Middle Ages.
45. Jonathan Wyn Shofer, *Confronting Vulnerability: The Body and the Divine in Rabbinic Ethics* (Chicago: University of Chicago Press, 2010).
46. Albrecht Classen, "Transgression and Laughter, the Scatological and Epistemological: New Insights into the Pranks of Till Eulenspiegel," *Medievalia et Humanistica* n.s. 33 (2007), 41–61; see also his "Farting and the Power

of Human Language, with a Focus on Hans Wilhelm Kirchhof's Sixteenth-Century *Schwänke*," *Medievalia et Humanistica* n. s. 35 (2009), 57–76.
47. Rose George, *The Big Necessity: Adventures in the World of Human Waste* (London: Portobello Books, 2008); the American subtitle is *The Unmentionable World of Human Waste and Why It Matters*. The book *Toilet: Public Restrooms and the Politics of Sharing* is edited by Harvey Molotch and Laura Noren (New York: New York University Press, 2010).
48. The scholarship on theoretical issues of the body is copious. One relevant starting point is Caroline Walker Bynum, "Why All the Fuss about the Body? A Medievalist's Perspective," *Critical Inquiry* 22 (1995), 1–33.
49. On gendered ideas of filth and pollution, see Alexandra Cuffel, *Gendering Disgust in Medieval Religious Polemic* (Notre Dame: University of Notre Dame Press, 2007).
50. George Lakoff and Mark Johnson, *Metaphors We Live By* (Chicago: University of Chicago Press, 1980); Howard Margolis, *Patterns, Thinking, and Cognition* (Chicago: University of Chicago Press, 1987); George Lakoff, *Women, Fire, and Dangerous Things* (Chicago: University of Chicago Press, 1987).
51. On these see Mark Johnson, *The Body in the Mind: The Bodily Basis of Meaning, Imagination, and Reason* (Chicago: University of Chicago Press, 1987); George Lakoff and Mark Johnson, *Philosophy in the Flesh: The Embodied Mind and its Challenge to Western Thought* (New York: Basic Books, 1999); Andy Clark, *Being There: Putting Brain, Body and World Together Again* (Cambridge, MA: MIT Press, 1997).
52. Lakoff and Johnson, *Philosophy*, p. 6.
53. Ibid., p. 555.
54. L. William Countryman, *Dirt, Greed, and Sex: Sexual Ethics in the New Testament and their Implications for Today* (Philadelphia: Fortress Press, 1988).
55. Peter Brown, *The Body and Society: Men, Women, and Sexual Renunciation in Early Christianity* (New York: Columbia University Press, 1988); *The Cult of the Saints: Its Rise and Function in Latin Christianity* (Chicago: University of Chicago Press, 1981).
56. Caroline Walker Bynum, *Fragmentation and Redemption: Essays on Gender and the Human Body in Medieval Religion* (New York: Zone Books, 1991).
57. The most comprehensive work in the field is perhaps Jean Delumeau, *Sin and Fear: The Emergence of a Western Guilt Culture 13th–18th Centuries*, trans. Eric Nicholson (New York: St. Martin's Press, 1990).
58. *The English Text of the Ancrene Riwle: Ancrene Wisse*, ed. J. R. R. Tolkien, EETS o.s. 249 (London: Oxford University Press, 1962), pp. 142–43. I have supplied punctuation and capitalization and expanded abbreviations. It is translated with commentary at *Ancrene Wisse* part 4: *Anchoritic Spirituality: Ancrene Wisse and Associated Works*, trans. with an introduction by Anne Savage and Nicholas Watson (New York: Paulist Press, 1991), pp. 149 and 384 n. 110. The translation here is my own.
59. *Fasciculus Morum: A Fourteenth-Century Preacher's Handbook*, ed. and trans. Siegfried Wenzel (University Park: Pennsylvania State University Press, 1989), p. 94. Wenzel translates this passage but for copyright reasons this is my own translation.
60. *Der Ackermann aus Böhmen*, ed. L. L. Hammerich and G. Jungbluth (Heidelberg: Carl Winter, 1951), cap. XXIV, p. 53.
61. *Death and the Plowman*, trans. Ernest N. Kirrmann (Chapel Hill: University of North Carolina Press, 1958), p. 23. Kirrman is translating from a

somewhat different version than used in the edition by Hammerich and Jungbluth quoted above.
62. In addition to the social scientists cited below, disgust has also been studied in literature by William Ian Miller, *The Anatomy of Disgust* (Cambridge, MA: Harvard University Press, 1997). On these issues in the early modern period see Keith Thomas, "Cleanliness and Godliness in Early Modern England," in *Religion, Culture and Society in Early Modern Britain: Essays in Honour of Patrick Collinson*, ed. A. J. Fletcher and P. R. Roberts (Cambridge: Cambridge University Press, 1994), pp. 56–83 and idem, "Health and Morality in Early Modern England," in *Morality and Health*, ed. Allan M. Brandt and Paul Rozin (New York: Routledge, 1997), pp. 15–34. On views of disgust from the eighteenth century and later see Winfried Menninghaus, *Disgust: The Theory and History of a Strong Sensation*, trans. Howard Eiland and Joel Golb (Albany: State University of New York Press, 2003).
63. Paul Rozin, Jonathan Haidt, Clark McCauley and Sumio Imada, "Disgust: Preadaptation and the Cultural Evolution of a Food-Based Emotion," in *Food Preferences and Taste: Continuity and Change*, ed. Helen Macbeth (Providence: Berghahn Books, 1997), pp. 65–82 at p. 72.
64. Steven Pinker, *How the Mind Works* (New York: Norton, 1997), p. 383.
65. Paul Rozin, Linda Millman and Carol Nemeroff, "Operation of the Laws of Sympathetic Magic in Disgust and Other Domains," *Journal of Personality and Social Psychology* 30 (1986), 703–12.
66. Paul Rozin, M. Markwith and C. R. McCauley, "Sensitivity to Indirect Contacts with Other Persons: AIDS Aversion as a Composite of Aversion to Strangers, Infection, Moral Taint, and Misfortune," *Journal of Abnormal Psychology* 103 (1994), 495–505.
67. Valerie Curtis and Adam Biran, "Dirt, Disgust, and Disease: Is Hygiene in our Genes?" *Perspectives in Biology and Medicine* 44 (2001), 17–31 at p. 25.
68. A. Angyal, "Disgust and Related Aversions," *Journal of Abnormal and Social Psychology* 36 (1941), 393–412 at pp. 394–95.
69. Jonathan Haidt, Paul Rozin, Clark McCauley and Sumio Imada, "Body, Psyche, and Culture: The Relationship between Disgust and Morality," *Psychology and Developing Societies* 9 (1997), 107–31 at p. 109.
70. Ibid., p. 111.
71. Jonathan Haidt, Clark McCauley and Paul Rozin, "Individual Differences in Sensitivity to Disgust: A Scale Sampling Seven Domains of Disgust Elicitors," *Personality and Individual Differences* 16 (1994), 701–13; Paul Rozin, Jonathan Haidt and Clark R. McCauley, "Disgust: The Body and Soul Emotion," *Handbook of Cognition and Emotion*, ed. Tim Dalgleish and Mick J. Power (Chichester: Wiley, 1999), pp. 429–45. An alternate classificatory scheme of five categories has been made by Curtis and Biran: bodily excretions and body parts; decay and spoiled food; particular living creatures; certain categories of "other people"; and violations of morality or social norms. See Curtis and Biran, "Dirt," p. 21.
72. Curtis and Biran, "Dirt," p. 21.
73. Haidt et al., "Body, Psyche, and Culture," p. 115.
74. http://www.sas.upenn.edu/sasalum/newsltr/fall97/rozin.html. Accessed July 29, 2010.
75. Ernest Becker, *The Denial of Death* (New York: Free Press, 1973). On the school of thought founded by Becker, see, for example, *Death and Denial: Interdisciplinary Perspectives on the Legacy of Ernest Becker*, ed. Daniel Liechty (Westport, CT: Praeger, 2002).
76. www.bbc.co.uk/science/humanbody/mind/disgust/index.shtml; accessed April 3, 2005.

77. Rozin et al., "Sensitivity to Indirect Contacts."
78. Ibid.
79. Haidt et al., "Individual Differences," pp. 703, 710.
80. J. L. Goldenberg, T. Pyszczynski, J. Greenberg, S. Solomon, B. Kluck and R. Cornwell, "I am NOT an Animal: Mortality Salience, Disgust, and the Denial of Human Creatureliness," *Journal of Experimental Psychology: General* 130 (2001), 427–35 and J. L. Goldenberg, T. Pyszczynski, J. Greenberg, S. K. McCoy and S. Solomon, "Death, Sex, Love, and Neuroticism: Why Is Sex Such a Problem?" *Journal of Personality and Social Psychology* 77 (1999), 1173–87. A related study involved household products found in supermarkets, where, in testimony to the biological nature of everyday life, six of the top ten best-selling nonfood products were regarded by consumers as "disgusting." These included trash bags, cat litter and diapers. Subjects proved to be significantly less likely to want to eat food such as chocolate chip cookies if the packages had been in physical contact with packages of "disgusting" products such as sanitary napkins. The horror of bodily functions and the "law of contagion" is amply illustrated here. See Andrea C. Morales and Gavan J. Fitzsimons, "Product Contagion: Changing Consumer Evaluations through Physical Contact with 'Disgusting' Products," *Journal of Marketing Research* 44 (2007), 272–83.
81. Chen-Bo Zhong and Katie Liljenquist, "Washing away your Sins: Threatened Morality and Physical Cleansing," *Science* 313, no. 5792 (2006), 1451–52, with the quotation on p. 1452. Erroneous numbers were entered into the tables initially, mistakenly giving the percentages as 66.7% and 33.3%; a correction was posted on the *Science* website on October 13, 2006. On related topics see also Jana Schaich Borg, Debra Lieberman and Kent A. Kiehl, "Infection, Incest, and Iniquity: Investigating the Neural Correlates of Disgust and Morality," *Journal of Cognitive Neuroscience* 20 (2008), 1529–46.
82. For an overview of these arguments in light of recent experiments, see Paul Rozin, Jonathan Haidt and Katrina Fincher, "Psychology: From Oral to Moral," *Science* 323, no. 5918 (2009), 1179–80.
83. See H. A. Chapman, D. A. Kim, J. M. Susskind and A. K. Anderson, "In Bad Taste: Evidence for the Oral Origins of Moral Disgust," *Science* 323, no. 5918 (2009), 1222–26 and Rozin et al., "Psychology."
84. Simone Schnall, Jonathan Haidt, Gerald L. Clore and Alexander H. Jordan, "Disgust as Embodied Moral Judgment," *Personality and Social Psychology Bulletin* 34 (2008), 1096–1109.
85. Schnall et al., "Disgust," p. 1097. The book referred to is A. R. Damasio, *Descartes' Error: Emotion, Reason, and the Human Brain* (New York: Avon, 1994).
86. Richard A. Shweder, Nancy C. Much, Manamohan Mahapatra and Lawrence Park, "The 'Big Three' of Morality (Autonomy, Community, Divinity) and the 'Big Three' Explanations of Suffering," *Morality and Health*, ed. Allan M. Brandt and Paul Rozin (New York: Routledge, 1997), pp. 119–69.
87. Paul Rozin, Laura Lowery, Sumio Imada and Jonathan Haidt, "The CAD Triad Hypothesis: A Mapping between Three Moral Emotions (Contempt, Anger, Disgust) and Three Moral Codes (Community, Autonomy, Divinity)," *Journal of Personality and Social Psychology* 76 (1999), 574–86.
88. In some cases they may also evoke disgust; see Chapman et al., "In Bad Taste," and Rozin et al., "Psychology."
89. See, for instance, Roy Porter, *Flesh in the Age of Reason* (London: Allen Lane, 2003), on the Enlightenment.
90. Christopher Hamlin, "Good and Intimate Filth," in *Filth*, ed. Cohen and Johnson, pp. 3–29 at p. 5, citing Becker, *The Denial of Death*, p. 32.

91. See, for instance, A. Rosenblatt, J. Greenberg, S. Solomon, T. Pyszczynski and D. Lyon, "Evidence for Terror Management Theory: I. The Effects of Mortality Salience on Reactions to Those Who Violate or Uphold Cultural Values," *Journal of Personality and Social Psychology* 57 (1989), 681–90; J. Greenberg, T. Pyszczynski, S. Solomon, A. Rosenblatt, M. Veeder, S. Kirkland and D. Lyon, "Evidence for Terror Management Theory II: The Effects of Mortality Salience on Reactions to Those Who Threaten or Bolster the Cultural Worldview," *Journal of Personality and Social Psychology* 58 (1990), 308–18; and J. L. Goldenberg, T. Pyszczynski, J. Greenberg and S. Solomon, "Fleeing the Body: A Terror Management Perspective on the Problem of Human Corporeality," *Personality & Social Psychology Review* 4 (2000), 200–18.
92. Haidt et al., "Individual Differences," p. 712.
93. David Nirenberg, *Communities of Violence: Persecution of Minorities in the Middle Ages* (Princeton: Princeton University Press, 1996), p. 127. Nirenberg cites "Arxiu de la Corona d'Aragó: Cancellaria Reial 437:101 v (1330/6/22)" and Josefa Mutgé Vives, *La ciudad de Barcelona durante el reinado de Alfonso el Benigno (1327–1336)* (Madrid: Consejo Superior de Investigaciones Científicas, 1987), p. 277.
94. On the Jews as exemplars of unrighteousness, see Martha Bayless, "The Story of the Fallen Jew and the Iconography of Jewish Unbelief," *Viator* 34 (2003), 142–56.
95. Ernest L. Sabine, "Latrines and Cesspools of Mediaeval London," *Speculum* 9 (1934), 303–21 at p. 306, citing (n. 5) "*Plea and Memoranda Rolls*, preserved in the archives of the Guidhall Rec. Off. (London), A 50, m 4^v."
96. Angyal, "Disgust and Related Aversions"; Paul Rozin and April E. Fallon, "A Perspective on Disgust," *Psychological Review* 94 (1987), 23–41 at p. 29.
97. Haidt et al., "Body, Psyche, and Culture," p. 113.
98. Augustine, *Enarrationes in Psalmos I-L*, in *Aurelii Augustini Opera* pars X, 1, ed. E. Dekkers and J. Fraipont, CCSL 38 (Turnhout: Brepols, 1956), pp. 388–89 (ps. 37: 7–9).
99. Gregory the Great, *Moralia in Iob. Libri I-X*, ed. M. Adriaen, CCSL 143 (Turnhout: Brepols, 1979), p. 120 (Book III, vii, 10).
100. Gregory the Great, *Moralia in Iob. Libri I-X*, ed. Adriaenn, p. 152 (Book III, xxxi, 60).
101. Bynum, "Why All the Fuss?" Among the numerous works demonstrating different aspects of this variety, see, for example, John W. Baldwin, *The Language of Sex: Five Voices from Northern France around 1200* (Chicago: University of Chicago Press, 1994).
102. Bynum, "Why All the Fuss?" p. 7.
103. Ibid., p.15.
104. Although eating would not be necessary in heaven, it was agreed that the resurrected body was capable of eating, as demonstrated by Jesus in Luke 24:41–43 and Acts 10:41.
105. Thomas Aquinas, *Summa Theologiae*, 5 vols. (Matriti: La Editorial Catolica, 1955–61), vol. 5, pp. 446–47.
106. Ibid., vol. 5, p. 449.
107. Francesc Eiximenis, *Dotzè llibre del Crestià*, ed. Xavier Renedo et al. (Girona: University of Girona, 2005), p. 291 (book 2, ch. 133). The complete version of the passage is given in Chapter 4.
108. From Francis of Assisi, "*I Fioretti di San Francesco*," *Riveduti su un nuovo Codice da Benvenuto Bughetti* (Quaracchi: Collegio San Bonaventura, 1926), printed in *Fonti Francescane*, new edition, ed. Ernesto Caroli (Padua: Editrici Francescane, 2004), p. 1188 (cap. 29).

109. Francis of Assisi, *Francis of Assisi: Early Documents*, ed. Regis J. Armstrong, J. A. Wayne Hellmann and William J. Short, 3 vols. (New York: New City Press, 1999–2001), vol. III, pp. 618–19 (ch. 29).
110. For example, Francis of Assisi, *The Little Flowers of Saint Francis of Assisi*, trans. and ed. Cardinal Manning (London: T. N. Foulis, 1915), p. 92.

NOTES TO CHAPTER 2

1. Paul Rozin and April E. Fallon, "A Perspective on Disgust," *Psychological Review* 94 (1987), 23–41 at pp. 33–34.
2. *Le Vilain Asnier*, in Willem Noomen and Nico H. J. van den Boogaard, *Nouveau Recueil complet des fabliaux* [NRCF], 10 vols. (Assen: Van Gorcum, 1983–98), vol. 8, pp. 213–14. Tubach, *Index Exemplorum* 3645, cites other versions of the story in a number of languages.
3. From Giovanni Della Casa's *Galateo* (Geneva, 1609), cited by Norbert Elias, "The History of Manners," trans. Edmund Jephcott, vol. 1 of *The Civilizing Process* (Oxford: Blackwell, 1969), pp. 131 and 277.
4. Colin Platt, *The English Medieval Town* (London: Secker and Warburg, 1976), p. 69.
5. *The Cambridge Urban History of Britain. Volume 1: 600–1540*, ed. D. M. Palliser (Cambridge: Cambridge University Press, 2000), p. 178.
6. Ernest L. Sabine, "Latrines and Cesspools of Mediaeval London," *Speculum* 9 (1934), 303–21 and "City Cleaning in Mediaeval London," *Speculum* 12 (1937), 19–43. The story of the man escaping his creditors is in the *Calendar of Early Mayor's Court Rolls Preserved among the Archives of the Corporation of the City of London at the Guildhall, AD 1298–1307*, ed. A. H. Thomas (Cambridge: Cambridge University Press, 1924), p. 247.
7. Derek Keene, *Survey of Medieval Winchester*, Winchester Studies 2, 2 vols. (Oxford: Clarendon Press, 1985), vol. II, p. 854. Even more distinctive is the "one-and-a-half-seater" privy for a mother and child, of unknown date, in a churchyard at Selling, Kent: see Roger Kilroy, *The Compleat Loo: A Lavatorial Miscellany* (London: Gollancz, 1984), p. 21.
8. P. E. Jones, "Whittington's Longhouse," *London Topographical Record* 23 (1972), 27–34.
9. D. J. Keene, "Rubbish in Medieval Towns," *Environmental Archaeology in the Urban Context*, ed. A. R. Hall and H. K. Kenward, The Council for British Archaeology Research Report 43 (London: Council for British Archaeology, 1982), pp. 26–30 at p. 26. See also A. Higounet-Nadal, "Hygiène, salubrité, pollutions au Moyen Age: l'exemple de Périgueux," *Annales de démographie historique* [no volume number] (1975), 81–92 and Jean-Pierre Leguay, *La rue au Moyen Age* (Rennes: Ouest France, 1984), pp. 53–63.
10. Sabine, "City Cleaning," passim.
11. Sabine, "Latrines," p. 306 and passim.
12. *Calendar of Coroners Rolls of the City of London AD 1300–1378*, ed. Reginald R. Sharpe (London: Richard Clay and Sons, 1913), 219–220.
13. Sabine, "City Cleaning," pp. 21, 27; André E. Guillerme, *The Age of Water: The Urban Environment in the North of France, A.D. 300–1800* (College Station: Texas A&M University Press, 1988), p. 165.
14. Sabine, "City Cleaning," pp. 29–31.
15. Sabine, "Latrines," p. 320, citing *Liber Custumarum*, ii, Pt. II, pp. 449–450.
16. Ibid., p. 306, citing "*Plea and Memoranda Rolls*, preserved in the archives of the Guidhall Rec. Off. (London), A 50, m 4^v."

Notes   191

17. *Calendar of Close Rolls*, 1354–60 (London: Stationary Office, 1908), p. 422, quoted by Paul Strohm, "Sovereignty and Sewage," in *Lydgate Matters: Poetry and Material Culture in the Fifteenth Century*, ed. Lisa H. Cooper and Andrea Denny-Brown (New York: Palgrave Macmillan, 2008), pp. 57–70 at p. 62 and n. 14.
18. Strohm, "Sovereignty," p. 62.
19. Guillerme, *The Age of Water*, p. 164. On France see also Jean-Pierre Leguay, *La Pollution au Moyen Age dans le royaume de France et dans les grands fiefs* (Paris: Jean-Paul Gisserot, 1999).
20. Guillerme, *The Age of Water*, p. 165.
21. Sabine, "City Cleaning," p. 39.
22. Kathy Stuart, *Defiled Trades and Social Outcasts: Honor and Ritual Pollution in Early Modern Germany* (Cambridge: Cambridge University Press, 1999), p. 27. The code is edited by Christian Meyer, *Das Stadtbuch von Augsburg, insbesondere das Stadtrecht vom Jahre 1276* (Augsburg, 1872).
23. Stuart, *Defiled Trades*, p. 27. The executioner was also responsible for guarding grain in the marketplace and judging the quality of milk sold; these duties seem to have been associated with his role as overseer of the public market.
24. Guillerme, *Age of Water*, p. 166.
25. For an overview of medieval water systems and sanitary arrangements, see Klaus Grewe et al., *Die Wasserversorgung im Mittelalter*, Geschichte der Wasserversorgung 4 (Mainz am Rhein: Philipp von Zabern, 1991). For Continental arrangements, particularly those of Zurich, see, for instance, Martin Illi, "Wasserentsorgung in spätmittelalterlichen Städten," *Die Alte Stadt* 20 (1993), 221–28.
26. Sabine, "City Cleaning," p. 32.
27. Sabine, "Latrines," p. 312.
28. Ibid., p. 313.
29. Keene, *Survey of Medieval Winchester*, vol. I, p. 64.
30. Guillerme, *Age of Water*, p. 165.
31. Donald Reid, *Paris Sewers and Sewermen: Realities and Representations* (Cambridge, MA and London: Harvard University Press, 1991), pp. 92 and 208 n. 25, citing Alfred Franklin, *La Vie privée d'autrefois: L'hygiene* (Paris, 1890), pp. 15, 57–58.
32. Margaret Wood, *The English Mediaeval House* (1965; repr. London: Studio Editions, 1994), p. 385.
33. Reid, *Paris Sewers*, pp. 10 and 186 n. 2, citing A. Mille, *Assainissement des villes par l'eau, les égouts, les irrigations* (Paris, 1885), p. 98.
34. D. Portman, *Exeter Houses 1400–1700* (Exeter: University of Exeter, 1966), p. 15.
35. Doris M. Stenton, *The Earliest Lincolnshire Assize Rolls A.D. 1202–1209*, Publications of the Lincoln Record Society 22 (n.p., 1926 for 1924), Assize 479, no. 646, p. 114.
36. Sabine, "City Cleaning," p. 33.
37. Ibid., p. 33.
38. Ibid., p. 34.
39. Ibid., p. 35.
40. Sabine, "Latrines," p. 308.
41. Ibid.
42. Guillerme, *Age of Water*, p. 167.
43. Ibid., pp. 167–68.
44. Sabine, "City Cleaning," p. 32.
45. Guillerme, *Age of Water*, p. 106.
46. Ibid., p. 107.

47. Reid, *Paris Sewers*, p. 12.
48. Ibid. Further information and citations on French arrangements and complaints, which are very similar to the English, are provided by Leguay, *La rue au Moyen Age*, pp. 53–63.
49. Roberta Magnusson and Paolo Squatriti, "The Technologies of Water in Medieval Italy," in *Working with Water in Medieval Europe*, ed. Paolo Squatriti (Leiden: Brill, 2000), pp. 217–65 at p. 255.
50. Bryan Ward-Perkins, *From Classical Antiquity to the Middle Ages: Urban Public Building in Northern and Central Italy AD 300–850* (Oxford: Oxford University Press, 1984), p. 134.
51. Many of these are addressed in Ronald E. Zupko and Robert A. Laures, *Straws in the Wind: Medieval Urban Environmental Law: The Case of Northern Italy* (Boulder: Westview, 1996).
52. Ibid., p. 256.
53. Guillerme, *Age of Water*, p. 156.
54. Ibid., pp. 156–57.
55. Keene, "Rubbish in Medieval Towns," p. 28.
56. Caroline Davidson, *A Woman's Work Is Never Done: A History of Housework in the British Isles 1650–1950* (London: Chatto and Windus, 1982), p. 142, quoting from Joseph Taylor, *A Journey to Edenborough in Scotland, by Joseph Taylor . . .* (Edinburgh: W. Brown, 1903), p. 136.
57. Davidson, *A Woman's Work*, p. 142, quoting from Torbuck and E. Rider, *A Collection of Welsh Travels and Memoirs of Wales* (Dublin, 1743), p. 64, and James Hall of Walthamstow, *Tour Through Ireland; particularly the interior and least known parts . . .* (London, 1813), vol. I, p. 233.
58. Miriam C. Davis, "The English Medieval Urban Environment before the Black Death: Learned Views and Popular Practice," *Medieval Perspectives* 13 (1998), 69–83.
59. See Davis, "English Medieval Urban Environment" and Sabine, "Latrines" and "City Cleaning."
60. Leguay, *La rue au Moyen Age*, pp. 56–63.
61. Carlo M. Cipolla, *Public Health and the Medical Profession in the Renaissance* (Cambridge: Cambridge University Press, 1976), ch. 1, "The orgin and development of the Health Boards," pp. 11–33.
62. W. G. Hoskins, *The Age of Plunder: King Henry's England 1500–1547* (London: Longman, 1976), p. 2. Hoskins does not cite his source, and no works by Erasmus appear in his "Select Bibliography"; hence I have been unable to identify the source of this quotation.
63. Da Vinci began to design plans for cities in the 1480s, after several episodes of plague had afflicted Milan. His designs were greatly concerned with sanitation systems, featuring canals to carry away waste and hydraulic water systems within houses. As this example demonstrates, he was also concerned with sanitation even on a small scale. This passage is from *The Notebooks of Leonardo da Vinci*, trans. Edward MacCurdy, 2 vols. (London: Jonathan Cape, 1938), vol. II, p. 424.
64. From the *Brunswick Court Regulations*, cited in Elias, *The History of Manners*, pp. 131 and 278.
65. Quoted in Elias, *The History of Manners*, pp. 132 and 278. The passage has two possible dates: October 9, 1694 and August 25, 1718; the August 1718 date seems more likely, judging by the "extreme heat" mentioned by the Duchess.
66. *English Historical Documents 1042–1189*, ed. David C. Douglas and George W. Greenaway (New York: Oxford University Press, 1953), vol. II, p. 878. The original is in F. Liebermann, *Die Gesetze der Angelsachsen*, 3 vols. (Halle a.S.: M. Niemeyer, 1898–1916), vol. I, pp. 444–53.

67. Georges Duby, *Rural Economy and Country Life in the Medieval West*, trans. Cynthia Postan (London: Edward Arnold, 1968), p. 104.
68. J. L. Bolton, *The Medieval English Economy 1150–1500* (London: J. M. Dent, 1980), p. 34.
69. Ibid.
70. Duby, *Rural Economy*, pp. 24–25.
71. Ibid., p. 104.
72. Marc Bloch, *French Rural History*, trans. Janet Sondheimer (Berkeley: University of California Press, 1966), p. 25. For instances of valuing dung amongst a variety of cultures, see Colin Richmond, *The Penket Papers* (Gloucester: Sutton, 1986), ch. 12, pp. 113–37.
73. For two post-medieval witnesses to the use of dung as fuel for fires, see Eric Kerridge, *The Farmers of Old England* (Totowa, NJ: Rowman and Littlefield, 1973), p. 28, where Kerridge cites an "old saw": "Lincolnshire, where the pig shits soap and the cow shits fire!"
74. D. E. Earl, *Forest Energy and Economic Development* (Oxford: Clarendon Press, 1975), p. 22.
75. Celia Fiennes, *The Illustrated Journeys of Celia Fiennes 1685–c. 1712*, ed. Christopher Morris (London: MacDonald, 1982), p. 144.
76. Davidson, *A Woman's Work*, pp. 76–77.
77. Edward Daniel Clarke, *A Tour through the South of England, Wales, and Part of Ireland, Made during the Summer of 1791* (London, 1793), pp. 116–17. A number of other post-medieval citations are given by Davidson, *A Woman's Work*, pp. 76–77.
78. Ibid., p. 77.
79. On longhouses see, for instance, Jane Grenville, *Medieval Housing* (London and Washington: Leicester University Press, 1997), pp. 134–41, and Jean Chapolet and Robert Fossier, *The Village and House in the Middle Ages*, trans. Henry Cleere (Berkeley: University of California Press, 1985), pp. 223–46.
80. Walter King, "How High Is Too High? Disposing of Dung in Seventeenth-Century Prescot," *Sixteenth Century Journal* 23 (1992), 443–57.
81. Ibid., p. 447.
82. Ibid., p. 447, citing "The Order Book of Ormskirk, 1613–1721," in *A Lancashire Miscellany*, ed. R. Sharpe France (Chester: Lancashire & Cheshire Record Society, 1965), p. 46.
83. *Le Registre d'inquisition de Jacques Fournier évêque de Pamiers (1318–1325)*, ed. Jean Duvernoy, 3 vols. (Toulouse: Édouard Privat, 1965), I.459–60; Emmanuel Le Roy Ladurie, *Montaillou: Cathars and Catholics in a French Village 1294–1324*, trans. Barbara Bray (Harmondsworth: Penguin, 1980), p. 256.
84. Duvernoy, *Registre* III, p. 45; Le Roy Ladurie, *Montaillou*, pp. 146–47.
85. "Esne mnemor quod te nudum nudamque capellam / In feno vidi mane jacere fimi?" ("Do you remember when I saw you both naked, lying in the dung and hay one morning?") Marc Wolterbeek, *Comic Tales of the Middle Ages: An Anthology and Commentary* (New York: Greenwood Press, 1991), pp. 216–17, lines 457–58. The accusations in the poem vary from incredible to merely low and unrefined; it may be that this is one of the unlikely accusations, but in light of Arnaud de Verniolles's experiences, and coupled as it is with another accusation which certainly reflects a commonplace activity, it seems plausible that this reflects reality to some degree. The charge that the subject is a goat, copulating like a filthy animal, may stem from the fact that he lies on a dungheap, rather than vice versa.
86. *Le Sacristain* is edited in *NRCF*, vol. 7, pp. 140–89.

87. General Prologue, line 530, *The Riverside Chaucer*, ed. Larry D. Benson, 3rd ed. (Oxford: Oxford University Press, 1988), p. 32.
88. *Monachus Sangallensis De Carolo Magno*, bk. I, ch. 34, edited in *Bibliotheca Rerum Germanicarum*, ed. Philipp Jaffé, vol. IV: *Monumenta Carolina* (Berlin, 1867), p. 666.
89. Ibid., bk. I, ch. 31, p. 663.
90. John Schofield, *Medieval London Houses* (New Haven: Yale University Press, 1994), pp. 87 and 247 n. 136, citing *London Viewers and Their Certificates, 1508–1558*, ed. Janet Senderowitz Loengard, London Record Series 26 (London: London Record Society, 1989), p. 170.
91. Roberta J. Magnusson, *Water Technology in the Middle Ages* (Baltimore: Johns Hopkins University Press, 2001), p. 157. The excavation is described in Colin Platt and Richard Coleman-Smith et al., *Excavations in Medieval Southampton 1953–1969*, 2 vols. (Leicester: Leicester University Press, 1975), vol. I, pp. 34, 293.
92. Wood, *The English Mediaeval House*, p. 379.
93. Ibid., pp. 377–88.
94. Ibid., pp. 381–82.
95. Ibid., p. 382.
96. On this system see J. Patrick Greene, *Medieval Monasteries* (Leicester: Leicester University Press, 1992), pp. 109–11, and T. Tatton-Brown, "The Precincts [sic] Water Supply," *Canterbury Cathedral Chronicle* 77 (1983), 45–52. On similar systems see Magnusson, *Water Technology*, pp. 53–115.
97. Greene, *Medieval Monasteries*, pp. 111–14. The article cited by Greene (W. H. St. John Hope, "London Charterhouse and Its Old Water Supply," *Archaeologia* 58 (1903), 293–312), is not in that location, but in *Archaeologia* 8 (1902), 293–312.
98. For further examples of ways English monasteries coped with clearing their latrines, see Richard Holt, "Medieval England's Water-Related Technologies," *Working With Water in Medieval Europe*, ed. Paolo Squatriti (Leiden: Brill, 2000), pp. 51–100 at p. 94.
99. For example, Greene, *Medieval Monasteries*, pp. 28, 121.
100. It is reproduced with extensive commentary by Walter Horn and Ernest Born, *The Plan of St. Gall*, 3 vols. (Berkeley: University of California Press, 1979). The section on "Sanitary Facilities" is vol. II, pp. 300–313.
101. Ibid., II, p. 302.
102. Ibid., II, pp. 310–11.
103. Ibid., II, pp. 311–12.
104. The classic study and interpretation is Richard Neudecker, *Die Pracht der Latrine. Zum Wandel öffentlicher Bedürfnisanstalten in der kaiserzeitlichen Stadt* (Munich: Verlag Dr. Friedrich Pfeil, 1994). A nicely illustrative photo of the fourth-century communal Roman latrine from Ostia is provided by Horn and Born, *St. Gall*, vol. II., p. 303 (fig. 498).
105. Among the substantial literature on Roman latrines, see Zena Kamash, "Which Way to Look? Exploring Latrine Use in the Roman World," in *Toilet: Public Restrooms and the Politics of Sharing*, ed. Harvey Molotch and Laura Noren (New York: New York University Press, 2010), pp. 47–63.
106. Horn and Born, *St. Gall*, vol. II., p. 305, citing *Usus antiquiores ordinis cisterciensis*, part I, chap. 72, ed. Julianus Paris, 1664; ed. Hugo Séjalon, 1892, 172.
107. Horn and Born, *St. Gall*, II, pp. 304–305.
108. Ekkehard IV, *Casus sancti Galli: St. Galler Klostergeschichten*, ed. Hans F. Haefele (Darmstadt: Wissenschaftliche Buchgesellschaft, 1980), p. 188 (chap. 91).
109. Rule of St. Benedict 8.4.

110. *Vita et regula SS. P. Benedicti: una cum expositione regulae a Hildemaro tradita*, ed. Rupert Mittermüller (Regensburg, 1880), p. 333 (cap. xxii).
111. Greene, *Medieval Monasteries*, p. 150.
112. Bindeswar Pathak, "History of Toilets," paper given at the International Symposium on Public Toilets, Hong Kong, May 25–27, 1995 <http://www.sulabhtoiletmuseum.org/pg02.htm>.
113. United Nations Development Programme, Human Development Report 2006, *Beyond Scarcity: Power, Poverty, and the Global Water Crisis* (New York: Palgrave Macmillan, 2006), p. v.
114. Sybil Marshall, *A Pride of Tigers: A Fen Family and its Fortunes* (Harmondsworth: Penguin, 1995), p. 108.
115. Joan Benson, pers. comm.
116. Rebecca Mead, "Letter from Finland: Getting to Know You," *The New Yorker*, Oct. 14–21, 2002, pp. 82–91 at p. 84.
117. H. Hinz, "Abort," *Reallexikon der Germanischen Altertumskunde*, ed. H. Jankuhn et al., vol. I. (Berlin and New York: W. de Gruyter, 1973), pp. 15–16.
118. Ibid.
119. *Gregorii Episcopi Turonensis Libri Historiarum X*, ed. Bruno Krusch and Wihelm Levison, MGH, Scriptores rerum Merovingicarum I, pars I (Hanover: Impensis Bibliopolii Hahniani, 1951), book II, ch. 23, lines 10–17 (p. 68).
120. The poem is quoted as the epigraph to this book; it is edited by E. Dümmler, MGH, Poetac Latini Aevi Carolini I (Berlin, 1881), p. 321.
121. Wolterbeek, *Comic Tales*, p. 152, couplets 17–18.
122. Wolterbeek's translation: ibid., p. 153.
123. *Urbanus Magnus Danielis Becclesiensis*, ed. J. Gilbart Smyly (Dublin: Hodges, Figgis and Co., 1939), ll. 1090–92 (p. 38).
124. Hinz, "Abort," pp. 15–16. Maori use of the latrine is recounted in F. Allan Hanson, "Method in Semiotic Anthropology: Or, How the Maori Latrine Means," in *Studies in Symbolism and Cultural Communication*, ed. F. Allan Hanson, Publications in Anthropology 14 (Lawrence: University of Kansas Press, 1982), 74–89.
125. *Laxdœla Saga*, ed. Einar Ól. Sveinsson, Íslenzk Fornrit 5 (Reykjavik, 1934), p. 145 (ch. 47).
126. *The Laxdoela Saga*, trans. A. Margaret Arent (Seattle: University of Washington Press, 1964), pp. 123–24 (ch. 47).
127. Kenneth Macaulay, *The History of St. Kilda* (1764; repr. Edinburgh: J. Thin, 1974), pp. 44–46. Macauley writes, "These ashes so exactly laid out, they cover with a rich friable sort of earth . . . " The "rich friable sort of earth" has been universally interpreted as dung by scholars; see, for example, Mary Harman, *An Isle Called Hirte: History and Culture of the St Kildans to 1930* (Waternish, Isle of Skye: Maclean, 1997), p. 145.
128. Macauley, *History of St. Kilda*, pp. 46, 44.
129. Quoted by Harman, *An Isle called Hirte*, pp. 146–47, from *Episode in the Life of the Rev. Neil MacKenzie, at St. Kilda from 1829 to 1843*, ed. J. B. MacKenzie (1911; privately printed), p. 11.
130. John Lanne Buchanan, *Travels in the Western Hebrides from 1782 to 1790* (London, 1793), p. 93. Buchanan confirms the practice on St. Kilda on pp. 132–33. The title page of the book mistakenly gives "Lane" for "Lanne."
131. George Hill, *Facts from Gweedore, compiled from the notes of Lord George Hill*, 5th ed., with an introduction by E. Estyn Evans (5th ed. published 1887; repr. with new introduction published in Belfast: Queen's University of Belfast, Institute of Irish Studies, 1971), pp. 17, xi and xx n. 32, citing the *Report*

from the *Select Committee on Destitution, Gweedore and Cloughaneely*, H.C. 412 (1957–58), 367.
132. Buchanan, *Travels*, p. 40.
133. Godfrid Storms, *Anglo-Saxon Magic* (The Hague: Martinus Nijhoff, 1948), p. 64.
134. Storms, *Anglo-Saxon Magic*, pp. 64–65 (Leechbook I, xxvi, xxxi, xxxviii; Leechbook III, xxxv, lii, xxiv).
135. Warren R. Dawson, *A Leechbook or Collection of Medical Recipes of the Fifteenth Century* (London: Macmillan, 1934), p. 20 (no. 15) and p. 34 (no. 62).
136. Ibid., p. 24 (no. 30).
137. Ibid., p. 58 (no. 141).
138. Lynn Thorndike, *A History of Magic and Experimental Science*, 8 vols. (New York: Columbia University Press, 1923–58), vol. II, p. 484.
139. On the recipe and the use of heat see Thorndike, *History of Magic*, vol. II, p. 817.
140. Benedictine Rule 8.4.
141. Cited with references by Horn and Born, *St. Gall*, II, p. 304.
142. Many of these are described and discussed by Robert Burchfield, "An Outline History of Euphemisms in English," in *Fair of Speech*, ed. D. J. Enright (Oxford: Oxford University Press, 1985), pp. 13–31.
143. Dawson, *Leechbook*, p. 69 (no. 167). The recipe is to relieve "Collica Passio."
144. *Lanfrank's 'Science of Cirurgie*,' ed. R. V. Fleischhacker, Early English Text Society o.s. 102 (London, 1894), p. 12.
145. Ibid., variants from Ashmole 1396.
146. Keith Allan and Kate Burridge, *Euphemism and Dysphemism: Language Used as Shield and Weapon* (New York: Oxford University Press, 1991), p. 57.
147. Ibid.
148. From "Een bispel van ii. clerken," a Flemish analogue to Chaucer's Reeve's Tale; see Peter G. Biedler, "The *Reeve's Tale* and its Flemish Analogues," *Chaucer Review* 26 (1992), 282–92 (at p. 285).
149. Various forms of the expression are found, for instance, in two sagas: *Eyrbyggja Saga*, ed. Einar Ól. Sveinsson and Matthías Thorðarson (Reykjavik, 1935), ch. 4 and 9, p. 10 and 15, and *Bárðar Saga*, ed. and trans. Jón Skaptason and Phillip Pulsiano (New York: Garland, 1984), ch. 4, p. 18. The implication seems to be that the elves are disgusted or offended by excretion and hence flee.
150. Geoffrey Chaucer, *The Riverside Chaucer*, gen. ed. Larry D. Benson, 3rd. ed. (Oxford: Oxford University Press, 1988), p. 162, lines 1950–51.
151. *Barbour's Bruce*, ed. Matthew P. McDiarmid and James A. C. Stevenson, 2 vols. (Edinburgh: Scottish Text Society, 1980–85), vol. II, p. 128 (book V, ll. 566–68).
152. Marguerite de Navarre, *L'Heptaméron*, ed. Michel François (Paris: Garnier, 1969), p. 88 (onziesme nouvelle). Similar expressions have persisted. Pudney reports, "The French speak of *aller ou le roi va à pied*. The Bulgarians ... still speak regally of *kadeto i Tzara hodi pesha*—going where even the Tzar goes on foot. The royalist Danes excuse themselves with *At gå hvor selv Kongen gar alene*, referring to the place where the king goes alone"; quoted from John Pudney, *The Smallest Room* (New York: Hastings House, 1955), p. 97. The humbling effect of excretion is clear from these expressions.
153. Miguel de Cervantes Saavedra, *Don Quijote de la Mancha*, ed. Martín de Riquer (Barcelona: Editorial Juventud, 1958), p. 185 (book I, cap. XX).
154. Daniel of Beccles, *Urbanus Magnus*, lines 1270–1273, p. 44: "Illo pro more solito gumpho residente / Accipias manibus fenum uel stramina; binas / Carpe

tuis busias digitis grossas, bene pressas, / Quas prestare pares patrono, cum petit illas."
155. *Early English Meals and Manners*, ed. Frederick J. Furnivall (London, 1868), pp. 63–64, lines 931–38.
156. On cloth, see Magnusson, *Water Technology*, p. 159.
157. Furnivall, *Early English Meals*, p. 64, n. 1, says, "From a passage in William of Malmesbury's autograph *De Gestis Pontificum Anglorum* it would seem that water was the earlier cleanser." I have not located this passage.
158. *The Demaundes Joyous: A Facsimile of the First English Riddle Book*, ed. John Wardroper (London: Gordon Fraser Gallery, 1971). Wardroper does not provide page numbers for his facsimile; the riddle is on the second full page of text, with translation on pp. 23–24.
159. Thomas W. Ross, "Taboo-Words in Fifteenth-Century English," in *Fifteenth-Century Studies: Recent Essays*, ed. Robert F. Yeager (Hamden, CT; Archon Books, 1984), pp. 137–60; s.v. "schit" *et passim*.
160. Ross, "Taboo-Words," p. 140. The manuscript is British Library Add. 37075, dated to the last quarter of the fifteenth century.
161. Ibid.
162. *Jouglet* is edited in *NRCF*, vol. 2, pp. 204–14; *La Crote* is edited in *NRCF*, vol. 6, pp. 31–32. On medieval French scatology see also Albert Gier, "Skatologische Komik in der französischen Literatur des Mittelalters," *Wolfram-Studien* VII, ed. Werner Schröder (Berlin: Erich Schmidt, 1982), pp. 154–83.
163. The French *Demandes joyeuses* appeared in a number of very similar versions; the texts are edited by Bruno Roy, *Devinettes françaises du moyen âge* (Montreal: Bellarmin, 1977). On the correspondences with the English version, see p. 34 n. 84. The English *Demaundes Joyous* was printed by Wynkyn de Worde in 1511. A facsimile was printed by Wardroper, *The Demaundes Joyous*.
164. Roy, *Devinettes*, p. 164, no. 535.
165. Wardroper, *Demaundes Joyous*, second full page of facsimile.
166. Ibid., third full page of facsimile.
167. On Shitteborwelane and its analogues in Romford and Oxford, see Eilert Ekwall, *Street-Names of the City of London* (Oxford: Clarendon Press, 1954), pp. 155–56. On Shitelane see Keene, *Survey of Medieval Winchester*, vol. II, p. 1430. On the Scitebroc in Lincoln see Doris M. Stenton, *Earliest Lincolnshire Assize Rolls, A.D. 1202–1209*, Publications of the Lincoln Record Society 22 (n.p., 1926 for 1924), p. 114; in Exeter, see Portman, *Exeter Houses*, p. 15. On Scitewelle and others see J. E. B. Gover, A. Mawer and F. M. Stenton in collaboration with F. T. S. Houghton, *The Place-Names of Warwickshire* (Cambridge: Cambridge University Press, 1936), p. 271.
168. Ekwall, *Street-Names*, p. 155.
169. Magnusson, *Water Technology*, p. 100.
170. Leguay, *La rue*, p. 56.
171. Omer Jodogne, "*Audigier* et la chanson de geste, avec une édition nouvelle du poème," *Le Moyen Age* 66 (1960), 495–526.
172. *Gesta Abbatum Monasterii Sancti Albani*, ed. Henry Thomas Riley, 3 vols. (London, 1867–69), vol. II, p. 399.
173. Wood, *The English Mediaeval House*, p. 379, citing "Exchequer, King's Remembrance Accounts, 489, 16." The phenomenon of corbelled latrines is also remarked on by L. F. Salzman, *Building in England Down to 1540* (Oxford: Clarendon Press, 1952; repr. 1992), pp. 282–83.

174. Salimbene de Adam, *Cronica*, ed. Giuseppe Scalia, CCCM 125–125A, 2 vols. (Turnhout: Brepols, 1998–99), vol. II, p. 558 (a. 1250); *The Chronicle of Salimbene*, trans. Baird et al., pp. 368–69.
175. I have quoted the episode involving St. Francis in Chapter 1 and Chapter 3; it is found at *Francis of Assisi: Early Documents*, ed. Regis J. Armstrong, J. A. Wayne Hellmann and William J. Short, 3 vols. (New York: New City Press, 1999–2001), vol. III, pp. 618–19 (ch. 29). In Chapter 1, I have quoted the legend attributing the phrase to Bernard, as retailed by Philipp Melanchthon; it is found in Melanchton's *Historia quaedam recitatae inter publicas lectiones*, section X, printed in *Philippi Melanthonis Opera quae Supersunt Omnia*, ed. K. G. Bretschneider and H. E. Bindseil, *Corpus Reformatorum* vol. 20 (Brunsviga, 1854), col. 523.
176. Sabine, "Latrines and Cesspools," p. 307, citing the *Calendar of Early Mayors' Court Rolls*, p. 255.
177. *Urbanus Magnus* ll. 1083–89, p. 38.
178. Ibid., l. 1093, p. 38: "Purgato uentre leua contersio fiat."
179. On these see Eckehard Simon, "The Rustic Muse: *Neidhartschwänke* in Murals, Stone Carvings, and Woodcuts," *Germanic Review* 46 (1971), 243–56 and figs.; and *Neidhartrezeption in Wort und Bild*, ed. Gertrud Blaschitz (Krems: Medium Aevum Quotidianum, 2000).
180. Simon, "The Rustic Muse," p. 243.
181. From Erasmus's *De civilitate morum puerilium* (1530), cited by Elias, *The History of Manners*, pp. 130 and 277.
182. From Giovanni Della Casa's *Galateo* (Geneva, 1609), cited by Elias, *The History of Manners*, pp. 131 and 277.
183. Antonio de Beatis, *The Travel Journal of Antonio de Beatis*, trans. J. R. Hale and J. M. A. Lindon (London: Hakluyt Society, 1979), p. 164.
184. Quoted in Elias, *The History of Manners*, pp. 131 and 277.
185. Cited by Elias, *The History of Manners*, pp. 131 and 277–78.
186. From Johann Christian Barth, *The Gallant Ethic, in which it is shown how a young man should commend himself to polite society through refined acts and complaisant words* (Dresden and Leipzig, 1731), p. 288, cited by Elias, *The History of Manners*, pp. 131 and 279.
187. Louis Simond, *Journal of a Tour and Residence in Great Britain during the Years 1810 and 1811*, 2 vols. (Edinburgh, 1815–17), vol. I, pp. 49–50.
188. The occasion was a dance at a private house, and the incident was preceded by a joking discussion about the derivation of a vulgar word. Then, "On proceeding to the Pot in the Cupboard it soon became full on which the Court door was opened Frank Floodgate bawls out, Hoollo! here's an opposition pot—Ay, says Rice in one you have a Yard for your pot, and in the other a pot for your Yard . . ." This was evidently funny enough to be worth describing. Letter to George and Tom Keats, January 5, 1818, in John Keats, *Letters of John Keats*, ed. Robert Gittings (Oxford: Oxford University Press, 1970), p. 47.

NOTES TO CHAPTER 3

1. Caroline Walker Bynum, "Why All the Fuss about the Body? A Medievalist's Perspective," *Critical Inquiry* 22 (1995), 1–33 at p. 15 n. 43.
2. George Lakoff and Mark Johnson, *Philosophy in the Flesh: The Embodied Mind and its Challenge to Western Thought* (New York: Basic Books, 1999), p. 6.
3. The image is that of Lakoff and Johnson, *Philosophy*, p. 36 and passim.
4. Ibid., p. 117.

5. George Lakoff and Mark Johnson, *Metaphors We Live By* (Chicago: University of Chicago Press, 1980), p. 22.
6. This system is also summarized by Stephen Toulmin and June Goodfield, *The Discovery of Time* (New York: Harper & Row, 1965), pp. 65–68.
7. On the phenomenon of religion and space see also Kim Knott, *The Location of Religion: A Spacial Analysis* (London: Equinox, 2005); on the interrelation of holy spaces and the moralized body, Dawn Marie Hayes, *Body and Sacred Place in Medieval Europe, 1100–1389* (New York: Routledge, 2009).
8. On this see also Robert Hertz, "The Pre-eminence of the Right Hand: A Study in Religious Polarity," in *Right and Left: Essays on Dual Symbolic Classification*, ed. Rodney Needham (Chicago: University of Chicago Press, 1973), pp. 3–31, and in Robert Hertz, *Death and the Right Hand*, trans. Rodney and Claudia Needham (Glencoe, IL: The Free Press, 1960), pp. 89–113.
9. The use of opposites is discussed, with particular regard to the twelfth century, by Constance Brittain Bouchard, *"Every Valley Shall Be Exalted": The Discourse of Opposites in Twelfth-Century Thought* (Ithaca, NY: Cornell University Press, 2003).
10. Augustine, *Confessionum libri XIII*, ed. Lucas Verheijen, CCSL 27 (Turnhout: Brepols, 1981), VII.X.16, p. 103. On this theme, see Charles Dahlberg, *The Literature of Unlikeness* (Hanover, NH: University Press of New England, 1988).
11. Augustine, *De trinitate libri XV*, ed. W. J. Mountain and Fr. Glorie, CCSL 50–50A (Turnhout: Brepols, 1968), lib. VI, cap. 12, ll. 150–52 (p. 266).
12. Hugh of St. Victor, *In Salomonis Ecclesiasten Homiliae XIX*, PL 175, cols. 114–256 at 191–92 (ch. 12).
13. On these see, for instance, Edward Grant, "Celestial Incorruptibility in Medieval Cosmology 1200–1687," in *Physics, Cosmology and Astronomy 1300–1700: Tension and Accommodation*, ed. Sabetai Unguru (Dordrecht: Kluwer, 1991), pp. 101–27 and Edward Grant, *Planets, Stars and Orbs: The Medieval Cosmos 1200–1687* (Cambridge: Cambridge University Press, 1994).
14. John Trevisa, *On the Properties of Things: John Trevisa's Translation of Bartholomaeus Anglicus De Proprietatibus Rerum*, Vol. I, ed. M. C. Seymour (Oxford: Clarendon Press, 1975), p. 451 (lib. XIII, cap. 2).
15. Trevisa, *On the Properties of Things*, p. 445 (lib. XIII, cap. 1).
16. Isidore of Seville, *Isidori Hispalensis Episcopi Etymologiarum Sive Originum Libri XX*, ed. W. M. Lindsay, 2 vols. (Oxford: Clarendon Press, 1911), vol. II, book XIV, ch. ix, 10–11. Isidore goes on to quote the opinion of the philosophers, that *inferus* comes from *ferantur*, because the souls are carried (*ferantur*) there.
17. Gossouin, *L'Image du monde de Maitre Gossouin*, ed. O. H. Prior (Lausanne and Paris: Payot, 1913), pp. 60–61. Gossouin's *Imago mundi* is a redaction of an expanded version of the *Imago mundi* of Honorius Augustodunensis, which first appeared in 1110; for the history of the *Imago* and its later adaptations see R. E. Kaske with Arthur Groos and Michael W. Twomey, *Medieval Christian Literary Imagery: A Guide to Interpretation* (Toronto: University of Toronto Press, 1988), p. 190.
18. The topic is also treated briefly by C. A. Patrides, "Renaissance Ideas on Man's Upright Form," *Journal of the History of Ideas* 19 (1958), 256–58 and in *Hali Meðhad*, ed. Bella Millett, EETS o.s. 284 (London: Oxford University Press, 1982), p. 41 n. 13/3–8, where the idea is traced. The idea was also common in the pre-Christian era, where it is found, for instance, in Ovid, *Metamorphoses* Book I, 84–87 and Plato, *Republic* Book 9, 586a-b.
19. *Homilia*, IX, 2 (*PG* 29, col. 192), as cited and translated by A. B Chambers, "'I Was but an Inverted Tree': Notes toward the History of an Idea," *Studies in the Renaissance* 8 (1961), 291–99 at p. 293.

20. Augustine, *De Genesi contra Manichaeos, PL* 34, cols. 186–87 (book I, ch. 17).
21. He discusses the intimate relation between moral and physical uprightness in Sermo 80.2–4. It is in Bernard of Clairvaux, *S. Bernardi Opera*, ed. J. Leclerq, C. H. Talbot, and H. M. Rochais (Rome: Editiones Cistercienses, 1957–77), vol. II, p. 278. Bernard uses the image again in *Epistola* 11.5 (*S. Bernardi Opera*, vol. VII, p. 56) and in *De moribus et officio episcoporum tractatus, PL* 182, cols. 809–34 at cols. 814–15 (cap. II).
22. Bernard of Clairvaux, *Sermo* 80.2, in *S. Bernardi Opera*, vol. II, p. 278.
23. Sermo 24, in *S. Bernardi Opera*, vol. I, p. 157–58.
24. Bernard of Clairvaux, *The Works of Bernard of Clairvaux*, Vol. III: *On the Songs of Songs* II, trans. Kilian Walsh, Cistercian Fathers Series 7 (Kalamazoo: Cistercian Publications, 1976), pp. 46–47 (sermon 24.6).
25. Sermon XC, *PL* 171, cols. 762–63.
26. Peter Comestor, Sermon XLVII, *PL* 198, cols. 1836–38 at col. 1836. On Anselm see Robert Pouchet, *La "Rectitudo" chez Saint Anselme* (Paris: Études Augustiniennes, 1964). The idea was still current in the late medieval and early modern periods, as for example in Alessandro Benedetti's *Historia corporis humani*, written in the 1490s and published in 1502, and in the *Microcosmographia* of Helkiah Crooke (1615). The relevant passages are in Alessandro Benedetti, *Historia corporis humani sive Anatomice*, ed. Giovanna Ferrari (Firenze: Giunti, 1998), p. 86; *Studies in Pre-Vesalian Anatomy: Biography, Translations, Documents*, trans. L. R. Lind (Philadelphia: American Philosophical Society, 1975), p. 83; and Helkiah Crooke, *Microcosmographia: A Description of the Body of Man* (London, 1615), pp. 3, 4–5, 11, 13. These latter two references are from the otherwise unrelated article by Patricia Simons, "Manliness and the Visual Semiotics of Bodily Fluids in Early Modern Culture," *Journal of Medieval and Early Modern Studies* 39 (2009), 331–73, notes 2–4.
27. Text and translation from *Three Eleventh-Century Anglo-Latin Saints' Lives*, ed. and trans. Rosalind C. Love (Oxford: Clarendon Press, 1996), pp. 80–81.
28. This correlation forms part of a larger understanding of physical imperfection as an indicator of sin; on this the most comprehensive treatment is Irina Metzler, *Disability in Medieval Europe: Physical Impairment in the High Middle Ages, c. 1100–c. 1400* (London: Routledge, 2006).
29. Guibert de Nogent, *Guibert de Nogent: Autobiographie*, ed. Edmond-René Labande (Paris: Société d'Edition 'Les Belles Lettres', 1981), p. 120 (book 1, ch. 15).
30. Tubach, *Index* 1921.
31. Jerome, *Adversus Jovinianum, PL* 23, cols. 211–338 at col. 260 (lib. 1, par. 36).
32. See also Barbara Obrist, "Les deux visages du diable," in *Diables et Diableries. La représentation du diable dans la gravure des XV et XVI siècles* (Geneva: Cabinet des estampes, 1976), pp. 19–30. An alternate and to my mind less convincing analysis of the phenomenon is offered by James J. Paxson, "The Nether-Faced Devil and the Allegory of Parturition," *Studies in Iconography* 19 (1998), 139–76.
33. Now in the Bayerische Staatsgemäldesammlung; it is reproduced in, for example, Robert Hughes, *Heaven and Hell in Western Art* (New York: Stein and Day, 1968), p. 256.
34. A photo of the devils from Troyes (from *c.* 1170) is found in Janetta Rebold Benton, *Holy Terrors: Gargoyles on Medieval Buildings* (New York: Abbeville, 1997), p. 108; it is now in the Victoria and Albert Museum, London. There are three examples from Bourges, dating from the second half of the thirteenth century, on the central porte of the west facade.

35. *Jacob's Well*, ed. Arthur Brandeis, EETS o.s. 115 (London, 1643–), p. 263.
36. *Acta sanctorum*, ed. J. Bollandus et al. (1643), Jun. IV, p. 166.
37. *The Alphabetum Narrationum* was formerly thought to be by Étienne de Besançon, but is now assigned to Arnold of Liège. The text was translated into English as *An Alphabet of Tales: An English 15th Century Translation of the Alphabetum Narrationum of Etienne de Besançon*, ed. Mary MacLeod Banks, EETS o.s. 126–27 (London, 1904–05; repr. Millwood, NY: Kraus, 1987), no. 696 (pp. 466–67). The motif is Tubach, *Index* 2882.
38. Ranulph Higden, *Polychronicon Ranulphi Higden Monachi Cestrensis*, vol 5, ed. Joseph Rawson Lumby (London, 1882; repr. Wiesbaden: Kraus, 1964), p. 170, with facing medieval translation.
39. Ibid.
40. *An Alphabet of Tales*, ed. Banks, pp. 466–67.
41. Ibid., no. 35, pp. 25–26 at 26. Tubach, *Index* 295.
42. The punctuation in the Latin version is original. The passage comes from a series of *distinctiones* appearing in more than 70 manuscripts, cited by Edwin D. Craun, *Lies, Slander and Obscenity in Medieval English Literature: Pastoral Rhetoric and the Deviant Speaker* (Cambridge: Cambridge University Press, 1997), p. 68.
43. *Le Registre d'inquisition de Jacques Fournier évêque de Pamiers (1318–1325)*, ed. Jean Duvernoy, 3 vols. (Toulouse: Édouard Privat, 1965), vol. I, p. 147.
44. From Francis of Assisi, "*I Fioretti di San Francesco*," *riveduti su un nuovo Codice da Benvenuto Bughetti* (Quaracchi: Collegio San Bonaventura, 1926), printed in *Fonti Francescane*, new edition, ed. Ernesto Caroli (Padua: Editrici Francescane, 2004), p. 1188 (cap. 29).
45. Francis of Assisi, *Francis of Assisi: Early Documents*, ed. Regis J. Armstrong, J. A. Wayne Hellmann and William J. Short, 3 vols. (New York: New City Press, 1999–2001), vol. III, pp. 618–19 (ch. 29).
46. See Alfred Thomas, "Alien Bodies: Exclusion, Obscenity, and Social Control in *The Ointment Seller*," in *Obscenity: Social Control and Artistic Creation in the European Middle Ages*, ed. Jan Ziolkowski (Leiden: Brill, 1998), pp. 214–30 at pp. 221–22.
47. John D. Niles, *Homo Narrans: The Poetics and Anthropology of Oral Literature* (Philadelphia: University of Pennsylvania Press, 1999), p. 70.
48. Edited by Willem Noomen and Nico H. J. van den Boogaard, *Nouveau Recueil complet des fabliaux* [*NRCF*], vol. 4 (Assen: Van Gorcum, 1988), pp. 19–21, and *The French Fabliau B. N. MS. 837*, ed. and trans. Raymond Eichmann and John DuVal, 2 vols. (New York: Garland, 1984–85), vol. II, pp. 44–47.
49. *NRCF* vol. V, pp. 368–70; *The French Fabliau*, ed. and trans. Eichmann and DuVal, vol. II, pp. 242–45.
50. The banner dates from the fifteenth or sixteenth century. It is reproduced by Ruth Mellinkoff, *Outcasts: Signs of Otherness in Northern European Art of the Late Middle Ages*, 2 vols. (Berkeley: University of California Press, 1993), vol. II, no. I.76 and Claude Gaignebet and Jean-Dominique Lajoux, *Art profane et religion populaire au Moyen Age* (Paris: Presses Universitaires de France, 1985), unnumbered page following p. 212.
51. *The English Text of the Ancrene Riwle: Ancrene Wisse*, ed. J. R. R. Tolkien, EETS o.s. 249 (London: Oxford University Press, 1962), pp. 142–43. I have supplied punctuation and capitalization and expanded abbreviations.
52. Photos of a number of these figures, from French misericords and church carvings of the fifteenth century, are printed in Gaignebet and Lajoux, *Art profane*, pp. 153, 212–15, and passim.

53. The history of Marcolf is outlined with particular attention to this motif by Malcolm Jones, "Marcolf the Trickster in Late Mediaeval Art and Literature or: The Mystery of the Bum in the Oven," in *Spoken in Jest*, ed. Gillian Bennett (Sheffield: Sheffield Academic Press, 1991), pp. 139–74.
54. Jan M. Ziolkowski, *Solomon and Marcolf* (Cambridge, MA: Department of the Classics, Harvard University, 2008).
55. Walter Map, *De Nugis Curialium: Courtiers' Trifles*, ed. and trans. M. R. James, rev. C. N. L. Brooke and R. A. B. Mynors (Oxford: Clarendon Press, 1983), p. 102 (Dist. i, c. 25). My translation. As Map explains in the same chapter, the Cistercians eschewed underwear.
56. I. Shachar, *The Judensau: A Medieval Anti-Jewish Motif and its History* (London: Warburg Institute, 1974); Alan Dundes, *Life is Like a Chicken Coop Ladder: A Portrait of German Culture Through Folklore* (New York: Columbia University Press, 1984), pp. 121–22.
57. *Guibert de Nogent*, ed. Labande, pp. 430–31 (book III ch. 17). On witchcraft and inversion see also Stuart Clark, "Inversion, Misrule and the Meaning of Witchcraft," *Past and Present* 87 (1980), 98–127.
58. Walter Map, *De Nugis Curialium*, pp. 120–21 (Dist. i, c. 30).
59. Alan of Lille, *Alani de Insulis De Fide Catholica contra Haereticos Sui Temporis*, PL 210, col. 366 (book 1, cap. LXIII).
60. Malcolm Barber, *The Trial of the Templars* (Cambridge: Cambridge University Press, 1978), p. 180. For a further description of the charges see Jeffrey Burton Russell, *Witchcraft in the Middle Ages* (Ithaca, NY: Cornell University Press, 1972), pp. 160–61 and Bernd-Ulrich Hergenmöller, "Black Sabbath Masses: Fictitious Rituals and Real Inquisitions," in *The Fall of the Angels*, ed. Christoph Auffarth and Loren T. Stuckenbruck (Leiden: Brill, 2004), pp. 176–91.
61. Barber, *Trial*, pp. 181 and 280 n. 14, citing Guillaume de Paris, *De Legibus*, in *Opera Omnia*, 1 (Amiens, 1674), p. 83.
62. Barber, *Trial of the Templars*, pp. 182–83.
63. An illustration is printed by Sara Lipton, *Images of Intolerance: The Representation of Jews and Judaism in the* Bible moralisée (Berkeley: University of California Press, 1999), p. 89 (fig. 62), from the *Bible moraliseé* in Vienna, Österreichische Nationalbibliothek cod. 1179, fol. 171d.
64. On this see Shachar, *The Judensau*. The more usual depiction has Jews suckling from the sow, but the kissing motif is also found.
65. Russell, *Witchcraft in the Middle Ages*, pp. 161–62; with caveats as to Russell's credulity.
66. *The Malleus Maleficarum of Heinrich Kramer and James Sprenger*, trans. Montague Summers (1928; repr. Mineola, NY: Dover, 1971), p. 96 (part I. qu. 1 ch. 1). The quotation is not translated by Summers.
67. Oxford, Bodleian Library Rawl. D 410, fol. 1); Paris, Bibliothèque Nationale fr. 961, fol. 1; and Brussels, Bibliotheque Royale 11209, fol. 3. These are reproduced and discussed by Franck Mercier, "Un trompe-l'œil maléfique: l'image du sabbat dans les manuscrits enluminés de la cour de Bourgogne (à propos du Traité du crisme de Vauderie de Jean Taincture, vers 1460–1470)," *Médiévales* 44 (2003), 97–115, with the images on pp. 101, 102 (both in the central image and in the margin) and 103. The Brussels image is in Norman Cohn, *Europe's Inner Demons: An Enquiry Inspired by the Great Witch-Hunt* (New York: Basic Books, 1975), Plate 1, and the Paris image in Gaignebet and Lajoux, *Art profane et religion populaire au Moyen Age*, p. 209. On early modern witchcraft and the *osculum infame*, see Jonathan Durrant, "The *Osculum Infame*: Heresy, Secular Culture and the Image of the Witches' Sabbath," in *The Kiss in History*, ed. Karen Harvey (Manchester: Manchester University Press, 2005), pp. 36–59.

68. The trials and confessions of the supposed diabolists are recounted by Andrew McCall, *The Medieval Underworld* (London: Hamish Hamilton, 1979), pp. 253–57, without references to the primary sources of Pierre de Broussart.
69. Enguerrand de Monstrelet, *The Chronicles of Enguerrand de Monstrelet*, trans. Thomas Johnes, 2 vols. (London, 1849), vol. 2, p. 270 (a. 1459).
70. Pierrette Paravy, "À propos de la genèse médiévale des chasses aux sorcières: Le traité de Claude Tholosan, juge dauphinois (vers 1436)," *Mélanges de l'École française de Rome* 91 (1979), 333–79 at p. 355.
71. The *Errores Gazariorum* is edited in Joseph Hansen, *Quellen und Untersuchungen zur Geschichte des Hexenwahns und der Hexenverfolgung im Mittelalter* (1901; repr. Hildesheim: G. Olms, 1963), pp. 118–22.
72. Barber, *Trial*, p. 223.
73. Anne Gilmour-Bryson, "Italian Templar Trials: Truth or Falsehood?," in *Knighthoods of Christ: Essays on the History of the Crusades and the Knights Templar*, ed. Norman Housley (Burlington, Vermont and Aldershot: Ashgate, 2007), pp. 209–28 at p. 218, citing Anne Gilmour-Bryson, *The Trial of the Templars in the Papal State and the Abruzzi* (Vatican City: Biblioteca apostolica vaticana, 1982), p. 149.
74. Many examples are given by Barber: *Trial*, pp. 45, 57–62, 67, 99, 143, 145, 147, 150, 163, 165, 168–69, 180–81, 183, 223, 249, 280 n. 17.
75. Barber, *Trial*, p. 223.
76. Tertullian, *Adversus Iudaeos* in *Tertulliani Opera* pars II, CCSL 2 (Turnhout: Brepols, 1954), XI.4 (p. 1381).
77. On clothing and physiognomy see Mellinkoff, *Outcasts*.
78. *Acta Sanctorum*, ed. J. Bollandus et al. (1643–), April vol. II, 424, cols. 1–2.
79. William of Malmesbury, *Gesta pontificum Anglorum: The History of the English Bishops*, ed. and trans. M. Winterbottom with R. M. Thomson, 2 vols. (Oxford: Clarendon Press, 2007), vol. I, pp. 656–57 (book V, cap. 275).
80. The *Gesta Herwardi* is edited in *Lestorie des Engles solum la translacion Maistre Geffrei Gaimar*, ed. Thomas Duffus Hardy and Charles Trice Martin, 2 vols. (London, 1888–89), vol. I, pp. 339–404 with the incident at p. 389. It is translated in *Three Lives of the Last Englishmen*, trans. Michael Swanton (New York: Garland, 1984), pp. 45–88 with the incident at p. 78.
81. Salimbene de Adam, *Cronica*, ed. Guiseppe Scalia, CCCM 125–125A, 2 vols. (Turnhout: Brepols, 1998–99), vol. II, p. 558 (a. 1250). This is my translation; the published translation is *The Chronicle of Salimbene de Adam*, trans. Joseph L. Baird et al. (Binghamton, New York, 1986), pp. 368–69.
82. Barber, *Trial*, pp. 199 and 283 n. 33, citing D. Wilkins, *Concilia Magnae Britanniae et Hiberniae*, vol. II (London, 1737), p. 359.
83. Reproduced in Mellinkoff, *Outcasts*, vol. II, no. X.28 and in Gaignebet and Lajoux, *Art profane*, p. 57.
84. Herzogenburg Monastery, Panel of the Aggsbach Altar; reproduced by Mellinkoff, *Outcasts*, vol. II, no. X.12.
85. Crucifixion by the Hamburg Master, Hamburg Kunsthalle; reproduced by Mellinkoff, *Outcasts*, vol. II, no. III.44.
86. Nuremberg, Germanisches Nationalmuseum; reproduced by Mellinkoff, *Ouctasts*, vol. II, no. VIII.14.
87. Louvain, Church of Saint-Pierre; reproduced in Brigitte de Patoul, Roger Van Schoute, et al., *Les primitifs flamands et leur temps* (Tournai: La Renaissance du Livre, 1998), p. 261.
88. Winnipeg, Canada, Winnipeg Art Gallery; reproduced by Mellinkoff, *Outcasts*, vol. II, no. X.25.
89. Würzburg, Mainfrankisches Museum; reproduced by Mellinkoff, *Outcasts*, vol. II, no. X.16.

90. Mellinkoff, *Outcasts*, vol. II, no. VII.39.
91. Ghent, Museum voor Schone Kunsten.
92. The Hague, Koninklijke Bibliothek 135.E.19, fol. 62v.
93. Melk Monastery, Panel of the Melk Altar; reproduced by Mellinkoff, *Outcasts*, vol. 2, no. X.6.
94. Nuremberg, Germanisches Nationalmuseum; reproduced by Mellinkoff, *Outcasts*, vol. 2, no. II.26.
95. Munich, Alte Pinakothek; reproduced by Mellinkoff, *Outcasts*, vol. 2, no. II.15.
96. Panel of the Ciudad Rodrigo Retable by Fernando Gallego and assistants, Tucson, University of Arizona Museum of Art; reproduced by Mellinkoff, *Outcasts*, vol. 2, no. IX.31.
97. Washington, D.C., National Gallery of Art, Rosenwald Collection; reproduced by Mellinkoff, *Outcasts*, vol. 2, no. I.58.
98. Karlsruhe, Kunsthalle; reproduced by Mellinkoff, *Outcasts*, vol. 2, no. VIII. 8.
99. Stuttgart, Staatsgalerie; reproduced by Mellinkoff, *Outcasts*, vol. 2, no. II. 43.
100. San Francisco, Fine Arts Museums; reproduced by Mellinkoff, *Outcasts*, vol. 2, no. II.12.
101. Vienna, Österreichische Galerie; reproduced by Mellinkoff, *Outcasts*, vol. 2, no. II.8.
102. From the altarpiece of St. George, Valencia, Spain; London, Victoria and Albert Museum; reproduced by Mellinkoff, *Outcasts*, vol. 2, no. X.24.
103. Painted by a Danube artist; Nuremberg, Germanisches Nationalmuseum; reproduced by Mellinkoff, *Outcasts*, vol. 2, no. I.60.
104. Rogier van der Weyden's Martyrdom of St. John the Baptist is in the Berlin Staatliche Museen; Memlic's Triptych is in the Hôpital Saint-Jean, Bruges. Both are reproduced in *Les primitifs flamands et leur temps*, ed. de Patoul et al., pp. 355 and 466.
105. See Rudolf Glanz, "The 'Jewish Execution' in Medieval Germany," *Jewish Social Studies* 5 (1943), 3–26; Guido Kisch, "The 'Jewish Execution' in Mediaeval Germany," *Historia Judaica* 5 (1943), 101–32; and Esther Cohen, "Symbols of Culpability and the Universal Language of Justice: The Ritual of Public Executions in Late Medieval Europe," *History of European Ideas* 11 (1989), 407–16.
106. See Solomon Grayzel, *The Church and the Jews in the XIIIth Century*, vol. II, ed. with additional notes by Kenneth Stow (Detroit: Wayne State University Press, 1989), p. 333. For illustrations see Heinz Schreckenberg, *The Jews in Christian Art: An Illustrated History* (New York: Continuum, 1996), pp. 250 (fig. 3) and 263.
107. See, for example, Bernard's *De moribus et officio episcoporum tractatus*, PL 182, cols. 814–15 (cap. II.5).
108. Cohen, "Symbols of Culpability," p. 411.
109. Bernard of Morval, *De Contemptu Mundi*, ed. H. C. Hoskier (London: B. Quaritch, 1929), p. 19 (I.545–48).
110. *The Siege of Jerusalem*, ed. Ralph Hanna and David Lawton, EETS o.s. 320 (Oxford: Oxford University Press, 2003), p. 47, line 701.
111. Exegesis on the passage is outlined by Frederick M. Biggs and Laura L. Howes, "Theophany in the Miller's Tale," *Medium Aevum* 65 (1996), 269–79.
112. Biggs and Howes, "Theophany," pp. 273 and 278 n. 17, citing Lyons, *Opera omnia in universum Sanctam Scripturam* [sic] (1669), VI, fol. 59r and VI, fols. 186v–187r.
113. Alain Boureau, *The Myth of Pope Joan*, trans. Lydia G. Cochrane (Chicago: The University of Chicago Press, 2001), p. 76.

114. Ruth Mellinkoff, "Riding Backwards: Theme of Humiliation and Symbol of Evil," *Viator* 4 (1973), 153–76 at pp. 154–55.
115. Boureau, *Myth of Pope Joan*, pp. 76–77 and 342 n. 9, citing Francesco Cancellieri, *Storia de' solenni possessi de' Sommi Pontefic i...* (Rome, 1802), 8–9 n.1.
116. Caesarius of Heisterbach, *Dialogus Miraculorum*, ed. Joseph Strange (Cologne, 1851; repr. Ridgewood, NJ, 1966), vol. II, p. 332 (dist. 12, ch. XXII); *The Dialogue on Miracles*, trans. H. von E. Scott and C. C. Swinton Bland, 2 vols. (London: Routledge, 1929), vol. II, p. 309.
117. Examples are legion. In addition to the many mentioned by Mellinkoff, "Riding Backwards," there is, for instance, another in a fifteenth-century wooden choir stall from the Church of Notre Dame, Aerschot, Belgium (a Jew riding backwards on a goat, holding its tail), reproduced in Joshua Trachtenberg, *The Devil and the Jews: The Medieval Conception of the Jew and its Relation to Modern Antisemitism* (1943; repr. Skokie, IL: Varda Books, 2001), p. 45.
118. From an early twelfth-century German manuscript, Oxford, Bodleian Library Bodley 352, fol. 6v; described in Mellinkoff, "Riding Backwards," p. 166.
119. John H. Arnold, *Belief and Unbelief in Medieval Europe* (London: Hodder Arnold, 2005), p. 214.

NOTES TO CHAPTER 4

1. See, for instance, Caroline Walker Bynum, *The Resurrection of the Body in Western Christianity 200–1336* (New York: Columbia University Press, 1995), plates 3, 6, 12–16 and 28–32 and pp. 192–95, and Robert M. Durling, "Deceit and Digestion in the Belly of Hell," in *Allegory and Representation*, ed. Stephen J. Greenblatt (Baltimore: Johns Hopkins University Press, 1980), pp. 61–93.
2. On this see Jean-Pierre Albert, *Odeurs de Sainteté: La Mythologie chrétienne des aromates* (Paris: École des Hautes Études en Sciences Sociales, 1990).
3. Augustine, *De Genesi contra Manichaeos*, PL 34, cols. 173–220 at col. 186.
4. On these issues, see for instance many passages in Thomas Aquinas cited by Caroline Walker Bynum, *Fragmentation and Redemption: Essays on Gender and the Human Body in Medieval Religion* (New York: Zone Books, 1991), p. 396 n. 16.
5. The work of Valentinus exists only in fragments. The statement in question survives only in a quotation in Clement of Alexander's *Stromata* (also called *Stromateis*) 3.59. The Greek text is edited by Otto Stählin, *Clemens Alexandrinus*, vol. II (Berlin: Akademie-Verlag, 1960), p. 223, lines 12–16 (*Stromata* III, cap. VII, 59.3). It is translated by Bentley Layton in *The Gnostic Scriptures* (London: SCM, 1987), p. 239. This passage is discussed at some length in Chapter 5.
6. M. R. James, *Latin Infancy Gospels* (Cambridge: Cambridge University Press, 1927), p. 70, translation from p. xxi.
7. James, *Latin Infancy Gospels*, p. 71. My translation.
8. *Le Registre d'inquisition de Jacques Fournier évêque de Pamiers (1318–1325)*, ed. Jean Duvernoy, 3 vols. (Toulouse: Édouard Privat, 1965), vol. II, p. 94.
9. "et vertens verba sua ad dictum Ramundum, dixit: "Et tu scis qualiter Deus factus fuit?", et dictus Ramundus respondit: "Ego dicam tibi, factus fuit

'foten e mardan'", et hoc dicens percutens unam manum suam cum alia", "and turning his words to the aforementioned Raymond, he said, "And do you know how God was made?" And the aforementioned Raymond replied, "I'll tell you, he was made 'fucking and shitting out,' and saying this, he hit one of his hands against the other." Duvernoy, *Registre*, II, p. 120.

10. Joseph Kimhi, *The Book of the Covenant*, trans. Frank Talmage (Toronto: Pontifical Institute of Mediaeval Studies, 1972), pp. 36–37. Talmage's text mistakenly reads *borm* for *born*.
11. On this see Steven F. Kruger, "Medieval Christian (Dis)identifications: Muslims and Jews in Guibert of Nogent," *New Literary History* 28 (1997), 185–203.
12. Guibert of Nogent, *Tractatus de incarnatione contra Judaeos*, PL 156, cols. 489–528 at 499 (book II, ch. 1).
13. Ibid., col. 499 (book II, ch. 1).
14. John H. Arnold, *Belief and Unbelief in Medieval Europe* (London: Hodder, 2005), p. 226.
15. Heriger of Lobbes mentions the issue in *De corpore et sanguine domini*, PL 139, col. 188; Alger of Liège is edited in *De sacramentis corporis et sanguinis domini*, PL 180, cols. 739–854, with heresies at 739–40. On the history of the controversy see the *Dictionnaire de théologie catholique*, ed. A. Vacant, E. Mangenot et al., 15 vols. (Paris: Letouzey et Ané, 1915–50), s.v. "Stercoranisme" (vol. 14, pp. 2590–2612).
16. Guitmund, *De corporis et sanguinis Christi veritate in eucharista*, PL 149, cols. 1427–94. The controversy is outlined by Gary Macy, "The Theological Fate of Berengar's Oath of 1059: Interpreting a Blunder Become Tradition," in his *Treasures from the Storeroom: Medieval Religion and the Eucharist* (Collegeville, MN: Liturgical Press, 1999), pp. 20–35.
17. Bandinelli has been problematically identified as the future pope Alexander III (1159–81). Roland Bandinelli's *Sentences* is edited in *Die Sentenzen Rolands nachmals Papstes Alexander III*, ed. A. M. Gietl (Freiburg, 1891), with this argument at pp. 232–33.
18. Gerald of Wales (Giraldus Cambrensis), *Gemma ecclesiastica*, ed. J. S. Brewer (1862; repr. Wiesbaden: Kraus, 1964), p. 54 (dist. I. cap. 18). The story is also found in an exemplum from a collection compiled in the 1270s: *Liber exemplorum ad usum praedicantium*, ed. A. G. Little (Aberdeen: Typis Academicis, 1908), p. 9 (part 1, ch. 17).
19. Giraldus Cambrensis, *Gemma ecclesiastica*, p. 54 (dist. I, cap. 18).
20. Albertus Magnus, "De sacramentis," in *Alberti magni ordinis fratrum praedicatorum opera omnia*, vol. 26 (Aschendorff, 1958), IV Sent. d.9.a.5 *in fine*; quoted by Miri Rubin, *Corpus Christi: The Eucharist in Late Medieval Culture* (Cambridge: Cambridge University Press, 1991), p. 338.
21. *Middle English Sermons Edited from British Museum MS. Royal 18 B. xxiii*, ed. Woodburn O. Ross, Early English Text Society o.s. 209 (London: Oxford University Press, 1940), p. 65.
22. Norman P. Tanner, *Heresy Trials in the Diocese of Norwich, 1428–31* (London: Royal Historical Society, 1977), pp. 44–45.
23. *Registre*, ed. Duvernoy, I, p. 461. Also quoted by Emmanuel Le Roy Ladurie, *Montaillou: Cathars and Catholics in a French Village 1294–1324*, trans. Barbara Bray (Harmondsworth: Penguin, 1980), p. 299. This translation is mine.
24. Guibert of Nogent, *Tractatus*, PL 156, cols. 489–528 at col. 499 (lib. II cap. 1).
25. *De civitate Dei* XIII.xvi as quoted in Augustine, *The City of God*, ed. T. E. Page et al., trans. Philip Levine, Loeb Classical Library (Cambridge, MA: Harvard University Press, 1966).
26. Francesc Eiximenis, *Dotzè llibre del Crestià*, ed. Xavier Renedo et al. (Girona: University of Girona, 2005), p. 291 (book 2, ch. 133).

27. Martin Luther, *D. Martin Luthers Werke: Kritische Gesamtausgabe*, vol. 42 (Weimar: Hermann Böhlaus, 1911), p. 70.
28. Martin Luther, *Lectures on Genesis, Chapters 1–5*, in *Luther's Works*, ed. Jaroslav Pelikan, vol. 1 (St. Louis: Concordia, 1958), pp. 92 (2:9).
29. Luther, *D. Martin Luthers Werke*, vol. 42, p. 84.
30. Luther, *Lectures on Genesis*, ed. Pelikan, pp. 110–11 (2:16, 17).
31. Caesarius of Heisterbach, *Dialogus miraculorum*, ed. Joseph Strange, 2 vols. (Cologne, 1851; repr. Ridgewood, NJ, 1966), vol I, p. 243 (book 4, ch. LXXVI); *The Dialogue on Miracles*, trans. H. von E. Scott and C. C. Swinton Bland, 2 vols. (London: Routledge, 1929), vol. I, p. 276.
32. Francesco di Giorgio Martini, *Trattati di architettura ingegneria e arte militare*, ed. Corrado Maltese, 2 vols. (Milan: Edizioni il Polifilo, 1967), vol. II, p. 335.
33. Caroline Walker Bynum, *Fragmentation and Redemption*.
34. On these see, for instance, Kathleen Cohen, *Metamorphosis of a Death Symbol: The Transi Tomb in the Late Middle Ages and the Renaissance* (Berkeley: University of California Press, 1973).
35. Saul N. Brody, *The Disease of the Soul: Leprosy in Medieval Literature* (Ithaca, NY: Cornell University Press, 1974), pp. 64–66, 79, 85–86; R. I. Moore, *The Formation of a Persecuting Society: Authority and Deviance in Western Europe 950–1250*, 2nd ed. (Oxford: Blackwell, 2007), pp. 57–61. On leprosy see also Carole Rawcliffe, *Leprosy in Medieval England* (Woodbridge: Boydell, 2006).
36. On these see Moore, *Formation*, p. 57.
37. On *contemptus mundi* literature see Jean Delumeau, *Sin and Fear: The Emergence of a Western Guilt Culture 13th–18th Centuries*, trans. Eric Nicholson (New York: St. Martin's Press, 1990).
38. Guillelmus abbas, *Meditationes orationes*, PL 180, cols. 205–48, at *Meditatio* IX, col. 233.
39. Lotario dei Segni (Pope Innocent III), *De miseria condicionis humane*, ed. Robert E. Lewis (Athens: University of Georgia Press, 1978), pp. 204–06 (part III, ch. 1).
40. A related argument is made by Michal Kobialka, who argues that early medieval representational practices were founded on the representation of the body of Christ; Kolbialka is referring to more learned arguments on a higher level than the more popular-based views I am describing. Michal Kobialka, *This Is My Body: Representational Practices in the Early Middle Ages* (Ann Arbor: University of Michigan Press, 1999).
41. Quoted by G. R. Owst, *Literature and Pulpit in Medieval England* (Oxford: Basil Blackwell, 1961), pp. 404–05.
42. *Fasciculus Morum: A Fourteenth-Century Preacher's Handbook*, ed. and trans. Siegfried Wenzel (University Park: Pennsylvania State University Press, 1989), p. 94. Wenzel translates the passage but this translation is mine, so as not to exceed the permissible number of words quoted. The passage attributed to Bernard is found in Lotario dei Segni (Pope Innocent III), *De miseria condicionis humane*, ed. Lewis, part I ch. 8, p. 105.
43. Bernard of Clairvaux, *De moribus et officio episcoporum tractatus* (ep. 42), in *S. Bernardi Opera*, ed. J. Leclercq, C. H. Talbot and H. Rochais, 8 vols. (Rome: Editiones Cistercienses, 1957–77), vol. VII, p. 107.
44. *Hali Meiðhad*, ed. Bella Millett, EETS o.s. 284 (London: Oxford University Press, 1982), p. 6.
45. Quoted by Caroline Walker Bynum, *Holy Feast and Holy Fast: The Religious Significance of Food to Medieval Women* (Berkeley: University of California Press, 1987), pp. 36 and 321 n. 21. Bynum is quoting the translation of Herbert Musurillo, "The Problem of Ascetical Fasting in the Greek Patristic

Writers," *Traditio* 12 (1956), 1–64 at p. 13, with the original in Clement of Alexandria, *Eclogae propheticae* 14.2, *Clemens Alexandrinus*, ed. Otto Stählin, vol. 3, Die griechischen christlichen Schriftsteller der ersten Jahrhunderte 17 (Berlin: Akademie-Verlag, 1970), p. 140.

46. For examples see Bynum, *Holy Feast*, pp. 84, 91, 136.
47. Bernard of Clairvaux, *Apologia ad Guillelmum*, PL 182, 895–918 at cols. 914–16 (cap. 12).
48. See Jeremy Goldberg, "John Skathelok's Dick: Voyeurism and 'Pornography' in Late Medieval England," in *Medieval Obscenities*, ed. Nicola McDonald (Woodbridge, Suffolk: Boydell and Brewer/York Medieval Press, 2006), pp. 105–23 at pp. 108–09.
49. From Erasmus's *De civilitate morum puerilium* (1530), cited by Norbert Elias, *The History of Manners*, trans. Edmund Jephcott, vol. 1 of *the Civilizing Process* (1939; repr. New York: Pantheon, 1978), pp. 130 and 277.
50. *Vita et regula SS. P. Benedicti: una cum expositione regulae a Hildemaro tradita*, ed. Rupert Mittermüller, 3 vols. in 1 (Regensburg, 1880), p. 333 (cap. xxii).
51. The motif was in circulation as early as Clement of Alexandria (c. 100–c.175), who wrote of the misguided priorities of gluttons, "They partake of luxurious dishes, which a little after go to the dunghill. But we who seek the heavenly bread must rule the belly, which is beneath heaven." Note also the vertical/moral orientation of the body and the heavens in the passage. *Paedagogus* book II ch. 1.
52. Ernst Dümmler, *Epistolae Karolini Aevi*, vol. 2, MGH Epist. 4 (Berlin, 1895), ep. 65, p. 108.
53. Lotario dei Segni (Pope Innocent III), *De miseria condicionis humane*, ed. Robert E. Lewis (Athens: University of Georgia Press, 1978), part II ch. 18, p. 167. The satirical poem "Inter membra singula," quoted by Salimbene de Adam in his thirteenth-century *Cronica*, makes the same point: *Cronica*, ed. Guiseppe Scalia, CCCM 125–125A, 2 vols. (Turnhout: Brepols, 1998–99), vol. II, p. 669 (s.v. 1250)
54. *Fasciculus Morum*, ed. and trans. Wenzel, pp. 638. My translation.
55. Ibid., pp. 628. My translation.
56. Ibid., pp. 692–93.
57. Ibid., pp. 692–93.
58. Salimbene de Adam, *Cronica*, ed. Scalia, vol. II, p. 645 (a. 1250); *The Chronicle of Salimbene de Adam*, trans. Joseph L. Baird et al. (Binghamton, NY: Medieval and Renaissance Texts and Studies, 1986), pp. 432–33.
59. Salimbene de Adam, *Cronica*, ed. Scalia, vol. I, p. 502 (a. 1249); *The Chronicle of Salimbene*, trans. Baird, p. 330.
60. Lactantius, *Divinae Institutiones et epitome divinarum institutionum*, ed. Samuel Brandt, CSEL 19 (Vienna, 1890), p. 165 (lib. II.14).
61. Caesarius of Heisterbach, *Dialogus miraculorum*, ed. Strange, vol. 1, pp. 293–94 (book 5, ch. XV).
62. My translation; the translation in Caesarius of Heisterbach, *The Dialogue on Miracles*, trans. Scott and Bland (vol. I, pp. 334–36) is expurgated.
63. Peter Damian, *De Sacramentis per improbos administratis*, PL 145, cols. 523–30 at col. 523.
64. Roger of Wendover, *The Flowers of History*, ed. Henry G. Hewlett, vol. I (1886; repr. Vaduz: Kraus, 1965), A.D. 1199, p. 283.
65. *Chronicles of the Reigns of Edward I and Edward II*, ed. William Stubbs, 2 vols. (1882; repr. Wiesbaden: Kraus, 1965), I, p. 142.
66. *Annales Monastici*, ed. Henry Richards Luard, 5 vols. (1864–69; repr. London: Bernard Quaritch, 1936–71), III, p. 294.
67. The case of Andrew de Harclay is found in *Placitorum in domo capitulari Westmonasteriensi asservatorum Abbreviatio* (London, 1811), vol. I, p. 351;

Gilbert of Middleton in *Select Cases in the Court of King's Bench under Edward II*, ed. G. O. Sayles, 6 vols. (London: Bernard Quaritch,1936–71), IV (Publications of the Selden Society 74), pp. 77–78 (no. 29).
68. These are outlined by Willis Johnson, "The Myth of Jewish Male Menses," *Journal of Medieval History* 24 (1998), 273–95 and Paul-Augustin DeProost, "La mort de Judas dans l'*Historia apostolica* d'Arator (I, 83–102)," *Revue des études Augustiniennes* 35 (1989), 135–50.
69. The legends are described by Peter Dinzelbacher, *Judastraditionen* (Vienna: Selbstverlag des Österreichischen Museums für Volkskunde, 1977). For a brief account of legends concerning Judas's death see Janet Robson, "Fear of Falling: Depicting the *Death of Judas* in Late Medieval Italy," *Fear and its Representations in the Middle Ages and Renaissance*, ed. Anne Scott and Cynthia Kosso, Arizona Studies in the Middle Ages and the Renaissance 6 (Turnhout: Brepols, 2002), pp. 33–65 at pp. 51–52. The traditions are described more fully by Otfried Lieberknecht, "Death and Retribution: Medieval Visions of the End of Judas the Traitor," <www.lieberknecht.de/~diss/papers/p_judas.pdf> [accessed on August 9, 2007]. A summary is also provided by Nancy Caciola, *Discerning Spirits: Divine and Demonic Possession in the Middle Ages* (Ithaca, NY: Cornell University Press, 2003), pp. 201–05, and see Norbert Schnitzler, "Judas' Death: Some Remarks Concerning the Iconography of Suicide in the Middle Ages," *Medieval History Journal* 3 (2000), 103–18.
70. *Expositio Actuum Apostolorum*, in Bede, *Bedae Venerabilis Opera, Pars II, 4: Opera Exegetica*, CCSL 121 (Turnhout: Brepols, 1983), I, 18, pp. 12–13.
71. Drogo, *Sermo de sacramento dominicae passionis*, PL 166, cols. 1515–46 at 1527; Bernard of Clairvaux, *Meditatio in passionem et resurrectionem Domini*, cap. VII: PL 184, cols. 741–68 at 753.
72. Hincmar of Reims, *Capitula in Synodo apud S. Macram ab Hincmaro promulgata*, PL 125, cols. 1069–86 at col. 1074 (cap. V).
73. Jacob de Voragine, *Iacopo da Varazze: Legenda Aurea*, ed. Giovanni Paolo Maggioni, 2nd ed., 2 vols. (Sismel: Edizioni del Galluzzo, 1998), vol. I, pp. 280–81 (cap. XLV: St. Matthew).
74. Hrabanus Maurus's commentary on Acts is unedited; this account is taken from Johnson, "Myth," pp. 278–79.
75. *Biblia Latina cum glossa ordinaria: facsimile reprint of the editio Princeps Adolph Rusch of Strassburg 1480/81*, intro. Karlfried Froehlich and Margaret T. Gibson, 4 vols. (Turnhout: Brepols, 1992), IV, fol. 454 (commentary on Acts 1:18).
76. Jean Michel, *Le Mystère de la Passion*, ed. Omer Jodogne (Gembloux: J. Duculot, 1959), p. 347, lines 23977–84.
77. Ibid., p. 345, lines 23901–03.
78. *Fragmenta*, PG 5, cols. 1259–62; *Die Apostolischen Väter*, Part I, ed. Franz Xaver Funk, rev. Karl Bihlmeyer, 3rd. ed. (Tübingen: Mohr, 1970), p. 134.
79. Eusebius's *Ecclesiastical History* is in PG 19–24; the passage is in book 2.10.7.
80. Rufinus of Aquileia, *Historia Ecclesiastica*, X.14, in *Eusebius Werke*, ed. Eduard Schwartz and Theodore Mommsen, Die griechischen christlichen Schriftsteller 9, pts 1–2 (Leipzig, 1903–09), vol. 2, pt. 2, p. 979.
81. Willis Johnson, "The Myth of Jewish Male Menses," p. 277.
82. Arator, *De actibus apostolorum*, ed. Arthur Patch McKinlay, Corpus Scriptorum Ecclesiasticorum Latinorum 72 (Vienna: Hoelder-Pichler-Tempsky, 1951), pp. 38–39.
83. Arator, *Arator's On the Acts of the Apostles (De Actibus Apostolorum)*, ed. and trans. Richard J. Schrader, trans. Joseph L. Roberts III and John F. Makowski (Atlanta: Scholars Press, 1987), p. 38.

84. Gregory of Tours, *Gregorii Episcopi Turonensis Libri Historiarum X*, ed. Bruno Krusch and Wihelm Levison, MGH, Scriptores rerum Merovingicarum I, pars I (Hanover: Impensis Bibliopolii Hahniani, 1951), p. 68, lines 10–17 (book II, ch. 23).
85. Walafrid Strabo, *Passiones Vitaeque Sanctorum Aevi Merovingici*, ed. Bruno Krusch, MGH, Scriptores rerum Merovingicarum IV (Hannover and Leipzig, 1892), p. 325 (bk. II, ch. 17). The story is repeated in brief in the *De Casibus Monasterii S. Galli, PL* 126, cols. 1057–80 at col. 1061.
86. *Historia relationis s. Richarii* in *Acta Sanctorum quotquot toto orbe coluntur*, ed. J. Bollandus et al. (1643–), April vol. III, pp. 461–64 at p. 463, col. 2. Less serious texts may play upon the same themes. In Chaucer's Merchant's Tale, for example, the young wife May receives the first letter from her would-be seducer and, not wanting to alert her husband, withdraws to the privy to read it. Having decided to act on the opportunity, she tears the letter into pieces and "in the privy softely it cast." Here her decision to commit carnal—and comic—sin is figuratively expressed by the secrecy and symbolism of the privy.
87. Guibert de Nogent, *Guibert de Nogent: Autobiographie,* ed. Edmond-René Labande (Paris: Société d'Edition 'Les Belles Lettres,' 1981), pp. 176–77 (book 1, ch. 22).
88. Ibid., pp. 440–41 (book 3, ch. 18).
89. Ibid., pp. 458 (book 3, ch. 19).
90. *Acta Sanctorum,* ed. Bollandus et al., Mai II, p. 647 (cap. II).
91. *Expositio Actuum Apostolorum,* in Bede, *Bedae Venerabilis Opera, Pars II, 4: Opera Exegetica,* I, 18, pp. 12–13.
92. *Acta Sanctorum,* ed. Bollandus et al., Mai II, p. 648 (cap. II).
93. *An Alphabet of Tales: An English 15th Century Translation of the Alphabetum Narrationum of Etienne de Besançon,* ed. Mary MacLeod Banks, EETS o.s. 126–127 (London, 1904–05; repr. Millwood, NY: Kraus, 1987), no. 35, pp. 25–26 at 26. Frederic C. Tubach, Index Exemplorum: A Handbook of Medieval Religious Tales, FF Communications 204 (Helsinki: Suomalainen Tiedeakatedia, 1969), 295.
94. *Gesta abbatum monasterii Sancti Albani,* ed. Henry Thomas Riley, 3 vols. (London, 1867–69), I, p. 224. On the history and authorship of the text see Mark Hagger, "The *Gesta Abbatum Monasterii Sancti Albani*: Litigation and History at St. Albans," *Historical Research* 81 (2008), 373–98.
95. *An Alphabet of Tales,* ed. Banks, pp. 306–07 at 307 (no. 450). The motif is Tubach, *Index* 745, with eleven examples.
96. This manner of death was either a widely circulating motif or a frequently practiced means of murder, or both; it appears in a number of other reports, for example, the murder of Godfrey Bocard by the henchmen of Robert the Frisian; a weapon was thrust into Bocard's lower parts as he was sitting *ad requisita naturae.* See William of Malmesbury, *Gesta regum Anglorum: The History of the English Kings,* ed. R. A. B. Mynors, R. M. Thomson and M. Winterbottom, 2 vols. (Oxford: Clarendon Press, 1998–1999), vol. I, p. 656–57 (book iv, section 373.4).
97. Henry, Archdeacon of Huntingdon, *Historia Anglorum: The History of the English People,* ed. and trans. Diana Greenway (Oxford: Clarendon Press, 1996), pp. 360–61.
98. *Vita Sancti Martini* in Sulpicius Severus, *Sulpicii Severi Libri qui Supersunt,* ed. C. Halm, CSEL 1 (Vienna, 1866), p. 127 (cap. 17); or in *Vita di Martino,* ed. and trans. Fabio Ruggiero (Bologna: Edizioni Dehoniane Bologna, 2003), p. 120 (cap. 17.7).
99. *Liber Eliensis,* ed. E. O. Blake, Camden Third Series 92 (London: Royal Historical Society, 1962), p. 209 (Book II, ch. 129).

100. *Liber Eliensis: A History of the Isle of Ely*, trans. Janet Fairweather (Woodbridge: Boydell, 2005), pp. 247–48 (Book II, ch. 129).
101. Ælfric tells a variant of the story in the late tenth century: an entertainer skips a Lenten mass and instead goes to gulp down food in the bishop's kitchen and is predictably stricken with divine punishment. The latrine is absent here, but the twin sins of skipping the service and serving carnal desire are clear, along with the added element of failure to respect the bishop. The story is in *Ælfric's Lives of Saints*, ed. W. W. Skeat, EETS o.s. 76 (London, 1881), p. 264 (no. 12, Ash Wednesday).
102. On the hellmouth see Gary D. Schmidt, *The Iconography of the Mouth of Hell, Eighth-Century Britain to the Fifteenth Century* (Selinsgrove: Susquehanna University Press, 1995).
103. The scene from Bosch's Hell (the right panel of *The Garden of Earthly Delights*) is reproduced in Charles De Tolnay, *Hieronymus Bosch* (London: Eyre Methuen, 1966), p. 247.
104. A representative version of the text accompanies plate 10 in Thomas Kren and Roger S. Wieck, *The Visions of Tondal from the Library of Margaret of York* (Malibu: J. Paul Getty Museum, 1990), p. 49.
105. George Philip Krapp, *The Legend of Saint Patrick's Purgatory: Its Later Literary History* (Baltimore: John Murphy Co., 1900), p. 70.
106. The image is reproduced in Robert Hughes, *Heaven and Hell in Western Art* (London: Weidenfeld and Nicolson, 1968), p. 214.
107. Salimbene de Adam, *Cronica*, ed. Scalia, vol. II, p. 645 (a. 1250); *The Chronicle of Salimbene*, trans. Baird, p. 432.
108. Ibid., vol. I, p. 316 (a. 1247); *The Chronicle of Salimbene*, trans. Baird, pp. 199–200.
109. Gregory the Great, *Grégoire le Grand: Dialogues*, ed. Adalbert de Vogüé, Sources chrétiennes 265 (Paris: Éditions du Cerf, 1980), p. 190 (IV, 57, 11).
110. The poem itself is not comic, but it is edited in Marc Wolterbeek, *Comic Tales of the Middle Ages: An Anthology and Commentary* (New York: Greenwood Press, 1991), pp. 70–71. The same equation is found in Chaucer's Nun's Priest's Tale, where Chanticleer tells the story of a murderer who hid the corpse in a heap of dung in a dung-cart. Although the Nun's Priest's Tale as a whole has a comic cast, the story of the murderer is not meant to be comic, and draws on a popular horror of those who would reduce the human body to lifeless dung.
111. *The Cornish Ordinalia*, trans. Markham Harris (Washington, D.C.: Catholic University of America Press, 1969), p. 171.
112. *Tractatus de psalmo CXLI* in Jerome, *S. Hieronymi Presbyteri Opera*, part II: *Opera Homiletica*, ed. G. Morin, CCSL 78 (Turnhout: Brepols, 1958), p. 309.
113. See Zena Kamash, "Which Way to Look? Exploring Latrine Use in the Roman World," in *Toilet: Public Restrooms and the Politics of Sharing*, ed. Harvey Molotch and Laura Noren (New York: New York University Press, 2010), pp. 47–63 at p. 56.
114. The picture is printed in Kamash, "Which Way to Look?" fig. 3.3 (p. 57).
115. For a theologically and historically informed discussion of rabbinical literature and its attitudes to defecation, with extensive references, see Jonathan Wyn Shofer, *Confronting Vulnerability: The Body and the Divine in Rabbinic Ethics* (Chicago: University of Chicago Press, 2010), pp. 52–76.
116. Ibid.
117. Ibid., p. 75.
118. See Lloyd R. Bailey, "Gehenna: The Topography of Hell," *The Biblical Archaeologist* 49 (1986), 187–91.

119. Isidore of Seville, *Mysticorum expositiones sacramentorum seu quaestiones in Vetus Testamentum*, PL 83, col. 370 (cap. xxi); Bede, *In Pentateuchum commentarii*, PL 91, cols. 391–92 (cap. xxiii); Hrabanus Maurus, *Enarratio super Deuteronomium*, PL 108, col. 932 (lib. 3, cap. ix); Hincmar of Reims, *De divortio Lotharii regis et Tetbergae reginae*, PL 125, col. 703 (Interrogatio XII); Rupert of Deutz, *De trinitate et operibus ejus libri XLII in Deuteronomium*, PL 167, cols. 942–43 (cap. xxiv).
120. Gregory the Great, *Moralia in Iob. Libri XXIII–XXXV*, ed. M. Adriaen, CCSL 143B (Turnhout: Brepols, 1985), p. 1589 (book 31, ch. 27, section 54).
121. Bruno Astensis (Bruno of Segni), *Expositio in Pentateuchum*, PL 164, col. 527 (cap. 23).
122. Among those who attempted to interpret the passage were, for example, Philip of Harveng, *De institutione clericorum*, PL 203, cols. 1197–98 (cap. vi); and Peter Cantor, *Verbum Abbreviatum*, PL 205, cols. 349–50 (cap. cxlvi)
123. Helinand of Froidmont, *Cronicon*, PL 212; the *Vita* is in *Acta Sanctorum*, ed. Bollandus et al., Jun. V, with this episode at p. 203 (cap. III).
124. Helinand of Froidmont, *Cronicon*, PL 212, col. 854 (lib. 45).
125. *Allegoriae in sacram scripturam*, PL 112, cols. 1052–53. The *Allegoriae* was formerly attributed to Hrabanus Maurus, but is now thought to be perhaps the work of Garner or Warner of Rochefort (d. after 1255).
126. Gregory the Great, *Moralia in Iob. Libri I–X*, ed. M. Adriaen, CCSL 143 (Turnhout: Brepols, 1979), p. 120 (Book III, vii, 10).
127. Gregory the Great, *Moralia in Iob. Libri I–X*, p. 152 (Book III, xxxi, 60).
128. The image is found in a French Book of Hours from the second half of the fifteenth century, Huntington Library HM 1163, fol. 129v, reproduced in C. W. Dutschke with R. H. Rouse, *Guide to Medieval and Renaissance Manuscripts in the Huntington Library*, 2 vols. (San Marino, CA: The Library, 1989), vol. II, fig. 122.
129. See G. Bartz and E. König, "Die Illustration des Totenoffiziums in Stundenbüchen," in *Im Angesicht des Todes: Ein interdisziplinäres Kompendium*, ed. Hansjakob Becker, Bernhard Einig and Peter-Otto Ullrich, 2 vols. (St. Ottilien: EOS Verlag, 1987), vol. I, pp. 487–528; Lawrence L. Besserman, *The Legend of Job in the Middle Ages* (Cambridge, MA: Harvard University Press, 1979), pp. 56–64. Further examples of images of Job are contained in Samuel L. Terrien, *The Iconography of Job through the Centuries: Artists as Biblical Interpreters* (University Park: Pennsylvania State University Press, 1996).
130. On Margaret of Hungary see *Acta Sanctorum*, ed. J. Bollandus et al., Jan. II, p. 902 (cap. III); on John of Gorze, *Acta Sanctorum*, ed. J. Bollandus et al., Feb. III, p. 704 (caput IX), also in Michel Parisse, *La vie de Jean, abbé de Gorze* (Paris: Picard, 1999).
131. *In Genesim* II, vi, 21, in Bede, *Bedae Venerabilis Opera, Pars II, Opera Exegetica*, 1, p. 113.
132. *Commentary on Genesis* ch. VI, VI. B. 248. The text dates from 1535–45; it is edited in *Vorlesungen über 1. Mose* in Luther, *D. Martin Luthers Werke. Kritische Gesamtausgabe* vols. 42–44 (Weimar, 1911–15).
133. Other commentators who addressed the question of the arrangements for dung on the ark included the fifteenth-century Spanish theologian and bishop Alfonso Tostado de Madrigal (Alphonsus Abulensis).
134. Hugh of St. Victor, *De arca Noe morali*, PL 176, cols. 617–704 at col. 632 (bk I, ch. 4).
135. Hugh of St. Victor, *De arca Noe morali*, PL 176, cols. 632–33 (bk I, ch. 4).
136. Thomas de Chobham, *Summa de arte praedicandi*, ed. Franco Morenzoni, CCCM 82 (Turnhout: Brepols, 1988), pp. 104–05 (cap. IV).

137. Guitmund, *De corporis et sanguinis Christi veritate in eucharista*, PL 149, cols. 1427–94 at cols. 1450–51. Alan of Lille also reported that the stercoran heretics used Matthew 15:17 in support of their position: *Alani de Insulis De Fide Catholica contra Haereticos Sui Temporis*, PL 210, col. 363. See also Macy, "The Theological Statement," pp. 65–66, and Philip Lyndon Reynolds, *Food and the Body: Some Peculiar Questions in High Medieval Theology* (Leiden: Brill, 1999), pp. 5–7, 64.
138. *Homilia de nativitate Domini*, edited in Jerome, *S. Hieronymi Presbyteri Opera*, p. 524.
139. Aquinas, *Summa Theologiae*, vol. 5, 3a.54.4 ad. 2; *The Resurrection of the Lord (3a. 53–59)*, ed. and trans. C. Thomas Moore (New York: McGraw-Hill, 1976), pp. 30–31.
140. Ibid., vol. 5, pp. 446–47.
141. Ibid., vol. 5, p. 449.
142. Guibert of Nogent, *Tractatus*, PL 156, cols. 489–528 at col. 499 (lib. II cap. 1).
143. Ibid.
144. As quoted in this chapter; the original is at Francesc Eiximenis, *Dotzè llibre del Crestià*, ed. Renedo et al., p. 291 (book 2, ch. 133).
145. Hugh of St. Victor, *De arca Noe morali*, PL 176, cols. 625–26 (book I, ch. 2).
146. Yves Lefèvre, *L'Elucidarium et les lucidaires* (Paris: E. de Boccard, 1954), pp. 393–94 (book I, no. 179).
147. On such stories see Martha Bayless, "The Story of the Fallen Jew and the Iconography of Jewish Unbelief," *Viator* 34 (2003), 142–56.
148. Edited by Christoph Cluse, "'Fabula ineptissima': Die Ritualmordlegende um Adam von Bristol nach der Handschrift London, British Library, Harley 957," *Aschkenas: Zeitschrift für Geschichte und Kultur der Juden* 5 (1995), 293–330.
149. Document of January 16, 1205 to the King of France: Solomon Grayzel, *The Church and the Jews in the XIIIth Century*, rev. ed. (New York: Hermon Press, 1966), no. 14, pp. 104–08 at p. 108.
150. Adamnan, *Adamnan's De Locis Sanctis*, ed. Denis Meehan, Scriptores Latini Hiberniae 3 (Dublin: Dublin Institute for Advanced Studies, 1958), pp. 119–20 (book III, ch. v).
151. These are cited in John of Garland, *The Stella Maris of John of Garland*, ed. Evelyn Faye Wilson (Cambridge, MA: Medieval Academy, 1946), pp. 172–73, and Jean Gobi, *La Scala Coeli de Jean Gobi*, ed. Marie-Anne Polo de Beaulieu (Paris: Centre national de la recherche scientifique, 1991), p. 697.
152. On these charges see Miri Rubin, *Gentile Tales: The Narrative Assault on Late Medieval Jews* (New Haven: Yale University Press, 1999), pp. 65–72, 91.
153. Rubin, *Gentile Tales*, pp. 65–66.
154. Shlomo Simonsohn, *The Apostolic See and the Jews: Documents: 492–1404*, Pontifical Institute of Mediaeval Studies and Texts 94 (Toronto: Pontifical Institute of Mediaeval Studies, 1988), pp. 86–87 (no. 82, of July 15, 1205).
155. On this see Miri Rubin, *Gentile Tales*, p. 33 and p. 211 n. 129, quoting the Latin of Henry of Segusio, *Summa aurea* (Basle, 1573), c. 1204 and citing the Polish synod of Breslau in 1446 as well.
156. Malcolm Barber, *The Trial of the Templars* (Cambridge: Cambridge University Press, 1978), p. 180 and p. 279 n. 7, citing *Epistolae Saeculi XIII e Regestis Pontificum Romanorum*, ed. C. Rodenberg, in *Monumenta Germaniae Historica, Epistolae* I (Berlin, 1883), no. 537, pp. 432–34. For a further description

see Jeffrey Burton Russell, *Witchcraft in the Middle Ages* (Ithaca, NY: Cornell University Press, 1972), pp. 160–61.

157. An extensive account of the tale is provided in Bayless, "The Story of the Fallen Jew"; for further examples of the same motif see Anthony Paul Bale, *The Jew in the Medieval Book: English Antisemitisms, 1350–1500* (Cambridge: Cambridge University Press, 2006), pp. 31–34. A representative version, from continental traditions of the *Gesta Romanorum*, is in *Gesta Romanorum*, ed. Hermann Oesterley (1872; repr. Hildesheim, 1963), p. 633, no. 229, app. 33.

158. These are described by James H. Marrow, *Passion Iconography in Northern European Art of the Late Middle Ages and Early Renaissance*, Ars Neerlandica 1 (Kortrijk: Van Ghemmert, 1979), pp. 104–14 and R. Berliner, "Die Cedronbrücke als Station des Passionsweges Christi," in *Rudolf Berliner (1886–1967): "The Freedom of Medieval Art" und andere Studien zum christlichen Bild*, ed. Robert Suckale (Berlin: Lukas Verlag, 2003), pp. 23–27.

159. Quoted by Marrow, *Passion Iconography*, p. 110, with manuscript references on p. 299 n. 469.

160. W. Mushacke, *Altprovenzalische Marienklage des XIII. Jahrhunderts* (Halle a.S., 1890), p. 43. See also Thomas H. Bestul, *Texts of the Passion: Latin Devotional Literature and Medieval Society* (Philadelphia: University of Pennsylvania Press, 1996). Thomas Bestul informs me that the incident is lacking from a number of versions, notably the *Meditationes vitae Christi*, but does appear in others (still in manuscript) as early as the thirteenth century.

161. On this see also Ian Lancashire, "Moses, Elijah and the Back Parts of God: Satiric Scatology in Chaucer's *Summoner's Tale*," *Mosaic* 14:3 (1981), 17–30.

162. Alfred Thomas, "Alien Bodies: Exclusion, Obscenity, and Social Control in *The Ointment Seller*," in *Obscenity: Social Control and Artistic Creation in the European Middle Ages*, ed. Jan M. Ziolkowski (Leiden: Brill, 1998), pp. 214–30 at 223. Thomas cites Roman Jakobson, *Moudrost starych Cechu. Odveké základy národniho odboje* (New York, 1943), pp. 118–19.

163. On the *Inferno* see also Durling, "Deceit and Disgestion."

164. William of Malmesbury, *Gesta regum Anglorum: The History of the English Kings*, ed. and trans. Mynors et al., pp. 340–41 (cap. 190).

165. Tubach, *Index* 2445, citing four examples.

166. Wolterbeek, *Comic Tales*, pp. 70–71.

167. Colin Platt and Richard Coleman-Smith, et al., *Excavations in Medieval Southampton 1953–1969*, 2 vols. (Leicester: Leicester University Press, 1975), vol. I, pp. 34, 293.

168. *Bedfordshire Coroners' Rolls*, ed. R. F. Hunnisett, Bedfordshire Historical Record Society 41 (Streatley: Bedfordshire Historical Record Society Publications, 1961), p. 73.

169. *Registre*, ed. Duvernoy, vol. III, p. 45; Le Roy Ladurie, *Montaillou*, pp. 146–47.

170. An ape and a hybrid animal defecate coins into bowls in London, British Library Add. 29253, fols. 410v and 41v; these images are reproduced by Lester K. Little, "Pride Goes Before Avarice: Social Change and the Vices in Latin Christendom," *American Historical Review* 76 (1971), 16–49 at p. 44.

171. Lester K. Little, *Religious Poverty and the Profit Economy in Medieval Europe* (Ithaca: Cornell University Press, 1978), p. 34, citing *Narratio de Alberico presbytero et ejus sceleribus*, ed. E. Martène and U. Durand, *Veterum Scriptorum et Monumentorum amplissima Collectio*, I (Paris, 1724), 253–55.

172. Both examples from Little, *Religious Poverty*, p. 34.

173. See Alain Boureau, *The Myth of Pope Joan*, trans. Lydia G. Cochrane (Chicago: The University of Chicago Press, 2001), pp. 23, 48 and 338 n. 8, citing

Francesco Cancellieri, *Storia de' solenni possessi de' Sommi Pontefici* ... (Rome, 1802), 60–112.
174. Marc Dykmans, *Le cérémonial papal de la fin du Moyen Age à la Renaissance*, 4 vols., vol. 1, *Le cérémonial papal du XIIIe siècle* (Brussels: Institut historique belge de Rome, 1977), p. 177.
175. In addition to Boureau, *The Myth of Pope Joan*, see Craig M. Rustici, *The Afterlife of Pope Joan: Deploying the Popess Legend in Early Modern England* (Ann Arbor: University of Michigan Press, 2006), pp. 50–52 and 165 n. 7.
176. Bartolomeo Platina, *Platynae historici Liber de vita Christi ac omnium pontificum (aa. 1–1474)*, ed. Giacinto Gaida (Città di Castello: S. Lapi, 1932), p. 152.
177. Salimbene de Adam, *Cronica*, II, p. 857 (a. 1285); *The Chronicle of Salimbene*, trans. Baird, pp. 577–78.
178. On this and the following instances, see Chapter 1.
179. Gabriel Biel, *Gabrielis Biel Canonis Misse Expositio*, ed. Heiko A. Oberman and William J. Courtenay, 4 vols. (Wiesbaden: Franz Steiner, 1963–67), III, p. 27 (lectio LXII.F).
180. Salimbene, *Cronica*, Salimbene de Adam, *Cronica*, II, p. 857 (a. 1285); *Chronicle* trans. Baird, p. 577.

NOTES TO CHAPTER 5

1. Jonathan Wyn Shofer, *Confronting Vulnerability: The Body and the Divine in Rabbinic Ethics* (Chicago: University of Chicago Press, 2010), p. 74.
2. Ruth Mellinkoff, *Averting Demons: The Protective Power of Medieval Visual Motifs and Themes*, 2 vols. (Los Angeles: Ruth Mellinkoff, 2004), ch. vi: "Sexual and Scatological Display," vol. I, pp. 123–43. For reservations on Mellinkoff's approach see the review by Louise Marshall in *Speculum* 81 (2006), pp. 891–93 and the review by Malcolm Jones in *Profane Images in Marginal Arts of the Middle Ages*, ed. Elaine C. Block with Frédéric Billiet, Sylvie Bethmont-Gallerand and Paul Hardwick (Turnhout: Brepols, 2009), pp. 339–61.
3. Mellinkoff, *Averting Demons*, vol. I, pp. 123–42, with images in vol. II, pp. 209–98.
4. Ibid., vol. I, p. 124.
5. Ibid., vol. I, p. 127.
6. The manuscript is New York, Pierpont Morgan Library MS 729, fol. 268r. It is reproduced in Mellinkoff, *Averting Demons* vol. II, p. 219 (fig. VI.10).
7. Translation from *Alexandrian Christianity*, with introduction and notes by J. E. L. Oulton and Henry Chadwick (London: Westminster Press, 1954), p. 67. The original is at *Clemens Alexandrinus*, ed. Otto Stählin, vol. II (Berlin: Akademie-Verlag, 1960), p. 223.
8. *Clemens Alexandrinus*, ed. Stählin, vol. II, p. 223.
9. *The Gnostic Scriptures*, trans. Bentley Layton (London: SCM, 1987), p. 239.
10. Ismo Dunderberg, "The School of Valentinus," in *A Companion to Second-Century Christian "Heretics,"* ed. Antti Marjanen and Petri Luomanen (Leiden: Brill, 2008), pp. 64–99 at p. 74.
11. Piotr Ashwin-Siejkowski, *Clement of Alexandria on Trial: The Evidence of "Heresy" from Photius' Bibliotheca* (Leiden: Brill, 2010), p. 97.
12. Layton, *The Gnostic Scriptures*, p. 238.
13. Philip Lyndon Reynolds, *Food and the Body: Some Peculiar Questions in High Medieval Theology* (Leiden: Brill, 1999).

14. Layton, *The Gnostic Scriptures*, p. 238.
15. Translation from Layton, *The Gnostic Scriptures*, p. 238.
16. Larry W. Hurtado, *Lord Jesus Christ: Devotion to Jesus in Earliest Christianity* (Grand Rapids and Cambridge: William B. Eerdmans, 2003), p. 528.
17. Dunderberg, "The School of Valentinus," p. 74.
18. Ashwin-Siejkowski, *Clement of Alexandria*, p. 97.
19. *Diogenis Laertii Vitae philosophorum*, ed. Miroslav Marcovich, 3 vols. (Stuttgart: Teuber, 1999–2002). The standard English translation in *Diogenes Laertius: Lives of Eminent Philosophers*, trans. D. R. Hicks, 2 vols. (London: Heinemann, 1925) is expurgated. The modern French translation suggests for these precepts "'ne pas s'essuyer aux latrines à la lumière d'une torche,' 'ne pas pisser tourné vers le soleil' . . . 'ne pas uriner ni se placer sur des rognures d'ongles et des cheveux coupés'": "Do not wipe oneself in the latrines in the light of a torch," "do not piss turned toward the sun," "do not urinate nor place oneself on nail clippings or on hair cuttings." The notes give alternate readings based on parallels elsewhere, but conclude that the text forms "un interdit relatif à la défécation," "prohibitions about defecation." *Diogène Laërce: Vies et doctrines des philosophes illustres*, translated under the direction of Marie-Odile Goulet-Cazé (Paris: Librarie Générale Française, 1999), p. 955.
20. A French translation is available in *Diogène Laërce: Vies et doctrines*, p. 149. The English translation of Hicks, *Diogenes Laertius*, is euphemized at this point.
21. Ashwin-Siejkowski, *Clement of Alexandria*, p. 97.
22. April D. DeConick, "The Great Mystery of Marriage: Sex and Conception in Ancient Valentinian Traditions," *Vigiliae Christianae* 57 (2003), 307–42 at p. 315. The first example is in Jacques de Vitry, *The Historia Occidentalis of Jacques de Vitry*, ed. John Frederick Hinnebusch (Fribourg: University Press, 1972), pp. 87–88, and *Opus minus*, in Roger Bacon, *Fr. Rogeri Bacon opera quaedam hactenus inedita*, ed. J.S. Brewer, vol. 1 (London, 1859), pp. 373–74.
23. On this phenomenon see Caroline Walker Bynum, *Holy Feast and Holy Fast: The Religious Significance of Food to Medieval Women* (Berkeley: University of California Press, 1987) and Rudolph M. Bell, *Holy Anorexia* (Chicago: University of Chicago Press, 1985).
24. On the nature and identity of "residues," see Porphyry, *On Abstinence from Killing Animals*, trans. Gillian Clark (London: Duckworth, 2000), p. 180 n. 248. Clark writes, "Aristotle discusses residues, *perittômata*, in *GA* 1. They result from useful and from useless food, and may be formed before or after food becomes blood. Useless food makes no contribution to the organism, and causes harm if much is eaten (725a4–7). Useful residues include semen and menses (interpreted as the female contribution to the embryo), useless residues include excrement." The original of the passage is in *Porphyre: De l'abstinence*, 3 vols., vol. III, ed. and trans. M. Patillon and A. Segonds with L. Brisson (Paris: Les Belles Lettres, 1995).
25. Porphyry, *On Abstinence from Killing Animals*, trans. Clark, p. 101 (Book 4.2.3).
26. Guibert of Nogent, *Tractatus de incarnatione contra Judaeos*, PL 156, cols. 489–528 at col. 499 (lib. II cap. 1).
27. Francesc Eiximenis, *Dotzè llibre del Crestià*, ed. Xavier Renedo et al. (Girona: University of Girona, 2005), p. 291 (book 2, ch. 133).
28. The manuscript is Oxford, Bodleian Library Douce 49.
29. Susan Signe Morrison, *Excrement in the Late Middle Ages: Sacred Filth and Chaucer's Fecopoetics* (New York: Palgrave Macmillan, 2008), pp. 90–91.

30. 'Psalter with Calendar', MS. Douce 49. Roll 243.10, Frame 003 (late 13th century). <http://bodley30.bodley.ox.ac.uk:8180/luna/servlet/detail/ODLodl~1~1~43145~118695:Psalter-with-Calendar-?sort=Shelfmark%2CFolio_Page%2CRoll_%23%2CFrame_%23&fullTextSearch=fullTextSearch&qvq=q:crouches%2Ba%2Bglowering%2Bbrown%2Bdog;sort:Shelfmark%2CFolio_Page%2CRoll_%23%2CFrame_%23;lc:ODLodl~1~1&mi=0&trs=1>
31. There are now a number of collections that include scatological and related marginalia and carvings. The most compendious include *Profane Images*, ed. Elaine C. Block et al.; Ruth Mellinkoff, *Averting Demons*; Malcolm Jones, *The Secret Middle Ages* (Stroud: Sutton, 2002); Michael Camille, *Image on the Edge: The Margins of Medieval Art* (London: Reaktion, 1992); Claude Gaignebet and Jean-Dominique Lajoux, *Art profane et religion populaire au Moyen Age* (Paris: Presses Universitaires de France, 1985); Karl P. Wentersdorf, "The Symbolic Significance of Figurae Scatalogicae in Gothic Manuscripts," in *Word, Picture, and Spectacle*, ed. Clifford Davidson (Kalamazoo: Western Michigan University Press, 1984), pp. 1–21; Lester K. Little, "Pride Goes Before Avarice: Social Change and the Vices in Latin Christendom," *American Historical Review* 76 (1971), 16–49; and Lilian Randall, *Images in the Margins of Gothic Manuscripts* (Berkeley: University of California Press, 1966).
32. Morrison, *Excrement* , pp. 90–91.
33. Ibid., pp. 92–93.
34. Hugh of St. Victor, *De arca Noe morali*, PL 176, cols. 632–33 (bk I, ch. 4).
35. *Allegoriae in sacram scripturam*, PL 112, col. 871.
36. Ibid., col. 883.
37. Peter of Dacia, *Acta B. Christinae Stumbelensi*, in *Acta Sanctorum*, ed. J. Bollandus et al., June vol. V, p. 250, cols. 1–2. The episode in question is translated by Aviad M. Kleinberg, *Prophets in their Own Country: Living Saints and the Making of Sainthood in the Later Middle Ages* (Chicago and London: University of Chicago Press, 1992), pp. 50–51.
38. Peter of Dacia, *Acta Sanctorum*, ed. J. Bollandus et al., p. 255, col. 1.
39. Ibid., p. 252, col. 1.
40. Kleinberg, *Prophets*, p. 67.
41. Ibid., p. 51.
42. Ibid., p. 52.
43. The variants are edited in NRCF, vol. VII, pp. 140–89 as *Le Sacristan I, II, and III*. The plots are nearly identical, with varying degrees of detail. In this analysis I will be talking about *Le Sacristain II*, which appears in five manuscripts, to the one manuscript of each of the other versions. This version is translated, with facing French, in *Gallic Salt*, trans. Robert Harrison (Berkeley: University of California Press, 1974), pp. 85–137. The story has analogues in many languages. The Middle English version, *Dane Hew, Munk of Leicestre*, is edited by Melissa M. Furrow, *Ten Fifteenth-Century Comic Poems* (New York and London: Garland, 1985), pp. 163–74. The English version is less scatological—the dead monk is propped up against a wall rather than seated in the latrine—but compensates by being more sexual, as the horse at the end of the story is chasing a mare.
44. Line numbers are from the edition of *Le Sacristain II*, NRCF, vol. VII, pp. 153–73.
45. Harrison, *Gallic Salt*, p. 107.
46. Ibid., p. 131.
47. Norbert Elias, *Über den Prozess der Zivilisation: soziogenetische und psycogenetische Untersuchungen*, 2 vols. (Basel: Verlag Haus zum Falken, 1939). The book became especially influential when its first volume appeared in

English as *The History of Manners*, trans. Edmund Jephcott, vol. 1 of the *Civilizing Process* (Oxford: Blackwell, 1969).
48. Dominique Laporte, *Histoire de la Merde* (Paris: Christian Bourgois Éditeur, 1978). Translated as *History of Shit* [sic], trans. Nadia Benabid and Rodolphe el-Khoury (Cambridge, MA: MIT Press, 2000).
49. Hans-Peter Duerr, *Der Mythos vom Zivilisationsprozess*: vol. 1, *Nacktheit und Scham* (1988); vol. 2, *Intimität* (1994); vol. 3, *Obszönität und Gewalt* (1995); vol. 4, *Der erotische Leib* (1997), vol. 5, *Die Tatsachen des Lebens* (2002). (Frankfurt-am-Main: Suhrkamp). See also Michael Hinz, *Der Zivilisationsprozess: Mythos oder Realität?: wissenschaftssoziologische Untersuchungen zur Elias-Duerr-Kontroverse* (Opladen: Leske + Budrich, 2002).
50. See, for instance, among many others, Jack Goody, "Elias and the Anthropological Tradition," *Anthropological Theory* 2 (2002), 401–12, countered by Eric Dunning, "Some Comments on Jack Goody's 'Elias and the Anthropological Tradition,'" *Anthropological Theory* 2 (2002), 413–20.
51. A case study is provided by Albrecht Classen, "Farting and the Power of Human Language, with a Focus on Hans Wilhelm Kirchhof's Sixteenth-Century *Schwänke*," *Medievalia et Humanistica* n.s. 35 (2009), 57–76.
52. The connection between these subjects and the passage by Mather was first noted in Jonathan Haidt, Paul Rozin, Clark McCauley and Sumio Imada, "Body, Psyche, and Culture: The Relationship between Disgust and Morality," Psychology and Developing Societies 9 (1997), p. 113.
53. John Ray, *A Collection of English Proverbs* (1st ed., 1670), sig. A3v; (2nd ed., 1678), sig. A3v, as cited by Adam Fox, *Oral and Literate Culture in England 1500–1700* (Oxford: Clarendon Press, 2000), p. 167.

Bibliography

PRIMARY SOURCES

Abelard, Peter, *Theologia "Summi Boni,"* in *Petri Abaelardi Opera Theologica*, ed. E. M. Buytaert and C. J. Mews, CCCM 13 (Turnhout: Brepols, 1987)
Der Ackermann aus Böhmen, ed. L. L. Hammerich and G. Jungbluth (Heidelberg: Carl Winter, 1951)
Acta Sanctorum quotque orbe coluntur..., ed. J. Bollandus et al. (1643-)
Adamnan, *Adamnan's De Locis Sanctis*, ed. Denis Meehan, Scriptores Latini Hiberniae 3 (Dublin: Dublin Institute for Advanced Studies, 1958)
Ælfric, *Ælfric's Lives of Saints*, ed. W. W. Skeat, EETS o.s. 76 (London, 1881)
Alan of Lille, *Alani de Insulis De Fide Catholica contra Haereticos Sui Temporis*, PL 210
Alger of Liège, *De sacramentis corporis et sanguinis domini*, PL 180, cols. 739–854
Allegoriae in sacram scripturam, PL 112, cols. 849–1088
An Alphabet of Tales: An English 15th Century Translation of the Alphabetum Narrationum of Etienne de Besançon, ed. Mary MacLeod Banks, EETS o.s. 126–127 (London, 1904–1905; repr. Millwood, New York: Kraus Reprint, 1987)
Annales Monastici, ed. Henry Richards Luard, 5 vols. (1864–69, repr. London: Bernard Quaritch, 1936–71)
Antonio de Beatis, *The Travel Journal of Antonio de Beatis*, trans. J. R. Hale and J. M. A. Lindon (London: Hakluyt Society, 1979)
Die Apostolischen Väter, part I, ed. Franz Xaver Funk, rev. Karl Bihlmeyer, 3rd. ed. (Tübingen: Mohr, 1970)
Aquinas, Thomas, *The Resurrection of the Lord (3a. 53–59)*, ed. and trans. C. Thomas Moore (New York: McGraw-Hill, 1976)
———, *Summa Theologiae*, 5 vols. (Matriti: La Editorial Catolica, 1955–61)
Arator, *De actibus apostolorum* ed. Arthur Patch McKinlay, Corpus Scriptorum Ecclesiasticorum Latinorum 72 (Vienna: Hoelder-Pichler-Tempsky, 1951)
———, *Arator's On the Acts of the Apostles (De Actibus Apostolorum)*, ed. and trans. Richard J. Schrader, trans. Joseph L. Roberts III and John F. Makowski (Atlanta: Scholars Press, 1987)
Augustine, *The City of God*, ed. T. E. Page et al., trans. Philip Levine, Loeb Classical Library (Cambridge, Mass.: Harvard University Press, 1966)
———, *Confessionum libri XIII*, ed. Lucas Verheijen, CCSL 27 (Turnhout: Brepols, 1981)
———, *Enarrationes in Psalmos I-L*, in *Aurelii Augustini Opera* pars X, 1: ed. E. Dekkers and J. Fraipont, CCSL 38 (Turnhout: Brepols, 1956)
———, *De Genesi contra Manicheos*, PL 34, cols. 186–87

——, *De ordine*, ed. in *Aurelii Augustini Opera pars II, 2*, CCSL 29 (Turnhout: Brepols, 1970)
——, *De trinitate libri XV*, ed. W. J. Mountain and Fr. Glorie, CCSL 50–50A (Turnhout: Brepols, 1968)
Bacon, Roger, *Fr. Rogeri Bacon opera quaedam hactenus inedita*, ed. J. S. Brewer, vol. 1 (London, 1859)
Bandinelli, Roland, *Die Sentenzen Rolands nachmals Papstes Alexander III*, ed. A. M. Gietl (Freiburg, 1891)
Barbour's Bruce, ed. Matthew P. McDiarmid and James A. C. Stevenson, 2 vols. (Edinburgh: Scottish Text Society, 1980)
Bárðar Saga, ed. and trans. Jón Skaptason and Phillip Pulsiano (New York and London: Garland, 1984)
Bede, *In Pentateuchum commentarii*, PL 91
——, *Bedae Venerabilis Opera, Pars II, 1*, ed. C. W. Jones, CCSL 118A (Turnhout: Brepols, 1967)
——, *Bedae Venerabilis Opera, Pars II, 4: Opera Exegetica*, CCSL 121 (Turnhout: Brepols, 1983)
Benedetti, Alessandro, *Historia corporis humani sive Anatomice*, ed. Giovanna Ferrari (Firenze: Giunti, 1998)
——, *Studies in Pre-Vesalian Anatomy: Biography, Translations, Documents*, trans. L. R. Lind (Philadelphia: American Philosophical Society, 1975)
Bernard of Clairvaux, *Apologia ad Guillelmum*, PL 182, 895–918
——, *Meditatio in passionem et resurrectionem Domini*, PL 184, cols. 741–768
——, *De moribus et officio episcoporum tractatus*, PL 182, cols. 809–834
——, *S. Bernardi Opera*, ed. J. Leclerq, C. H. Talbot, and H. M. Rochais (Rome: Editiones Cistercienses, 1957–77)
——, *The Works of Bernard of Clairvaux*, Vol. III: *On the Songs of Songs* II, trans. Kilian Walsh, Cistercian Fathers Series 7 (Kalamazoo: Cistercian Publications, 1976)
Bernard of Morval, *De Contemptu Mundi*, ed. H. C. Hoskier (London: B. Quaritch, 1929)
Biblia Latina cum glossa ordinaria: facsimile reprint of the editio princeps (Adolph Rusch of Strassburg 1480/81), intro. Karlfried Frohelich and Margaret T. Gibson, 4 vols. (Turnhout: Brepols, 1992)
Bruno Astensis (Bruno of Segni), *Expositio in Pentateuchum*, PL 164
Buchanan, John Lanne, *Travels in the Western Hebrides from 1782 to 1790* (London, 1793)
Caesarius of Heisterbach, *Dialogus Miraculorum*, ed. Joseph Strange (Cologne, 1851; repr. Ridgewood, New Jersey: Gregg Press, 1966)
——, *The Dialogue on Miracles*, trans. H. von E. Scott and C. C. Swinton Bland, 2 vols. (London: Routledge, 1929)
Chaucer, Geoffrey, *The Riverside Chaucer*, ed. Larry D. Benson, 3rd ed. (Oxford: Oxford University Press, 1988)
Les Cent nouvelles nouvelles, ed. Franklin P. Sweetser (Geneva: Droz, 1966)
Cervantes Saavedra, Miguel de, *Don Quijote de la Mancha*, ed. Martín de Riquer (Barcelona: Editorial Juventud, 1958)
Clarke, Edward Daniel, *A Tour Through the South of England, Wales, and Part of Ireland, Made During the Summer of 1791* (London, 1793)
Clement of Alexandria, *Clemens Alexandrinus*, ed. Otto Stählin, vol. II (Berlin: Akademie-Verlag, 1960)
The Cornish Ordinalia, trans. Markham Harris (Washington, D.C.: Catholic University of America Press, 1969)
Crooke, Helkiah, *Microcosmographia: A Description of the Body of Man* (London, 1615)

Da Vinci, Leonardo, *The Notebooks of Leonardo da Vinci*, trans. Edward Mac-Curdy, 2 vols. (London: Jonathan Cape, 1938)
Dahlberg, Charles, *The Literature of Unlikeness* (Hanover, New Hampshire: University Press of New England, 1988)
Daniel of Beccles, *Urbanus Magnus Danielis Becclesiensis*, ed. J. Gilbart Smyly (Dublin: Hodges, Figgis and Co., 1939)
Death and the Plowman, trans. Ernest N. Kirrmann (Chapel Hill: University of North Carolina Press, 1958)
De Casibus Monasterii S. Galli, PL 126, cols. 1057–80
Delaborde, H.-François, *Oeuvres de Rigord et de Guillaume Le Breton, Historiens de Philippe-Auguste*, 2 vols. (Paris, 1882–1885)
The Demaundes Joyous: A Facsimile of the First English Riddle Book, ed. John Wardroper (London: Gordon Fraser Gallery, 1971)
Diogenes Laertius, *Diogène Laërce: Vies et doctrines des philosophes illustres*, trans. under the direction of Marie-Odile Goulet-Cazé (Paris: Librarie Générale Française, 1999)
———, *Diogenes Laertius: Lives of Eminent Philosophers*, trans. D. R. Hicks, 2 vols. (London: Wm. Heinemann, 1925)
———, *Diogenis Laertii Vitae philosophorum*, ed. Miroslav Marcovich, 3 vols. (Stuttgart: Teuber, 1999–2002)
Douglas, David C. and George W. Greenaway, eds., *English Historical Documents 1042–1189* (New York: Oxford University Press, 1953)
Drogo, *Sermo de sacramento dominicae passionis*, PL 166, cols. 1515–1546
Dümmler, Ernst, ed., *Epistolae Karolini Aevi*, vol. 2, MGH Epist. 4 (Berlin, 1895)
———, MGH, *Poetae Latini Aevi Carolini* I (Berlin, 1881)
Duvernoy, Jean, ed., *Le Registre d'inquisition de Jacques Fournier évêque de Pamiers (1318–1325)*, 3 vols. (Toulouse: Édouard Privat, 1965)
Eichmann, Raymond and John DuVal, *The French Fabliau B. N. MS. 837*, 2 vols. (New York: Garland, 1984–1985)
Ekkehard IV, *Casus sancti Galli: St. Galler Klostergeschichten*, ed. Hans F. Haefele (Darmstadt: Wissenschaftliche Buchgesellschaft, 1980)
Enguerrand de Monstrelet, *The Chronicles of Enguerrand de Monstrelet*, trans. Thomas Johnes, 2 vols. (London, 1849)
Eusebius, *Ecclesiastical History*, PG 19–24
Eyrbyggja Saga, ed. Einar Ól. Sveinsson and Matthías Thorðarson (Reykjavik, 1935)
Fasciculus Morum: A Fourteenth-Century Preacher's Handbook, ed. and trans. Siegfried Wenzel (University Park, Pennsylvania and London: Pennsylvania State University Press, 1989)
Fiennes, Celia, *The Illustrated Journeys of Celia Fiennes 1685-c. 1712*, ed. Christopher Morris (London and Sydney: MacDonald and Co., 1982)
Flateyjarbók, ed. S. Nordal et al., 4 vols ([n.p.], Prentverk Akraness, 1944–45)
Francesc Eiximenis, *Dotzè llibre del Crestià*, ed. Xavier Renedo et al. (Girona: University of Girona, 2005)
Francis of Assisi, *"I Fioretti di San Francesco," Riveduti su un nuovo Codice da Benvenuto Bughetti* (Quaracchi: Collegio San Bonaventura, 1926), printed in *Fonti Francescane*, new edition, ed. Ernesto Caroli (Padua: Editrici Francescane, 2004)
———, *Francis of Assisi: Early Documents*, ed. Regis J. Armstrong, J. A. Wayne Hellmann, and William J. Short, 3 vols. (New York: New City Press, 1999–2001)
———, *The Little Flowers of Saint Francis of Assisi*, trans. and ed. Cardinal Manning (London: T. N. Foulis, 1915)
Furrow, Melissa M., *Ten Fifteenth-Century Comic Poems* (New York and London: Garland, 1985)

Gabriel Biel, *Gabrielis Biel Canonis Misse Expositio*, ed. Heiko A. Oberman and William J. Courtenay, 4 vols. (Wiesbaden: Franz Steiner, 1963–67)
Gerald of Wales (Giraldus Cambrensis), *Gemma ecclesiastica*, ed. J. S. Brewer (1862; repr. Wiesbaden: Kraus Reprint, 1964)
Gesta Abbatum Monasterii Sancti Albani, ed. Henry Thomas Riley, 3 vols. (London, 1867–69)
Gesta Romanorum, ed. Hermann Oesterley (1872; repr. Hildesheim: Olms, 1963)
Gobi, Jean, *La Scala Coeli de Jean Gobi*, ed. Marie-Anne Polo de Beaulieu (Paris: Centre national de la recherche scientifique, 1991)
Gossouin, *L'Image du monde de Maitre Gossouin* ed. O. H. Prior (Lausanne and Paris: Payot, 1913)
Gregory the Great, *Grégoire le Grand: Dialogues*, ed. Adalbert de Vogüé, Sources chrétiennes 265 (Paris: Éditions du Cerf, 1980)
———, *Moralia in Iob. Libri I-X*, ed. M. Adriaen, CCSL 143 (Turnhout: Brepols, 1979)
———, *Moralia in Iob. Libri XXIII-XXXV*, ed. M. Adriaen, CCSL 143B (Turnhout: Brepols, 1985)
Gregory of Tours, *Gregorii Episcopi Turonensis Libri Historiarum X*, ed. Bruno Krusch and Wihelm Levison, MGH, Scriptores rerum Merovingicarum I, pars I (Hanover: Impensis Bibliopolii Hahniani, 1951)
Guibert de Nogent, *Guibert de Nogent: Autobiographie*, ed. Edmond-René Labande (Paris: Société d'Edition 'Les Belles Lettres', 1981)
———, *Tractatus de incarnatione contra Judaeos*, PL 156, cols. 489–528
Guillelmus abbas, *Meditationes orationes*, PL 180, cols. 205–48
Guitmund, *De corporis et sanguinis Christi veritate in eucharista*, PL 149, cols. 1427–94
Hali Meiðhad, ed. Bella Millett, EETS o.s. 284 (London: Oxford University Press, 1982)
Hardy, Thomas Duffus and Charles Trice Martin, eds., *Lestorie des Engles solum la translacion Maistre Geffrei Gaimar*, 2 vols. (London, 1888–1889)
Harington, Sir John, *Sir John Harington's A New Discourse of a Stale Subject, called The Metamorphosis of Ajax*, ed. Elizabeth Story Donno (London: Routledge and Kegan Paul, 1962)
———, *A New Discourse of a Stale Subject, Called the Metamorphosis of Ajax* (London, 1596)
Harrison, Robert, trans., *Gallic Salt* (Berkeley: University of California Press, 1974)
Helinand of Froidmont, *Cronicon*, PL 212
Henry of Huntingdon, *Historia Anglorum: The History of the English People*, ed. and trans. Diana Greenway (Oxford: Clarendon Press, 1996)
Heriger of Lobbes, *De corpore et sanguine domini*, PL 139, cols. 179–88
Higden, Ranulph, *Polychronicon Ranulphi Higden Monachi Cestrensis*, vol. 5, ed. Joseph Rawson Lumby (London, 1882; repr. Wiesbaden: Kraus, 1964)
Hildebert of Lavardin, *Sermo XC*, PL 171, cols. 761–65
Hill, George, *Facts from Gweedore, compiled from the notes of Lord George Hill*, 5th ed., with an introduction by E. Estyn Evans (5th edition published 1887; reprint: Queen's University of Belfast, Institute of Irish Studies, 1971)
Hincmar of Reims, *Capitula in Synodo apud S. Macram ab Hincmaro promulgata*, PL 125, cols. 1069–1086
———, *De divortio Lotharii regis et Tetbergae reginae*, PL 125
Hrabanus Maurus, *Enarratio super Deuteronomium*, PL 108
Hugh of St. Victor, *De arca Noe morali*, PL 176, cols. 617–704
———, *In Salomonis Ecclesiasten Homiliae XIX*, PL 175, cols. 114–256

Isidore of Seville, *Isidori Hispalensis Episcopi Etymologiarum Sive Originum Libri XX*, ed. W. M. Lindsay, 2 vols. (Oxford: Clarendon Press, 1911)
———, *Mysticorum expositiones sacramentorum seu quaestiones in Vetus Testamentum*, PL 83
Jacob de Voragine, *Iacopo da Varazze: Legenda Aurea*, ed. Giovanni Paolo Maggioni, 2nd ed., 2 vols. (Sismel: Edizioni del Galluzzo, 1998)
Jacob's Well, ed. Arthur Brandeis, EETS o.s. 115 (London, 1900)
Jacques de Vitry, *The Historia Occidentalis of Jacques de Vitry*, ed. John Frederick Hinnebusch (Fribourg: University Press, 1972)
Jerome, *Adversus Jovinianum*, PL 23, cols. 211–338
———, *S. Hieronymi Presbyteri Opera*, part II: *Opera Homiletica*, ed. G. Morin, CCSL 78 (Turnhout: Brepols, 1958)
John of Garland, *The Stella Maris of John of Garland*, ed. Evelyn Faye Wilson (Cambridge, Mass.: Medieval Academy, 1946)
Keats, John, *Letters of John Keats*, ed. Robert Gittings (Oxford: Oxford University Press, 1970)
Kimhi, Joseph, *The Book of the Covenant*, trans. Frank Talmage (Toronto: Pontifical Institute of Mediaeval Studies, 1972)
Lactantius, *Divinae Institutiones et epitome divinarum institutionum*, ed. Samuel Brandt, CSEL 19 (Vienna, 1890)
Lanfranco, *Lanfrank's 'Science of Cirurgie,'* ed. R. V. Fleischhacker, EETS o.s. 102 (Berlin, New York, and Philadelphia, 1894, repr. 1988)
Laxdœla saga, ed. Einar Ól. Sveinsson, Íslenzk Fornrit 5 (Reykjavik, 1934)
The Laxdoela Saga, trans. A. Margaret Arent (Seattle and New York: University of Washington Press, 1964)
Layton, Bentley, trans., *The Gnostic Scriptures* (London: SCM, 1987)
Liber Eliensis, ed. E. O. Blake, Camden Third Series 92 (London: Royal Historical Society, 1962)
Liber Eliensis: A History of the Isle of Ely, trans. Janet Fairweather (Woodbridge: Boydell, 2005)
Liber exemplorum ad usum praedicantium, ed. A. G. Little (Aberdeen: Typis Academicis, 1908)
Liebermann, F., ed., *Die Gesetze der Angelsachsen*, 3 vols. (Halle a.S.: M. Niemeyer, 1898–1916)
Lotario dei Segni (Pope Innocent III), *De miseria condicionis humane*, ed. Robert E. Lewis (Athens, Georgia: University of Georgia Press, 1978)
Love, Rosalind C., ed. and trans., *Three Eleventh-Century Anglo-Latin Saints' Lives* (Oxford: Clarendon Press, 1996)
Luther, Martin, *D. Martin Luthers Werke: Kritische Gesamtausgabe*, vols. 42–44 (Weimar: Hermann Böhlaus, 1911–15)
———, *D. Martin Luthers Werke. Kritische Gesamtausgabe. Tischreden*, 6 vols. (Weimar: Hermann Böhlaus, 1912–21)
———, *Lectures on Genesis, Chapters 1–5*, in *Luther's Works*, ed. Jaroslav Pelikan, vol. 1 (St. Louis: Concordia, 1958)
Macaulay, Kenneth, *The History of St. Kilda* (1764; repr.. Edinburgh: J. Thin, 1974)
The Malleus Maleficarum of Heinrch Kramer and James Sprenger, trans. Montague Summers (1928; repr. Mineola, NY: Dover, 1971)
Map, Walter, *De Nugis Curialium: Courtiers' Trifles*, ed. and trans. M. R. James, rev. C. N. L. Brooke and R. A. B. Mynors (Oxford: Clarendon Press, 1983)
Marguerite de Navarre, *L'Heptaméron*, ed. Michel François (Paris: Garnier, 1969)
Marshall, Sybil, *A Pride of Tigers: A Fen Family and its Fortunes* (Harmondsworth: Penguin, 1995)

Martini, Francesco di Giorgio, *Trattati di architettura ingegneria e arte militare*, ed. Corrado Maltese, 2 vols. (Milan: Edizioni il Polifilo, 1967)
Melanchthon, Philipp, *Philippi Melanchthon Opera quae Supersunt Omnia*, ed. K. G. Bretschneider and H. E. Bindseil, Corpus Reformatorum 20 (Brunsvige, 1854)
Meyer, Christian, *Das Stadtbuch von Augsburg, insbesondere das Stadtrecht vom Jahre 1276* (Augsburg, 1872)
Michel, Jean, *Le Mystère de la Passion*, ed. Omer Jodogne (Gembloux: J. Duculot, 1959)
Mittermüller, Rupert, ed., *Vita et regula SS. P. Benedicti: una cum expositione regulae a Hildemaro tradita* (Regensburg, 1880),
Mombritius, Boninus (Bonino Mombrizio), *Sanctuarium seu Vitae Sanctorum*, 2 vols. (Hildesheim: Georg Olms Verlag, 1978)
Monachus Sangallensis De Carolo Magno, ed. in *Bibliotheca Rerum Germanicarum*, ed. Philipp Jaffé, vol. IV: *Monumenta Carolina* (Berlin, 1867)
Noomen, Willem and Nico van den Boogaard, eds., *Nouveau Recueil complet des fabliaux*, 10 vols. (Assen: Van Gorcum, 1983–98)
Papias of Hierapolis, *Fragmenta*, PG 5, cols. 1255–62
Parisse, Michel, *La vie de Jean, abbé de Gorze* (Paris: Picard, 1999)
Peter Cantor, *Verbum Abbreviatum*, PL 205
Peter Comestor, Sermon XLVII, PL 198, cols. 1836–38
Peter Damian, *De Sacramentis per improbos administratis*, PL 145, cols. 523–30
Peter the Venerable, *De Miraculis*, PL 189
Philip of Harveng, *De institutione clericorum*, PL 203
Placitorum in domo capitulari Westmonasteriensi asservatorum Abbreviatio (London, 1811)
Platina, Bartolomeo, *Platynae historici Liber de vita Christi ac omnium pontificum (aa. 1–1474)*, ed. Giacinto Gaida (Città di Castello: S. Lapi, 1932)
Porphyry, *Porphyre: De l'abstinence*, ed. and trans. M. Patillon and A. Segonds with L. Brisson, 3 vols. (Paris: Les Belles Lettres, 1995)
——, *On Abstinence from Killing Animals*, trans. Gillian Clark (London: Duckworth, 2000)
Rodulphus Cluniacensis, *Vita Domni Petri Abbatis*, PL 189
Roger of Wendover, *The Flowers of History*, ed. Henry G. Hewlett, vol. I (1886, repr. Vaduz: Kraus Reprint Ltd., 1965)
Ross, Woodburn O., ed., *Middle English Sermons Edited from British Museum MS. Royal 18 B. xxiii*, EETS o.s. 209 (London: Oxford University Press, 1940)
Rufinus of Aquileia, *Historia Ecclesiastica*, in *Eusebius Werke*, ed. Eduard Schwartz and Theodore Mommsen, Die grieschen christlichen Schriftsteller 9, pts 1–2 (Leipzig, 1903–9)
Rupert of Deutz, *De trinitate et operibus ejus libri XLII in Deuteronomium*, PL 167
Salimbene de Adam, *Cronica*, ed. Guiseppe Scalia, CCCM 125–125A, 2 vols. (Turnhout: Brepols, 1998–1999)
——, *The Chronicle of Salimbene de Adam*, trans. Joseph L. Baird et al. (Binghamton, New York, 1986)
Savage, Anne and Nicholas Watson, trans. and intro., *Anchoritic Spirituality: Ancrene Wisse and Associated Works* (New York and Mahwah, NJ: Paulist Press, 1991)
Sayles, G. O., ed., *Select Cases in the Court of King's Bench*, 6 vols. (London: Bernard Quaritch, 1936–71)

Sharpe, Reginald R., ed. *Calendar of Coroners Rolls of the City of London AD 1300–1378* (London: Richard Clay and Sons, 1913)
The Siege of Jerusalem, ed. Ralph Hanna and David Lawton, EETS o.s. 320 (Oxford: Oxford University Press, 2003)
Simonsohn, Shlomo, *The Apostolic See and the Jews: Documents: 492–1404*, Pontifical Institute of Mediaeval Studies and Texts 94 (Toronto: Pontifical Institute of Mediaeval Studies, 1988)
Walafrid Strabo, *Passiones Vitaeque Sanctorum Aevi Merovingici*, ed. Bruno Krusch, MGH, Scriptores rerum Merovingicarum IV (Hannover and Leipzig, 1892)
Stubbs, William, ed., *Chronicles of the Reigns of Edward I and Edward II*, 2 vols. (1882, repr. Wiesbaden: Kraus, 1965)
Sulpicius Severus, *Sulpicii Severi Libri qui Supersunt*, ed. C. Halm, CSEL 1 (Vienna, 1866)
———, *Vita di Martino*, ed. and trans. Fabio Ruggiero (Bologna: Edizioni Dehoniane Bologna, 2003)
Swanton, Michael, trans., *Three Lives of the Last Englishmen* (New York: Garland, 1984)
Tertullian, *Adversus Iudaeos* in *Tertulliani Opera* pars II, CCSL 2 (Turnhout: Brepols, 1954)
Thietmar of Merseberg, *Die Chronik des Bischofs Thietmar von Merseburg*, ed. Robert Holtzmann, MGH, Scriptores Rerum Germanicarum n.s. IX (Berlin: Weidman, 1955)
Thomas de Chobham, *Summa de arte praedicandi*, ed. Franco Morenzoni, CCCM 82 (Turnhout: Brepols, 1988)
Thomas, A. H., ed., *Calendar of Early Mayor's Court Rolls Preserved among the Archives of the Corporation of the City of London at the Guildhall, AD 1298–1307* (Cambridge: Cambridge University Press, 1924)
Tolkien, J. R. R., ed., *The English Text of the Ancrene Riwle: Ancrene Wisse*, EETS o.s. 249 (London: Oxford University Press, 1962)
Trevisa, John, *On the Properties of Things: John Trevisa's Translation of* Bartholomaeus Anglicus De Proprietatibus Rerum, Vol. I, ed. M. C. Seymour (Oxford: Clarendon Press, 1975)
William of Malmesbury, *Gesta pontificum Anglorum: The History of the English Bishops*, ed. and trans. M. Winterbottom with R. M. Thomson, 2 vols. (Oxford: Clarendon Press, 1998–1999)

SECONDARY LITERATURE

Albert, Jean-Pierre, *Odeurs de Sainteté: La Mythologie chrétienne des aromates* (Paris: École des Hautes Études en Sciences Sociales, 1990)
Allan, Keith and Kate Burridge, *Euphemism and Dysphemism: Language Used as Shield and Weapon* (New York and Oxford: Oxford University Press, 1991)
Angyal, A., "Disgust and Related Aversions," *Journal of Abnormal and Social Psychology* 36 (1941), 393–412
Arnold, John H., *Belief and Unbelief in Medieval Europe* (London: Hodder Arnold, 2005)
Ashwin-Siejkowski, Piotr, *Clement of Alexandria on Trial: The Evidence of "Heresy" from Photius' Bibliotheca* (Leiden: Brill, 2010)
Bailey, Lloyd R., "Gehenna: The Topography of Hell," *The Biblical Archaeologist* 49 (1986), 187–91

Bakhtin, Mikhail, *Rabelais and His World*, trans. Helene Iswolsky (Cambridge, Mass.: MIT Press, 1968)
Baldwin, John W., *The Language of Sex: Five Voices from Northern France Around 1200* (Chicago: University of Chicago Press, 1994)
Bale, Anthony Paul, *The Jew in the Medieval Book: English Antisemitisms, 1350–1500* (Cambridge: Cambridge University Press, 2006)
Barber, Malcolm, *The Trial of the Templars* (Cambridge: Cambridge University Press, 1978)
Bartz, G. and E. König, "Die Illustration des Totenoffiziums in Stundenbüchern," in *Im Angesicht des Todes: Ein interdisziplinäres Kompendium*, ed. Hansjakob Becker, Bernhard Einig, and Peter-Otto Ullrich, 2 vols. (St. Ottilien: EOS Verlag, 1987), I, pp. 487–528
Bataille, Georges, *Visions of Excess: Selected Writings 1927–1939*, trans. Allan Stoekl with Carl R. Lovitt and Donald M. Leslie Jr. (Minneapolis: University of Minnesota Press, 1985)
Bayless, Martha, "The Story of the Fallen Jew and the Iconography of Jewish Unbelief," *Viator* 34 (2003), 142–56
Becker, Ernest, *The Denial of Death* (New York: Free Press, 1973)
Bell, Rudolph M., *Holy Anorexia* (Chicago: University of Chicago Press, 1985)
Benton, Janetta Rebold, *Holy Terrors: Gargoyles on Medieval Buildings* (New York: Abbeville Press, 1997)
Berliner, R., "Die Cedronbrücke als Station des Passionsweges Christi," in *Rudolf Berliner (1886–1967): "The Freedom of Medieval Art" und andere Studien zum christlichen Bild*, ed. Robert Suckale (Berlin: Lukas Verlag, 2003), pp. 23–27
Besserman, Lawrence L., *The Legend of Job in the Middle Ages* (Cambridge, Mass.: Harvard University Press, 1979)
Bestul, Thomas H., *Texts of the Passion: Latin Devotional Literature and Medieval Society* (Philadelphia: University of Pennsylvania Press, 1996)
Biedler, Peter G., "The *Reeve's Tale* and its Flemish Analogues," *Chaucer Review* 26 (1992), 282–92
Biggs, Frederick M. and Laura L. Howes, "Theophany in the Miller's Tale," *Medium Aevum* 65 (1996), 269–79
Biow, Douglas, *The Culture of Cleanliness in Renaissance Italy* (Ithaca, NY and London: Cornell University Press, 2006)
Blaschitz, Gertrud, ed., *Neidhartrezeption in Wort und Bild* (Krems: Medium Aevum Quotidianum, 2000)
Bloch, Marc, *French Rural History*, trans. Janet Sondheimer (Berkeley and Los Angeles: University of California Press, 1966)
Block, Elaine C. with Frédéric Billiet, Sylvie Bethmont-Gallerand and Paul Hardwick, eds., *Profane Images in Marginal Arts of the Middle Ages* (Turnhout: Brepols, 2009)
Bolton, J. L., *The Medieval English Economy 1150–1500* (London: J. M. Dent, 1980)
Borg, Jana Schaich, Debra Lieberman, and Kent A. Kiehl, "Infection, Incest, and Iniquity: Investigating the Neural Correlates of Disgust and Morality," *Journal of Cognitive Neuroscience* 20 (2008), 1529–46
Bouchard, Constance Brittain, *"Every Valley Shall Be Exalted": The Discourse of Opposites in Twelfth-Century Thought* (Ithaca: Cornell University Press, 2003)
Boureau, Alain, *The Myth of Pope Joan*, trans. Lydia G. Cochrane (Chicago and London, 2001)
Bourke, John G., *Scatalogic Rites of All Nations* (Washington, D.C.: Lowdermilk and Co., 1891)

Brody, Saul N., *The Disease of the Soul: Leprosy in Medieval Literature* (Ithaca, NY: Cornell University Pres, 1974)
Brown, Peter, *The Body and Society: Men, Women, and Sexual Renunciation in Early Christianity* (New York: Columbia University Press, 1988)
———, *The Cult of the Saints: Its Rise and Function in Latin Christianity* (Chicago: University of Chicago Press, 1981)
Burchfield, Robert, "An Outline History of Euphemisms in English," in *Fair of Speech*, ed. D. J. Enright (Oxford and New York: Oxford University Press, 1985), pp. 13–31
Bynum, Caroline Walker, *Fragmentation and Redemption: Essays on Gender and the Human Body in Medieval Religion* (New York: Zone Books, 1991)
———, *Holy Feast and Holy Fast: The Religious Significance of Food to Medieval Women* (Berkeley: University of California Press, 1987)
———, *The Resurrection of the Body in Western Christianity 200–1336* (New York: Columbia University Press, 1995)
———, "Why All the Fuss about the Body? A Medievalist's Perspective," *Critical Inquiry* 22 (1995), 1–33
Caciola, Nancy, *Discerning Spirits: Divine and Demonic Possession in the Middle Ages* (Ithaca and London: Cornell University Press, 2003)
Camille, Michael, *Image on the Edge: The Margins of Medieval Art* (London: Reaktion, 1992)
Chambers, A. B., "'I Was But an Inverted Tree': Notes toward the History of an Idea," *Studies in the Renaissance* 8 (1961), 291–99
Chapman, H. A., D. A. Kim, J. M. Susskind, and A. K. Anderson, "In Bad Taste: Evidence for the Oral Origins of Moral Disgust," *Science* 323, no. 5918 (2009), 1222–26
Chapolet, Jean and Robert Fossier, *The Village and House in the Middle Ages*, trans. Henry Cleere (Berkeley and Los Angeles: University of California Press, 1985)
Cipolla, Carlo M., *Public Health and the Medical Profession in the Renaissance* (Cambridge and New York: Cambridge University Press, 1976)
Clark, Andy, *Being There: Putting Brain, Body and World Together Again* (Cambridge, MA: MIT Press, 1997)
Clark, Stuart, "Inversion, Misrule and the Meaning of Witchcraft," *Past and Present* 87 (1980), 98–127
Classen, Albrecht, "Farting and the Power of Human Language, with a Focus on Hans Wilhelm Kirchhof's Sixteenth-Century *Schwänke*," *Medievalia et Humanistica* n. s. 35 (2009), 57–76
———, "Transgression and Laughter, the Scatological and Epistemological: New Insights into the Pranks of Till Eulenspiegel," *Medievalia et Humanistica* n.s. 33 (2007), 41–61
Cluse, Christoph, "'Fabula ineptissima': Die Ritualmordlegende um Adam von Bristol nach der Handschrift London, British Library, Harley 957," *Aschkenas: Zeitschrift für Geschichte und Kultur der Juden* 5 (1995), 293–330
Cockayne, Emily, *Hubbub: Filth, Noise and Stench in England 1600–1770* (New Haven, Conn.: Yale University Press, 2007)
Cohen, Esther, "Symbols of Culpability and the Universal Language of Justice: The Ritual of Public Executions in Late Medieval Europe," *History of European Ideas* 11 (1989), 407–16
Cohen, Kathleen, *Metamorphosis of a Death Symbol: The Transi Tomb in the Late Middle Ages and the Renaissance* (Berkeley: University of California Press, 1973)
Cohen, William A. and Ryan Johnson , eds., *Filth: Dirt, Disgust, and Modern Life* (Minneapolis: University of Minnesota Press, 2005)

Cohn, Norman, *Europe's Inner Demons: An Enquiry Inspired by the Great Witch-Hunt* (New York: Basic Books, 1975)
Corbin, Alain, *The Foul and the Fragrant: Odor and the French Social Imagination* (Cambridge, MA: Harvard University Press, 1986)
Countryman, L. William, *Dirt, Greed, and Sex: Sexual Ethics in the New Testament and Their Implications for Today* (Philadelphia: Fortress Press, 1988)
Craun, Edwin D., *Lies, Slander and Obscenity in Medieval English Literature: Pastoral Rhetoric and the Deviant Speaker* (Cambridge and New York: Cambridge University Press, 1997)
Cuffel, Alexandra, *Gendering Disgust in Medieval Religious Polemic* (Notre Dame: University of Notre Dame Press, 2007)
Curtis, Valerie and Adam Biran, "Dirt, Disgust, and Disease: Is Hygiene in Our Genes?", *Perspectives in Biology and Medicine* 44 (2001), 17–31
Davidson, Caroline, *A Woman's Work is Never Done: A History of Housework in the British Isles 1650–1950* (London: Chatto and Windus, 1982)
Davis, Miriam C., "The English Medieval Urban Environment Before the Black Death: Learned Views and Popular Practice," *Medieval Perspectives* 13 (1998), 69–83
Dawson, Warren R., *A Leechbook or Collection of Medical Recipes of the Fifteenth Century* (London: Macmillan, 1934)
DeConick, April D. "The Great Mystery of Marriage: Sex and Conception in Ancient Valentinian Traditions," *Vigiliae Christianae* 57 (2003), 307–42
De Tolnay, Charles, *Hieronymus Bosch* (London: Eyre Methuen, 1966)
Delumeau, Jean, *Sin and Fear: The Emergence of a Western Guilt Culture 13th-18th Centuries*, trans. Eric Nicholson (New York: St. Martin's Press, 1990)
de Patoul, Brigitte, Roger Van Schoute et al., *Les primitifs flamands et leur temps* (Tournai: La Renaissance du Livre, 1998)
DeProost, Paul-Augustin, "La mort de Judas dans l'*Historia apostolica* d'Arator (I, 83–102)," *Revue des études Augustiniennes* 35 (1989), 135–50
Dictionnaire de théologie catholique, ed. A. Vacant, E. Mangenot et al., 15 vols. (Paris: Letouzey et Ané, 1915–50)
Dinzelbacher, Peter, *Judastraditionen* (Vienna: Selbstverlag des Österreichischen Museums für Volkskunde, 1977)
Douglas, Mary, *Natural Symbols: Explorations in Cosmology*, 2nd ed. (London: Routledge, 1996)
———, *Purity and Danger: An Analysis of Concepts of Pollution and Taboo* (London and New York: Routledge, 1966)
Duby, Georges, *Rural Economy and Country Life in the Medieval West*, trans. Cynthia Postan (London: Edward Arnold, 1968)
Duerr, Hans-Peter, *Der Mythos vom Zivilisationsprozess*: vol. 1, *Nacktheit und Scham* (1988); vol. 2, *Intimität* (1994); vol. 3, *Obszönität und Gewalt* (1995); vol. 4, *Der erotische Leib* (1997), vol. 5, *Die Tatsachen des Lebens* (2002). (Frankfurt-am-Main: Suhrkamp)
Dunderberg, Ismo "The School of Valentinus," in *A Companion to Second-Century Christian "Heretics,"* ed. Antti Marjanen and Petri Luomanen (Leiden: Brill, 2008), pp. 64–99
Dundes, Alan, *Life is Like A Chicken Coop Ladder: A Portrait of German Culture Through Folklore* (New York: Columbia University Press, 1984)
Dunning, Eric, "Some Comments on Jack Goody's 'Elias and the Anthropological Tradition,'" *Anthropological Theory* 2 (2002), 413–20
Durling, Robert M., "Deceit and Digestion in the Belly of Hell," in *Allegory and Representation*, ed. Stephen J. Greenblatt (Baltimore: Johns Hopkins University Press, 1980), pp. 61–93

Durrant, Jonathan, "The *Osculum Infame*: Heresy, Secular Culture and the Image of the Witches' Sabbath," in *The Kiss in History*, ed. Karen Harvey (Manchester: Manchester University Press, 2005), pp. 36–59

Dutschke, C. W. with R. H. Rouse, *Guide to Medieval and Renaissance Manuscripts in the Huntington Library*, 2 vols. (San Marino, California: The Library, 1989)

Dykmans, Marc, *Le cérémonial papal de la fin du Moyen Age à la Renaissance*, 4 vols., vol. 1, *Le cérémonial papal du XIIIe siècle* (Brussels and Rome: Institut Historique Belge de Rome, 1977)

Earl, D. E., *Forest Energy and Economic Development* (Oxford: Clarendon Press, 1975)

Ekwall, Eilert, *Street-Names of the City of London* (Oxford: Clarendon Press, 1954)

Elias, Norbert, *The History of Manners*, trans. Edmund Jephcott, vol. 1 of *the Civilizing Process* (1939; repr. New York: Pantheon, 1978)

——, *Über den Prozess der Zivilisation: soziogenetische und psycogenetische Untersuchungen*, 2 vols. (Basel: Verlag Haus zum Falken, 1939)

Fox, Adam, *Oral and Literate Culture in England 1500–1700* (Oxford: Clarendon Press, 2000)

Freud, Sigmund, "Character and Anal Eroticism," in *Standard Edition of the Complete Psychological Works*, ed. James Strachey, 24 vols. (London: Hogarth Press, 1953–74), vol. 9, pp. 169–75

——, *Civilization and Its Discontents*, trans. Joan Riviere, rev. and newly ed. James Strachey (London: Hogarth Press and the Institute of Psycho-Analysis, 1969)

——, "On Transformations of Instinct as Exemplified in Anal Eroticism," in *Standard Edition of the Complete Psychological Works*, ed. James Strachey, 24 vols. (London: Hogarth Press, 1953–74), vol. 17, pp. 126–33

——, *Three Essays on the Theory of Sexuality*, trans. James Strachey (London: Hogarth Press and the Institute of Psycho-Analysis, 1962)

Furnivall, Frederick J., ed., *Early English Meals and Manners* (London, 1868)

Gaignebet, Claude and Jean-Dominique Lajoux, *Art profane et religion populaire au Moyen Age* (Paris: Presses Universitaires de France, 1985)

Gaignebet, Claude and Marie-Claude Périer, "L'homme et l'excretum," in *Histoire des Moeurs* vol. I: *Les Coordinnées de l'homme et la culture matérielle*, ed. Jean Poirier (Paris: Gallimard, 1990), pp. 831–93

George, Rose, *The Big Necessity: Adventures in the World of Human Waste* (London: Portobello Books, 2008)

Gier, Albert, "Skatologische Komik in der französischen Literatur des Mittelalters," *Wolfram-Studien* VII, ed. Werner Schröder (Berlin: Erich Schmidt, 1982)

Gilmour-Bryson, Anne, "Italian Templar Trials: Truth or Falsehood?" in *Knighthoods of Christ: Essays on the History of the Crusades and the Knights Templar*, ed. Norman Housley (Burlington, Vermont, and Aldershot: Ashgate, 2007), pp. 209–28

Glanz, Rudolf, "The 'Jewish Execution' in Medieval Germany," *Jewish Social Studies* 5 (1943), 3–26

Goldberg, Jeremy, "John Skathelok's Dick: Voyeurism and 'Pornography' in Late Medieval England," in *Medieval Obscenities*, ed. Nicola McDonald (Woodbridge, Suffolk: Boydell and Brewer/York Medieval Press, 2006), pp. 105–23

Goldenberg, J. L. T. Pyszczynski, J. Greenberg, S. K. McCoy, and S. Solomon, "Death, Sex, Love, and Neuroticism: Why is Sex Such a Problem?", *Journal of Personality and Social Psychology* 77 (1999), 1173–87

Goldenberg, J. L. T. Pyszczynski, J. Greenberg, and S. Solomon, "Fleeing the Body: A Terror Management Perspective on the Problem of Human Corporeality," *Personality & Social Psychology Review* 4 (2000), 200–218

Goldenberg, J. L. T. Pyszczynski, J. Greenberg, S. Solomon, B. Kluck and R. Cornwell, "I am NOT an Animal: Mortality Salience, Disgust, and the Denial of Human Creatureliness," *Journal of Experimental Psychology: General* 130 (2001), 427–35

Goody, Jack, "Elias and the Anthropological Tradition," *Anthropological Theory* 2 (2002), 401–12

Gover, J. E. B., A. Mawer and F. M. Stenton in collaboration with F. T. S. Houghton, *The Place-Names of Warwickshire* (Cambridge: Cambridge University Press, 1936)

Grant, Edward, "Celestial Incorruptibility in Medieval Cosmology 1200–1687," in *Physics, Cosmology and Astronomy 1300–1700: Tension and Accommodation*, ed. Sabetai Unguru (Dordrecht: Kluwer Academic Publishers, 1991), pp. 101–27

——, *Planets, Stars and Orbs: The Medieval Cosmos 1200–1687* (Cambridge: Cambridge University Press, 1994).

Grayzel, Solomon, *The Church and the Jews in the XIIIth Century*, rev. ed. (New York: Hermon Press, 1966)

Greenberg, J., T. Pyszczynski, S. Solomon, A. Rosenblatt, M. Veeder, S. Kirkland, and D. Lyon, "Evidence for Terror Management Theory II: The Effects of Mortality Salience on Reactions to Those Who Threaten or Bolster the Cultural Worldview," *Journal of Personality and Social Psychology* 58 (1990), 308–318

Greenblatt, Stephen, "Filthy Rites," *Daedalus* 111 (1982), 1–16

Greene, J. Patrick, *Medieval Monasteries* (Leicester: Leicester University Press, 1992)

Grenville, Jane, *Medieval Housing* (London and Washington: Leicester University Press, 1997)

Grewe, Klaus et al., *Die Wasserversorgung im Mittelalter*, Geschichte der Wasserversorgung 4 (Mainz am Rhein: Philipp von Zabern, 1991)

Guillerme, André E., *The Age of Water: The Urban Environment in the North of France, A.D. 300–1800* (College Station, Texas: Texas A&M University Press, 1988)

Hagger, Mark, "The *Gesta Abbatum Monasterii Sancti Albani*: Litigation and History at St. Albans," *Historical Research* 81 (2008), 373–98

Haidt, Jonathan, Clark McCauley, and Paul Rozin, "Individual Differences in Sensitivity to Disgust: A Scale Sampling Seven Domains of Disgust Elicitors," *Personality and Individual Differences* 16 (1994), 701–13

Haidt, Jonathan, Paul Rozin, Clark McCauley, and Sumio Imada, "Body, Psyche, and Culture: The Relationship between Disgust and Morality," *Psychology and Developing Societies* 9 (1997), pp. 107–31

Hamlin, Christopher, "Good and Intimate Filth," in *Filth*, ed. Cohen and Johnson, pp. 3–29

Hansen, Joseph, *Quellen und Untersuchungen zur Geschichte des Hexenwahns und der Hexenverfolgung im Mittelalter* (1901, repr. Hildesheim: G. Olms, 1963)

Hanson, F. Allan, "Method in Semiotic Anthropology: or, How the Maori Latrine Means," in *Studies in Symbolism and Cultural Communication*, ed. F. Allan Hanson, Publications in Anthropology 14 (Lawrence, Kansas: University of Kansas Press, 1982), 74–89

Harman, Mary, *An Isle called Hirte: History and Culture of the St Kildans to 1930* (Waternish, Isle of Skye: Maclean Press, 1997)

Hayes, Dawn Marie, *Body and Sacred Place in Medieval Europe, 1100–1389* (New York: Routledge, 2009)

Hergenmöller, Bernd-Ulrich, "Black Sabbath Masses: Fictitious Rituals and Real Inquisitions," in *The Fall of the Angels*, ed. Christoph Auffarth and Loren T. Stuckenbruck (Leiden: Brill, 2004), pp. 176–91

Hertz, Robert, *Death and the Right Hand*, trans. Rodney and Claudia Needham (Glencoe, Illinois: The Free Press, 1960), pp. 89–113
———, "The Pre-eminence of the Right Hand: A Study in Religious Polarity," in *Right and Left: Essays on Dual Symbolic Classification*, ed. Rodney Needham (Chicago: University of Chicago Press, 1973), pp. 3–31
Higounet-Nadal, A., "Hygiène, salubrité, pollutions au Moyen Age: l'exemple de Périgueux," *Annales de démographie historique* [no volume number] (1975), 81–92
Hinz, H., "Abort," *Reallexikon der Germanischen Altertumskunde*, ed. H. Jankuhn et al., vol. I. (Berlin and New York: W. de Gruyter, 1973)
Hinz, Michael, *Der Zivilisationsprozess: Mythos oder Realität?: wissenschaftssoziologische Untersuchungen zur Elias-Duerr-Kontroverse* (Opladen: Leske + Budrich, 2002)
Holt, Richard, "Medieval England's Water-Related Technologies," *Working With Water in Medieval Europe*, ed. Paolo Squatriti (Leiden: Brill, 2000), pp. 51–100
Horn, Walter and Ernest Born, *The Plan of St. Gall*, 3 vols. (Berkeley, Los Angeles and London: University of California Press, 1979)
Hoskins, W. G., *The Age of Plunder: King Henry's England 1500–1547* (London and New York: Longman, 1976)
Hughes, Robert, *Heaven and Hell in Western Art* (London: Weidenfeld and Nicolson, 1968)
Hunnisett, R. F., ed., *Bedfordshire Coroners' Rolls*, Bedfordshire Historical Record Society 41 (Streatley: Bedfordshire Historical Record Society Publications, 1961),
Hurtado, Larry W., *Lord Jesus Christ: Devotion to Jesus in Earliest Christianity* (Grand Rapids and Cambridge: William B. Eerdmans, 2003)
Hurtado, Martin, "Wasserentsorgung in spätmittelalterlichen Städten," *Die Alte Stadt* 20 (1993), 221–28
James, M. R., *Latin Infancy Gospels* (Cambridge: Cambridge University Press, 1927)
Jodogne, Omer, "*Audigier* et la chanson de geste, avec une édition nouvelle du poème," *Le Moyen Age* 66 (1960), 495–526
Johnson, Mark, *The Body in the Mind: The Bodily Basis of Meaning, Imagination, and Reason* (Chicago: University of Chicago Press, 1987)
Johnson, Willis, "The Myth of Jewish Male Menses," *Journal of Medieval History* 24 (1998), 273–95
Jones, Malcolm, "Marcolf the Trickster in Late Mediaeval Art and Literature or: The Mystery of the Bum in the Oven," in *Spoken in Jest*, ed. Gillian Bennett (Sheffield: Sheffield Academic Press, 1991), pp. 139–74
———, *The Secret Middle Ages* (Stroud: Sutton, 2002)
Jones, P. E., "Whittington's Longhouse," *London Topographical Record* 23 (1972), 27–34
Kamash, Zena, "Which Way to Look? Exploring Latrine Use in the Roman World," in *Toilet: Public Restrooms and the Politics of Sharing*, ed. Harvey Molotch and Laura Noren (New York: New York University Press, 2010), pp. 47–63
Kaske, R. E. with Arthur Groos and Michael W. Twomey, *Medieval Christian Literary Imagery: A Guide to Interpretation* (Toronto: University of Toronto Press, 1988)
Keene, D. J., "Rubbish in Medieval Towns," *Environmental Archaeology in the Urban Context*, ed. A. R. Hall and H. K. Kenward, The Council for British Archaeology Research Report 43 (London: Council for British Archaeology, 1982), pp. 26–30
Keene, Derek, *Survey of Medieval Winchester*, Winchester Studies 2, 2 vols. (Oxford: Clarendon Press, 1985)

Kerridge, Eric, *The Farmers of Old England* (Totowa, New Jersey: Rowman and Littlefield, 1973)
Kilroy, Roger, *The Compleat Loo: A Lavatorial Miscellany* (London: Gollancz, 1984)
King, Walter, "How High Is Too High? Disposing of Dung in Seventeenth-Century Prescot," *Sixteenth Century Journal* 23 (1992), 443–57
Kisch, Guido, "The 'Jewish Execution' in Mediaeval Germany," *Historia Judaica* 5 (1943), 101–32
Kleinberg, Aviad M., *Prophets in their Own Country: Living Saints and the Making of Sainthood in the Later Middle Ages* (Chicago and London: University of Chicago Press, 1992)
Knott, Kim, *The Location of Religion: A Spacial Analysis* (London: Equinox, 2005)
Kobialka, Michal, *This Is My Body: Representational Practices in the Early Middle Ages* (Ann Arbor: University of Michigan Press, 1999)
Krapp, George Philip, *The Legend of Saint Patrick's Purgatory: Its Later Literary History* (Baltimore: John Murphy Co., 1900)
Kren, Thomas and Roger S. Wieck, *The Visions of Tondal from the Library of Margaret of York* (Malibu: J. Paul Getty Museum, 1990)
Kristeva, Julia, *Powers of Horror: An Essay on Abjection*, trans. Leon S. Roudiez (New York: Columbia University Press, 1982)
Kruger, Steven F., "Medieval Christian (Dis)identifications: Muslims and Jews in Guibert of Nogent," *New Literary History* 28 (1997), 185–203
Lakoff, George, *Women, Fire, and Dangerous Things* (Chicago: University of Chicago Press, 1987)
Lakoff, George and Mark Johnson, *Metaphors We Live By* (Chicago: University of Chicago Press, 1980)
——, *Philosophy in the Flesh: The Embodied Mind and Its Challenge to Western Thought* (New York: Basic Books, 1999)
Lancashire, Ian, "Moses, Elijah and the Back Parts of God: Satiric Scatology in Chaucer's *Summoner's Tale*," *Mosaic* 14:3 (1981), 17–30
Laporte, Dominique, *Histoire de la Merde* (Paris: Christian Bourgois Éditeur, 1978)
——, *History of Shit*, trans. Nadia Benabid and Rodolphe el-Khoury (Cambridge, Mass.: MIT Press, 2000)
Larrington, Carolyne, "Diet, Defecation and the Devil: Disgust and the Pagan Past," in *Medieval Obscenities*, ed. Nicola McDonald (Woodbridge, Suffolk: Boydell and Brewer/York Medieval Press, 2006), pp. 138–55
Ladurie, Emmanuel Le Roy, *Montaillou: Cathars and Catholics in a French Village 1294–1324*, trans. Barbara Bray (Harmondsworth: Penguin, 1980)
Lefèvre, Yves, *L'Elucidarium et les lucidaires* (Paris: E. de Boccard, 1954)
Leguay, Jean-Pierre, *La Pollution au Moyen Age dans le royaume de France et dans les grands fiefs* ((Paris: Jean-Paul Gisserot, 1999)
——, *La rue au Moyen Age* (Rennes: Ouest France, 1984)
Lieberknecht, Otfried, "Death and Retribution: Medieval Visions of the End of Judas the Traitor," www.lieberknecht.de/~diss/papers/p_judas.pdf
Liechty, Daniel, ed., *Death and Denial: Interdisciplinary Perspectives on the Legacy of Ernest Becker* (Westport, CT; Praeger, 2002)
Lipton, Sara, *Images of Intolerance: The Representation of Jews and Judaism in the* Bible moralisée (Berkeley: University of California Press, 1999)
Little, Lester K., "Pride Goes Before Avarice: Social Change and the Vices in Latin Christendom," *American Historical Review* 76 (1971), 16–49
Macy, Gary, "The Theological Fate of Berengar's Oath of 1059: Interpreting a Blunder Become Tradition," in his *Treasures from the Storeroom: Medieval Religion and the Eucharist* (Collegeville, Minnesota: Liturgical Press, 1999), pp. 20–35

Magnusson, Roberta J., *Water Technology in the Middle Ages* (Baltimore and London: Johns Hopkins University Press, 2001)
Magnusson, Roberta and Paolo Squatriti, "The Technologies of Water in Medieval Italy," in *Working With Water in Medieval Europe*, ed. Paolo Squatriti (Leiden: Brill, 2000), pp. 217–65
Margolis, Howard, *Patterns, Thinking, and Cognition* (Chicago: University of Chicago Press, 1987)
Marrow, James H., *Passion Iconography in Northern European Art of the Late Middle Ages and Early Renaissance*, Ars Neerlandica 1 (Kortrijk: Van Ghemmert 1979)
Marshall, Louise, Review of Mellinkoff's *Averting Demons*, *Speculum* 81 (2006), 891–93
Mauss, Marcel, "Les techniques du corps," *Journal de Psychologie normale et pathologique* 32 (1935), 271–93
McCall, Andrew, *The Medieval Underworld* (London: Hamish Hamilton, 1979)
Mead, Rebecca, "Letter from Finland: Getting to Know You," *The New Yorker*, Oct. 14–21, 2002, pp. 82–91
Mellinkoff, Ruth, *Averting Demons: The Protective Power of Medieval Visual Motifs and Themes*, 2 vols. (Los Angeles: Ruth Mellinkoff, 2004)
———, *Outcasts: Signs of Otherness in Northern European Art of the Late Middle Ages*, 2 vols. (Berkeley: University of California Press, 1993)
———, "Riding Backwards: Theme of Humiliation and Symbol of Evil," *Viator* 4 (1973), 153–76
Menninghaus, Winfried, *Disgust: The Theory and History of a Strong Sensation*, trans. Howard Eiland and Joel Golb (Albany: State University of New York Press, 2003)
Mercier, Franck, "Un trompe-l'œil maléfique: l'image du sabbat dans les manuscrits enluminés de la cour de Bourgogne (à propos du *Traité du crisme de Vauderie* de Jean Taincture, vers 1460–1470)," *Médiévales* 44 (2003), 97–115
Metzler, Irina, *Disability in Medieval Europe: Physical Impairment in the High Middle Ages, c. 1100-c. 1400* (London: Routledge, 2006)
Miller, William Ian, *The Anatomy of Disgust* (Cambridge, Mass.: Harvard University Press, 1997)
Molotch, Harvey and Laura Noren (eds.), *Toilet: Public Restrooms and the Politics of Sharing* (New York: New York University Press, 2010).
Moore, R. I., *The Formation of a Persecuting Society: Authority and Deviance in Western Europe 950–1250*, 2nd ed. (Oxford: Blackwell, 2007)
Morales, Andrea C. and Gavan J. Fitzsimons, "Product Contagion: Changing Consumer Evaluations Through Physical Contact with 'Disgusting' Products," *Journal of Marketing Research* 44 (2007), 272–83
Morrison, Susan Signe, *Excrement in the Late Middle Ages: Sacred Filth and Chaucer's Fecopoetics* (New York: Palgrave Macmillan, 2008)
Mushacke, W., *Altprovenzalische Marienklage des XIII. Jahrhunderts* (Halle a.S., 1890)
Neudecker, Richard, *Die Pracht der Latrine. Zum Wandel öffentlicher Bedürfnisanstalten in der kaiserzeitlichen Stadt* (Munich: Verlag Dr. Friedrich Pfeil, 1994)
Niles, John D., *Homo Narrans: The Poetics and Anthropology of Oral Literature* (Philadelphia: University of Pennsylvania Press, 1999)
Nirenberg, David, *Communities of Violence: Persecution of Minorities in the Middle Ages* (Princeton: Princeton University Press, 1996)
Obrist, Barbara, "Les deux visages du diable," in *Diables et Diableries. La représentation du diable dans la gravure des XV et XVI siècles* (Geneva: Cabinet des estampes, 1976), pp. 19–30

Oulton, J. E. L. and Henry Chadwick, *Alexandrian Christianity* (London: Westminster Press, 1954)
Owst, G. R., *Literature and Pulpit in Medieval England* (Oxford: Basil Blackwell, 1961)
Palliser, D. M., ed., *The Cambridge Urban History of Britain. Volume 1: 600–1540* (Cambridge and New York: Cambridge University Press, 2000)
Paravy, Pierrette, "À propos de la genèse médiévale des chasses aux sorcières: Le traité de Claude Tholosan, juge dauphinois (vers 1436)," *Mélanges de l'École française de Rome* 91 (1979), 333–79
Paster, Gail Kern, *The Body Embarrassed: Drama and the Disciples of Shame in Early Modern England* (Ithaca: Cornell University Press, 1993)
———, "The Epistemology of the Water Closet: John Harington's *Metamorphosis of Ajax* and Elizabethan Technologies of Shame," in *Material Culture and Cultural Materialisms in the Middle Ages and Renaissance*, ed. Curtis Perry (Turnhout: Brepols, 2001), pp. 139–58
Pathak, Bindeswar, "History of Toilets," paper given at the International Symposium on Public Toilets, Hong Kong, May 25–27, 1995; http://www.sulabhtoiletmuseum.org/pg02.htm
Patrides, C. A., "Renaissance Ideas on Man's Upright Form," *Journal of the History of Ideas* 19 (1958), 256–58
Paxson, James J., "The Nether-Faced Devil and the Allegory of Parturition," *Studies in Iconography* 19 (1998), 139–76
Pinker, Steven, *How The Mind Works* (New York: W. W. Norton, 1997)
Platt, Colin, *The English Medieval Town* (London: Secker and Warburg, 1976)
Platt, Colin and Richard Coleman-Smith, et al., *Excavations in Medieval Southampton 1953–1969*, 2 vols. (Leicester: Leicester University Press, 1975)
Porter, Roy, *Flesh in the Age of Reason* (London and New York: Allen Lane, 2003)
Portman, D., *Exeter Houses 1400–1700* (Exeter: University of Exeter, 1966)
Pouchet, Robert, *La "Rectitudo" chez Saint Anselme* (Paris: Études Augustiniennes, 1964)
Pudney, John, *The Smallest Room* (New York: Hastings House, 1955)
Rawcliffe, Carole, *Leprosy in Medieval England* (Woodbridge: Boydell, 2006)
Reeves, William, "On the Céli-dé, commonly called Culdees," *Transactions of the Royal Irish Academy* 24 (1873), 119–263
Reid, Donald, *Paris Sewers and Sewermen: Realities and Representations* (Cambridge, Mass., and London: Harvard University Press, 1991)
Reynolds, Philip Lyndon, *Food and the Body: Some Peculiar Questions in High Medieval Theology* (Leiden: Brill, 1999)
Richmond, Colin, *The Penket Papers* (Gloucester: Sutton, 1986)
Robson, Janet, "Fear of Falling: Depicting the *Death of Judas* in Late Medieval Italy," *Fear and Its Representations in the Middle Ages and Renaissance*, ed. Anne Scott and Cynthia Kosso, Arizona Studies in the Middle Ages and the Renaissance 6 (Brepols: Turnhout, 2002), pp. 33–65
Rosenblatt, A., J. Greenberg, S. Solomon, T. Pyszczynski, and D. Lyon, "Evidence for Terror Management Theory: I. The Effects of Mortality Salience on Reactions to Those Who Violate or Uphold Cultural Values," *Journal of Personality and Social Psychology* 57 (1989), 681–90
Ross, Thomas W., "Taboo-Words in Fifteenth-Century English," in *Fifteenth-Century Studies: Recent Essays*, ed. Robert F. Yeager (Hamden, Conn.; Archon Books, 1984), pp. 137–60
Roy, Bruno, *Devinettes françaises du moyen âge* (Montreal: Bellarmin, 1977)
Rozin, Paul and April E. Fallon, "A Perspective on Disgust," *Psychological Review* 94 (1987), pp. 23–41

Rozin, Paul, Jonathan Haidt, and Katrina Fincher, "Psychology: From Oral to Moral," *Science* 323, no. 5918 (2009), 1179–80

Rozin, Paul, Jonathan Haidt, and Clark R. McCauley, "Disgust: The Body and Soul Emotion," *Handbook of Cognition and Emotion*, ed. Tim Dalgleish and Mick J. Power (Chichester and New York: Wiley, 1999), pp. 429–45

Rozin, Paul, Jonathan Haidt, Clark McCauley, and Sumio Imada, "Disgust: Preadaptation and the Cultural Evolution of a Food-Based Emotion," in *Food Preferences and Taste: Continuity and Change*, ed. Helen Macbeth (Providence: Berghahn Books, 1997), pp. 65–82

Rozin, Paul, Laura Lowery, Sumio Imada, and Jonathan Haidt, "The CAD Triad Hypothesis: A Mapping Between Three Moral Emotions (Contempt, Anger, Disgust) and Three Moral Codes (Community, Autonomy, Divinity)," *Journal of Personality and Social Psychology* 76 (1999), 574–86

Rozin, Paul, M. Markwith and C. R. McCauley, "Sensitivity to Indirect Contacts With Other Persons: AIDS Aversion as a Composite of Aversion to Strangers, Infection, Moral Taint, and Misfortune," *Journal of Abnormal Psychology* 103 (1994), 495–505

Rozin, Paul, Linda Millman, and Carol Nemeroff, "Operation of the Laws of Sympathetic Magic in Disgust and Other Domains," *Journal of Personality and Social Psychology* 30 (1986), 703–12

Rubin, Miri, *Corpus Christi: The Eucharist in Late Medieval Culture* (Cambridge: Cambridge University Press, 1991)

——, "Europe Remade: Purity and Danger in Late Medieval Europe," *Transactions of the Royal Historical Society*, 6th series, 11 (2001), 101–124

——, *Gentile Tales: The Narrative Assault on Late Medieval Jews* (New Haven and London: Yale University Press, 1999)

Russell, Jeffrey Burton, *Witchcraft in the Middle Ages* (Ithaca, NY: Cornell University Press, 1972)

Rustici, Craig M., *The Afterlife of Pope Joan: Deploying the Popess Legend in Early Modern England* (Ann Arbor: University of Michigan Press, 2006)

Sabine, Ernest L., "City Cleaning in Mediaeval London," *Speculum* 12 (1937), 19–43

——, "Latrines and Cesspools of Mediaeval London," *Speculum* 9 (1934), 303–21

Salzman, L. F., *Building in England Down to 1540* (Oxford: Clarendon Press, 1952, repr. 1992)

Schmidt, Gary D., *The Iconography of the Mouth of Hell, Eighth-Century Britain to the Fifteenth Century* (Selinsgrove: Susquehanna University Press, 1995)

Schnall, Simone, Jonathan Haidt, Gerald L. Clore, and Alexander H. Jordan, "Disgust as Embodied Moral Judgment," *Personality and Social Psychology Bulletin* 34 (2008), 1096–1109

Schnitzler, Norbert, "Judas' Death: Some Remarks Concerning the Iconography of Suicide in the Middle Ages," *Medieval History Journal* 3 (2000), 103–118

Schofield, John, *Medieval London Houses* (New Haven and London: Yale University Press, 1994)

Schreckenberg, Heinz, *The Jews in Christian Art: An Illustrated History* (New York: Continuum, 1996)

Shachar, I., *The Judensau: A Medieval Anti-Jewish Motif and its History* (London: Warburg Institute, 1974)

Shofer, Jonathan Wyn, *Confronting Vulnerability: The Body and the Divine in Rabbinic Ethics* (Chicago: University of Chicago Press, 2010)

Shweder, Richard A., Nancy C. Much, Manamohan Mahapatra, and Lawrence Park, "The 'Big Three' of Morality (Autonomy, Community, Divinity) and the 'Big Three' Explanations of Suffering," *Morality and Health*, ed. Allan M. Brandt and Paul Rozin (New York and London: Routledge, 1997), pp. 119–69

Simon, Eckehard, "The Rustic Muse: *Neidhartschwänke* in Murals, Stone Carvings, and Woodcuts," *Germanic Review* 46 (1971), 243–56

Simond, Louis, *Journal of a Tour and Residence in Great Britain during the Years 1810 and 1811*, 2 vols. (Edinburgh, 1815–17)

Simons, Patricia, "Manliness and the Visual Semiotics of Bodily Fluids in Early Modern Culture," *Journal of Medieval and Early Modern Studies* 39 (2009), 331–73

Spearing, Anthony, "*Purity* and Danger," *Essays in Criticism* 30 (1980), 293–310

Stallybrass, Peter and Allon White, *The Politics and Poetics of Transgression* (Ithaca: Cornell University Press, 1986)

Stenton, Doris M., *The Earliest Lincolnshire Assize Rolls A.D. 1202–1209*, Publications of the Lincoln Record Society 22 ([n.p.], 1926 for 1924)

Storms, Godfrid, *Anglo-Saxon Magic* (The Hague: Martinus Nijhoff, 1948)

Strohm, Paul, "Sovereignty and Sewage," in *Lydgate Matters: Poetry and Material Culture in the Fifteenth Century*, ed. Lisa H. Cooper and Andrea Denny-Brown (New York: Palgrave-Macmillan, 2008), pp. 57–70

Stuart, Kathy, *Defiled Trades and Social Outcasts: Honor and Ritual Pollution in Early Modern Germany* (Cambridge: Cambridge University Press, 1999)

Tanner, Norman P., *Heresy Trials in the Diocese of Norwich, 1428–31* (London: Royal Historical Society, 1977)

Tatton-Brown, T., "The Precincts [sic] Water Supply," *Canterbury Cathedral Chronicle* 77 (1983), 45–52

Terrien, Samuel L., *The Iconography of Job Through the Centuries: Artists as Biblical Interpreters* (University Park, PA; Pennsylvania State University Press, 1996)

Thomas, Alfred, "Alien Bodies: Exclusion, Obscenity, and Social Control in *The Ointment Seller*," in *Obscenity: Social Control and Artistic Creation in the European Middle Ages*, ed. Jan M. Ziolkowski (Leiden and Boston: Brill, 1998), pp. 214–230

Thomas, Keith, "Cleanliness and Godliness in Early Modern England," in *Religion, Culture and Society in Early Modern Britain: Essays in Honour of Patrick Collinson*, ed. A. J. Fletcher and P. R. Roberts (Cambridge: Cambridge University Press, 1994), pp. 56–83

———, "Health and Morality in Early Modern England," in *Morality and Health*, ed. Allan M. Brandt and Paul Rozin (New York and London: Routledge, 1997), pp. 15–34

Thorndike, Lynn, *A History of Magic and Experimental Science*, 8 vols. (New York and London: Columbia University Press, 1923–1958)

Toulmin, Stephen and June Goodfield, *The Discovery of Time* (New York: Harper & Row, 1965)

Trachtenberg, Joshua, *The Devil and the Jews: The Medieval Conception of the Jew and its Relation to Modern Antisemitism* (1943, repr. Skokie, Illinois: Varda Books, 2001)

Tubach, Frederic C., *Index Exemplorum: A Handbook of Medieval Religious Tales*, FF Communications 204 (Helsinki: Suomalainen Tiedeakatedia, 1969)

United States Development Program, Human Development Report 2006: *Beyond Scarcity: Power, Poverty, and the Global Water Crisis*

Velz, John W., "Scatology and Moral Meaning in Two English Renaissance Plays," *South Central Review* 1 (1984), 4–21

Ward-Perkins, Bryan, *From Classical Antiquity to the Middle Ages: Urban Public Building in Northern and Central Italy AD 300–850* (Oxford: Oxford University Press, 1984)

Wentersdorf, Karl P., "The Symbolic Significance of Figurae Scatalogicae in Gothic Manuscripts," in *Word, Picture, and Spectacle*, ed. Clifford Davidson (Kalamazoo: Western Michigan Universiy Press, 1984), pp. 1–21

Wolterbeek, Marc, *Comic Tales of the Middle Ages: An Anthology and Commentary* (New York: Greenwood Press, 1991)

Wood, Margaret, *The English Mediaeval House* (1965; repr. London: Studio Editions, 1994)

Yates, Julian, *Error, Misuse, Failure: Object Lessons from the English Renaissance* (Minneapolis and London: University of Minnesota Press, 2003)

Zhong, Chen-Bo and Katie Liljenquist, "Washing Away Your Sins: Threatened Morality and Physical Cleansing," *Science* 313, no. 5792 (2006), 1451–52

Ziolkowski, Jan M., *Solomon and Marcolf* (Cambridge, Mass. and London: Department of the Classics, Harvard University, 2008)

Žižek, Slavoj, *The Plague of Fantasies* (London and New York: Verso, 1997)

Zupko, Ronald E. and Robert A. Laures, *Straws in the Wind: Medieval Urban Environmental Law: The Case of Northern Italy* (Boulder: Westview Press, 1996)

Subject Index

A
Abelard, 7, 67
Ackermann aus Böhmen, Der, 13
Adamnán, 157
Ælfric, 115
Alcuin, xiii, 51, 119
Allegoriae in sacram scripturam, 143–44, 174–75
Ancrene Wisse 12, 82
Anselm, 74
Aquinas, Thomas, 26–27, 69, 151, 153, 155
Arator, 124, 129, 130
Arius, 125, 128–29, 130, 133, 142, 178
Ashwin-Siejkowski, Piotr, 169
Audigier, 60
Augustine (of Hippo), 5–7, 22, 67–68, 72, 101, 109, 163

B
Bacon, Roger, xix, 170–71
Baegert, Jan, 94
Bakhtin, Mikhail, 9, 165
Bandinelli, Roland, 106
Barbour, John, 57
Bartholomaeus Anglicus, 70–71
Baxter, Margery, 107
Becker, Ernest, 16, 19, 20
Bede, 124, 126, 128, 133, 141, 146, 147
Berengar of Tours, 105
Berger, Balthasar, 94
Bernard of Clairvaux, St., 3, 5, 61, 73–74, 114, 115–16, 117, 125, 134
Bernard of Cluny, 95
"Big Three" of Morality, 18–19
Biow, Douglas, 11
Biran, Adam *see* Valerie Curtis
Boccaccio *see* Decameron
Boke of Nurture, 57–58
Bouts, Thierry, 90
bowels, as dwelling-place of demons, 122–23, 135, as origin of sin 123–28
Breu, Jörg, the Elder, 90, 92, 94
Brown, Peter, 11–12
Bruno of Segni, 142
buttocks, baring of as insult, 60–61, 83, 88, 89, 92, 94
Bynum, Caroline Walker, 12, 25, 65

C
Caesarius of Heisterbach, 3, 96, 111, 122, 162
Canterbury Cathedral Priory, conduit of, 46–47
Cathars *see* Heretics
Cent nouvelles nouvelles, 3, 162
Cervantes, Miguel de *see Don Quijote*
Charlemagne, 45
Chaucer, Geoffrey, xviii, 10, 44, 179; Merchant's Tale 57; Miller's Tale xviii, 31, 60, 181; Summoner's Prologue and Tale, 60, 159, 60, 181
Christ *see* Jesus
Christina of Stonnelm, xxi, 175–76
Classen, Albrecht, 10
Cockayne, Emily, 11
Corbin, Alain, 11
Countryman, L. William, 11
Curtin, Valerie, and Adam Biran, 16–17

D
Daniel of Beccles, 51–52, 57, 61

240 Subject Index

Dante, xviii, 159
Da Vinci, Leonardo, 41, 61, 192n63
Decameron, 36
DeConick, April, 170, 171
Demaundes Joyous/Demaundes Joyeuses, 58, 59
demons *see* devils
Devil/devils/demons/Satan/Lucifer, xix, 1–5, 7, 25, 27, 61, 66, 67, 68, 75, 76–77, 81, 82, 83, 84–85, 86, 88, 89, 96, 106, 121, 122–23, 125, 126, 127, 128, 131–32, 133, 134–35, 136, 137, 138–39, 140, 144, 149, 157, 162, 163, 164, 175, 176, 178, 180, 182. *See also osculum infame*
Diogenes Laertius, 169, 170
disgust, scholarly literature on, 13–22, 30, 31
Don Quijote, 57
Douglas, Mary, xiii, 8–9
Duerr, Hans-Peter, 179
Dunderberg, Ismo, 168, 169
Dundes, Alan, 10
Dürer, Albrecht, 89, 94

E
Edmund Ironside, 135
Elias, Norbert, 58, 179
Elucidarium see Honorius of Autun
Erasmus, 41, 62, 118
Eucharist, xix, 99, 103, 105, 106–7, 115, 123, 153, 170, 171
euphemisms, 56–57, 58–60
Exeter, 33, 37, 59

F
fabliaux, xxi, 25, 59, 60, 167, 177–78, 217n43; *Du Con qui fu fez a la besche*, 82; *La Crote*, 5; *Jouglet*, 59; *Le Pet au villain*, 82. *See also Le Sacristain*
farting, xvii, 25, 31, 60, 61, 82, 88, 92, 105, 138, 139, 165, 185–86n56, 218n51
"fasting girls," 116, 170–71
fertilizer, dung as, 32–33, 42–44, 166
Francesc Eiximensis, xv, 27, 109, 110, 153, 172
Francis, St. xxi, 27–28, 61, 172–75
Francisca/Francesca of Rome, 3
Freud, Sigmund, 9–10, 138
France, sanitary practices in, 34–35, 37, 38, 39, 40, 41–42, 60

G
Gallego, Fernando, 94
gender, 11, 156
George, Rose, 11
Gerald of Wales, 106
Gesta abbatum monasterii Sancti Albani, 133–34
Gesta Herwardi, 88
Glossa ordinaria, 127
Gossuin of Metz, 71
Gregory of Tours, 51, 130, 178
Gregory the Great, 2, 23–24, 121, 140, 145
Grünewald, Matthias, 94
Guibert of Nogent, 3, 75, 84, 104–105, 108, 109, 131–32, 152–53, 172, 178
Guillerme, André, 34, 38, 40
Guitmund of Bec, 106

H
Harington, Sir John, 1, 4, 5, 10
Heimelike Passie, 158–59
Helinand of Froidmont, 143
hell, xvii, 66, 71, 95, 98, 128, 132, 133, 137, 138, 140, 159, 163
Henry of Huntingdon, 135
Henry of Segusio, 157
heretics, 84, Arian 128–29; Bogomils 100; Cathars xix, 80, 84, 100, 107–108; Manicheans 101. *See also* Arius
heresy, stercoran xix, 105, 150
Hildebert of Lavardin, 74
Hincmar of Reims, 141
Holy Maidenhood, 116
Honorius of Autun, 69–70, 155, 158
Hrabanus Maurus: 127, 141
Hugh of St. Victor 69, 147–48, 154–55, 158, 174

I
Icelanders, sanitary practices of, 52, 56, 57
Isidore, 71, 141
Italy, sanitary practices in, 39, 41

J
Jerome, 75, 124, 139, 150–51
Jesus, xxi, 65, 81, 95, 100, 106, 117, 138–39, 156, 157; ate after resurrection, 24; condition of birthplace, 146, 150–51; insulted by the backside, 61,

Subject Index   241

90–94; purity of, 102–103, 104, 126, 127, 174; question of digestion and excretion of, 100–102, 108–109, 152–56, 168–72; sayings on contamination, 148–150; tormented by dung during Passion, 158–59. *See also* Eucharist

"Jewish execution," 94–95

Jews, sanitary practices of, 8, 39, unbelief/sins of 21, 81, 84, 94, 95, 96, 104, 107, 108, 140, 152, 156, 157–58, 159, 205n117

Job, 23–24, 143–45, 146, 150–51, 175, 176

John de Trevisa, 70–71

Johnson, Mark *see* Lakoff, George

Johnson, Willis, 129

Judas, xix, 90, 124–28, 129, 130, 132, 133, 143

Juliana, Passion of St., 3

Juvencus, 124, 129

K

Kenelm, Life of St., 74–75

Kimhi, Joseph, 104

Kleinberg, Aviad, 176

Kristeva, Julia, 10, 165

L

Lakoff, George and Mark Johnson, xvii–xviii, 11, 65–66, 113

Laporte, Dominique 10, 179

Laxdæla saga, 52

lepers/leprosy, 23, 35, 112, 121, 138

Liber Eliensis, 136–37

London, sanitary practices in, 21, 33, 34, 35–36, 37–38, 39, 40, 43, 45, 47, 59, 60, 61

Luther, Martin, xix, 5, 110, 157, 179, 180, 181

M

Mankind, 60

manure *see* fertilizer

Manuscripts: London, British Library, Add. MS 47682 (Holkham 666) (the Holkham Bible Picture Book): vii, 126; London, British Library, Royal 2.B.Vii (the Queen Mary Psalter): vii, 77, 164; London, British Library, Stowe 17 (the Stowe Missal): vii, 96, 97; New York, Pierpont Morgan Library, William S. Glazier Collection 24: vii, 76; Oxford, Bodleian Library, Douce 49 (the Saint-Omer Psalter): vii, 172–32; Oxford, Bodleian Library, Rawlinson D.410: vii, 86; Vienna, Österreichische Nationalbibliothek 2561: vii, 36; Yolande of Soissons Psalter/Hours: 167

Map, Walter, 83–84

Marguerite de Navarre, 57

Martini, Francesco di Giorgio, 111

Mary, Virgin 21, 102–103, 108, 132, 157, 174

Mather, Cotton, 179–80, 181,

medicine, dung in, 55, 56–57, 150, 164

Melanchthon, Philipp, 3, 5

Mellinkoff, Ruth, 165, 166–67

Memlic, Hans, 94

mooning *see* buttocks, baring of as insult

Morrison, Susan Signe, xv, 10, 172–73, 174

N

Nider, Johannes, 3

Niles, John D., 81–82

Notker Balbulus, 45

O

osculum infame, 85, 86

Owl and the Nightingale, The, 60

P

Peter Comestor, 74

Peter of Dacia, 175

Peter the Venerable, 2

Pinker, Steven, 14

Platina (Bartolomeo Sacchi), 161–62

Porphyry, 171–72

Prose Rule of the Céli Dé, 2–3

prostitution, 35

Pythagoras, 169, 170

R

Ratgeb, Jörg, 92

Rectitudines Singularum Personarum, 42

Romans, sanitary arrangements of, 48–49, 118

Ross, Thomas W., 58–59

Rozin, Paul, 16, 18, 99, 114, 117, 139
Rupert of Deutz, 141
Russell, John *see* Boke of Nurture
Rypon, Robert, 113–14

S

Sabine, Ernest, 21, 34, 38
Sacristain, Le (*The Sacristan*), xxi, 44, 57, 177–78, 217n43
St. Gall (monastery), 47–48, 49, 50, 57
St. Kilda (island), sanitary practices of, 53–54, 56
Salimbene de Adam, xi, 1–2, 7, 61 (Alberigo da Romano), 121, 138, 162, 163, 178
Satan *see* Devil/devils/demons/Satan/Lucifer
sedes stercoria/stercory seat, 161–62
Shofer, Jonathan Wyn, 10, 140, 164
Southampton, 45–46, 160
Strohm, Paul, 34
Sulpicius Severus, 136, 137

T

Templars, charges against, 84, 85, 86–87, 88
Terror Management Theory, 20

Þáttr Þorsteins skelks, 3, 162
Thietmar of Merseburg, 2
Thomas of Chobham, 149

U

Unibos, 51, 57, 160
urine, 56, 105, as desecration, 79; impurity of, 2, 9, 17, 26, 104, 113, 114, 146, 152; in public 41, 63–64; rules about, 41, 49, 61, 62, 169–70, 216n19; uses of, 40, 42, 54

V

Valentinus, xxi, 102, 168–72
van der Weyden, Rogier, 94
Van Heemskerck, Maarten, 92
Veilchenschwank, 62
Vitae Patrum, 120–21

W

Wade, Alice, 35, 180
Walafrid Strabo, 131
William of Malmesbury, 58, 159
Winchester, 33
witches, 85, 86

Z

Žižek, Slavoj, 10, 165

Index of Biblical Passages

Genesis 1:27, 117
   3, 117
   3:17–19, 23
   3:20, 118
   6:21–22, 147
   7:16, 147
   18:27, 24, 145
Exodus 33:20, 95, 96
   33:23, 95–96
Deuteronomy 23:12–14, 1, 141–42
   28:27, 87
Judges 3:22, 142, 143
1 Samuel 2:8, 161
   5:6, 87
1 Kings 2:4, 139
   24, 149
2 Kings 17:23, 124–25
   19:9:,124–25
3 Kings 14:10, 141
4 Kings 9:37, 113
   10:27, 140
Esdras 2:13, 140
   12:31, 140
1 Corinthians 12:27, 140
2 Chronicles 21:15–19, 141
Job 2:7–8, 23, 24, 143, 144
   5:7, 174
   20:7, 143
Psalms 16:10, 169
   18:15, 158
   37:6, 22
   68:3, 158
   77:66, 87
   79:8, 6
   82:11, 113, 121
   87:5, 158
   87:7, 158
   90:11–12, 83
   113:7, 151
   141, 139
Proverbs 26:11, 14, 175
Ecclesiastes 7:30, 72
Canticles 1:3, 22
Ecclesiasticus 9:28, 153
Isaiah 5:25, 141
Jeremiah 8:2, 141
   9:22, 141
   16:4, 141
Lamentations 4:5, 143, 144
Joel 1:17, 115, 116, 120–21, 138, 143
Matthew 7:6, 174, 175
   12:34, 80
   15:17–18: 148–50, 213n137
   17:1, 96
   27:5, 124
Mark 7:18–21: 148, 150
Luke 24:33, 102
   24:41–43, 189n104
John 6:27, 169
Acts 1:18, 124–25, 143
   10:41, 189n104
1 Corinthians 15:45, 148
2 Corinthians 2:15, 22
Galatians 5:16–25, 99–100
Ephesians 2:2, 124–25
   6:16–17: 101
Philippians 3:2, 175
   3:8, 117
Revelations 22:15, 174